M000287031

47.95

Purchased by:_____

Heather James examines the ways in which Shakespeare handles the inheritance and transmission of the Troy legend. She argues that Shakespeare's use of Vergil, Ovid, and other classical sources demonstrates the appropriation of classical authority in the interests of developing a national myth, and goes on to distinguish Shakespeare's deployment of the myth from "official" Tudor and Stuart ideology. James traces Shakespeare's reworking of the myth in *Titus Andronicus*, *Troilus and Cressida*, *Antony and Cleopatra*, *Cymbeline*, and *The Tempest*, and shows how the legend of Troy in Queen Elizabeth's day differed from that in the time of King James. The larger issue the book confronts is the directly political one of the way in which Shakespeare's textual appropriations participate in the larger cultural project of finding historical legitimation for a realm that was asserting its status as an empire.

Cambridge Studies in Renaissance Literature and Culture 22

Shakespeare's Troy

Cambridge Studies in Renaissance Literature and Culture

General editor
STEPHEN ORGEL
Jackson Eli Reynolds Professor of Humanities, Stanford University

Editorial board
Anne Barton, *University of Cambridge*
Jonathan Dollimore, *University of Sussex*
Marjorie Garber, *Harvard University*
Jonathan Goldberg, *Duke University*
Nancy Vickers, *Bryn Mawr College*

Since the 1970s there has been a broad and vital reinterpretation of the nature of literary texts, a move away from formalism to a sense of literature as an aspect of social, economic, political and cultural history. While the earliest New Historicist work was criticised for a narrow and anecdotal view of history, it also served as an important stimulus for post-structuralist, feminist, Marxist and psychoanalytical work, which in turn has increasingly informed and redirected it. Recent writing on the nature of representation, the historical construction of gender and of the concept of identity itself, on theatre as a political and economic phenomenon and on the ideologies of art generally, reveals the breadth of the field. Cambridge Studies in Renaissance Literature and Culture is designed to offer historically oriented studies of Renaissance literature and theatre which make use of the insights afforded by theoretical perspectives. The view of history envisioned is above all a view of our own history, a reading of the Renaissance for and from our own time.

Recent titles include

The marketplace of print: pamphlets and the public sphere in early modern England
ALEXANDRA HALASZ, Dartmouth College

Courtly letters in the age of Henry VIII: literary culture and the arts of deceit
SETH LERER, Stanford University

The culture of slander in early modern England
M. LINDSAY KAPLAN, Georgetown University

Narrative and meaning in early modern England: Browne's skull and other histories
HOWARD MARCHITELLO, Texas A & M University

The homoerotics of early modern drama
MARIO DIGANGI, Indiana University

A complete list of books in the series is given at the end of the volume

Shakespeare's Troy

Drama, politics, and the translation of empire

Heather James

University of Southern California

PUBLISHED BY THE PRESS SYNDICATE OF THE UNIVERSITY OF CAMBRIDGE
The Pitt Building, Trumpington Street, Cambridge CB2 1RP, United Kingdom

CAMBRIDGE UNIVERSITY PRESS
The Edinburgh Building, Cambridge CB2 2RU, United Kingdom
40 West 20th Street, New York, NY 10011–4211, USA
10 Stamford Road, Oakleigh, Melbourne 3166, Australia

First published 1997

Printed in the United Kingdom at the University Press, Cambridge

Typeset in Times 10/12pt

A catalogue record for this book is available from the British Library

Library of Congress cataloguing in publication data

James, Heather,
Shakespeare's Troy: drama, politics, and the translation of empire /
Heather James.
    p. cm. – (Cambridge studies in Renaissance literature and culture; 22)
ISBN 0 521 59223 2 (hardback)
1. Shakespeare, William, 1564–1616. Troilus and Cressida.
2. Shakespeare, William, 1564–1616 – Political and social views.
3. Politics and literature – Great Britain – History – 17th century.
4. Political plays, English – History and criticism.
5. Troilus (Legendary character) in literature.
6. Trojan War – Literature and the war.
7. Troy (Extinct city) – In literature.
8. English drama – Roman influences.
9. Imperialism in literature.   10. Myth inliterature.
I. Title.   II. Series.
PR2836.J36   1997
822.3′3 – dc21   96–51770   CIP

ISBN 0 521 59223 2 hardback

CE

To my parents, Jan and Jerry James,
and in loving memory of George S. James

Contents

Illustrations

All items are reproduced by the kind permission of The Huntington Library, San Marino, California.

Acknowledgements

I have incurred many pleasureful debts in writing this book. Of my earliest teachers, Harry Berger, Jr., taught me never to be satisfied with a convenient answer, even if no substitute was in sight, and Michael Warren, who read the manuscript with scrupulous care and less alarm than I had feared, taught me to mistrust an untheatrical one. W. S. Anderson and John Lynch made it possible to pursue classical as well as renaissance literature and culture. Patricia Parker first made the translation of empire fascinating on literary and political grounds. At the University of California at Berkeley, Joel Altman, Patrick Cook, Helen Deutsch, Teresa Faherty, Brad Johnson, Laura King, Steven Knapp, and the late William Nestrick sustained the work that led to my dissertation, and Jeffrey Knapp offered timely advice and support. To Janet Adelman, whose critical rigor and kindness were unstinting, I owe thanks above all.

The project largely turned into the present book at Yale University, where I was fortunate to have financial support in the form of two A. Whitney Griswold research grants in 1992 and 1995 and, even more valuably, resident and visiting colleagues who set a high standard of collegiality. The Yale junior faculty works-in-progress group provided invaluable responses to my work at a pivotal stage, and I am particularly grateful to Ian Duncan, Elizabeth Fowler, Suzanne Keen, and Katherine Rowe for their inexhaustible supply of knowledge, insights, and acts of friendship. Elizabeth Freund read an early draft of my argument about *Titus Andronicus* with encouragement and insight, and Jonathan Bate's kind interest in my work led to stimulating discussions of both Ovid and *Titus*. From the early stages of reconceiving the project, David Quint was generous with his knowledge of the field and practical advice, and Eugene Waith prompted me to revisit its foundations toward the end. Richard Brodhead and Susanne Wofford offered welcome, detailed insights into the article on *Antony and Cleopatra* that formed the basis of my chapter. Geoffrey Hartman gave me the opportunity to present my work on *Troilus and Cressida* to the Text Club, of whose members I especially thank Leslie Brisman, Paul Fry, Thomas M. Greene, Geoffrey Hartman, David Quint, Claude Rawson, and Alexander Welsh. Although he had little time to do so, Lawrence Manley read the manuscript with characteristic shrewdness and warmth and solved the problem of the book's title.

I wish to thank Lars Engle, who urged me to extend my argument about Shakespeare's ambition to secure cultural legitimacy for the theater, and Stephen Orgel, who encouraged the project and steered me through some bad moments with expertise and wit. I am grateful to the deans of the University of Southern California for providing a timely research grant to secure the illustrations. Leonard Barkan knew where I might find the perfect Trojan horse for the book's cover; many thanks to him.

My husband, Gregory Kuntz, seized every opportunity to support even those labors that took me from circulation in our household. My sister, Sharon L. James, always believed in my work, and my grandfather made sure I was able to complete it. My longest-standing debt, in literary and other matters, is to my parents, whose intelligence and good humor made this book possible.

Introduction: Shakespeare's fatal Cleopatra

This study investigates Shakespeare's use of the political and literary tradition derived from imperial Rome to legitimate the cultural place of the theater in late Elizabethan and early Stuart London. It began in efforts to understand why a playwright unpretentious about his learning should introduce explicit textuality and even books at moments of crisis in plays that seek to shape English cultural identity in relation to imperial Rome. Although the citational force of the following scenes remains to be seen, I refer to the entrance of Lavinia, previously a Vergilian figure, "her hands cut off and her tongue cut out, and ravished" according to Ovidian and Petrarchan conventions; Achilles' crisis of exemplarity, in which he is reduced to his constituent histories or redactions; Antony's manful attempt to resist Vergil's derisive portrait of his choices; Imogen's disturbing laments over what she takes to be Posthumus' headless body, an image that crosses the *pietà* with the fallen body of Priam in *Aeneid* 2; and finally, Prospero's use of the incantations of Ovid's Medea to renounce his rough and Vergilian magic and to drown his book.

The strikingly visual or emblematic character of these scenes is tied to a complex textuality unusual for the popular theater. Disentangling such knots led to an investigation of the generic character and historical occasions of a group of Shakespeare's plays I call "translations of empire," after the literary-political tradition dedicated to the transfer of authority from Troy to imperial Rome to London (Troynovant) and, although this aspect of its traffic is less often noted, from one social sphere to another within London.[1] The plays differ from the group dubbed "Roman plays" in that they share not the locale and political themes of republican and imperial Rome, but an innovative and politically veiled practice of confounding the interests of rival authorities within the Troy legend. Shakespeare's method of "contaminating" sources simply refers to the introduction of multiple texts in the creation of a new one, but in the early modern period often involves the unseemly joining of unlike texts.[2] Shakespeare's Achilles, to elaborate an example from chapter 3, is subjected to a crisis of identity that traces textual and

1

historical ambivalences in his figure from Homer to Chapman's Homer. The impetus for his crisis comes when Ulysses, head of the Greek secret service, confronts the great warrior with his inconsistent but equally traditional reasons for withdrawing from the Trojan war: Homeric honor, the medieval love of Polyxena, and homosexual love of Patroclus. First outed or "known" (3.3.193, 195) as a creature of Lydgate and Caxton in Homeric armor, then lovingly counseled by Patroclus to "rouse" himself and shake off, "like a dew-drop from a lion's mane" (3.3.222), the homosexual torpor of the "closet" tradition of critical commentary, Achilles faces his conflicting identities and confesses that his "mind is like a fountain stirr'd" and he cannot "see the bottom on't," i.e., he does not know to what source (*fons*) he owes his identity. By scraping the palimpsest-like identities from Achilles, Shakespeare disables Western civilization's greatest warrior as a character in the play and a usable exemplar in late Elizabethan England.

Along with the multiple genres of Achilles come questions of their associations with different social classes: Chapman's Homeric Achilles is dedicated to the Earl of Essex and an aristocratic code of honor discredited by the time of Shakespeare's play; Polyxena's lover, never greatly appreciated by courtly writers, befits the satirical ballads and broadsides that girls will sing about the hero gone astray, according to the taunting Ulysses; Patroclus' lover affirms the scholarly and homosocial interests of humanists who exchange ideas in critical margins and in scholarly Latin unavailable to popular audiences. The present study foregrounds the vested interests of classical, medieval, and early modern versions of the highly privileged tradition of the Troy legend and investigates the divergent uses to which Shakespeare and his contemporaries put competing versions as they sought to chart and influence shifts in the power and legitimacy of different cultural and political spheres in England, from the court to the Inns-of-Court, the universities, the city, and its underground as described by such men as Thomas Nashe, acerbic commentator on "Madame Troynovant" or London.[3]

Although differing agendas inform the uses of the Troy legend in Davies, Peele, Heywood, and Nashe, Shakespeare's overarching concern – and therefore mine – is the legitimacy of his developing national theater. Whether written under Elizabeth or James, his "translations of empire" take place in the interrogative mood,[4] or at less encomiastic and more restive moments in his relations with his two princes and their greatly differing styles of rule. Collectively the plays meditate what might constitute an English national politics rather than a narrow courtly politics; individually, they vary according to the historical stimuli that prompt Shakespeare to renew negotiations with court or city and produce a given "translation of empire." Historical occasions include contemporary preoccupations with female sovereignty and the depleted cult of the Virgin Queen in *Titus Andronicus*; in *Troilus and Cressida*, the fall of Essex and simultaneous collapse of the aristocratic culture of honor; the relationship of political and theatrical display in *Antony and Cleopatra*, the first Jacobean translation of empire; in *Cymbeline*, the growing separation of a strongly articulated royal absolutism and less heralded changes in English cultural identity, characterized by the beginnings of constitutional and legal struggles between James I and his parliaments; and in *The Tempest*, Shakespeare's valedictory meditation on the theater's relationship to stubborn differences between political theory and practice at a time when early Stuart England cast one eye on its increasingly equivocal status as a nation and another on its transatlantic expansion. This study aims to trace and historicize the repeated turns of Shakespeare's political thought as he renewed his experiments in undoing and regluing the idea of England in terms of authoritative books on England's cultural market. Recognizable as a social and political phenomenon since the rise of the Tudors, the tradition could be appropriated to promote the variously converging and conflicting interests of the market and the theater as well as its long-term benefactors, the court and the city.

We gain a sublime prospect on Shakespeare's quibbling authorities from the vantage point of Samuel Johnson's famous account of Shakespeare's wordplay as the "fatal Cleopatra for which he lost the world, and was content to lose it." When Johnson dramatizes a Herculean Shakespeare at the crossroads, he entertains the philosophical and political implications of choosing the licentious quibble over stable authority, whether linguistic or textual:[5]

A quibble is to Shakespeare, what luminous vapours are to the traveller; he follows it at all adventures; it is sure to lead him out of his way, and sure to engulf him in the mire. It has some malignant power over his mind, and its fascinations are irresistible. Whatever be the dignity or profundity of his disquisition, whether he be enlarging knowledge or exalting affection, whether he be amusing attention with incidents, or enchaining it in suspense, let but a quibble spring up before him, and he leaves his work unfinished. A quibble is the golden apple for which he will always turn aside from his career, or stoop from his elevation. A quibble, poor and barren as it is, gave him such delight, that he was content to purchase it, by the sacrifice of reason, propriety and truth. A quibble was to him the fatal *Cleopatra* for which he lost the world, and was content to lose it.

The quibble is a tragic weakness in Shakespeare, who abandons duty and authoritative language to chase after the impertinent attractions of a pun. The pleasures of doubt, for Johnson, lead to an artistic and ethical lapse reminiscent of the greatest political failure in the Western tradition: on 2 September 31 BC, Marc Antony, distracted by Cleopatra, followed her from the field at Actium and lost to Octavius Caesar both his claim to empire and his right to author his own reputation. When Johnson casts the scene of Shakespeare abdicating his poetic responsibilities as Antony at the fateful battle of Actium, he chooses an image of unusual potency: the Herculean Roman who unmans himself and assumes the woman's role of following. The heroic Antony himself becomes a tragic quibble, for as *Troilus and Cressida* states the paradox, he "is, and is not" Antony. Antony proves to be an apt, if tragic, exemplar of the way Shakespeare treats authority in all his translations of empire: as a victim of proliferating meanings.

When Johnson implicitly connects quibbling rhetoric, epistemology, gender, and politics, he performs an act of literary criticism felicitous to this study of Shakespeare's contaminated authorities. The passage invites readers to pause in the act of condemning quibbles in order to understand their doubtful charms, hauntingly revived through allusions to Eve's temptation in *Paradise Lost*. Cleopatra's retrospective prototype,[6] Milton's Eve is compared to an "amazed night-wanderer" when she encounters Satan's linguistic duplicity:[7]

> He leading swiftly rolled
> In tangles, and made intricate seem straight,
> To mischief swift. Hope elevates, and joy
> Brightens his crest, as when a wandering fire,
> Compact of unctuous vapour, which the night
> Condenses, and the cold environs round,
> Kindled through agitation to a flame,
> Which oft, they say, some evil spirit attends
> Hovering and blazing with delusive light,
> Misleads the amazed night-wanderer from his way
> To bogs and mires, and oft through pond or pool,
> There swallowed up and lost, from succour far.   (9.631–42)

Like Eve, Johnson's Shakespeare is a traveller distracted by "luminous vapours . . . sure to lead him out of his way, and sure to engulf him in the mire"; he, too, will "turn aside from his career" for the golden apple of a quibble and lose an Eden. Johnson compacts his linguistic will-o-the-wisp from Milton's account of Satan as a "wandering fire, / Compact of unctuous vapour" (9.634–5), who "Misleads the amazed night-wanderer from his way / To bogs and mires" where he is "swallowed up and lost" (lines 640–2) as surely as Johnson's Shakespeare is "engulf[ed] in the mire." Fascinating and "irresistible," the quibble exercises "malignant power" over Shakespeare, who recalls "Adventurous Eve" (9.921) in succumbing to verbal temptation and follows the brilliant but vaporous pun "to all adventures." By implicit comparison to Satanic rhetoric, which "casts between / Ambiguous words and jealousies to sound or taint integritie" (5.699–701), Johnson powerfully indicts Shakespeare's puns. Shakespeare's seduction from "reason, propriety and truth" represents no trivial failure of judgment: like Eve, he is distracted into pursuing a line of reasoning that alienates him from proprieties he once knew to be authoritative.

The pun lures Shakespeare into the indefinite meanings of language that takes issue with itself. Linguistically and socially subversive, the quibble will not commit to singular reference or allow any meaning to stand unchallenged by other meanings wishing to usurp the same sign. For Johnson, it epitomizes Shakespeare's general lack of "moral purpose" (p. 21) and his tendency to produce "stubborn" rhetorical and cognitive "entanglements" (p. 23). A quibble insists on differing with itself, and because it problematizes the grounds for knowledge, its philosophical terrain is epistemology. Although Johnson calls the quibble "poor and barren," it is far from meaningless: irresponsibly recreative, quibbling language generates more significances than it can contain and authorize and thus earns its name as Shakespeare's infinitely various, fertile, and fatally distracting Cleopatra.

Johnson's assessment of the Shakespearean quibble gains brilliance from his deep understanding of the linguistic charms he condemns: he reproduces in epitome Shakespeare's visceral attraction to quibbles and their co-ordinates in epistemology, gender, and politics. The political dimensions of quibbles, flagged by the erring figure of Antony, can be illuminated by the puns of Shakespeare's all-licensed fools, who include Falstaff, Hamlet, Lear's Fool, and the self-deposing antic in Richard II's head. The antic riddles and puns to disrupt comfort in social order. With the aid of quibbles, Falstaff turns himself into an unscrupulous and romantic authority opposed to "old father Antic, the law." Hamlet routs Claudius' court through the methodical madness of puns; the Fool uses song, riddles, and puns to force Lear's insight into the political and familial consequences of separating the name of king from its material basis in land; and in the ceremonial transfer of royal power to Henry IV, Richard II exploits the rivalrous, usurping resources of quibbles to discredit Bolingbroke's authority. Puns, like contaminations, create meanings that rival each other for primacy. Because the various meanings of a word or versions of a story are equally legitimate, they ultimately level notions of priority and hierarchy. The antic takes up the impudent pun as a form of language that opposes stable order, hierarchy, and the absolutist language of kingship. The pun is the antic's chief resource in upsetting assumptions of singular and hierarchical meaning – the sorts of assumptions that encourage editors to prioritize or disavow significances. Puns and contamination alike are indiscriminate: they mingle and mangle metaphors that ought to be kept discrete if they are to transport authority from one sphere to another.[8]

The present study adapts the epistemological and political model proposed by the recreative Shakespearean quibble and extends it to the playwright's use of imperial Roman authorities, primarily Vergil and Ovid, called to further political reckonings in Elizabethan and Jacobean England. These literary-political authorities had flourishing afterlives in Shakespeare's London, where their significances multiplied by the adaptability of the classics to elite and popular genres and to the sociopolitical interests of divergent audiences, illiterate and university-trained, courtly and civic. Both the classical texts themselves and their early modern coinages prompt Shakespeare's thinking about the shape and possibilities of his emergent theater and English national identity, which he routinely presents as a jeopardized possibility rather than a *fait accompli*. Reviving the excitement of classical authorities for Shakespeare's audiences, who generally if not uniformly understood the social and political valences at stake, is perhaps the greatest challenge to this study, undertaken at a time when we no longer look to classical allusions for witty topicality. Miranda is not the only pupil to find herself lulled to sleep after her father's quasi-Vergilian history of his calamities, but she is the only one compelled to do so. This study cheerfully appropriates methods from cultural studies and source studies, strange bedfellows that they are, arguing for the need to interpret the texts of the *translatio imperii studiique* as political metaphors rather than dead ones.

1   Shakespeare and the Troy legend

"Ingenium par imperio": the "Swan of Auon" and triumph of Britain

At least since the appearance of the *First Folio*, when Ben Jonson paid tribute to Shakespeare as the "Soule of the Age" and a poet "not of an age, but for all time," it has seemed incumbent upon critics to champion Shakespeare for his ability either to represent history or to rise above it.[1] Jonson, however, would be dismayed that his paradox about Shakespeare's art has come to underscore stubborn inconsistencies between Romantic transcendence and historical embeddedness, and disturbed at the notion that transcendent poetic skills detach the artist from history and politics. For a poet of Jonson's literary and social ambition, Shakespeare would most fully be the "Soule of the Age" when defying limitation in his own artistry and in England's political, geographical, and cultural borders. When Shakespeare bests the great dramatists of Greece and Rome, not to mention Elizabethan England, his credit wondrously affects England as an emergent nation. At the thematic and numerical center of his poem, Jonson dramatically shifts his address from Shakespeare to England itself. He moves – abruptly or seamlessly, depending on how prepared one is for conflations of art and politics – from Shakespeare's excellence in the theater to a political scene in which Britain personified triumphs over European rivals for cultural prestige:

> Leaue thee alone, for the comparison
> Of all, that insolent Greece, or haughtie Rome
> Sent forth, or since did from their ashes come.
> Triumph, my Britaine, thou hast one to showe,
> To whom all Scenes of Europe homage owe.
> He was not of an age, but for all time!   (lines 38–43)

Ageless art does not detach Shakespeare from contemporary England, but anchors him to the social and material conditions of his age that it makes visible to future generations: through the hybrid medium of published plays, Shakespeare makes the Elizabethan and Jacobean eras compelling enough to count historically. Defeating both "insolent Greece" and "haughtie Rome," he enters England triumphantly into the *translatio imperii studiique*, the myth by which cultural authority migrates from Troy to imperial Rome to England and rival European states.

On behalf of Shakespeare and England, Jonson revives the claims of Augustan poets to an immortality linked carefully to imperial expansion. He fulfills the promise at the close of his tribute, when he steps firmly into the vatic mode and shifts from remembrance to prophecy:

> Sweet Swan of Auon! what a sight it were
> To see thee in our waters yet appeare,
> And make those flights upon the bankes of Thames,
> That so did take Eliza, and our Iames!
> But stay, I see thee in the Hemisphere
> Aduanc'd, and made a Constellation there!
> Shine forth, thou Starre of Poets, and with rage,
> Or influence, chide, or cheere the drooping Stage;
> Which, since thy flight from hence, hath mourn'd like night,
> And despaires day, but for thy Volumes light.   (lines 71–80)

As the "Starre of Poets" and the "Swan of Auon" admired by royal spectators, Shakespeare merges with privileged signs of poetic and nationalistic ambition. Stellification, claimed in England by Sir Philip Sidney, the Astrophil mourned by a nation, derives most famously from the *Aeneid*, where it is the compensatory destiny that Jupiter awards Julius Caesar in the prophecy (*Aeneid* 1.261–96) whose centerpiece is Rome's claim to *imperium sine fine* (1.279). At the end of the *Metamorphoses*, Ovid first parodies Vergil's hint in an obsequious account of Julius Caesar's stellar apotheosis and then uses the triumph of imperial Rome as the basis of his poetic immortality. Hitching his own fame to Julius Caesar's, Ovid asserts that he, too, will be "borne beyond the stars" by means of his "indelible name." As a poet made immortal through Roman expansion, he will be quoted "wherever Roman power spreads over conquered lands": *perennis / astra ferar, nomenque erit indelebile nostrum / quaque patet domitis Romana potentia terris, / ore legar populi* (15.875–8).[2]

The swan's elegant and other-worldly flights, it turns out, are no more indifferent to conquest than the twinkling of the stars. The *locus classicus* for the image of the poet as swan (fig. 1) is Horace's Ode 2.20, a poem Jonson generously echoes throughout his commemoration of Shakespeare, from his emphasis on envy in the first passage to his celebration of the book as a source of immortality and a replacement for the tomb. Jonson reworks the Horatian demand to "give up the pointless tribute of a tomb" (*sepulcri / mitte supervacuos honores*, lines 23–4)[3] into a tribute,

Figure 1. "Insignia Poetarum." Andrea Alciati, *Emblemata* (Antwerp, 1577)

"Thou art a Moniment, without a tombe, / And art aliue still, while thy Booke doth liue" (lines 22–3), and exhortation to "Shine forth, thou Starre of Poets" (line 77) through "thy Volumes light" (line 80). Given his proprietary feelings about Horace and ambivalence about Shakespeare's fecund imagination, Jonson's choice of Horace's ode is key to understanding how he evaluated Shakespeare's art in retrospect: Jonson expected his rival's 1623 *Folio* not only to establish Shakespeare as a cultural icon but to witness and facilitate the cultural transformation of Britain itself.[4]

In 2.20, Horace establishes a model of poetic transcendence circumscribed by imperial expansion. In the first strophe, he declares that envy can no longer detain him from poetic flight as a *biformis vates* or "prophetic poet of double-form": man and bird, mortal writer of immortal verse, commoner accepted in the court. Galvanized by the tensions between his humble birth and summons to court by Maecenas, Rome's great aristocratic patron, Horace is launched towards his destiny: "not I, child of poor parents, not I, whom you call, beloved Maecenas, shall die" (*non ego pauperum | sanguis parentum, non ego, quem vocas, | dilecte Maecenas, obibo*, lines 5–7). Flight from civic discontents carries Horace, paradoxically, not to the heavens or to nature but to the further reaches of Rome's sprawling empire, where he surveys lands colonized by Rome and those still resisting assimilation. Horace names these lands and peoples in an elegiac travelogue, and like Ovid, who contemplates a readership among the conquered, Horace allows the possibility that the colonized peoples will read him to gain joint instruction in Roman norms and the means to endure their lost cultural autonomy. Horatian decorum invites both pleasure in, and anxiety over, Roman acquisition: lamenting Bosphorus may groan over more than its famously resounding ocean; the stoical Dacians only pretend not to fear Rome's toughest cohorts; the Hyperboreans, who dwell at the back of the North Wind, lack their customary representation as idyllic; the Geloni are only distant if Rome is the center of the world; and the Spaniards need no instruction from Rome to love reading and learning. Horace's elegiac adjectives for the colonized tactfully question the glory of cultural transformation, and his own example of metamorphosis into a swan suggests it is grotesque: "Now, even now the rough skin is settling on my shins, and I am changing into a snowy swan above, and light feathers are springing from my fingers and shoulders" (*iam iam residunt cruribus asperae | pelles, et album mutor in alitem | superne, nascunturque leves | per digitos umerosque plumae*, lines 9–12).[5]

Jonson omits the awkwardness of Horace's metamorphosis, preferring a miraculous vision of the "Sweet Swan of Auon" on the Thames. Nonetheless, he incorporates Horace's social motive for the problematic transformation from provincial origins to his destiny as an imperial Roman poet. When Jonson describes the Stratford playwright's commanding performances on the Thames, he adapts the socially liminal position from which Horace accepts and claims poetic authority. Shakespeare's identification with the Avon river, no mere bucolic tribute to his royal spectators, "Eliza, and our Iames,"[6] stresses his difference and autonomy from the center of English national identity in the royal court at London. For Jonson, the Thames serves as a geographical and semipermeable boundary between royal and theatrical authority. Steven Mullaney's conception of the physical and ideological place of the theaters helps illuminate the view in Jonson's poem:[7]

Born of the contradiction between Court license and City prohibition, popular drama in England emerged as a cultural institution only by materially embodying that contradiction, dislocating itself from the strict confines of the existing social order and taking up a place on the margins of society, in the Liberties located outside the city walls and, to the south, across the natural barrier of the Thames . . . When Burbage dislocated theater from the city, he established a social and cultural distance that . . . provided the stage with a culturally and ideologically removed vantage point from which it could reflect upon its own age with more freedom and license than had hitherto been possible.

The "Swan of Auon" visiting London's Thames becomes a dazzling intermediary between the theaters and London proper. A liminal figure, Jonson's Shakespeare is free to traffic in, not obliged to ventriloquize, the language of the court.

The Horatian swan, crossed with native English swans such as Leland celebrates in *Cygnea Cantio*, affirms Shakespeare's partial independence from the court-centered use of nationalist rhetoric and simultaneously confers on Shakespeare the power to make princely reputation. In Jonson's nostalgic image, the Spenserian "Eliza" and Jonsonian "our Iames" take on popular forms of royal self-representation and move to the Thames where Shakespeare performs an English cultural identity more inclusive and varied than what the princes might expect at court. To the extent that the Shakespearean swan commemorates England's national theater, he differs from those Ariostan swans who bestow immortality on generous princes (*Orlando furioso* 34–5). Richly invested with poetic and political significance, the image of the swan prepares for the moment when Jonson grows rapt with the vision of Shakespeare's apotheosis: "But stay, I see thee in the Hemisphere / Aduanc'd, and made a Constellation there!" The apotheosis is made possible by the publication of the "Volume" that elevates Shakespeare above the vagaries of theatrical production and confirms his status as a poet. When his audience widens to include posterity, Shakespeare becomes, posthumously, a poet who can influence the way in which Elizabeth, James, and the England that Jonson lovingly celebrates as "my Britain," are remembered and evaluated.

It should now be clear that Jonson explains the transcendent effect of Shakespeare's art in terms of a program of national ambition – the *translatio imperii studiique* – in which poets and princes participate alike, but not generally with the same shape of cultural authority in mind. The myth of political origins was adapted in imperial Rome to affirm Augustus' authority and vision of Rome's future, but also to propose dialogue with the receptive prince. The translation of empire is generally encomiastic, with ambition also to be advisory. A poet "translating empire" may be vague or hortatory about the exact constitution of the government he favors; and poet-advisers tend to imagine communities with greater latitude or distribution of cultural authority than the centralized and hierarchical one sought by absolutist princes.[8]

Since the Troy legend was promulgated in imperial Rome as a substitute history for the republic, the *translatio imperii* at times involves a shadowy *translatio republicae*. To understand what kind of government Jonson was translating in 1623, we may turn to the words that introduced the translation of empire – "insolent Greece" and "haughty Rome" – as they appear in the catalogue of eloquent statesmen that Jonson includes in *Timber, or Discoveries*. In his *scriptorum catalogus*, Jonson declares that Cicero was "the only wit that the people of Rome had equalled to their empire" – "*ingenium par imperio*" – and casts about for an English counterpart of the republican Cicero. His inventory of statesmen from the Henrician to Jacobean reigns moves through eloquent speakers on royal prerogative and the liberties of the subject from Thomas More to Thomas Smith, Nicholas Bacon to Sidney and Hooker, Essex to Raleigh and Savile, Edwin Sandys to Egerton and finally Francis Bacon, who[9]

hath filled up all numbers, and performed that in our tongue, which may be compared or preferred either to *insolent Greece, or haughty Rome*. In short, within his view, and about his times, were all the wits born, that could honour a language, or help study. Now things daily fall, wits grow downward, and eloquence grows backward: so that he may be named, and stand as the mark and ακμη of our language. (*Discoveries*, 79; my italics)

An elegiac figure in the drama of English oratory's growth and fall, Jonson's Bacon is less happy than Jonson's Shakespeare, who must be left "alone, for the comparison / Of all that *insolent Greece, or haughtie Rome* / Sent forth, or since did from their ashes come." Like Marcellus, the blighted figure of Rome's imperial promise who appears at the end of Anchises' catalogue of Roman heroes, the paradoxically *un*named Bacon stands at the despondent close of Jonson's survey of Tudor and Stuart statesmen. Many of these statesmen lived precariously, and several died violently, in service to the Tudor or Stuart courts, but none fell more humiliatingly than Francis Bacon: charged with bribery, he was impeached in 1621 by a strong common law Parliament led by his rival, Sir Edward Coke. Although both overgo "insolent Greece" and "haughty Rome," Shakespeare transcends where Bacon founders. Perhaps because Shakespeare worked in a versatile and popular medium aimed at large, diverse audiences, his was the *ingenium* equal to Britain's *imperium*; once published, his was the art that led Britain to march in triumph over European rivals for the authority conferred by the translation of empire.[10]

Jonson places Shakespeare at the center of Britain's political theater involving the *translatio imperii studiique*, the once thriving, now arcane tradition designed to transfer cultural authority from imperial Rome and, reaching further into the "dark backward and abysm of time," from Troy, imperial Rome's own lost site of national origins. Just as the poetic reputations of Vergil, Horace, and Ovid are linked to the enduring power of the Roman empire, so Shakespeare's art is inseparable from Britain's glory under Elizabeth and James. Since Jonson does not refer to a panegyrical style or to explicit topicality, the *First Folio*'s greatest tributary poem invites us to investigate other ways in which Shakespeare "translates empire," or uses privileged classical models to enchant and challenge Elizabeth and James, and perhaps to translate aspects of the Roman republic to haunt its centralized empire.

Royal flattery is not a mainstay of Shakespeare's translations of empire, although he is capable of praise ample enough to satisfy either Elizabeth I or James I. Witness to this talent is Cranmer's prophecy, at the close of *Henry VIII*, about the "maiden phoenix" and her "star-like" successor. Like Vergil's fourth eclogue, on which the prophecy is roughly based, the child will usher in a pastoral age in which "every man shall eat in safety / Under his own vine what he plants, and sing / The merry songs of peace to all his neighbors" (5.4.33–5); her "ashes" will "new create another heir / As great in admiration as herself" (lines 41–2), a prince able to transform the "peace, plenty, love, truth, terror" (line 47) of Elizabeth's reign into an imperial design. As Augustus was to the Roman empire, so will James be to Britain: "Where ever the bright sun of heaven shall shine, / His honor and the greatness of his name / Shall be, and make new nations" (lines 50–2). Cranmer's speech, which instantiates normative uses of classical imagery to translate authority from imperial Rome to the Tudor and Stuart courts, may serve as a counter to Shakespeare's allusive practices in the plays here called translations of empire. The idiosyncratic character of *Titus Andronicus*, *Troilus and Cressida*, *Antony and Cleopatra*, *Cymbeline*, and *The Tempest* should be viewed against encomiastic uses of the Troy legend in histories, lyric, masques, and pageantry and within the context of the interrogative tradition suggested by Vergil, launched by Ovid, Englished by Chaucer and Spenser, and strategically debased by Nashe.

The ideological legacy of Troy

The Troy legend, canonized by Vergil to ease Rome's painful transitions from republican to triumviral and finally imperial government under Augustus Caesar, became a privileged topos for nationalistic endeavors in early modern Europe.[11] Homer supplied Vergil with a heroic context to assuage Rome's recent political trauma and a prestigious origin for Rome's emergent imperial character. Revising Homeric epic allowed Vergil to mythologize and antedate the origins of Roman imperial identity so that Troy, not the conflicts of the triumvirate and ruins of the republic, would be treated as the prehistory and source of Augustus' power. Yet he offers a Janus-faced perspective on the Roman empire: the ideological mirror that promises Augustan peace simultaneously reflects the confusions and compromises of history. Throwing into relief the republican heritage that the Troy legend displaces, Vergil's poem insists on its revisionary and analytic character.

Vergil's ambitions to fashion an imperial ideology out of a fictitious past and to evaluate the actual histories pre-empted (the republic) and stigmatized (the civil wars between Octavius and Antony) almost immediately yielded a tradition that opposes, rather than reconciles, Vergil's own attitudes toward Roman history and ideology. In *Epic and Empire*, David Quint takes up the republican *Pharsalia*'s antagonistic imitation of the imperial *Aeneid* and argues that the rival traditions he associates with Lucan and Vergil[12]

define an opposition between epics of the imperial victors and epics of the defeated, a defeated whose resistance contains the germ of a broader republican or antimonarchical politics.

Time made possible an antiphonal voice to the imperial ideology of Vergil, and Quint productively analyzes the uses to which Milton puts Lucan's nostalgia for a republic long since displaced by the tyranny of such Augustan successors as Tiberius, Caligula, and Nero. Yet Quint's pairing of Vergil and Lucan, appropriate to the study of Milton's restoration politics, should not be taken to mean that Lucan was consistently heralded as Vergil's ideological opponent. In the late Elizabethan and early Stuart periods, that poet was Ovid, Vergil's younger and irreverent contemporary, eventually exiled by Augustus for acts not always romanticized in Shakespeare's England: Lodge, for example, prefaces his remarks on censorship by stating flatly, "I like not of a wicked *Nero* that wyll expell *Lucan* . . . I like not of an angrye *Augustus* which wyll banishe *Ovid* for envy."[13] This study, which joins Quint's in analyzing the interplay of ideology and form, proposes that for Shakespeare and his contemporaries, the insouciant Ovid offered an irresistible model of a poet able to promote the interests of the socially mobile (e.g., players) and the politically recalcitrant (e.g., the early Stuart parliaments). For breadth of representation, Shakespeare's England looked to its mixed monarchy, celebrated by Sir John Fortescue and Sir Thomas

Smith for its emphasis on political as well as royal government. Lucan's republican epic of the defeated awaited its welcome by anti-monarchical Englishmen grumbling under a more absolutist Stuart.

Vergil reaps more credit for encomia than criticism of empire, since the precedent he set by adopting the authoritative poetic legacy of Greece to predict the emergence of the Roman empire pleased not only Augustus but hosts of emergent nation-states and aspiring princes in the renaissance. The Troy legend became a transcultural, transhistorical model onto which poets such as Ariosto and Ronsard might graft indigenous myths of origin. The political authority inscribed in Vergil's epic and its Trojan myth awaited only transcription into the culture, history, and language of European governments in need of a legitimate history. France had its Francus, son of Priam; Denmark claimed Danus; Ireland, Hiberus; Saxony, Saxo. In his *History of the Kings of England*, Geoffrey of Monmouth, claiming to translate from a *vetustissimus liber* (sic), revealed the royal lineage: Adam, Noah, Priam, Aeneas, Ascanius, Silvius, Brutus. In an adventure narratively structured on Vergil's Aeneas' journey from Troy to Rome, Brutus traveled from Rome to England to establish Troynovant, later named London[14] (figs. 2 and 3). When Wace translated the legend into French and the history of Brittany, he prompted Layamon to wrest it back into the English language and culture, and the skirmishes among emergent European nations increased the legend's currency and prestige.

As the legend's geographical and temporal itinerary indicates, only in fiction does cultural authority migrate with the sureness of fate from one locale to another. Chroniclers, poets, and aristocrats regarded other roughly contemporary users of the legend as rivals, yet joined to assimilate Rome, the model user of the legend, to the legend's growing authority and body of exploitable material. Cultures, poets, and princes who once employed the myth of origins and its legendary heroes and events in the political undertakings of their day are themselves converted into the exemplary material used to mediate the political representations of later nations, poets, and princes. In light of its digestive function, the Troy legend is not only about the westering movement of cultural authority: it is also about the translation of historical moments, such as Rome's monumental shift from a republic to an empire, into a complex system of signs available both to claimants to, and critics of, political authority in search of precedent and ethical weight.

Shakespeare's contemporaries liberally employed the Troy legend to praise the virtues of Elizabeth, James, and London itself. Since Frances Yates' "Queen Elizabeth I as Astraea," critics have intensively examined the ways in which Elizabeth and her courtiers exploited the semiotics of

Figure 2. Title page from Richard Grafton, *Chronicle* (London, 1569)

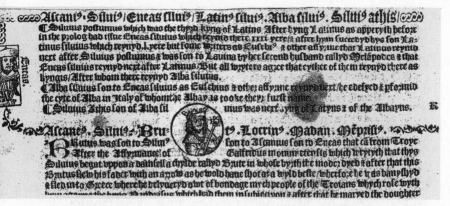

Figure 3. Leaf from John Rastell, *Cronycles of Englande* (London, 1536?)

the legend in her royal iconography, which featured classical figures of benign female governance.[15] Pre-eminent among her guises was the virgin Astraea, the classical goddess of justice whose return inaugurated Vergil's prophetic fourth eclogue – *iam redit et Virgo* – and whose departure in Ovid's *Metamorphoses* marked the fall from the golden to the bronze age. Supremely suited to Elizabeth I's needs, Astraea helped cast the virgin queen as a judicious restorer of the Protestant golden age in England. The rich Elizabethan tradition, well known from the epic poetry of Spenser, the pastoral poetry of Mary, Countess of Pembroke, the lyrics of Sir John Davies, and masques such as Peele's *Descensus Astraeae*, supplied a welcome celebration of Elizabeth's authority after the religious and political upheavals of Mary's reign. Thomas Heywood offers a typical gloss on Astraea in his *Life of Merlin*, written in the Stuart reign:

Astraea in whom is figured Justice (and here Queen Elizabeth personated) borrowing Ariadnes Crowne, which is one of the Celestiall constellations, who left the world in Saturnus Reigne, called the Golden Age, when the seven deadly sins began first to peep into the world, and clayme chiefe predominance on earth: who now at this restoration of true Religion, is said to descend from her place in the Zodiack, where she sate constell'd by the name of Virgo.

Heywood adds that Astraea now presides "over this blessed Queenes Tribunall, in which all Justice (with mercy mixed) was continually exercised."[16] His parenthetical remark that Elizabeth mixed mercy with rigorous justice underscores the use of classical myth to overlay historical compromises such as the beheading of Mary, Queen of Scots in 1587.

Elizabeth's identification with Astraea and the return of the golden age of Protestantism formed a strong link with the potent *renovatio* of the Troy legend so important to earlier Tudors. Heywood's *Life of Merlin* places its celebration of Elizabeth as Astraea within a narrative that concludes in Charles I's assumption of the throne and begins with the legend of Brute, who descends from "Aeneas and Creusa, daughter of Priam," settles in Britain, and founds a city near the river Thames "which in remembrance of the late subverted *Troy*, he called *Troynovant*, or new *Troy*, now *London*." In developing the image of Elizabeth as Astraea and the queen's associations with Troy, Heywood elaborates an epideictic tradition firmly entrenched in Elizabethan iconography. In the 1591 entertainment at Elvetham, for example, Elizabeth inspires the natural renewal of cultural authority. She brings "unfeigned joy" to her subjects, music to nature, and Troy to Troynovant: "Now birds record new harmonie, / And trees doe whistle melodie" in the presence of Elizabeth, the "beauteous Queene of second Troy."[17]

Another tie to the *translatio imperii* was Elizabeth's association with Dido, the founder of Carthage, a leader whose heroism is evoked in her other name, Elissa. Even in the *Aeneid*, where Vergil introduces the historical Dido into the *Aeneid* only to make her fall victim to passion, Dido first appears as Aeneas' female equivalent. The connection of Elizabeth and the fortuitously named Elissa is best known from the *Shepheardes Calendar*, in which Spenser celebrates Elizabeth in the figure of "Eliza, Queene of shepheardes."[18] In the background of the Sieve Portrait, moreover, are columns with scenes from Book 1 of the *Aeneid* which stress Aeneas' position as suppliant to the gracious queen. After the Armada, when Elizabeth's popularity and nationalist pride soared alike, a celebratory medal appeared bearing the Vergilian inscription, *Dux Foemina Facti*.[19] In this line, Vergil both praises Dido's heroism in escaping her tyrannical brother and establishing her own city and dwells, with astonishment, on the incongruity of the leader (*dux*) being a woman (*mirabile dictu*). Elizabeth I encouraged her identification with heroism and martial prowess, as witness her armed appearance before the troops at the Armada, to whom she boldly declared, "I may have the body of a weak and feeble woman, but I have the heart and stomach of a king . . ."[20]

When James VI and I came from Scotland to ascend the English throne, the poets in charge of royal entertainments and triumphs took pains to foster the link of English royal authority to the classical models favored in imperial Rome. Like the fictional Cranmer in *Henry VIII*, Dekker and Middleton found a suitable heritage for James in the personal iconography of Elizabeth and her promise of the golden to replace that of his Catholic mother, Mary. In *The Magnificent Entertainment* of 1604, Zeal acknowledges the depressed uncertainty felt in England at the end of Queen Elizabeth's reign: "The populous globe of this our English isle / Seem'd to move backward at the funeral pile / Of her dead female majesty." But England stages a miraculous recovery, inspired by the "attractive wonder of man's majesty!'":

> And then so rich an Empyre, whose fayre brest,
> Contaynes foure Kingdomes by your entrance blest,
> By Brute divided, but by you alone,
> All are againe united and made One,
> Whose fruitfull glories shine so far and even,
> They touch not onely earth, but they kisse heaven,
> From whence Astraea is descended hither,
> Who with our last Queenes Spirit, fled up thither,
> Fore-knowing on the earth, she could not rest,
> Till you had lockt her in your rightfull brest.[21]

Astraea allows the new king to incorporate Elizabeth's popularity and authority, for the spirits of both the goddess of justice and the Tudor queen are "lockt . . . in [his] rightfull brest." Not until James' pacifist attitude towards Spain, mounting debts, and dislike of crowds led to his widespread unpopularity did the figure of Elizabeth serve to chastise rather than compliment the king.[22] By the time James established his style of rule, as Muriel Bradbrook remarks,

the relatively stable and widely accepted images of Elizabeth as Astraea, Belphoebe or Diana, which had met the specific needs of the religious-political adjustments embodied in the Elizabethan Settlement, could not be simply reproduced . . . since the nature of the social pressures defined [political conflict] eventually as one between Crown and Commons.[23]

At the time the new king first entered London, however, the Jacobean Astraea took unprecedented interest in his project to unite England and Scotland.

Under the Stuarts, civic pageantry also recycled Elizabeth's iconography while suppressing her witness to effective female magistracy. In the Caroline entertainment, *Brittannia's Honor*, Dekker presents London as so "famous . . . for her *Buildings*, that Troy has leap'd out of her own Cinders, to build Her Wals." The second presentation, *New Troyes Tree of Honor*, opens to discover "A *Person* in a rich *Romane* Antique Habit, with an ornament of Steeples, Towers, and Turrets on her head, Sits in a queint Arbor, Interwoven with several Branches of Flowers." The ancient Roman "Leader and Conductresse of a Mighty People," then reaches into the arbor with her right hand to grasp a tree with "Twelve Maine and Goodly Branches." She represents London, and the branching tree "(guarded and supported by her) the 12 Superior Companies." Once the Stuarts were on the throne, the anomaly of a woman being the "Leader and Conductresse of a Mighty People" – *dux foemina facti* – becomes less disruptive, for she is London personified. Dekker includes the companies in his praise of London's strength, but there is no question that the primary recipient of the compliment is Charles: Sol declares, "O how I ioy / To view a Kingdome, and a New-built Troy / So flourishing, so full, so faire, so deare / To th' Gods: they leave love's Court to revell here." Charles' court could, after a fashion, be called nearer to the gods than his father's, for the son insisted even more strenuously than the ardent James on the divine right of kings.

Vergilian themes also dominated James' triumph. In his *Magnificent Entertainment*, Dekker adapted Anchises' prescription of "imperial acts" to Aeneas to "establish peace, spare the conquered, and battle down the proud."

> Tu Regere Imperio populos Iacobe memento,
> Hac tibi erunt Artes, Pacique imponere morem,
> Parcere Subiectis, et debellare Superbos.

These words, which conclude James' *Basilikon Doron*, adorned the arch – "over the Gate, in golden Caracters" – through which James passed on his way into London.[24] With the substitution of *Iacobe* for *Romane*, James need only accept Vergilian authority in order to match Aeneas' assumption of imperial Roman identity. Ben Jonson also labored to construct a potent Vergilian iconography for the king's entrance. He composed a speech to begin with a recollection of Troy – "The long laments I spent for ruin'd Troy / Are dried" – and to promise England a "lasting glory to AUGUSTUS state."[25] Jonson habitually affirmed James' Vergilian heritage: "*Aeneas*, the sonne of *Venus*, *Vergil* makes through-out the most exquisit patterne of *Pietie*, *Justice*, *Prudence*, and all other Princely vertues, with whome (in way of that excellence) I conferre my Soveraigne."[26] This tribute from *The Haddington Masque* emphasizes that James' classical heritage is a gift of poets. Jonson seeks a model of political authority in which prince and poet rely upon each other: he adopts the Augustan system of patronage to negotiate for political authority within the court as the undisputed center of England's power. Jonson's courtly ideal differs from the working model in Shakespeare's translations of empire, which appropriate the classical authority for more public uses in the theater.

The *translatio imperii* offered authority so apparently unimpeachable that the complicated histories and ethics behind key figures seem mostly not to intrude upon the iconographical scene. Elizabeth could be represented as a second Dido, strictly associated with the heroic and chaste founder of Carthage, uncompromised by the subsequent disaster that forms the most widely read and affecting scenes of Vergil's *Aeneid*. James could identify with Aeneas without having to explain why his exemplary model loved and abandoned Dido. Alternately, he could cast himself as the new Augustus, the imperial prince who restored order to Rome without suffering, for example, from the role Augustus played in the proscriptions against fellow citizens enacted by the triumvirate of Octavius, Antony, and Lepidus.[27] As it was adapted in the courts and pageants of Elizabeth and James, the legend was detached from its original embeddedness in the complex, ambivalent texts of Vergil's *Aeneid* and Ovid's *Metamorphoses*. Employed in a highly controlled manner, the legend resembled ideological images of imperial authority like the frieze on the shield of Aeneas. It bore the mark of abstracted and politically usable authority.

The path that the *translatio imperii* and its attendant cultural prestige took to reach Tudor and Stuart England, however, was more arduous and devious than the easy step from Anchises' speech in Vergil's Underworld to Dekker's triumphal arch. The Troy legend was subjected to stinging skepticism among historians and antiquarians, and the slights of a Polydore Vergil or John Selden make their way into Shakespeare's *Troilus and Cressida*, where the cultural legacy of the Troy legend amounts to the syphilitic diseases that accompany the degeneration of exemplars into social tropes – pandars, Cressids, a Hector or Achilles. Such tropes parody more pointed cultural uses of the historical and legendary figures to oppose or champion dominant court politics. Heywood, for example, cites the Troy legend to oppose Stuart absolutism. Stressing the "uncontroulable authority" and "absolute power" of the Roman equivalents to England's mayors, he takes pains to point out that there was no greater office than the one comparable to the Lord Mayor's, "till *Julius Cæsar* aiming at the Imperiall Purple, was not content with that annuall *honour*, which was to passe successively from one to another, but he caused himselfe to be Elected *Perpetuus Dictator*, which was in effect no lesse than Emperor."[28] When Heywood translates something of the republican form of senatorial counsel into the empire founded by a Caesar, he follows the great medieval constitutionalist, Sir John Fortescue, who writes that Julius

on account of this arrogance of his being at last put to death, Octavianus, a man of the mildest character, being raised to the monarchy of the whole world, governed it not only royally only but politickly by the advice of the Senate.[29]

For the purposes of his own constitutionalist argument, Fortescue chooses to view Augustan empire as a proto-English mixed monarchy.

The Achilles' heel of the Troy legend is, finally, its long, tortuous history. Its transmission through varied eras, nations, and vested interests radically affects the precious univocality of its authority and its singularly affirmative character in political commentary. While history deepens the tradition's authority, it also disperses it through nationalistic competition: European nations sprouted their lineal branch from the Trojans in response to the epic and chronicle accounts composed for rival nations. When the goal was *imperium sine fine*, the need to translate the legend into one's own idiom and culture was pressing indeed. Under pressure from within, the ostensibly monolithic Troy legend could be broken down into the multiple and competing versions which make up a seamless continuum only in panegyric. There is nothing novel in the suspicion that Trojan authority might arise from propaganda and force. Even before historians took up increasingly rigorous historical methodology and classical scholarship, skepticism haunted the tradition: Vergil himself repeatedly endangers his own authority, not least through the figure of Fama, who becomes a champion for later authors to challenge the truth and ethics of the Troy legend.

The legacy of Fame: authority and ambiguity in the Troy legend

The emperor's court is like the house of Fame,
The palace full of tongues, of eyes and ears.   (*Titus Andronicus*, 2.1.126–7)

Travelling backwards through literary history reveals the ways in which poets shape disparate interpretive traditions from sources as multivalent as the *Aeneid*. From the perspective of Elizabethan and Stuart iconography, Vergil offered a treasury of images through which artists might safely conduct classical authority to the English court. As the last section indicates, even literary forms more open-ended than pageants and masques could use the Troy legend to essentially iconographic effect. Shakespeare does so when he praises Elizabeth, in *A Midsummer Night's Dream*, as an "imperial vot'ress" (2.1.163): like the "little western flower" (line 166) shot with Cupid's shaft, the "fair vestal throned by the west" (line 158) is rhetorically tied to empire by allusions to the westering movement of authority in the *translatio imperii*.[30] Yet strong readers of textual knots and ambiguities may choose instead to respond critically and creatively to works that have been canonized on political, as well as aesthetic, grounds.

When Chaucer conspicuously fails to rewrite the *Aeneid* in the *Hous of Fame*, it is because the figure of Dido brings him to an interpretive crossroads. He ably paraphrases the Latin epic up to the moment that

Dido begins to lament, at which point Chaucer finds himself rehearsing, with feeling, the complaints of Ovid's Dido and a chorus of abandoned women from Ovid's *Heroides*. Unable to recover from the tragic crisis of the *Aeneid*, Chaucer is scarcely able to finish Aeneas' story and ends the first part of his work in confusion. At this point in the *Hous of Fame*, Chaucer founders in his Vergilian labors over problems of empathy, and continues his literary search for "tydynges / Of Loves folk" (2.644–5)[31] in a more Ovidian frame of mind. The problems that Dido raises for Chaucer are symptoms of a larger crisis of interpreting Vergil's authoritative text about empire and the reactive literary tradition launched by Ovid. When Chaucer at last enters the house of Fame, he confronts the fundamental problem of the Vergilian tradition: the Troy legend is made up of ideologically warring parts.

In Fame's house, Chaucer's narrator spies the iron pillar of Troy's reputation, shouldered by "gret Omer; / and with him Dares and Tytus / Before, and eke he Lollius, / And Guido eke de Columpnis, / And Englyssh Gaufride eke, ywis" (3.1466–70). The group of authorities at the pillar of Troy is more than the bibliography that the heaped up "ekes" suggest. Great Homer has priority in the inventory, but Dares and Dictys come "before," presumably because each claims to bear eyewitness to the Trojan War. Just as the casual joining of the pro-Trojan Dares with the pro-Greek Dictys conceals ironies about the authors' solidarity, so does the introduction of Lollius, an authority known only to Chaucer. When he passes the torch to Guido della Colonne, the Troy legend crosses the boundaries of epic and chronicle into historical romance. And when "Englyssh" Geoffrey takes over, Troy's fame enters into the political teleology of the *translatio imperii* and becomes a matter of English nationalism. The conflicts so ill-concealed by the monolithic presentation of names become explicit when the narrator inspects the *auctores*' positions closely:

> And ech of these, as have I joye,
> Was besy for to bere up Troye.
> So hevy therof was the fame
> That for to bere hyt was no game.
> But yet I gan ful wel espie,
> Betwex hem was a litil envye.
> Oon seyd that Omer made lyes,
> Feynynge in his poetries,
> And was to Grekes favorable;
> Therfor held he hyt but fable.   (3.1471–80)

The strain of supporting the iron pillar of Troy's fame comes from the *auctores*' struggle to wrest the national and ideological bearings of Troy from the hands of their literary competitors. As Chaucer observes, the efforts of one writer to undermine Homer's authority thrust the entire legend out of the realm of history and into fable. Reading the Troy legend in its many versions induces in Chaucer a crisis of authority parallel, although less emotionally vexing, to the original one over the Didos of Vergil and Ovid.

Vergil's *Aeneid* constitutes the *locus classicus* for an unquestionable imperial authority as well as its impeachment: Vergil himself formulated two distinct approaches to Augustan empire in the *Aeneid*, one panegyrical and the other interrogative. The first tradition is based upon the *Aeneid*'s structural principles, which seek the harmonious alignment of the narrative, Augustan ideology, and the cosmos. This tradition also trades on the poem's images of a centralized and paternalistic authority, such as the figure of Augustus in the center of Aeneas' shield, surrounded by the chaos generated by Antony and Cleopatra.[32] The second tradition emanates from many unanswerable questions, scattered throughout the poem, about the costs of empire and the reasons – myth or misadventure – for historical events. The struggle between the two implied versions of the poem is summed up by the ambiguous questions Vergil asks of sacrifice. Upon her death, Aeneas' nurse gives "eternal fame" to the shores that Vergil and his original readers patriotically celebrate as "ours." "And if this glory matters in the end" (*si qua est ea gloria*, 7.4), Vergil continues, "Your name tells of your grave in great Hesperia."[33] If the question is read rhetorically, the reader enjoys the proud thrill of *assuming* the compensatory value in death for Rome and pleasure in naming one of the monuments on the map of the empire Aeneas charts on his way to found Rome. If the question is read grammatically, the reader is liable to founder, as Aeneas himself frequently does, on epistemological grounds. Who is to say that there is glory in the deaths of Caieta, Misenus, Palinurus, and Pallas? Literary tradition is not always known for its justice, and so the panegyrical tradition is, in the renaissance, mostly known as Vergilian while the interrogative tradition is more often associated with Ovid, the poet who used the questions Vergil left dangling to structure an alternate version of the Troy legend. The figure that Ovid, like Chaucer after him, uses to sponsor his revision of the *Aeneid* is Vergil's Fama, appropriately used against her original author, since she stands for incomplete, misleading, narration.

A monstrous personification allegory, Fama erupts from Vergil's narrative, immediately after Dido and Aeneas consummate their passion in the cave, and wreaks havoc on the stable narrative frame of the epic.[34] A titaness with an epic genealogy and a heavily iconographic body, she is

monstrum horrendum, ingens, cui quot sunt corpore plumae,
tot vigiles oculi subter (mirabile dictu),
tot linguae, totidem ora sonant, tot subrigit auris.   (4.181-3)

> a monster vast,
> And dreadful. Look, how many plumes are placed
> On her huge corps, so many waking eyes
> Stick underneath; and, which may stranger rise
> In this report, as many tongues she bears,
> As many mouths, as many listening ears.   (Ben Jonson, *Poetaster* 5.1)

Her grotesque body emblematizes her linguistic mixture of truths and half-truths: *pariter facta atque infecta canebat* (4.190). *Infecta*, which verbally mirrors *facta* and is usually translated as "falsehood," literally refers to something unfinished. The difference between a lie and a partial truth is crucial to understanding Vergil's project at this moment in the *Aeneid* and, in fact, in the poem as a whole. Vergil uses Fama to raise questions about the vested interests that help shape events into *facta*, or usable fictions.

Fama's disconcerting language issues an epistemological challenge to the poem's official ideology. It takes a leap of faith to believe that Fama represents a linguistic duplicity to which Vergil's own authoritative language is opposed, for Vergil's poem, imbued with ambiguity, is rigorously selective about its certainties. Vergil's figure for faulty language and epistemological doubt, Fama appears directly after a rare assertion of indisputable fact: Dido, he tells us, no longer contemplates a secret love affair, but calls it marriage and "with this name covers her guilt" (*hoc praetexit nomine culpam*, 4.172). There is, as one critic puts it, "no getting around the fact that Vergil's Dido ends as a fallen woman, conscious of her sin, betrayed and abandoned."[35] Yet despite her self-condemnation, powerfully seconded by the poem's pro-Augustan forces, other factors in the *Aeneid* rise up to confute the resounding judgment against her. Dido bases her understanding of the event on cosmic, natural, and emotional signs and the goddess of marriage herself validates Dido's view: however ill-motivated, Juno vows to be present at the joining of Dido and Aeneas and to consecrate their union in a fixed marriage (*conubio iungam stabili propriamque dicabo*, 4.126). For Vergil, certainty is a lure: all readers of the episode must weave the events in the cave – the verb *praetexo* bears on the Roman idea of a poem or text as something woven – into a coherent narrative with a usable moral. Aeneas does so when he reminds Dido that no laws bind him to her: "I never held the torches of a bridegroom," he says, "or entered into that bond" (*nec coniugis umquam / praetendi taedas aut haec in foedere veni*,

4.338–9). Aeneas is on shaky legal ground, however, for cohabitation constituted a binding marriage in Rome.

In the figure of Fama, Vergil personifies the crisis of authority induced by competing plausible interpretations of the events in the cave, which ultimately lead to Rome's Punic wars. If we trust in the authority of indictment – and Vergil evidently uses his own voice to pronounce her guilt – what are we to believe when we hear, moments later, Fama issue an equally authoritative judgment? Through indirect speech, we learn what Fama has been singing:

> venisse Aenean Troiano sanguine cretum,
> cui se pulchra viro dignetur iungere Dido;
> nunc hiemem inter se luxu, quam longa, fovere
> regnorum immemores turpique cupidine captos.   (4.191–4)

how Aeneas, born of Trojan blood, has come, to whom lovely Dido has deigned to join herself; now between themselves they warm the long winter in luxury, unmindful of their kingdoms, prisoners of bitter lust.

A weaver of fictions, Fama sings (*canat*) an account of Dido and Aeneas' story that compresses rather than distorts the poem that Vergil himself undertook to sing with the words, *arma virumque cano*. Fama speaks neither bald lies nor bare facts but, instead, a jumbled version of the very judgments and implied genres that Vergil dexterously weaves into his own narrative. Every detail in the passage is saturated with warm romance or poisonous censure. Dido's loveliness and Aeneas' high birth make them "such a mutual pair" that the world almost admits they "stand up peerless" and turn kingdoms to "clay," as Shakespeare's Antony puts it. Fama supplies an attractive glimpse of the couple's intimacy as they "warm the winter" (*fovere hiemem*), a view disrupted by the intrusion, in the center of line 193, of the "Roman thought" of luxury, a concept that meant to the Romans what "idle" meant to Elizabethans. With unguarded pleasure so effectively nipped in the bud, critics feel doomed, perhaps, to accept the stinging indictment of the final line, which reduces love to lust and castigates the couple for thinking of desire rather than public duty.[36] All of Fama's words, however, not just those uncongenial to empire, are gossipy and opinionated. It is deeply unsettling to hear in the mouth of Fama the perspective and diction familiar from the decrees of Jupiter and the supposedly absolute judgment of Vergil on Dido's guilt. In sum, Dido is guilty and the love affair shameful only if the reader assumes that the pro-imperial interests of the poem throw into shadow the counter-evidence of literary, legal, and historical implication. Fama, Vergil's personification for the interrogative mood of his epic, erupts from a tear in the pro-Augustan fabric of the *Aeneid*.

In Ovid's *Metamorphoses* 12, Fama has risen to a higher social position: no longer a prodigious birth, created by Earth to defy the gods – Vergil's *foeda dea* – she presides over a house composed of sounding brass. Standing open to catch and release all news, her palace resounds and repeats what it hears, *tota fremit vocesque refert iteratque quod audit* (12.47):

> veniunt, leve vulgus, euntque
> mixtaque cum veris passim commenta vagantur
> milia rumorum confusaque verba volutant;
> e quibus hi vacuas inplent sermonibus aures,
> hi narrata ferunt alio, mensuraque ficti
> crescit, et auditis aliquid novus adicit auctor.   (12.53–58)

shifting throngs come and go, and everywhere wander fictions mixed with truth, thousands of rumors, and confused words fly. Some of these fill idle ears with gossip, and others tell the stories they have heard to someone else; the size of the fiction grows, and each new author adds something to what he or she has heard.

By revising Vergil's Fama into a courtly and gossipy figure, Ovid simultaneously defines his own project of revision. He is the *novus auctor* – author and augmenter – who adds something new to the story he heard from Vergil which, in its day, filled idle ears at court with gossip. What Ovid heard from Vergil was the myth of the *translatio imperii*, the story of Aeneas, which he proceeds to retell from the Trojan war to the foundation of Rome.

In Ovid's theory of imitation, new authors in a tradition gradually but inexorably displace earlier authorities. He is keenly aware that

[t]ranslatio always involves a relation to a previous authority or figure of the proper. Whether considered as the basis of a theory of history (*translatio imperii*) or literature (*translatio studii*), or as a general rhetorical term that encompasses all kinds of tropes (figurative language, in which there is a substitution of one term for another), *translatio* articulates a movement away from the authoritative, the proper, and an establishment of another authority or propriety.[37]

What Ovid adds to the translation of empire is his own establishment as a counter-authority and master of impropriety. His innovation is to reverse the relationship Vergil established between the *Aeneid*'s stable narrative frame and its unsettling episodes. Vergil chose to support Augustan ideology in the formal design of the *Aeneid* and test it through "impertinent" questions dispersed throughout the poem, such as the ones raised by Fama. Ovid flamboyantly marks his poem's difference from the *Aeneid* when he uses Vergil's Fama to introduce his rivalrous version of the Trojan war. By casting Fama as the sponsor of the *translatio imperii*, Ovid strips the newly-canonized Troy legend of authority. Through a catalogue of personification allegories who populate Fama's house in the *Metamorphoses*, Ovid gives us a précis of his view of the Troy legend and a foretaste of his own political retelling of it:

> illic Credulitas, illic temerarius Error
> vanaque Laetitia est consternatique Timores
> Seditioque recens dubioque auctore Susurri . . .   (12.59–61)

Here's credulity, here bold error, empty pleasure, anxieties, fresh sedition, and whispers from an untrustworthy source.

Having modeled literary and political history on the language of rumor, Ovid uses the rest of his *Metamorphoses* to launch a critique of Aeneas' mission to found the Augustan empire.[38]

The final third of his poem metamorphoses into a relentlessly uninspiring and erratic imitation of the *Aeneid*. At every opportunity, Ovid evinces boredom with his heroic material. Surly because someone else is invulnerable to the sword, Achilles the petulant crushes Cygnus to death, and comes back from the dead to demand the sacrifice of Polyxena. He, the blockish Ajax, and the duplicitous Ulysses collude to exhaust the epideictic powers of epic. Ovid then turns the *Aeneid* inside-out by flattening Vergil's protagonists and developing his minor characters. Anius, priest of Apollo, tells the story of his daughters' metamorphosis into Venus' doves, who led Vergil's Aeneas to the golden bough. Achaemenides, whom Vergil invented to testify against Ulysses, gains from Ovid a tale of his own and friends interested in hearing it. Ovid's Diomedes, the fearsome Iliadic warrior who sent word in the *Aeneid* of his refusal to fight once more against the Trojans, now wants to share his war stories and the problems he faced in resocializing. Vergil's Polyphemus, a mostly Homeric and blood-thirsty monster, enjoys a translation into his Theocritean identity as the pathetic lover of Galatea, and even the Sybil regains her love life with Apollo. No Vergilian detail is too trivial for Ovid, who elaborates on the lives of Caenus and Picus: of the almost Ovidian figures who exist on the fringe of Vergil's narrative, one metamorphosed from a woman to a man, while Circe changed the other from a man to a bird.[39] Throughout the master narrative of Aeneas' journey, Ovid defies Vergilian constraints and pauses to let characters narrate their own stories. By subjecting the *Aeneid* to a wandering narrative structure, flamboyant rhetoric, and reversal of the values attached to erotic and political themes, Ovid causes Vergil's poem to testify against its proposed ideal of erotic restraint. Narratively and thematically, he unravels the *Aeneid* at the seams.

As for the principal characters in Vergil's poem, Aeneas is mechanically conveyed from one port of his journey to another, coolly unaffected by the path of destruction he leaves in his wake. Where Vergil lavishes pathos – the fall and suicide of Dido – Ovid bestows only a lethal transition:

> cum iam prope litus adessent
> Ausonium, Libycas vento referuntur ad oras.
> excipit Aenean illic animoque domoque
> non bene discidium Phrygii latura mariti
> Sidonis; inque pyra sacri sub imagine facta
> incubuit ferro deceptaque decipit omnes.
> rursus harenosae fugiens nova moenia terrae . . .   (14.76–82)

when they had almost reached the Ausonian shore, they were borne back by the wind to the Libyan coast. There the Sidonian queen received Aeneas in her heart and home – she who would ill endure her Phrygian husband's divorce. On a pyre, built under pretense of sacred rites, she lay down upon his sword; deceived, she deceived all. Leaving once more the new city built upon the sandy shore . . .[40]

Since regrets do not compensate for the sacrifices marking each step of Aeneas' journey, Ovid omits them. He endorses Dido's perspective on her relationship with Aeneas when he refers to the divorce (*discidium*) of her husband (*maritus*) and to Aeneas' deceit (*decipio*). However, although he employs the legal vocabulary Vergil scrupulously avoids, Ovid drastically minimizes the episode. Saving complaints for the *Heroides*, Ovid here stresses the indifference of empire to individual voice. It is no wonder that Augustus, a fairly patient ruler and good reader, finally exiled the audacious poet from Rome. Chaucer, an even better reader of the tradition, lost faith in the *Aeneid* by reading Ovid and never recovered his trust in the Troy legend. At the end of the *Hous of Fame*, a "man of gret auctoritee" – possibly Vergil – bursts onto the scene and appears to be on the verge of conquering Fama's ambiguities. At this moment, Chaucer's poem comes to its inconclusive end: for the last time, Chaucer fails to tell the story of the *Aeneid*.

Reading literary history, as this brief examination of Vergil's Fama and her legacy demonstrates, uncovers the Troy legend's self-marring history of ideological appropriation. The stakes are high, because it is *the* literary tradition invested with originary cultural authority, to which its distinctive examples and metaphors are expected to grant safe conduct through time. The tradition's generic, evaluative, and ideological transformations have a cumulative effect that differs from the reconstitution of authority that takes place in any one of its translations: the united and teleological appearance of the *translatio imperii* breaks down. In the face of this phenomenon, Chaucer decides not to translate Vergil's *Aeneid* and, by extension, empire. But poets who set themselves the task of translating empire must confront the problem of the tradition's history of appropriation and change and, in particular, its dual sponsorship by Vergil and Ovid as Prince of Poets and Lord of Misrule. The ready solution of encomiastic pageantry is to ignore differences and use famous motifs to simple iconographic effect.

A more sophisticated response, adopted by Spenser, is to negotiate diplomatic relations between the Vergilian and the Ovidian traditions. In *The Faerie Queene* III.ix-x, Britomart inherits the Vergilian mantle, while Hellenore, warmed to Ovidian pleasures by Paridell, ends her career in the embraces of those rudimentary Ovidians, the satyrs.[41] Within Spenser's encomiastic work, Ovidian parody achieves a place, albeit subordinate to the higher ambitions of Vergilian epic. Spenser both engages and protects the divisive tradition by employing a complex form of contamination. Yet diplomatic relations among ideologically warring texts are not always desired: Spenser prefers an irreconcilable clash between Redcrosse's Vergilian and Protestant ethic of labor and the knight's lapse with Duessa by the Ovidian pool in I.vii. In a similar bid for disjunction, Shakespeare contaminates the translation of empire in ways that jeopardize the very authority that the legend should convey in stately triumph from Troy, through imperial Rome, and finally to England.

Quibbling with authority: Shakespeare's translations of empire

> sorrow's eye, glazed with blinding tears,
> Divides one thing entire to many objects,
> Like perspectives, which rightly gaz'd upon
> Show nothing but confusion; ey'd awry,
> Distinguish form.   (*Richard II*, 2.2.16–20)

By the time Shakespeare sought out the legends of Troy for use in his theater, the *translatio imperii* had high visibility in civic and courtly pageantry and a degree of notoriety due to internal conflicts that fanned skepticism in sober antiquarians and playful Ovidians. Familiar and controversial by the 1590s, the *translatio imperii* allowed Shakespeare to draw on courtly iconography and test it against its origins in the imperial, but ambivalent, texts of Vergil and Ovid. In his translations of empire, he radicalizes the skepticism that Chaucer, Ariosto, and Spenser used to lay bare the history of ideological appropriation that destabilizes authority, quite against the conservative political interests of the Troy legend. Shakespeare's dramatic imagination and social ambition, sparked by the possibility of translating cultural and political authority from imperial Rome, Troy, and Troynovant, brought him to crack the ideological lens that "ey'd awry" the tradition in order to "distinguish form." He subjects the legend to its anamorphic properties, dividing "one thing entire to many objects" which "show nothing but confusion." Summoning two or more authorities, he sets them in implicit debate about the success of the *translatio imperii*.

As a glance at Geoffrey Bullough's eight-volume *Narrative and Dramatic Sources of Shakespeare* tells us, Shakespeare often forges plays from disparate sources without particular consideration of the sources' authority or ideological consistency.[42] In *Julius Caesar*, for example, the differences in accounts by Plutarch, Tacitus, and Appian do not underpin the play's differing perspectives on Roman government in an expressly citational manner. The Roman plays do not, collectively, trade on problematic conflations of sources in order to represent and generate a crisis of authority. The plays I call "translations of empire" are distinguished from the Roman plays partly by their contaminations of disparate sources, which, on a specifically textual level, audit the treasury of stable authority and identity inherited from imperial Rome. The plays studied here – *Titus Andronicus, Troilus and Cressida, Antony and Cleopatra, Cymbeline*, and *The Tempest* – are linked by their engagement of the imperial theme and formation of peculiar relations with their textual authorities. In these plays, Vergil, Ovid, Horace, Plutarch, and Livy, as well as Lydgate and Holinshed, refuse to fade into the background or, having failed the first law of decorum, refuse even to establish congenial relations with each other. These plays cite and mingle exemplary models in ways that emphasize, rather than naturalize, the imperious nature of strong fictions or histories.

A contemporary playgoer might expect Shakespeare to privilege a single authority, such as Geoffrey, Lydgate, or Vergil, or to choose his authorities for their consistency. After all, poets rarely reflect on the ways in which classical models, such as Aeneas or Achilles, have undergone multiple transformations in order to support opposed interests and values. Moreover, one does not anticipate methodological or representational risks when the subject matter intimately concerns the myths of national origins used by the reigning monarch. Yet when Shakespeare selects multiple authorities and highlights the differences among them, he repudiates the kind of imitation that honors its model and hopes to transport some essential value from the original. His Aeneas is not only Vergil's duty-bound hero, but also *Cymbeline*'s "false Aeneas" and *Titus Andronicus*' "wandering prince," who is hardly to be distinguished from Spenser's Paridell. If these versions of Aeneas were discretely kept apart, little could be said of the significance of Shakespeare's alternating perceptions of Rome's founder. Yet in *Titus, Antony and Cleopatra, Cymbeline*, and *The Tempest*, Vergil's empire-builder and Ovid's cad rub elbows. When this happens in the figure of *Cymbeline*'s Posthumus, for example, Shakespeare generates a crisis that endangers the exemplarity of both the British Posthumus and Roman Aeneas. And when a national hero's exemplarity is jeopardized, so is the triumph that Britain is supposed to enjoy through inheritance.

The narrative histories of Achilles reveal that Aeneas does not suffer from multiple personalities alone. Conflicting accounts of a particular event throw into question elements of the legend which, unlike Aeneas' choice of empire over love, are meant to be assumed, not contested. A survey of Achilles' histories reveals that we cannot be sure what motivated Western literature's greatest warrior even in his most celebrated acts, such as his refusal to fight. Did he withdraw from the Trojan war to preserve his honor? or to negotiate in secret for the hand of Polyxena in marriage? Is he to be interpreted according to the accounts of Homer or Ovid and the medieval chroniclers? In *Troilus and Cressida*, Shakespeare disturbs his audiences' confidence in self-evident identity, an illusion produced by the tireless reproductions of an exemplar since the beginning of Western literature. We do not, in fact, know who is onstage simply because his name is Achilles, Ulysses, or Troilus, and Shakespeare conducts us into serious doubts that we can know a man if we "ever saw him before and knew him," as Cressida puts it (1.2.66). In this play, Shakespeare extends the destabilizing function of literary history from a single hero to the entire Troy legend: and when a writer demands that we confront the divisions internal to the myth of national origins itself, then the very authority which is its theme and *raison d'être* can only emerge as vitiated. Like Chaucer, Shakespeare poses fundamental questions about the portability of classical authority through metaphor and example. Chaucer, however, presents such questions as his own interpretive trial; for Shakespeare, writing after the *translatio imperii* had become canonized in Tudor propaganda, they impose a cultural crisis on English audiences, able to contrast the Troy legend's inconsistency in Shakespeare's theater or Nashe's prose with its assumed integrity in royal or civic pageantry.

Timothy Hampton considers a similar problem of narrative inconsistency in humanist accounts of the classical exemplar:[43]

. . . the specific relationship between modern imitators and ancient exemplars is far from stable. This instability is produced by the mode of transmission: the heroic life is presented as narrative. The form of the narrative undermines the persuasive power of the exemplar . . . [since] the story of the great life can be unfolded to include and describe an infinite variety of actions; the life of the hero can easily be sliced into a multitude of discrete metonymically related segments or moments. Some of these may connote virtue, but some may suggest vice, and their interaction always produces conflict and moral dialectics, with the potential to turn back and subvert the pedagogical intent of the humanist who evoked the exemplar as a model for his student or reader in the first place. . . [T]he persuasive function of the name may be undermined by the ambiguity of certain of the hero's acts.

The narrative of a hero's life may lead us to wonder how finally to evaluate him. The problem is compounded when readers confront the multiple and ideologically motivated narratives of an exemplar's life: the many alterations that "new authors add to what they have heard," as Ovid puts it, radicalize the basic instability Hampton identifies in narrative. Within the privileged tradition of the translation of empire, Shakespeare's contaminations of textual authorities collectively raise the question central to that most disruptive play, *Troilus and Cressida*: "what's aught but as 'tis valu'd?" This question, posed by Troilus and seconded by Hector, the "ethical Trojan," assaults the values of central authority that Ulysses champions in his speech on degree. To compose plays that raise this question structurally rather than thematically both circumvents the censor and devastates the idea of transmissible value.

To contaminate the Troy legend is to cast in epistemological doubt the ideological ground on which the Tudors had based their myths of political origin. An alternative to topical polemics, Shakespeare's icono-clastic translations of empire adopt a generally interrogative stance to empower the theater as an instrument for social commentary, a partly autonomous cultural institution that might endorse or quibble with politics and social norms. On stage, classical emblems and models favored in courtly art forms, from Astraea and Dido to Achilles, Augustus, and Vergil, learn to speak a different language (not necessarily to curse), and help Shakespeare establish the theater as an independent sphere of cultural authority. As an alternative to the city (i.e., the mayor and aldermen bent on shutting down the theaters), pulpit (sympathetic to anti-theatrical sentiment), parliament, and court (equipped with the powers of patronage and censorship), the theater can traffic in the discourses of the established domains of social influence without being obliged to replicate any particular set of interests. By translating authority from imperial Rome for use in the theater, Shakespeare might convey enough cultural authority from the civic and courtly circles to establish the theater's difference from these established centers, a project consonant with the semi-autonomous model of the London theaters Ben Jonson proposes when he carefully places "Eliza, and our Iames" on the Thames to watch, in amazement, the "Sweet Swan of Auon."

It is now possible to thicken the plot and pose a question implied in the idea of a fatal Cleopatra: why do women preside over the male protagonists' textual crises of identity and, what is more, over contaminations at their most subversive?[44] Achilles is effeminized at the moment he faces inconsistencies in his historical identities, and Prospero identifies with an Ovidian witch when he renounces his magic. While Ovid's Medea presides over Prospero's conversion, his Procne supervises Titus' shift from a Vergilian to an Ovidian identity. Antony and hosts of critics hold Cleopatra responsible for Antony's loss of his "visible form," or coherence, after he half-hysterically plays out different legends about himself, from generous commander and libertine to Hercules *furens*. It is unsurprising that Cleopatra presides over Antony's crisis, but startling that Imogen plays the same role for Posthumus. In fact, Cleopatra reintegrates Antony in her dream of the emperor Antony, while Imogen, hovering over the headless body she believes to belong to her husband, rhetorically sums up the way his identity is scattered among texts from ancient and renaissance Rome, ancient and Italianate Britain. For Imogen to join company with Cleopatra and Medea suggests that the destabilizing role played by women in Shakespeare's plays has less to do with character than with the trope of Fortune as the "feminine" principle in capricious or lucky events. The most material instance of this trope appears in *Titus Andronicus*, where the transgressive semiotics sparked by literary contamination are gendered in Tamora's "pit": in this unnerving place – set in the wilderness outside of Rome and closely associated with the libidinous and vengeful queen of the Goths – texts and men are digested, undone, and made to produce strange new meanings.

In these plays, Shakespeare engages the heroic tradition committed to political and ethical order, yet deliberately unmans it and binds it to mutability and variety, feminized arch-enemies in the tradition of Spenser's Mutabilitie or Machiavelli's Fortuna. Shakespeare's theatrical translations of empire enact on the level of representation rather than theme the conflict between male virtue and female fortune that Johnson dramatizes in his account of Shakespeare's encounter with the "fatal Cleopatra" of a quibble and that J. G. A. Pocock outlines in *The Machiavellian Moment*:

Virtue and fortune . . . were regularly paired as opposites, and the heroic fortitude that withstood ill fortune passed into the active capacity that remolded circumstances to the actor's advantage and thence into the charismatic *felicitas* that mysteriously commanded good fortune. This opposition was frequently expressed in the image of a sexual relation: a masculine active intelligence was seeking to dominate a feminine passive unpredictability which would submissively reward him for his strength or vindictively betray him for his weakness.[45]

To what end does Shakespeare forswear the heroic tradition and gender as female the transgressive semiotics resulting from contamination or "mingle-mangle?" The answer begins in the habit critics have of

associating Shakespeare's art with Cleopatra's "infinite variety" and
Prospero's magic, itself identified with Ovid's Medea. Shakespeare
adapts the feminine trope of variety and change, even at the risk of
political instability, to betoken the difference between the social and
political language of his theater and those of the court or city. Although
formally the same on either side of the Thames and the city walls, the
signs inherited from the Troy legend do not signify identically in the
court and the theater. The feminine trope for Shakespeare's transgressive semiotics marks the theater's status as an alternate sphere of
cultural authority: metaphorically speaking, he places next to the
Globe's emblem of "Hercules and his load" a banner blazoned with the
fatal Cleopatra, icon of the Shakespearean play on meanings. Strikingly
pejorative when viewed from the perspective of Stoics or anti-theatricalists,[46] the image is also ground-clearing and exuberantly recreative,
suggesting the difference of a theater seeking debate and affirming the
role of popular consent.

Contaminating authorities in the *translatio imperii* bears indirectly on
politics, but it is by no means clear that Shakespeare intends audiences
and readers to develop a political practice from his iconoclasm. We
might ask, then, why Shakespeare fashions a dramatic method which
produces more radical meanings than would be feasible to translate into
a political practice. Even the need to evade censorship does not explain
the difference between dramatic effect – Tamora's appearance as Astraea,
or the textual breakdown of Achilles – and a practical response.
Shakespeare's representational choices manifestly distress the courtly
model of transporting original value through metaphor, but what is an
audience to do after a play has disturbed faith in the portability of stable
authority? What move from *gnosis* to *praxis*, as Sidney puts it in the
Defense of Poesie, might Shakespeare desire?[47]

Shakespeare does not play to potential Jack Cades in the audience or
even the rebel thoughts peopling the minds of civic-minded auditors,
although "the constant fear of riot and tumult in the theaters is an
indirect index to the extent to which they promoted social activism."[48]
My candidate for Shakespeare's ideal audience is Michael Williams,
Henry V's doubting but loyal subject. On the eve of battle, when the
disguised Henry baits Williams to question the justice of the king's cause,
the soldier meditates on the costs of battle but finally asserts that "to
disobey [the king] were against all proportion of subjection" (4.8.145–6).
When Henry, this time in his royal person, stages a second confrontation,
Williams unexpectedly insists upon his right privately to differ with the
king. Trapped into revealing potentially treasonous thoughts about royal
prerogatives and the liberties of the subject, Williams refuses to accept

punishable responsibility for his rebuff on the eve of Agincourt and becomes the play's first character to trace blame to Henry:

Your Majesty came not like yourself. You appear'd to me but as a common man; witness the night, your garments, your lowliness; and what our Highness suffer'd under that shape, I beseech you take it for your own fault and not mine; for had you been as I took you for, I made no offense; therefore I beseech your Highness pardon me. (4.8.50–6)

Williams insists upon the subject's right to think his own thoughts without legal meddling. Freedom of thought belongs to the common man as fully as it does to the aristocrat, like the rebellious Earl of Essex, who bases his liberties and privileges on ancient laws exalting the rights of the nobility against both the prince and the "base upstarts" he has favored with advancement.[49] The questions Essex asked of Egerton – "cannot princes Erre? and can not subiectes receyve wronge? is an earthlie power an authoritie infinite? Pardon me, pardon me, my lorde, I can never subscribe to these Principles"[50] – mean something more radical when placed in the mouth of a common soldier.[51] While Essex protects feudal rights, Michael Williams charges the absolutist state, responsible for protecting the commonwealth, not to exploit the ancient liberties of its subjects. What Shakespeare presents as politically imaginable, rather than practical, is surprising in view of the conservatism often assumed in his work. The non-conformist, even radical, dimension of his translations of empire abides through his career under both Elizabeth I and James I.

The choice of a model audience in Michael Williams, who privately deliberates the prerogatives and responsibilities of both the sovereign and his subjects and then publicly resists Henry V's charismatic absolutism, is sentimental and historical: Williams is Shakespeare's affectionate personification of the popular or "politicke" side of England's mixed constitution, *dominium politicale et regale* in Fortescue's phrase. Fortescue claimed a Roman heritage for England's mixed monarchy in the figure of Octavius Caesar, whose reliance on senatorial advice and popular consent forms a telling contrast with the tyrannical absolutism Fortescue attributes to Julius Caesar. Appearing in *Henry V* to negotiate English "brotherhood" in terms closer to political theory than the patriotism that Henry thrillingly mobilizes, Williams' private debate and public rebuttal wryly invoke the issues of advice and consent defined as essentially English in Fortescue's *De Laudibus Regnum Anglorum* (available in Edward Whitechurch's 1545–46 edition) and Sir Thomas Smith's *De Republica Anglorum* (1583)[52] and co-opted at every opportunity by Shakespeare's Henry V. As a personification of social relations from political theory,[53] Michael Williams brings into focus the constitutional dimension of Shakespeare's political thinking and, consequently, a

strong historical reason for him to develop plays whose continuity –
methodological, generic, political – is as important as their attention
both to general differences between his sovereigns' popular and absolutist
styles of rule and to particular turns in England's cultural history from
Titus Andronicus to *Antony and Cleopatra* and *The Tempest*.

Quoting the text: actors and allusion

> *Enter Lucius' son, and* Lavinia *running after him, and the Boy flies from*
> *her with his books under his arm.*
>
> TITUS.   . . . what book is that she tosseth so?
> BOY.   Grandsire, 'tis Ovid's *Metamorphoses*;
>   My mother gave it me . . .
> TITUS.   Soft, so busily she turns the leaves!
>   What would she find? Lavinia, shall I read?
>   This is the tragic tale of Philomel,
>   And treats of Tereus' treason and his rape –
>   And rape, I fear, was root of thy annoy.
> MARCUS.   See, brother, see: note how she quotes the leaves.
>
> (4.1.41–3, 45–50)

In his study of imitation in the renaissance, G. W. Pigman III wryly
formulates the "less than inspiring principle" that "a reader must be very
cautious in even calling a similarity between two texts an imitation or an
allusion, much less in analyzing the use or significance of the similarity"
(p. 12).[54] Other readers may not agree on the relevance of the allusion, or
even recognize its presence. Malcolm Smuts, a deft reader of political
implication in Stuart arts, cautions against reliance on allusion, since "it
is generally impossible to determine whether the hidden meanings
discovered by a modern critic were intended by the author or recognizable to a seventeenth-century audience." When he remarks further, in
exasperation, that there is "no way of controlling the imaginative
fecundity of a critic intent on showing that dramatists were expressing
the political ideas he would like to attribute to them,"[55] the critic
becomes something of a truant chasing his fatal Cleopatra of an allusion,
heedless of scholarly restraints. Although it is not always easy to
distinguish his methodological from his interpretive skepticism,[56] Smuts'
call for interpretive controls raises the compelling issue of the historical
grounds for construing classical allusion, particularly in the drama.

Appropriate as it is to task the critic with the need for adequate
historical rigor, it is hard to envision a practice of allusion – especially a
political one – that does not require interpretive risks from audiences
and readers as well as critics. While it is fair to require critics not to
attribute their own political ideas to a seventeenth-century dramatist, it

is somewhat perverse to request that students of allusion use history as a prophylactic, rather than a stimulus, to "imaginative fecundity": the author or player who alludes politically knows that his readers and auditors will exercise interpretive license. At times he even anticipates enough controversy to bring additional audiences and revenue to the theater. The question that arises from considering both invention and restraint, whether those of early modern writers, readers, and auditors or of modern critics, is how to situate a consistent allusive practice within the social institutions which give the allusions contemporary force.

To furnish a critical theory of allusion itself is manifestly beyond the limits of a study of the literary-political dimensions of five Shakespearean plays set in the context of the *translatio imperii*; what it hopes to contribute, on a modest scale, is a clearer sense of how inclusive of the literary, historical, and cultural methods of interpretation such a theory would need to be. To mount its arguments, this study relies on both traditional and newer scholarship. A partial list includes studies of imitation; censorship; the history of the Troy legend; its uses in various quarters of Elizabethan social life; the appearance of manuscripts and translations available to the reading public;[57] Elizabeth I's political iconography; James I's predilection for the style and politics of imperial Rome and Roman civil law; the place of the stage in early modern England; the composition of Shakespeare's audiences and the different theaters for which he composed;[58] and Shakespeare's education.[59]

This study assumes that allusions underscore meanings in a given play, rather than import issues otherwise unavailable, and that the Troy legend's many social points of reference – from royal iconography to ballads – shore up rather than scatter the political force of an allusion, allowing for multiple points of entry. Based on such moments as the player's tale of Priam's fall in *Hamlet*, Antony's revision of the *Aeneid*, and Lavinia's physical pursuit of the *Metamorphoses*, it also assumes that Shakespeare took seriously the potential of a classical text to stand for less tangible authority and to prompt audiences to speculate. Such moments fire the starting shot, but do not indicate to audience or critic when the chase is over. The degree of ungovernable license involved in allusion is a liability in criticism, but not in the theater. Yet Shakespeare's theatrical medium and venue raise another fundamental question about critical discussions of allusion, the hallmark of highly literary poetry. Should not an allusion be actable if it is to be interpretable?

How does an actor playing Achilles *act* a textual crisis of identity? How does an actor representing Lavinia, to anticipate a question central to the next chapter, *act* a critique of empire based on myths of rape?

Would Shakespeare entrust the theatrical translation of imperial Roman authority to a text-bound medium that apparently disregards normal acting protocols? Shakespeare, of course, far too successful a playwright to attempt an unactable method of composition and repeat it throughout his career, did no such thing. The actors need only imitate Achilles' identity crisis and Lavinia's trauma. Actors are in no way required to "act out" the relation of their respective plights to the books cited and even brought onstage as props. The book Ulysses uses to precipitate Achilles' identity crisis underscores the textual crisis in Achilles' admission to incompatible but equally traditional motives for his withdrawal from the war. The passage emblematically enacts the textualized identity more familiar in Coriolanus' wish to be author of himself, or King John's lamentation, "I am a scribbled form, drawn with a pen / Upon a parchment" (5.7.32–3). Lavinia goes so far as to compare herself directly with her textual source: "note how she quotes the leaves," her uncle says as she physically imitates the story she has turned to – and turned into – in Ovid's *Metamorphoses*.

Shakespeare, moreover, designed his plays to work without his immediate supervision. The foolproof *A Midsummer Night's Dream* contains built-in critiques of bad acting and reading, and *Henry V* relies on dramatic structure to present its critique of conquest. Even if Henry's wooing of Katherine of France is played with winning charm – as it should, despite the fact that her consent is being negotiated in the next room by Henry's council – it inevitably echoes Henry's terrible speech before Harfleur, where rape haunts the scene of conquest.[60] The doubled character of wooing and conquest coalesces in an image the French king uses to comment on Henry's zeal for dominion by conquest or marriage: "you see them perspectively, the cities turned into a maid; for they are all girdled with maiden walls that war hath never ent'red" (5.2.320–3). Henry acknowledges the link of sexual and political conquest when he responds that he is content to wed the already Anglicized Kate "so the maiden cities you talk of may wait on her; so the maid that stood in the way for my wish shall show me the way to my will" (lines 326–8). The internal allusions in *Henry V* work similarly to allusions to external texts, whether or not they are brought onstage as props. The classical allusions liable to be cut from modern performances were likely to carry political connotations in Shakespeare's day: playwrights interested in making political commentary without winding up in a Star Chamber interrogation turned from English history to Roman history after Essex's rebellion and the publication of Hayward's seditious history of Henry IV, which dwelled favorably on the deposition of Richard II.

In the cases of both internal and external allusions, what matters most is the relation of the allusion to dominant preoccupations in a given play. Many allusions reinforce meanings in a narrative sequence that does not depend upon their recognition. In the frame of Kyd's *The Spanish Tragedy*, for example, the references to the *Aeneid*'s Underworld support but do not constitute the psychological hell pervading the play. But not all allusions, even to famous texts, are immediately obvious. The popular myth of Actaeon is readily identifiable in *The Merry Wives of Windsor* and *Cymbeline*, but is not aggressively presented in *The Tempest*, where Prospero orders a pack of spirits, disguised as hunting hounds and equipped with names reminiscent of those of Actaeon's dogs in the *Metamorphoses*, to track down and torment Caliban, Stephano, and Trinculo. This allusion calls for interpretive tact and close attention to its relation to shifts in the dramatic plot that it must underscore if the allusion is to have meaning at all. Since an underdeveloped or submerged allusion is wholly dependent upon support from the independent discourses, themes, and plots of the new text, the myth of Actaeon must coincide with concerns already developing in *The Tempest* or it can only be irrelevant. Not strong enough to import issues and judgments into the play, the allusion nonetheless helps key themes to coalesce and marks transitions in the plot. In the case of Prospero's allusion to Actaeon, Ovid's text suggests that the hounds of desires, who are chasing down the rebels, are agents of Prospero's own transgression into the domain of divine authority.

I have deliberately chosen a weak allusion as a test case for imitations which inform the *plot* and *dramatic structure* of Shakespeare's plays rather than simply illuminating aspects of the dramatic *moment* without carrying resonances beyond the scene and without advancing the plot. Shakespeare, of course, often uses allusions to epiphanic effect rather than narrative purpose. Any interest that Shakespeare may have in Hecuba, for instance, is subordinate to Hamlet's troubled fascination with mimicry and widowed mothers. In the translations of empire, however, imitations play a structural role in the arguments of the plays. Because the plays interrogate the bases for authority, partly as it is transmitted through specific texts, the imitations reflect ideological positions. They serve a function similar to characters who give voice to particular positions within larger discourses, such as the prerogatives of the monarch in *Henry V* or New World discovery in *The Tempest*, where the *Aeneid* and the *Metamorphoses* constitute positions within the discourse of empire and colonialism. These authoritative textual voices, like the characters, personify discursive stances in the play's larger project.

Strong allusions, even official citations, of Vergil in *Titus Andronicus* make little sense when taken as epiphanic images which illuminate local aspects of the dramatic moment and then obligingly disappear after the utterance. Here is the view of Robert Miola, an observant and sensitive reader of Vergilian allusion in Shakespeare:[61]

Shakespeare invokes Vergil to help shape character and theme in *Titus Andronicus*. Yet the effort is comparatively clumsy and juvenile: the allusions to Aeneas and Lavinia are crudely and baldly inappropriate rather than ironic. They are stitched on to the play rather than woven into its fabric. Shakespeare is clearly excited by the *Aeneid* as subtext but he is overwhelmed by it as well, unable to control fully the powerful resources at his disposal.

Miola sensibly assumes that an allusion should "shape character and theme" and "illustrate" the dramatic moment, or reverse that process and underscore dramatic irony. In either case, decorum, harmony, and verisimilitude are prized commodities. For Miola, Shakespeare's allusions in *Titus Andronicus* are failures precisely because they are not epiphanic. Worse, their crude impropriety does not dissipate with the dramatic moment: the bad fit between tenor and vehicle, character and model lingers onstage to disturb the audience.

Allusions in *Titus Andronicus* refuse to perform an illustrative and epiphanic role because their energies are directed elsewhere: perhaps more than any character, allusions help constitute the play's plot to undermine authority. The play is set just before the fall of the Roman empire, and it is fitting that Vergilian values should survive only in empty forms. If one stripped from the play its many allusions to Roman literary authorities, nothing could happen: Titus could not establish himself as a Vergilian exemplar, Chiron and Demetrius would not have the tale of Tereus and Philomela on which to model their rape of Lavinia, and Titus would not have the precedent of Procne's revenge to exceed. Nor would Shakespeare have the resources of Vergil, Ovid, Seneca, and Horace to represent authority and its interrogation. The allusions which Miola properly identifies as "indecorous shreds from the original robes" (p. 243) are instructive of the play's overall plot, for they enact on the textual level the same ideological violence – even dismemberment – that the characters enact on the dramatic level. The use of imitations to embody ideological conflicts and the problematic transmission of authority from model to user are at the heart of Shakespeare's translations of empire.

2   Blazoning injustice: mutilating Titus Andronicus, Vergil, and Rome

> And now he writes to heaven for his redress.
> See, here's "to Jove," and this "to Mercury,"
> This "to Apollo," this "to the god of war":
> Sweet scrolls to fly about the streets of Rome!
> What's this but libelling against the senate
> And blazoning our injustice everywhere?   (4.4.13–18)[1]

Trimming the laurels of triumph: poetic and political inscriptions

Titus Andronicus poses problems of response all the more vexed by the characters' habit of citing cultural authorities from Vergil and Ovid to Hecuba and Virginius for their gory exploits in rape, mutilation, and cannibalism. Also disturbing is Shakespeare's palpably felt hand in the play's learned butchery – he discursively re-enacts the physical violence performed by his characters – which critics generally chalk up to youthful exuberance and bad taste.[2] Yet Shakespeare rivals, absorbs, and transforms the authorities of imperial Rome in a programmatic manner that has yet to be explained.[3] His status as a relative newcomer to the London theatrical scene partly explains his aggressive stance toward classical models: by taking up violent, classically allusive drama, Shakespeare both joins and rivals Kyd and Marlowe in a collective struggle to transform the theater into a legitimate sphere of social influence. In *Titus Andronicus*, Shakespeare inaugurates his own artistic program to commandeer classical themes and events for the purposes of drama: when he manhandles the classical iconography generally reserved and polished for the court, he disturbs the normative uses for Roman authority and claims no small share of this authority for his theater. *Titus Andronicus'* aggressive imitations do nothing less than perform a critique of imperial Rome on the eve of its collapse and, in doing so, glance proleptically at Elizabethan England as an emergent nation.

This is a lot to claim for a play whose overwrought rhetoric and violent excesses have brought down on Shakespeare's head the famous charge that it is "a most incorrect and indigested piece" and "rather a heap of Rubbish than a Structure."[4] It is no wonder that critics are affronted by *Titus Andronicus*, which of all Shakespeare's plays cites the most Latin, yet hacks up the most bodies; trades on puns and body parts; and, after ransacking Lavinia's "treasury" (1.1.631/2.1.132), drags onstage the dismal sign of its "trim sport" (5.1.93–6) in Lavinia, trimmed of her hands and tongue, then trimmed in petrarchan poetry. But *Titus Andronicus'* rhetoric and spectacles are not gratuitously outrageous: the play gains its status as a translation of empire because, not in spite, of them. Hard to stomach, the play's perverse links between language and action, rhetoric and violence, relate to the cultural distresses of late imperial Rome. For this grim state of civic affairs, we may call as witness the unfortunate clown who mistakes Jupiter for "gibbetmaker" (4.3.80) and loses his life over a pun.

Titus himself affirms the politics of citational violence in his quirky feats of political activism: his barbed allusions include a bundle of arrows wrapped in a Horatian ode; the use of the Zodiac for topical target practice; and, as his *pièce de résistance*, the allusive pie he makes for Tamora to "digest." Critics who satirize the play's allusions and language fail to recognize Shakespeare's keen understanding of the political stakes of disintegrative rhetoric: his outrageous language and trim invention betoken Rome's impending cultural disintegration. When an Elizabethan speculates on the beginnings and end of imperial Roman politics, moreover, he inevitably trains one eye on the emergent British nationhood to which Rome's empire cedes. The question, then, is not whether *Titus* has a political dimension, but whether its critique is confined to the late Roman empire. Do Shakespeare's tropes deface Roman authority and prepare for a *renovatio imperii* in Elizabethan England? Or do they outface the Tudor notion of a political authority made portable through classical iconography?

These questions emerge, perhaps unexpectedly, from thinking about Shakespeare's use of classical sources – a scholarly field often assumed to settle rather than unearth literary and cultural matters. Source studies of *Titus Andronicus* address Ovid's tale of Philomela and sometimes Senecan tragedy; they mostly regard allusions to other Roman authorities, such as Vergil and Horace, as local embroidery on the wholecloth of Ovid, accepted as Shakespeare's primary source. It has not yet been recognized that Ovid dominates the central acts of the play at a direct cost to Vergil as a source of cultural decorum for Titus, Rome, and the play itself. No sooner is Vergilian authority installed through the ritual events and ceremonious speeches of the first act than it is deposed by a specifically Ovidian insouciance, marked by the once humorless Titus' laughter upon receiving his severed hand and his sons' heads: "Ha, ha, ha!" (3.1.265).[5] When Shakespeare wrenches the play world from Vergilian to Ovidian coordinates, he unleashes the floodgates to the outrageous puns, violence, and schematic disjunctions that subsequently pervade the play. For a play to invoke and then displace Vergilian authority is momentous: *Titus Andronicus* asserts its idiosyncratic position in the translation of empire.

The turning-point from the imperial epic of Vergil to the counter-epic of Ovid is Lavinia's entrance after her rape, made more painful by her assaulters' adherence to the *Metamorphoses*. This grisly fulcrum functions logically in the poetics of cultural disintegration, for Rome was mythically founded on rape: the rape of the Sabine women, the rape of Lucrece, the rape of Ilia (raped by Mars, this vestal virgin bore Romulus and Remus), and Aeneas' dynastic marriage to Lavinia, which threatened to repeat the rape of Helen of Troy.[6] Aeneas' affair with Dido, of special interest to Shakespeare, relates ambiguously to the paradigm of conquest through rape: despite her willing participation in the love affair, Dido's seduction, effected by the gods of love as well as Aeneas' heroism and eloquence, is so overdetermined that singular agency is impossible to isolate.[7] That Shakespeare has in mind the problems of Dido's fall is clear from allusions dispersed throughout the play, notably her "counsel-keeping cave" (2.2/3.24), Vergil's simile of her as a wounded doe, and the "sad-attending ear" with which she listened to Aeneas' tale (5.3.81). Shakespeare uses these allusions and the figure of Lavinia to raise the problem of accountability in Dido's fall, a simultaneously ethical and political issue in the *Aeneid*. In Lavinia's rape, Shakespeare contaminates the fall of Dido by the rape of Philomela, whose tale he reprises and splices onto the Great Rapes that helped found Rome. When he conflates Vergil's Dido and Ovid's Philomela, Shakespeare performs an Ovidian critique of Rome whose *imperium* was not, after all, *sine fine*.[8] Meticulously citing Rome's own authorities, Shakespeare suggests that the founding acts of empire contain the seeds of its ruin.

Such literary-political themes loom over Shakespeare's deviant uses of the emblems, images, and characters popular in the Elizabethan chapter of the *translatio imperii* and Elizabethan political iconography. Lavinia, "her hands cut off and her tongue cut out, and ravished," is the woeful figure of Shakespeare's literary-political project: a "map of woe" (3.2.12) from whom Titus "wrests an alphabet" (line 44) of revenge, she is also Shakespeare's extreme image of Rome's cultural disintegration and his calling card as an Elizabethan cultural critic. First mutilated into a citation of Ovid's Philomela, then refigured as a petrarchan blazon, she

Figure 4. Daphne and Apollo. Barthelemy Aneau, *Picta Poesis* (Lyons, 1552)

"quotes the leaves" (4.1.50) of the *Metamorphoses* and petrarchan sonneteers. She acquires striking textual significations that her rapists are first to comment on: "See how with signs and tokens" (2.3/4.5) they jeer, she can "scrowle" (quarto) or "scowle" (Folio). Her gestures conflate scowls with scrolls, and anticipate the "sweet scrowles" Titus uses to "blazon" Rome's injustices (Folio, 2009–11).[9]

Following the examples of Ovid's Apollo and of Petrarch, Shakespeare appropriates the laurel tree as his image for his poetic project: his practice of disjoining icons from their normative political significances, such as Daphne (triumph) and Astraea (justice), derives from a careful reading of Ovid as a poet who preferred criticizing the politics of Augustan Rome to praising them. The *Metamorphoses*, which complicates and politicizes the nature of poetic reference, sets forth its poetic project in the story of Daphne's transformation into a laurel to escape rape by Apollo (fig. 4). Having lost the nymph in human form, the god of poetry settles for her arboreal figure, which he appropriates as a pleasureful "figure of speech" and his personal emblem.[10] The laurel's boughs, Ovid remarks, seem to nod: *factis modo laurea ramis | adnuit utque caput visa*

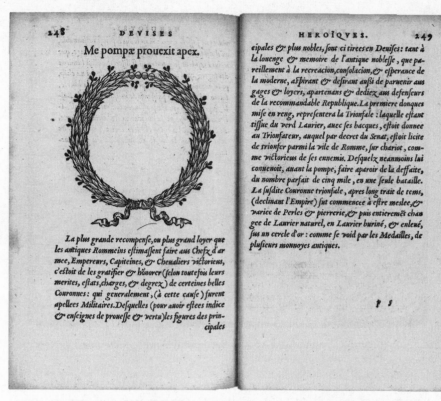

Figure 5. Laurel boughs. Claude Paradin, *Emblemes Heroïques* (Lyons, 1557)

est agitasse cacumen, 1.566–7 ("the laurel nodded its newly made branches and the top seemed to shake its head"). The boughs form a tree-top or a head, depending on the degree of human agency that the viewer attributes to their movements. Branches blowing in the wind may signify consent (as the verb *adnuo* implies), as Apollo and some critics assume, or dissent.[11] On the other hand, their agitation (*agitasse*) may mean nothing at all, since a viewer is required to create meaning from their movement (as the phrase *visa est* implies). Ovid's tale dramatizes the ambiguity of signs and exposes the motives for variable readings: power and passion affix meaning to words, bodies, and gestures. At the end of his narrative, when Ovid sets those equivocal laurel boughs on Augustus' portals and the brows of Rome's military commanders, he suggests a political origin for love lyric (figs. 5 and 6).

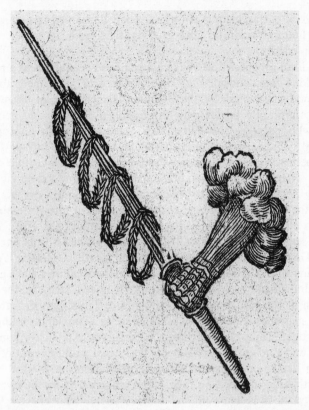

Figure 6. Sword ringed with laurels. Claude Paradin, *Emblemes Heroïques* (Lyons, 1557)

Ovid's story is an aetiological tale of political and poetic appropriation through tropes and iconography. *Titus Andronicus* inherits the full ambivalence of Daphne's legacy, from the triumphant entrance of "Andronicus, bound with laurel boughs" (1.1.77) to the grimly petrarchan appearance of Lavinia, "lopped and hewed and made . . . bare / Of her two branches, those sweet ornaments" (2.3/4.17–18). Refusing to naturalize the citational violence, Shakespeare uses the extreme physical abuse of Lavinia and the sumptuous description of her mutilated body to scrutinize the art of petrarchan representation itself. Lavinia becomes a palimpsest bearing the literary and ideological inscriptions of Vergil, Ovid, Petrarch, and finally, Shakespeare. A troubling *tour de force*, Shakespeare's performance rivals the strongest adaptations of petrarchism that English poets developed to comment on both the literary tradition and the political uses it served in the Elizabethan court.

There is little prospect that Shakespeare praises Elizabeth as a restorer of the golden age, considering *Titus Andronicus'* sustained abuse of classical models favored by the Tudors. His critique of Elizabethan political iconography begins with the figure of Lavinia and ends with Tamora, who parodies the guises that Queen Elizabeth appropriated from Vergil – Dido, Astraea, and the *Venus armata*. The link of Tamora and Elizabeth through iconography adds interest to the Gothic queen's fate as a character-turned-iconic-monster. Tamora ultimately gains nothing by her maternity and her concrete motives for revenge: in the course of the play, she undergoes a transformation into an emblem of malice – in effect, the personified Revenge she stages for Titus. Aaron, the play's self-styled devil, fares better: although he is "this barbarous Moor, / This ravenous tiger, this accursed devil" (5.3.4–5), Aaron's villainy wins him a degree of glory with audiences, and his paternity deepens him characterologically. As the Romans struggle for social equilibrium at the end of the play, they praise Titus, punish Aaron but grudgingly spare his son, and unleash their cultural anxieties on the other "ravenous tiger, Tamora" (5.3. 194), who deserves to be thrown unburied "to beasts and birds of prey: / Her life was beastly and devoid of pity, / And being dead, let birds on her take pity" (lines 197–9).[12] For an empire mythically founded on rape – and empowered by the overthrow of Cleopatra – it is tempting to achieve social recovery by troping internal social threats as female and Gothic.[13]

Although cast as opposites, Tamora and Lavinia both render up their bodies and become metaphors advancing Shakespeare's cultural critique. In the course of the play, the bodies of Tamora and Lavinia are twinned and understood as sites of physical mayhem and literary contamination. Tamora's pit and Lavinia's body are the play's extreme signs of violation, and on them is writ large the discourse of cultural disintegration that generally informs the play's plot, dramatic structure, and allusive practice. As conflations of Vergil and Ovid, they are metaphors transporting Roman origins to their apocalyptic end. Shakespeare causes their bodies to oscillate between the natural and politically iconographic, suggesting a hybrid of character and emblem that curiously relates to the political body of Elizabeth I: for *Titus Andronicus*, Shakespeare ransacks Elizabeth's iconographic body to insist that her body politic was part of the general cultural treasury and therefore available to the self-authorizing gestures of his emerging theater.[14]

Deforming Vergil: the failure of Roman institutions

The *Aeneid* begins with a portentous storm which comes to stand for political and emotional upheaval, or *furor*. *Titus Andronicus* begins with a political and domestic conflict whose passions resonate in imagery of storms, thunder, and furies. Social and psychological turbulence appears variously as a "shipwreck" (1.1.523/2.1.24), "tempest" (1.1.463), "storm" (1.1.524/2.1.25, 2.2/3.23, 2.3/4.54), and "fury" (1.1.443), and as "furious" (1.1.575). At the play's beginning, Rome is beleaguered by Goths, its own legal institutions, and its worn out myths – particularly its latter-day Romulus and Remus, who vie for the imperial seat and for Titus' daughter. The last Caesar has died, and his sons rally their factions to determine the succession. Saturninus invokes primogeniture while Bassianus appeals to free election and to "virtue consecrate, / To justice, continence and nobility" (1.1.14–15). But when Titus enters the Roman stage directly from his military victory over the Goths, the people elect him as the true successor to Rome's military Caesars (fig. 7).

Entering Rome with a personification and epic simile on his lips, Titus seems to restore his city's equilibrium with the breath of authority and order:

> Hail, Rome, victorious in thy mourning weeds!
> Lo, as the bark that hath discharged his freight
> Returns with precious lading to the bay
> From whence at first she weighed her anchorage,
> Cometh Andronicus, bound with laurel boughs,
> To resalute his country with his tears,
> Tears of true joy for his return to Rome.   (1.73–9)

Through a deeply traditional simile and address, Titus transforms the political scene from chaos to stately triumph. Indirectly, he has the effect of Vergil's Neptune as he calms the sea-storm in *Aeneid* 1 (fig. 8), and with surprising specificity, he imitates the august citizen in Vergil's simile for Neptune:

> ac veluti magno in populo cum saepe coorta est
> seditio saevitque animis ignobile vulgus,
> iamque faces et saxa volant, furor arma ministrat,
> tum, pietate gravem ac meritis si forte virum quem
> conspexere, silent arrectisque auribus astant;
> ille regit dictis animos et pectora mulcet.   (1.148–53)

as, when political revolt has risen in a great nation, and the common mob rages angrily, and now torches and rocks fly – passion supplies weapons – then, if by chance they see a man dignified by his patriotic duty and service, they fall silent and stand with attentive ears; he rules their spirits with words and softens their hearts.

Figure 7. "Optimus civis." Claude Paradin, *Emblemes Heroïques* (Lyons, 1557)

That Titus resembles this exemplary magistrate would be evident to audiences used to his once frequent appearances in moral philosophy. He crops up not only in, for example, Daniel Tuvill's *Essays Politic and Moral* (1608), where he inaugurates Tuvill's classical references, but also in Shakespeare, who shows persistent interest in the dramatic potential of Vergil's simile. Shakespeare favorably recalls Vergil's official in the scene he contributed to *Sir Thomas More*, where More's eloquence calms an incipient rebellion, and makes him the butt of a joke in the first scene of *The Tempest*, when the boatswain snaps at Gonzalo for interfering with his struggle against the storm: "You are a councillor; if you can command these elements to silence, and work the peace of the present,

**Law.
Comaun=
Dementes.**

Figure 8. Neptune calming the waves. Initial "T" from Richard
Grafton, *Chronicle* (London, 1569)

we will not hand a rope more – use your authority" (1.1.20–3).[15] Like
the civic official, Titus Andronicus enters to bind scattered and disruptive
forces and command the political stage.

Known for "uprightness and integrity" (1.1.51), the Andronici virtually claim the *Aeneid* as family history. When Marcus announces that the
people "have by common voice / In election for the Roman empery /
Chosen Andronicus, surnamed Pius" (1.1.21–3), he derives Titus' claim
to the imperial seat from his spiritual descent from the *pius* Aeneas as
well as the popular vote. In fact, the people's role in honoring Titus tends
to disappear in Marcus' epideictic speech which catalogues Titus' virtues
and refers its values to the *Aeneid*. For a ten laborious years that recall
the Trojan war, Rome's "Patron of virtue" (line 68) fought "weary wars
against the barbarous Goths" and "chastised with arms / Our enemies'
pride" (lines 28, 32–3). To ears trained by Vergil, Titus' military acts
against the Goths and their Queen recall Rome's ancient wars with
Carthage, the enemy civilization founded by another queen, Vergil's
Dido. Moreover, they satisfy Anchises' instructions to Aeneas in the
Underworld: *tu regere imperio populos, Romane, memento | (hae tibi erunt
artes), pacique imponere morem, | parcere subiectis et debellare superbos*

("Remember, Roman, by your power to rule the people (for these will be your arts), to impose the custom of peace, spare the conquered, and battle down the proud," 6.851–3). Titus has buried twenty-one of his "five-and-twenty valiant sons, / Half the number that King Priam had" (lines 82–3), suggesting that he begets sons according to epic precedent and sacrifices them to the state. For his sole daughter, he chooses the name of Aeneas' Latin bride: Lavinia, "Rome's rich ornament" (1.1.55) for whom Saturninus and Bassianus fight. To crown his Vergilian achievements, Titus enters Rome with a conquered Cleopatra in Tamora, "brought to Rome / To beautify [his] triumphs" (lines 112–13).

Yet Vergilian *pietas* has ossified over the centuries. Titus' religious and patriotic observances conform to the letter rather than the spirit of the law. No longer a creative force of order, form is emblematically entwined with death: the Andronici's five-hundred-year-old tomb, which Titus has "sumptuously re-edified" (1.1.356), contains too many sons to suggest a thriving family religion in which living sons revere their ancestors.[16] Titus' burial rites contribute to the gloomy atmosphere, for they demand human sacrifice. Before he buries the sons who died in the wars, he interrogates his own piety:

> Titus, unkind and careless of thine own,
> Why suffer'st thou thy sons unburied yet
> To hover on the dreadful shore of Styx?   (1.1.89–91)

His question is not merely rhetorical, but citational: as J. C. Maxwell points out, Titus alludes to the souls of the unburied in *Aeneid* 6: *haec omnis, quam cernis, inops inhumataque turba est . . . volitantque haec litora circum* ("This crowd you see, poor and unburied . . . flutter about the shore," 325–9). Titus calls on Vergil to initiate a burial rite and authorize a dubious act of piety: the human sacrifice of Tamora's eldest son, despite her plea for pity. In Titus' practices, Roman institutions pervert the virtues they were designed to protect.

For Titus, in fact, the step is short between sacrificing the enemy's son and executing one's own. The sacrifices of Alarbus and Mutius dramatically frame Titus' role in determining the succession. As T. J. B. Spencer notes, Titus adjudicates not only among men but, anachronistically, among rival political institutions in Rome's history.[17] Rejecting his own election by popular vote, he settles on Saturninus, the brother conspicuously undeserving except by primogeniture. Implicitly dismissing the republican-minded claims of the younger Bassianus, Titus agrees to give his daughter in marriage to Saturninus. In a move that would irk playgoers from England's Inns of Court, Titus severs the "politicke" from the "royal" function of the mixed government that Fortescue celebrated as essentially English and traced to Augustus Caesar:[18] quelling the rising threat to empire posed by Rome's republican and plebeian institutions, Titus seeks to base his own political power on a dynastic claim. His *fiat* is a political and familial disaster, however, because Lavinia is already betrothed to Bassianus. Instead of resolving Rome's civil conflicts, Titus inadvertently amplifies the brothers' political competition and re-centers it on Lavinia as a dynastic figure: he nearly plunges Rome once again into the second half of the *Aeneid*. Titus can hardly be unaware of his family's prior commitments to Bassianus, and we witness his fury when his word fails to dissolve the allegiance. When his sons help Bassianus seize *"suum cuique"* (1.1.284), he does not blame the prince for seizing his own "in justice" (line 285). Enraged at his mutinous sons, however, Titus silences Mutius: crying, "What, villain boy, barr'st me my way in Rome?" (line 295), Titus kills his twenty-second son.[19] With these baldly ambitious words, Titus establishes himself as a tyrant, dismissive of the idea that sovereign authority derives from popular consent and intolerant of institutional or personal opposition.

Within the first three hundred lines of the play, the Vergilian virtues through which Titus understands himself emerge as bankrupt. In the name of *pietas*, Titus commits the act unthinkable in the *Aeneid*, despite his family's horror at his "impiety" and "barbarous" acts (1.1. 360, 383). Titus' execution of Mutius directly follows the public enumeration of his credentials as a Vergilian hero, and reflects on the father-son relations represented in the *Aeneid*. Aeneas leaves burning Troy clasping his son's hand and carrying his father on his back in hopes that he may bring to Rome his most prized value, the love between father and son (fig. 9). This bond represents the *amor* that Aeneas later equates with *patria* when he explains to Dido that he is leaving her for Rome: *hic amor, haec patria est* (4.347). But as the *Aeneid* presses to its conclusion, Aeneas' paternal devotion turns to institutional violence. Human sacrifice appears first in Aeneas' burial rites for Pallas, his adoptive son, and last in his murder of Turnus.[20] In the poem's closing lines, Aeneas calls upon the memory of Pallas to ratify human sacrifice, despite Turnus' plea for mercy:

> "tune hinc spoliis indute meorum
> eripiare mihi? Pallas te hoc vulnere, Pallas
> immolat et poenam scelerato ex sanguine sumit."   (12.947–9)

Do you seek to deprive me of my rewards? Pallas, with this wound, Pallas stabs you and exacts punishment from your criminal blood.

When Aeneas displaces his agency onto Pallas and describes Turnus' blood as "criminal" – *sceleratus* is the opposite of *pius* – he suggests that the wrathful but impartial arm of justice takes Turnus' life. At the end of

Figure 9. Aeneas carrying Anchises from burning Troy. Andrea Alciati, *Toutes les Emblemes* (Lyons, 1558)

the *Aeneid,* Vergil warns that law may threaten the single uncompromised love known to Aeneas, the self-sacrificing love of father for son. When Titus, at the outset of Shakespeare's play, murders his own son for obstructing his social ascent in Rome – "What, villain boy, / Barr'st me my way in Rome?" – he effectively picks up where the *Aeneid* left off.

Tamora, who entered as the subjugated enemy of Rome, assumes a choral role as witness to Rome's barbarous rites: "O cruel, irreligious piety!" (1.1.131). Her memorable cry signals the oxymoronic destructiveness of the Roman ethic of *pietas.* Titus' by-the-book judgments provisionally sway audience sympathies towards Tamora. When he pitilessly condemns the Gothic Queen's son and then slays his own, she is temporarily permitted a role other than that of dangerous foreigner, a seductive Cleopatra infiltrating Rome by marriage to the emperor. When one of her two remaining sons invokes "The self-same gods that armed the Queen of Troy / With opportunity of sharp revenge / Upon the Thracian tyrant" (1.1.139–41), she identifies with Ovid's Hecuba, justified in revenge against the tyrant Polymestor, who robbed and killed her youngest son, Polidorus. When Titus sinks to an ethical nadir, Tamora momentarily assumes the role of a sympathetic avenger.

The *Aeneid* suffers its greatest warping in the next act, whose plot turns on repeated displacements of Dido's seduction. To celebrate the reconciliations of Tamora and Titus, Saturninus and Bassianus, the court arranges a royal hunt which proves more dire than the one that brought Dido and Aeneas to the cave in which they consummated their desires. The plot begins when Aaron finds Tamora's two sons mooning over Lavinia and ludicrously acting like fratricidal Romans – such as Romulus and Remus or the *Aeneid*'s contenders for the original Lavinia. Borrowing a metaphor from poaching, Demetrius boasts of his skills in adultery: "What, hast not thou full often struck a doe, / And borne her cleanly by the keeper's nose?" (1.1.593–4/2.1.94–5). Aaron wrenches the figure of speech into a rally call to rape Lavinia during the next day's hunt:

> The forest walks are wide and spacious,
> And many unfrequented plots there are,
> Fitted by kind for rape and villainy.
> Single you thither then this dainty doe,
> And strike her home by force . . .   (1.1.614–18/2.1.115–19)

The boys jubilantly adopt the metaphor Aaron uses to pervert their chosen genre of courtly love and twist adultery into rape. The boys themselves, once translated from love-struck lyricists, exult unnervingly in the displacements of metaphor. Wresting pleasure from the idea of a figurative hunt which – ironically, in their eyes – promises far greater brutality than the merely literal hunt that will take place around them, they exit crowing, "we hunt not, we, with horse nor hound, / But hope to pluck a dainty doe to ground" (2.1/2.25–6).

The metaphor gains its power to chill the blood in part because it has been violently wrenched from its original context in Vergil's magnificent simile of the impassioned Dido as a wounded deer:[21]

> uritur infelix Dido totaque vagatur
> urbe furens, qualis coniecta cerva sagitta,
> quam procul incautam nemora inter Cresia fixit
> pastor agens telis liquitque volatile ferrum
> nescius: illa fuga silvas saltusque peragrat
> Dictaeos; haeret lateri letalis harundo.   (4.68–73)

Unhappy Dido burns and wanders in a frenzy through the city, even as an unwary doe, struck by an arrow, whom a shepherd hunting with darts in the Cretan woods has unwittingly pierced from far off, and left in her the flying steel. She, fleeing, wanders through the woods and dales of Dicte; the fatal shaft clings to her side.

The image, which appears in the *Aeneid* just before the fateful hunt during which Dido abandons her chastity, appears in *Titus Andronicus* immediately before the court hunt, as quoted above, and directly afterwards, when Marcus presents Lavinia to her father, saying he "found her, straying in the park, / Seeking to hide herself, as doth the deer / That hath received some unrecuring wound" (3.1.89–91). The grotesque transposition of Dido's fatal passion onto Lavinia's mutilated and raped body invites both comparison of the fates of the two women and speculation on the ways rhetoric manipulates judgment. If Shakespeare's breach of decorum earns a groan, the scene appears as a failed invocation of Vergil's poem – as "indecorous shreds from the original robes."[22] He violates convention, however, to dramatize the distance between the worlds and ethics of the *Aeneid* and *Titus Andronicus* and to suggest that the bloody horrors of the latter stem from the compromises and sacrifices of the former. The Latin epic and the English revenge tragedy comment upon each other, but the play has the final word when it asserts by citation that its degeneracies are genetic, and that Vergil is the imperial father.

Upon hearing the doe simile, Titus takes the opportunity to pun in Latin and English. He seizes upon the image of the "unrecuring wound," standard in Elizabethan petrarchism, and invents a pun on *cura*, a word Vergil uses for a beloved or dear care: "It was my dear, and he that hath wounded her / Hath hurt me more than he had kill'd me dead . . . that which most gives my soul the greatest spurn / Is dear Lavinia, dearer than my soul" (3.1.92–3, 102–3). The multiple puns, characteristic of the Ovidian tradition, on unrecuring wounds, deer, dear, and *cura*, help Titus translate the Vergilian metaphor of Lavinia as a wounded deer into his own irremediable wound. The resurgence of Dido's simile is a startling reminder of the *Aeneid*'s importance to Titus' construction of his own identity. The mutilated allusion – displaced into the thick of the Ovidian plot of Philomela's rape, which properly has nothing to do with the losses calculated into empire-building – measures the changes the *Aeneid* has suffered since the beginning of the play.

The play interweaves the rape of Lavinia with Tamora's love affairs, which simultaneously confirm and distort the echoes of Dido's simile. Tamora's first resemblance to Dido comes when Saturninus woos her as "lovely Tamora, Queen of Goths, / That like the stately Phoebe 'mongst her nymphs / Dost overshine the gallant'st dames of Rome" (1.1.320–2).

The compliment alludes to Dido's first appearance and the simile *(NB)*
comparing her to Diana as she leads her chorus of nymphs and, in
Phaer's translation, "overshines" them all:

> qualis in Eurotae ripis aut per iuga Cynthi
> exercet Diana choros, quam mille secutae
> hinc atque hinc glomerantur Oreades; illa pharetram
> fert umero gradiensque deas supereminet omnis.   (1.498–501)

As on Eurotas' bank or Cynthus' ridge Diana trains her dancers, and a thousand
followers, mountain-nymphs, gather about her on each side; she bears her quiver
on her shoulder and as she steps, she overshines all the goddesses.

Vergil's simile emphasizes Dido's stately grace, chastity, and regal
authority; but because it translates almost verbatim the simile used to
describe the lovely Nausicaa in *Odyssey* 6, it also prepares for Dido's
erotic attraction to Aeneas. The complex and tragic ironies of comparing
Dido to Diana are simply parodic when transferred to Tamora.

The iconographical attributes of Diana that Saturninus does not
mention are the bow and arrow that Tamora gains during the hunt in act
2. Diana's chastity and Tamora's lack of it become issues when she
herself calls upon Dido as precedent for her amorous desires: she lyrically
solicits Aaron the Moor to enjoy the *locus amoenus* such as the
"wandering prince and Dido once enjoyed, / When with a happy storm
they were surprised, / And curtained with a counsel-keeping cave" (2.2/
3.22–4). When Aaron redirects her passion from sexuality to revenge, *(NB)*
pat on cue enter Lavinia and Bassianus, who proceed to deride Tamora
as an obscene parody of Vergil's *Venus armata* from *Aeneid* 1, where
Venus disguises herself as a follower of Diana. In this paradoxically
erotic and chaste form,[23] she appears to Aeneas and directs him to
Carthage and Dido. The *Venus armata*, who synthesized eroticism and
chastity, was also incorporated into the iconography of the Virgin
Queen. When Bassianus and Lavinia discover Tamora soliciting Aaron,
they accost "this queen, / This goddess, this Semiramis, this nymph, /
This siren" (1.1.520–3/2.1.21–4) with sarcastic comparisons to Diana:

> Who have we here? Rome's royal empress,
> Unfurnished of her well-beseeming troop?
> Or is it Dian, habited like her,
> Who hath abandoned her holy groves
> To see the general hunting in this forest?   (2.2/3.55–9)

Elizabethan audiences may never have witnessed so violent a yoking
together of Venus and Diana or, for that matter, a more startling
promise of the ways in which a play would treat the iconography of their

"Sovereigne Lady," "The English Diana, the great Britton mayde," as Puttenham calls Elizabeth I.[24]

Tamora, no slouch at barbed allusions, rises to the occasion. Shredding the neoplatonic robes of the allusion, she warns the prying couple that Diana punished Actaeon for seeing too much. In her shift of allusions, she makes a decisive move from a Vergilian to an Ovidian precedent and turns their acid reference to her ill-fitting robes as "Rome's royal empress" into a threat to use her new-found political powers:

> Saucy controller of my private steps!
> Had I the power that some say Dian had,
> Thy temples should be planted presently
> With horns, as was Actaeon's, and the hounds
> Should drive upon thy new-transformed limbs,
> Unmannerly intruder as thou art.   (2.2/3.60–5)

As the political-literary struggle mounts, Lavinia reminds Tamora of the (renaissance) association of Actaeon to cuckoldry and implicitly threatens to expose the queen's adultery: "Under your patience, gentle empress, / 'Tis thought you have a goodly gift in horning . . . Jove shield your husband from his hounds today: / 'Tis pity they should take him for a stag" (lines 66–7, 70–1). The battle of allusions ends in textual and sexual conflations: the mention of Diana generates scenarios of seduction, rape, castration, and dismemberment, all of which grotesquely mingle in Tamora's revenge. Tamora finds satisfaction in her son's vow to rape Lavinia and, on pain of being "an eunuch," to "Drag hence her husband to some secret hole, / And make his dead trunk pillow to our lust" (lines 129–30). This revenge, Tamora inclusively claims, is "the honey we desire" (line 131). "Away with her," she continues, "and use her as you will: / The worse to her, the better loved of me" (lines 166–7). Tamora's parting words again link her sexual exploits to her sons' rape: "Now will I hence to seek my lovely Moor, / And let my spleenful sons this trull deflower" (lines 190–1) (see fig. 10).

Although Tamora leaves the stage, the play pursues the displacement of her lust, making her sexualized body the metaphorical site of revenge. The next scene replaces the rape of Lavinia with the strange fate of Titus' sons, Martius and Quintus, swallowed up in the pit. It is a "subtle hole . . . Whose mouth is covered with rude-growing briers / Upon whose leaves are drops of new-shed blood / As fresh as morning dew distilled on flowers" (lines 198–201). It is a "very fatal place" (line 202), an "unhallowed and bloodstained hole" (line 210), a "detested, dark, blood-drinking pit" (line 224), and "this fell devouring receptacle, / As hateful as Cocytus' misty mouth" (lines 235–6). The pit, into which Chiron and Demetrius have thrown Bassianus' body, sends a "chilling sweat"

Figure 10. Statue of modesty. Andrea Alciati. *Toutes les Emblemes*
(Lyons, 1558)

through the "trembling joints" (line 212) of Titus' sons. They suffer an
"uncouth fear" (line 211) until they grow faint and are "plucked into the
swallowing womb" (line 239). At that very moment, Tamora's sons
"pluck" Lavinia the dainty doe to the ground in another part of the
woods. When Martius strangely compares Bassianus to "Pyramus /
When he by night lay bathed in maiden blood" (lines 231–2), the
imagery of defloration helps foreground the representational multiplicity
of the scene in which the pit substitutes for the offstage scenes of
Lavinia's rape and Tamora's erotic tryst with revenge.[25]

   The anatomy of the pit should be read iconographically as the site of
textual, as well as sexual, aggression. As a stage metaphor, the pit
enables the perverse conflation of Lavinia's rape and Tamora's sexual
pleasures: the "subtle Queen of Goths" (1.1.397) presides over the

"subtle hole" (2.2/3.198) which unnerves Quintus and Martius. To find
sexual imagery in a pit, which miraculously appears in answer to Tamora's
wish for Dido's "counsel-keeping cave," neither reduces the play's artistic
status nor removes it from historical and political contexts: on the
contrary, Shakespeare's use of sexual imagery casts a lurid light on those
Roman myths of empire founded on rape and generates epistemological
problems for the play's audience that parallel those suffered by Quintus
and Martius as they are drawn into the pit[26] (see fig. 11).

Allusions to Vergil's Dido and her cave provide the imaginative impetus
for the pit's creation, yet the product of the pit's violent activities is
Ovidian. When Lavinia enters, *her hands cut off and her tongue cut out,
and ravished,* her uncle invokes Ovid's tale of Philomela as the mythical
backdrop for the bewildering rhetorical ornamentation of her plight. His
niece's maimed body inspires Marcus to outdo Ovid in disjoining rhetoric
and referent:

> Speak, gentle niece, what stern ungentle hands
> Hath lopped and hewed and made thy body bare
> Of her two branches, those sweet ornaments
> Whose circling shadows kings have sought to sleep in
> And might not gain so great a happiness
> As half thy love? Why dost not speak to me?
> Alas, a crimson river of warm blood,
> Like to a bubbling fountain stirred with wind,
> Doth rise and fall between thy rosed lips,
> Coming and going with thy honey breath.
> But sure some Tereus hath deflowered thee
> And, lest thou shouldst detect him, cut thy tongue.
> Ah, now thou turn'st away thy face for shame,
> And notwithstanding all this loss of blood,
> As from a conduit with three issuing spouts,
> Yet do thy cheeks look red as Titan's face,
> Blushing to be encountered with a cloud.
> Shall I speak for thee? shall I say 'tis so?
> O that I knew thy heart, and knew the beast,
> That I might rail at him to ease my mind! . . .
> Fair Philomela, why she but lost her tongue,
> And in a tedious sampler sewed her mind:
> But, lovely niece, that mean is cut from thee.
> A craftier Tereus, cousin, hast thou met,
> And he hath cut those pretty fingers off,
> That could have better sewed than Philomel.   (2.3/4.16–35, 38–43)

Ovidian ornamentation is not meant to offer a magical escape from the
spectacle of Lavinia's body, as critics sometimes suppose.[27] Shakespeare

Figure 11. Sacrificial pit in foundation rituals. Andrea Alciati,
Emblemata (Antwerp, 1577)

uses the theatrical medium to radicalize Ovid's habit of disconnecting
events from their poetic representations. When the figure of Philomela
metaphorically emerges from Dido's "counsel-keeping cave," Shakespeare achieves an extraordinary contamination of Ovid and Vergil, and
proposes a revision of the *Aeneid* from the perspective of Ovid's violent
domestic tale.

The encounter of Marcus and Lavinia stages a collision of readerly
and dramatic modes of representation. Shakespeare adapts this practice
from Ovid but improves on his master's technique. Ovid habitually
exploits differences between violent events and their ornate descriptions,

but his reader may minimize the discontinuities and distresses. When Orpheus compares Hyacinthus, struck by a javelin, to

> Broosd violet stalkes or Poppie stalkes growing on
> Brown spindles, streight they withering droope with heavy heads
>   and are
> Not able for too hold them up, but with their tops doo stare
> Uppon the ground. So *Hyacinth* in yeelding of his breath
> Chopt downe his head. His neck bereft of strength by means of death
> Was even a burthen too itself, and downe did loosely wrythe
> On both his shoulders, now a tone and toother lythe.   (10.199–206)

Ovid's reader may visualize at will images of bruised poppies or the boy's mangled head. Shakespeare's medium stages the difference between things and their descriptions more sharply, for his audience has no escape from the spectacle of Lavinia's mutilated body ornamented by imagery and citations. When Marcus speaks of Lavinia's body made "bare / Of her two branches, those sweet ornaments, / Whose circling shadows kings have sought to sleep in" (lines 17–19), her "crimson river of warm blood, / Like to a bubbling fountain stirr'd with wind," and her cheeks, "red as Titan's face / Blushing to be encountered with a cloud" (lines 31–2), he re-animates vigorously, if inadvertently, Ovid's original critique of the motives of eloquence in the tale of Daphne.[28] Unwittingly, Marcus produces the play's most bizarre conflict of rhetoric and referent and transforms Lavinia's body into a site for a skeptical analysis of metaphor.

Ovid frequently makes trouble for the *Aeneid* and its imperial values through metaphors, particularly those that obscure their biases. Shakespeare, whom Francis Meres called the Elizabethan Ovid, adopts Ovid's contentious imitations in the speech he gives to Marcus, who inadvertently turns Lavinia's maimed body into an emblem of Vergil's contamination by Ovid. At no other point in his citation-heavy play, not even when he brings onstage a copy of the *Metamorphoses* as a prop, does Shakespeare offer his playgoers a greater temptation to pick up Ovid's book and read. Through the strategic contamination of Dido by Philomela in *Titus Andronicus*, Shakespeare invites his audiences particularly to compare the simile of Philomela with both Vergil's famous simile of Dido as a wounded doe and Shakespeare's own stage version of it. When Philomela is raped, she is "like the wounded Lambe which from the Wolves hore teeth / New shaken thinkes hir selfe not safe," or "as the Dove that seeth / Hir fethers with hir own bloud stayned." Ovid did not design this simile to recall Vergil's simile of Dido as a wounded doe: such similes of victimized maidens as vulnerable prey are conventional and generally establish no special relationship with prior models. Yet by

conflating Dido with Philomela, Shakespeare proposes that we read
Dido's fall through the double lens of Philomela's rape and simile.
Consequently, Dido's fall becomes a scene of violation in which responsibility cannot be obscured, as it is in Vergil's simile of her as a doe
wounded by the arrow of an unwitting shepherd.

Even the conspicuous Ovidian indulgence in the grotesque description
of Philomela's tongue as it writhes like a snake in its dying attempt to
return to its mistress has a critical edge:

> But as she yirnde and called ay upon hir fathers name,
> And strived to have spoken still, the cruell tyrant came,
> And with a paire of pinsons fast did catch hir by the tung,
> And with his sword did cut it off. The stumps whereon it hung
> Did patter still. The tip fell downe, and quivering on the ground
> As though that it had murmured it made a certaine sound,
> And as an Adders tayle cut of doth skip a while: even so
> The tip of *Philomela's* tongue did wriggle to and fro,
> And nearer to hir mistresseward in dying still did go.   (6.707–15)

Ovid places enormous pressure on the epic simile, normally used to
aestheticize heroic violence. The simile cannot make rape and mutilation
conform to epic decorum. Ovid seizes upon the prestigious technique,
meant to represent the glorious or elegiac, and assigns it the degrading
work of presenting contemptible acts. Ovid seems to have a double use
for the sophisticated equipment Tereus carries on his person: Tereus'
forceps or pincers can be viewed as Ovid's analogue of the epic simile
used to describe the rape. In Ovid's hands, they recall the poetic
technologies used to describe violence. Moreover, Ovid seems to have in
mind a specific precedent: Philomela's tongue wriggling its way back to
its mistress parodies a severed hand suffering death paroxysms in the
Aeneid, where a young warrior looks for his lopped-off hand and sees his
dying fingers pulsate and grope for a sword (*te decisa suum, Laride,
dextera quaerit | semianimesque micant digiti ferrumque retractant*,
10.395–6).

In *Titus Andronicus*, Shakespeare adopts Ovid's knack for irreverent
allusions to Vergil and demonstrates his sympathy for interrogative, even
transgressive imitations. He could not have contaminated two more
startlingly relevant episodes: Dido's agentless seduction turns to Philomela's rape; Aeneas' *pietas* to Tereus' *impietas*, a word that pervades
Ovid's tale; Dido feeding the wound of love changes to Tereus and his
too concrete food of passion or madness (*cibus furoris*); the silencing of
Dido gives way to the cutting out of Philomela's tongue; and Dido's
curse to Procne and Philomela's revenge. There is no tradition of treating
this particular tale as a critique of Dido's function in the *Aeneid*, yet a

violent wrenching of the epic's purpose is precisely what Shakespeare accomplishes in his contamination.[29] Shakespeare appears to find in Ovid's *Metamorphoses* a narrative and critical practice which he assimilates to the semiotics of the pit, which substitutes, inverts, confuses, appropriates, swallows up, and engenders meanings. Yet Shakespeare genders and metaphorizes the politics of imitation more insistently than Ovid does. His audience confronts the art of contamination in the forms of the pit and Lavinia's body, which turn into brutal signs of social disorder.

An unlikely character to do so, Marcus contributes to the violation of representational norms which Shakespeare condenses in the image of the pit. The pit metamorphically assumes the shapes of Tamora, Lavinia, Philomela, Dido, Dido's cave, the classical Underworld, and even the Andronici's tomb, the "sacred receptacle" retaining Titus' sons. Marcus' speech identifies both the Ovidian text that will replace Vergil's as the shaping myth of this late Roman society, and the violent poetics that separates decorative signifiers from their gory referents. He also transforms Lavinia's body into an iconographic sign of violation, affecting the literary, rhetorical, cultural, and epistemological reaches of the play: it is the final version of that pit. Her body, inscribed with Philomela's fate, haunts the audience's imagination. Her significances are nightmarishly hard to escape, as her nephew learns when she chases him to get hold of his copy of the *Metamorphoses*, a gift from his mother – he is perhaps afraid that she will serve him as Philomela and Procne did Itys. That mutilated, voiceless, but overly signifying body becomes a spectacle that sucks up and annihilates Marcus' golden poetry. The pit and Lavinia's body condense the play's tendency to conflate and warp literary sources. Because they simultaneously produce and consume meaning, these gendered signs violate the norms of representation. They are semiotic black holes.

Imperial rape and the poetic blazon

It is time to pause in the pursuit of Shakespeare's Ovidian deformations of Vergil to address the second order of disfiguration inscribed on Lavinia's body: Elizabethan petrarchism, to which the Ovidian critique of imperial authority proleptically relates. Marcus' rhetorical embellishment draws on Ovid and Petrarch interchangeably. His comparison of Lavinia's severed arms to "two branches" alludes to Petrarch's Laura as well as Ovid's Daphne, and the "circling shadows" resonate with expressly petrarchan images of erotic obsession.[30] His account of her maimed body parts recalls Ovidian metamorphoses into trees, rivers

(Arethusa), and bubbling fountains (Byblis), and also constitutes a gruesome blazon, the inventory of the petrarchan lady's body, such as Lavinia's "rosèd lips," "honey breath," and "lily hands." Ovid mingles well with Petrarch, who figured his own love and ambition through Ovid's Apollo, and modeled his blazon on Apollo's chase of Daphne and praise of those beauties destined to adorn the heads of poets and conquerors. The link of poetry to conquest, traced from Ovid to Petrarch and his courtly Elizabethan legatees, identifies a signal reason for the Elizabethan adoption of petrarchism as the language for praise, blame, and negotiation in the court of the Virgin Queen. The courtly and topical context for Ovidian–Petrarchan tropes motivates Shakespeare's startling disfigurations in Marcus' notorious speech and his parallel assault on the cult of the Virgin Queen in the figure of Tamora.[31]

It is not Ovid's Apollo, however, but Tereus who presides over the petrarchan ornamentation, rape and mutilation of Lavinia. The tale of Tereus plunges the *Metamorphoses* into a world of human depravity, absent gods, and brutal injustice. The abrupt shift in Ovid's tone challenges readers who sentimentalized earlier tales and, persuaded by rhetoric and genre, transmuted rape into seduction. Tereus' violent desires, conceived in the narrative space allotted to the description of Philomela's beauties, compels attention to linguistic and narrative parallels with the tale of Apollo. Both men burn like ripe grain, and the god of poetry, despairing of Daphne's consent, attempts to seize what she refuses to give. It is not clear that Tereus, the fiery barbarian from Thrace, needs the warming effects of rhetorical description. He conceives his desire to rape Philomela at the moment Ovid mentions the kind of description he forgoes:

> ecce venit magno dives Philomela paratu,
> divitior forma; quales audire solemus
> naidas et dryadas mediis incedere silvis,
> si modo des illis cultus similesque paratus.   (6.451–4)

Behold, Philomela entered, rich in her splendid apparel, but even richer in beauty; *such as we are accustomed to hear* of nyads and dryads when they step through the deep woods – if only you were to grant them refinement and clothing like hers.

Tereus may not need the poetic stimulus that inspired Apollo's chase, but the rape narrative nonetheless requires that Ovid acknowledge the breached custom of leisurely perusal of each beauty.

Renaissance poets enjoyed exposing the denaturing effects of petrarchan comparison, as witness Spenser's False Florimell, a Frankenstein-like monster composed of snow, wax, vermilion, golden wire for hair, burning lamps for eyes, and silver sockets to set them in, and a fallen "Spright to rule the carkasse dead" (III.viii.7). Even when engaging in the light ironies of fashionable travesties, English petrarchists reveal a simultaneous revulsion and attraction to the way that petrarchan poetics and particularly the blazon appropriate, objectify, and fragment the lady's body, as John Freccero and Nancy Vickers have shown.[32] Elizabethan petrarchists often use parody to expose the implicit violence against the woman's body, as well as the exclusion of her will. A prose blazon inspires Musidorus to attempt the rape of Pamela in Sidney's original *Arcadia*.[33] Spenser's Florimell appears as a stock petrarchan blazon pursued by a "griesly Foster" bent on raping her (III.i.17). The villain turns out to represent every man's response to her various attractions: the old fisherman and Proteus do their best to rape her, and even Arthur would be hard put to find something different to do with Florimell if he had the misfortune to catch up with her in Book III. In the anti-epithalamium that concludes *Parthenophil and Parthenope*, Barnabe Barnes presents the final resort of his petrarchan lover: frustrated by the failure of rhetoric to persuade, he uses magical arts to have his lady placed on a black goat and conveyed to the woods, where he rapes her.[34] In the poem's concluding moments, the speaker tells the weeping lady, "cease thy teares," before issuing legalistic language of retaliation: "all the fierie element I bare / Tis now acquitted," he says, and "as she once with rage my bodie kindled, / So in hers am I buried this night."

Shakespeare's presentation of rape and rhetoric needs to be placed in the context of other Elizabethan struggles with violence, dismemberment, and rape in petrarchan sequences. Shakespeare inherited his interest in the problem of feminine subjectivity, or the woman's alienation when her body is appropriated for loving decoration and redesigned to record the poet's own privileged subjectivity. Through the theatrical medium, though, Shakespeare radicalizes the Elizabethan critique of rhetoric: the actor who plays Lavinia offers a living body to quicken our empathy for the fictional woman who has been raped and mutilated, and is now being translated into petrarchan rhetoric. Marcus' rhetorical ornamentation painfully intensifies the effect of Lavinia's mutilation, which is to strip her of agency and voice. The theatrical medium has critical resources surpassing those of the printed text, for the play retains Lavinia's body as a stage prop bearing witness to her victimization by poetic devices as well as Tamora's sons. *Titus Andronicus* never allows us to forget Lavinia: it formally seals us off from her interiority and diagnoses the loss as symptomatic of petrarchan description.

While Marcus' blazon appears to take as its point of departure the critique of English petrarchists such as Spenser, Sidney, and Barnes, it innovates in singling out for elegiac ornamentation those body parts that are physically "trimmed." Curiously, Shakespeare presents the distorting and fragmenting effects of petrarchan comparisons before he produces the words themselves. In fact, everything about the situation Shakespeare forces upon Marcus and the audience is reversed from its customary petrarchan placement. And the most striking reversal is that Lavinia has already been raped. As the works of Sidney, Spenser, and Barnes indicate, the way that a poetic sequence ends is crucial. When the poet completes a blazon or a *gradatio*, he may abandon his quest for bliss, turn from erotic to divine love, or despondently resume his original posture. In rare cases, he may move from theory to practice, with or without consent: Spenser's *Amoretti* successfully conclude in an epithalamion, and Barnes' sequence ends in a vindictive rape. Lavinia's body is the figurative page on which Shakespeare analyzes poetic devices which distort and fragment the female body and may lead teleologically to rape. The goal of sexual conquest ties the lyric comparison, so bizarrely heaped on Lavinia, to the play's interrogation of empire founded on rape.

Marcus, Lavinia's well-intentioned uncle, has a different set of reasons for poetic ornamentation, which allows him both to acknowledge ceremoniously and to deflect momentarily realities too oppressive for his niece to survive and for him to grasp.[35] The problems of the speech have nothing to do with Shakespeare's dramatic incompetence or with insensitivity on the part of Marcus. Marcus founders because he has no way to know if his speech gives even partial voice to Lavinia's mind: "O that I knew thy heart, and knew the beast, / That I might rail at him to ease my mind!" (34–5). Knowing the culprit would ease the strain of his "dialogue of one": diverting attention to agents and causes would grant a reprieve from his painful confrontation with Lavinia and her literally inexpressible agony. Marcus' speech "fails" extravagantly because he can only blunder ahead verbally with no assurance that he is speaking for Lavinia instead of imposing his own emotions and words on her. He is unable surely to inhabit Lavinia's thoughts and emotions, and so he falls into an epistemological abyss – a "pit" in the terms of the play. He takes us with him, for at the moment we would most want to feel a "sympathy of woe," as Titus puts it, we have no access to Lavinia's interiority: this is lost when her agency and eloquence – hands and tongue – have been cut from her. It is no coincidence that Marcus uses the language of love poetry and finds himself suffering in the extreme from a condition routinely experienced by Ovidian and petrarchan love poets. Like Apollo chasing Daphne, Narcissus at his pool, Pygmalion romancing his stone, and scores of petrarchan lovers, Marcus does not know if his poetry stirs up sympathetic vibrations or if it merely sticks to the surface of the lady's body. Unlike some of these artists, Marcus cares intensely about the woman's will, and creates his comparisons in the hopes of conforming his mind to hers, not of forming her in the image of his desires.

Despite his intentions, Marcus' poetry obeys the play's metaphorizing activity and attempts a second rape or seizure of Lavinia's body. Since it cannot persuade, it seeks to coerce her body into complying with the laws of rhetorical decorum and once again being "Rome's rich ornament." Her body resists the verbal alchemy through which Marcus poignantly attempts to reclaim his niece. Yet the simile, at times fantastically successful in *Titus Andronicus*, cannot transform her and, for the first time in the play, begins to lose its creative powers of order. The first important simile came from Titus: his very first words were an epic simile, which helped generate order out of the socially chaotic moment at the beginning of the play, when the two princes threatened to stir up civil war. An epic simile, a sacrifice, a burial ritual, and a choice to privilege primogeniture: the resources of epic are Titus' means to impose creative order on the threatened Roman empire. Also at this moment Shakespeare stages a critique of the petrarchan blazon as appropriative and ultimately mutilating. Epic and erotic poetry meet a simultaneous critique in Lavinia's disfigured and ornamented body because they share an appropriative and colonizing nature.[36] Like the epic simile, the lyric blazon produces systematically acquisitive comparisons – hence the familiar analogy of the beloved's body to "my America, my new-found land," in John Donne's phrase. In Shakespeare's diagnosis, rape, as a metaphor for imperial conquest, is also the aim of the lyric blazon.

As the "craftier Tereus" that Marcus wonders about and the source of the "trim invention" Aaron admires in himself, Shakespeare may lay claim to being the greatest "shake-scene" of the Elizabethan stage. What remains to be suggested is that his iconoclastic handling of the imperial–petrarchan tradition has a powerfully unsettling context in the Elizabethan language for negotiating cultural and political authority. In the figure of Lavinia, Shakespeare has seized upon and contaminated an imperial body – "Rome's rich ornament," blazoned with Vergilian and Ovidian counter-perspectives on empire and conquest – as an image of and surrogate for the Queen's "body iconographic." *Titus Andronicus* makes visible a Shakespeare who ransacks Queen Elizabeth's treasury of imperial icons, meant to denote her political legitimacy, in poetry like Puttenham's blazon of her silver forehead, ebony brows, fringed gold tresses, ruby lips

Like leaues to shut and to unlock.
As portall dore in Princes chamber:
A golden tongue in mouth of amber . . .
Her bosome sleake as Paris plaster,
Helde up two balles of alabaster,
Eche byas was a little cherrie:
Or els I thinke a strawberie.

As Puttenham goes on to note, "all the rest that followeth" in the blazon "may suffice to exemplifie your figure of *Icon*" (p. 244). On stage, such emblems sustain a cross-examination that ties Shakespeare to Ovid on political as well as literary grounds: the Elizabethan Ovid follows his transgressive predecessor in sabotaging the established representative of imperial authority. If one accepts the seriousness of Shakespeare's quirky representations in *Titus Andronicus* – and his mass of theatrical "footnotes" suggests he is establishing his credentials – one gains a Shakespeare willing to pirate courtly images for cultural use in the theater.

Titus' cultural wars

In the second half of the play, Titus develops his own brand of Ovidian semiosis, in which he both metaphorizes and genders literary imitations. Through mock-heroic feats of literalism and displacement, Titus seeks poetic justice for the familial and ideological violence that caused his suffering. He does not, however, enjoy Ovid's constructive brand of *serio ludere*, but subverts referentiality in order to wreak havoc on his enemies and on the system of values, as encoded in Augustan literature, that has disappointed him. Once we have entered the Ovidian woods of the second act, where physical and epistemological violence may occur at any moment, the play's audience and characters never return to secure Vergilian foundations.

At the beginning of the play, Titus exemplifies the stoic belief that "to endure misfortune is to reveal one's true self – a pure essence of *virtus* – and, simultaneously, to discover that the universe is significantly ordered."[37] The epic genre which consecrated the imperial origins of Rome and offered a model of self-containment to Titus, the triumphant warrior but grieving father who marked his entrance to Rome with an epic simile. When Titus acknowledges that Rome is no grieving, victorious matron granting him harbor after his sacrifice, he rediscovers her as a "wilderness of tigers" and proceeds to undercut epic convention and stoicism alike:

Marcus, we are but shrubs, no cedars we,
No big-boned men framed of the Cyclops' size,

But metal, Marcus, steel to the very back,
Yet wrung with wrongs more than our backs can bear.   (4.3.46–9)

Before he embraces his role as revenger, Titus ritually exhausts epic's fortifying resources. Its similes, hyperboles, and mythological precedents are a source of pain to Titus, who formally disclaims the cedars of epic similes for common shrubs and the titanic "big-boned men" of heroic song for androids.

Heroic standards and golden age visions have no place in Titus' iron-age rhetoric, a discourse most famously recorded in *Metamorphoses* 1. Ovid's description of the degeneration of the golden to the iron age is appropriate to *Titus Andronicus*, where there is no Saturn, only Saturninus. Titus' world does not even have a Jupiter to overthrow his pacific father: the most memorable trace of the god is the Clown's malapropism, so grimly proleptic of his own death, "gibbet-maker." Ovid's tale of the second creation of humankind from stone leaves a strong mark on Titus. After narrating the tale of Deucalion and Pyrrha, Ovid comments, "Of these are we the crooked ympes, and stonie race in deede, / Bewraying by our toyling life, from whence we doe proceede" (1.493–4). Titus, who wasted his tears and lamentations on stone rather than the obdurate tribunes, despairs at the stoniness of iron age humanity. Whereas Aeneas shouldered responsibility for Rome's future, Titus understands Rome's destiny as torture "more than our backs can bear."

Experience in specifically Ovidian woods causes Titus to loosen his hold on the linguistic, cultural, and psychological integrity that Vergilian authority represents for him. Once Titus grasps a copy of the *Metamorphoses* in his hand, he reinscribes the "ruthless, vast and gloomy woods" as an Ovidian *locus horrendus* "Patterned by that the poet here describes, / By nature made for murders and for rapes" (4.1.53, 57–8). At the play's turning point, Titus abandons his Andronican heritage of "uprightness and integrity," beginning with his language. After Titus sacrifices his hand to buy his sons' lives, a messenger enters with the severed hand and his children's heads. At last dropping the reins of stoicism, Marcus attempts to rouse an epic fury: "Now is a time to storm" (3.1.264), he cries. But Titus, no longer an epic hero, announces his generic transformation: "Ha, ha, ha!" (line 265).

Titus comes undone in puns which strikingly contrast with the formal decorum of his former, Vergilian identity. The dear-deer-*cura* puns come directly after an allusion to the Troy legend: "What fool has added water to the sea, / Or brought a faggot to bright-burning Troy?" (3.1.69–70). And when Marcus foolishly mentions the word "hands" after Titus and Lavinia have lost theirs, Titus cries out that Marcus bids him, like

Aeneas, to "tell the tale twice o'er / How Troy was burnt and he made miserable," and then produces one of the play's worst puns, "O handle not the theme, to talk of hands" (3.2.27–9). At such moments, the *Aeneid* looms over the play as a dismembered, mutilated text of Rome's former greatness.

Marcus consistently serves to point up the shift in genre that Titus has undergone. When Marcus, Titus, and his grandson discover the identities of Lavinia's rapists, Marcus urges them to revenge, calls young Lucius "Roman Hector's hope," a thriving Astyanax, and invokes the rape of Lucrece to guide the Andronici's revenge against tyrants. They are to swear "as with the woeful fere / And father of that chaste dishonoured dame, / Lord Junius Brutus swore for Lucrece' rape – / That we will prosecute by good advice / Mortal revenge upon these traitorous Goths" (4.1.89–93). Although Marcus self-deceptively identifies with the model of Junius Brutus, Titus knows that they resemble the disguised and politically wronged Brutus less than the devastated husband and father of Lucrece. Marcus' impulses tend to be regressive, to hark back to when the Andronici were defenders and not victims of Rome.

Titus avoids his brother's rite, rejects the model of resurrection offered by the figure of Astyanax, and instead imitates the feigned imbecility of Brutus, Rome's early champion. Instead of pursuing a successful campaign against tyranny, he perversely contaminates the precedent of Brutus with that of Procne, whose domestic tragedy is antithetical to epic, and in doing so, undermines Marcus' normative perspective on exemplarity and authority. From this point on, the brothers' interaction onstage represents the conflict of obsolete (Marcus) and emergent (Titus) ethics and epistemologies. Shakespeare heightens the contrast when Titus forbids young Lucius to deliver a message to Tamora's sons "with [his] dagger in their bosoms" (4.1.118). While Marcus wrongly assumes that Titus has committed himself to stoic patience, Titus plots his assault on heroic models: when he teaches young Lucius "another course," he makes weapons of the literature that encodes Rome's celebrated virtues. Titus seeks revenge by exploiting the elastic nature of Roman exemplars, whose vulnerability to hyperbolic expansion and satiric reduction makes life seem absurd to Titus.

The text of his first lesson is a celebrated Augustan poem: Titus sends to Chiron and Demetrius a bundle of arrows in a scroll inscribed with Horace's famous ode, *Integer vitae, scelerisque purus, / Non eget Mauri iaculis, nec arcu* (4.2.20–1). With arrows wrapped up in a poem about the bow and arrows of the Moor, Titus produces, quite literally, a barbed allusion. The poem, however, has degenerated into no more than a schoolboy's verse: Chiron immediately identifies it as "a verse in Horace,

I know it well: / I read it in grammar long ago" (lines 22–3). Part of
Titus' conceit is to exploit the ode's authoritative status. As a mere poetic
tag, stripped of both its context and its power to stir the mind, these too
famous lines offer Tamora's sons nothing to interpret. If the poem has
degenerated into meaningless authority, the boys will fail to see its new
referents: themselves, Aaron the Moor, and Titus himself, who is no
longer physically whole (*integer*) and does not intend to remain free of
crime. Whom or what does Titus seek to wound with his barbed allusion?
It hardly seems worth the trouble to humiliate Tamora's foolish and
villainous sons in a literary contest. His revenge on them will be exacting,
but Titus' immediate opponent is Horace's magnificent ode itself, which
he proves to be a dead metaphor, apt only as a figure for lifeless Roman
virtue.

Titus next gathers his family to solicit the gods for justice, using an
innovative method: using bow and arrow, they send petitions to the
Zodiacal signs on the Capitoline Hill. Titus is staging no supplication but
an elaborate attack on Tamora, Saturninus, and his court. He initiates
the event by citing Ovid's words about the flight of justice: "*Terras
Astraea reliquit*: be you remembered, Marcus, / She's gone, she's fled"
(4.3.4–5). After shooting arrows at Jove, Apollo, Pallas, and Mercury,
Titus cracks the first topical joke: "'To Saturn', Caius – not Saturnine: /
You were as good to shoot against the wind" (4.3.57–8). The Andronici
then unite in hurling shafts of wit at the court when Lucius strikes
Virgo's lap, Publius shoots off one of Taurus' horns, and Marcus
completes the family joke about the cuckolded emperor:

> This was the sport, my lord: when Publius shot,
> The Bull, being galled, gave Aries such a knock
> That down fell both the Ram's horns in the court,
> And who should find them but the empress' villain!
> She laughed, and told the Moor he should not choose
> But give them to his master for a present.   (4.3.70–5)

Titus' arrows undermine the pretensions that Saturninus and his queen
might have to divine status as represented by the Zodiacal signs. They
also strip the Zodiac of its power to support the traditional Roman
sense of order and justice. Shot in the lap, Astraea, virgin goddess of
justice and forerunner among Elizabeth I's celebratory guises, is anato-
mically exposed as the whoring queen of Goths. To the compliments to
Elizabeth I in *A Midsummer Night's Dream* and pageant plays, Bradbrook contrasts

the oblique and tragic reflection of the image of Astraea in *Titus Andronicus*,
when Titus, despairing of justice, shoots his arrows against the heavens . . .
Instead of using the images of pageantry, of the Accession Tilts or the lyric poets,

Shakespeare evolved a counter-image, an evil figure with every quality opposed to Astraea.

Bradbrook hesitates to see parody before the Stuart period, but one may glimpse Shakespeare alongside of his Andronici, shooting barbs at a contemporary Astraea. When he daringly inverts Elizabeth's personal iconography in Tamora, he unleashes "a demonic energy that . . . steals the show." [38]

Tamora renders herself vulnerable to Titus' deadly literalisms because she does not realize that he has lost faith in Roman legends and, like her, exploits ideological forms for personal ends. She seeks power over Titus by staging herself as a version of poetry: "I will enchant the old Andronicus / With words more sweet, and yet more dangerous, / Than baits to fish" (4.4.88–90) she tells her husband, "I can smooth and fill his aged ears / With golden promises that, were his heart / Almost impregnable, his old ears deaf, / Yet should both ear and heart obey my tongue" (lines 95–8). A sophisticated reader of the Vergilian Titus, she believes that the most incantatory poetry at her disposal is Vergil's electrifying Fury, Allecto. Accompanied by her two sons, she seeks Titus in his accustomed haunt, "his study, where they say he keeps / To ruminate strange plots of dire revenge" (5.2.5–6). She enters the stage "in this strange and sad habiliment" to tell Titus that she is "Revenge, sent from below" (5.2.1.3), "Revenge, sent from th' infernal kingdom / To ease the gnawing vulture of thy mind / By working wreakful vengeance on thy foes" (lines 30–2).

By casting herself as Revenge, Tamora supplies Titus with the means to exact revenge on her and, simultaneously, harrow Vergil's Underworld. Although Titus at first feigns reluctance – "how can I grace my talk, / Wanting a hand to give it action?" (lines 17–18) – he at last welcomes the "dread Fury" to his "woeful house" (line 82). At this point in his metamorphosis from a Vergilian hero, Titus no longer requires a hand to enact his designs: a personification better suits the anti-hero who displaces agency onto literature. He persuades her to rename her sons Rape and Murder, and in these forms he is able to "lesson" his enemies (line 110) and "o'erreach them in their own devices" (line 143). He refers the competition to its literary mediators: "worse than Philomel you used my daughter, / And worse than Progne I will be revenged" (lines 194–5), he tells Chiron and Demetrius just before he slits their throats. The punch line to Titus' joke is that he knows full well that he has finally got his remaining hand on the empress' two sons. For all his self-dramatization, Titus knows the difference between living throats and dead texts: he is able to suspend his rage at ideology and take action against rapists, murderers, and bad emperors (fig. 13).

Titus empties out precedents much as he drains the blood from the bodies of Tamora's sons. Calling Lavinia to hold a basin in her stumps to receive the blood, he tells Tamora's sons,

> You know your mother means to feast with me,
> And calls herself Revenge and thinks me mad.
> Hark, villains, I will grind your bones to dust,
> And with your blood and it I'll make a paste,
> And of the paste a coffin I will rear,
> And make two pasties of your shameful heads,
> And bid that strumpet, your unhallowed dam,
> Like to the earth swallow her own increase.   (lines 184–91)

In describing Tamora as the earth, an "unhallowed dam," swallowing her own increase, Titus recalls the pit, that "unhallowed . . . hole" and "swallowing womb" (2.3.210, 239). Audiences digest the allusion while Chiron and Demetrius recognize their destiny as Ovidian allusions for their mother to digest. Titus enjoys the rhetorical drama of his recipe and then, flamboyantly dressed as a chef, serves to the Queen the flesh of her sons baked in a crust of their ground-up bones, a pie the English called – Shakespeare is charmed by the perverseness – "coffin" (fig. 12).

Lavinia's body, the other primary site for the play's metaphorizing activity, also bears the burden of Titus' literalisms. When he gathers his remaining family to swear revenge, he holds the head of one son, gives the other to Marcus, and sets in Lavinia's mouth his severed hand:

> The vow is made. Come, brother, take a head,
> And in this hand the other will I bear.
> And, Lavinia, thou shalt be employed:
> Bear thou my hand, sweet wench, between thy teeth.   (3.1.280–3)

These lines and Titus' ceremony generate considerable distress among editors. Wells and Taylor follow the Cambridge editor who proposed that Shakespeare or a corrector, "to soften what must have been ludicrous in representation, wrote 'Armes' above 'teeth' as a substitute for the latter" and emend these lines to "And *Lavinia* thou shalt be imployde, / Bear thou my hand sweet wench betweene thine Armes."[39] They accept that Lavinia originally bore the severed hand between her teeth, but use the correction of the previous line (line 281) to pry Titus' hand from her teeth and nestle it more decorously between her arms. Even if the lines are not altered to reduce the ludicrous and abrasive, editors may offer staging suggestions to soften the character of the oath. Waith proposes that the Andronici engage in a "simple ritual, such as handshaking."[40] Although Titus still has one hand to shake, a ceremony involving hands – involving four live but not altogether whole people, six

IMPOTENTIS VINDICTAE
FOEMINA.

Figure 12. Philomela and Procne cook Itys. Barthelemy Aneau, *Picta Poesis* (Lyons, 1552)

heads, and a mixture of whole arms, stumps, and a severed hand – can hardly be "simple."

Waith's suggestion conjures the wonderful image of the actors using the oath of revenge to exploit the problem of hands. Titus might raise his stump aloft and join his remaining hand with those of his family, after placing his dead hand between the handless Lavinia's teeth. His "hand-maid of revenge," Lavinia becomes the centerpiece of Titus' emblem about his commitment to dismemberment – corporeal, social, and linguistic – as his new and potent resource. His emblem dramatizes what he lacks, which is the "victorious hand" that, as Katherine Rowe suggests, witnessed his agency in "the affiliative relations among persons and between individuals and the sovereign state," as well as his choice to revel in what Rowe calls a "fetishizing tradition that makes the capacity

Non fine caufa.

Figure 13. "Non sine causa." Claude Paradin, *Emblemes Heroïques* (Lyons, 1557)

for effective action contingent on disability"[41] (figs. 13 and 14) and that also makes Ovid's Philomela a compelling exemplar.

Titus insistently focuses his gruesome play with literalized signs on Lavinia's body, which figuratively grounds the refashioning of his cultural myths, his course of action, and his very identity. He calls her a "map of woe, that thus dost talk in signs," and further says, "Thou shalt

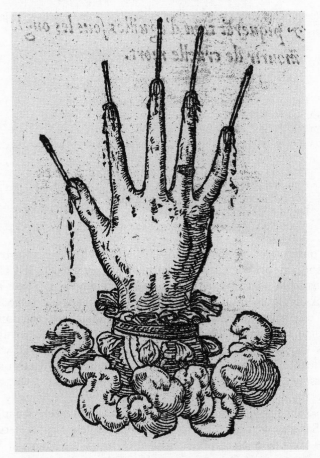

Figure 14. Bloody hand. Claude Paradin, *Emblemes Heroïques* (Lyons, 1557)

not sigh, nor hold thy stumps to heaven, / Nor wink, nor nod, nor kneel, nor make a sign, / But I of these will wrest an alphabet / And by still practice learn to know thy meaning" (3.2.12, 42–5). Her body suggests to Titus the course of his revenge and prepares for the comical appearance of the book itself: *Titus Andronicus* advertises its bookishness when it trots out a copy of the *Metamorphoses* and makes Lavinia chase it down. Turning to Philomela's tale, Lavinia provides Titus with an authoritative text to replace his obsolete Vergil, and Titus, in a faithful act of literary digestion, concocts his revenge from Ovid's plot.

As Lavinia's body inspires Titus' literary revenge, so it serves as the text to reveal, authorize, and complete it. Titus issues his challenge to Saturninus in the form of a deadly logical proof:

> My lord the emperor, resolve me this:
> Was it well done of rash Virginius
> To slay his daughter with his own right hand,
> Because she was enforced, stained, and deflowered?
> SATURNINUS. It was, Andronicus.
> TITUS. Your reason, mighty lord?
> SATURNINUS. Because the girl should not survive her shame,
> And by her presence still renew his sorrows.
> TITUS. A reason, mighty, strong, and effectual;
> A pattern, precedent, and lively warrant
> For me, most wretched, to perform the like.
> Die, die, Lavinia, and thy shame with thee,
> And with thy shame thy father's sorrow die.   (5.3.35–46)

It takes only fifteen lines more for Titus to clarify the nature of his revenge and Tamora's meal, and a further three for Titus to kill Tamora, Saturninus to kill Titus, and Lucius to kill the emperor. These are the aftershocks of Titus' murder of his daughter. Perhaps most shockingly, Lavinia's death provides the occasion for Titus' final heroic-demonic raid on paradigms of virtue. He does not endorse Virginius' example: he considers Virginius "rash" and himself "wretched." Moreover, when he first learned of Lavinia's rape, Titus responded with extraordinary tenderness, not with Virginius' severity. Marcus presented her, saying, "This *was* thy daughter" (3.1.63) to which Titus answered simply, "Why Marcus, so she *is*" (line 64). Titus shifts responsibility for his daughter's death to Saturninus, who authorized the example despite the reservations that Titus takes pains to emphasize. He also aims a death blow at Virginius, whose exemplarity Titus tarnishes through his perverse repetition.

Yet Titus cannot, finally, endure existence or death without a "pattern, precedent, and lively warrant," for he covertly affirms the example of Lucrece, the raped matron who took her life rather than live in shame. Titus continues secretly to identify with and to affirm virtuous Romans, for it is he who gets to play the illustrious Roman woman. The point becomes inescapable when one compares Titus' revenge play to the tale he invokes. Lavinia's rape, Titus' death, and especially his desire to die, strikingly differ from the *Apius and Virginia* presented on the Elizabethan stage in 1575.[42] Virginius kills his daughter to *prevent* her shame, and once he has done so in this morality play, he is spared from self-recriminations by the handy appearance of Comfort, who proposes that Virginius "be not dismayde" (a pun worthy of *Titus Andronicus*) and send Virginia's head to Apius in court: "This wil be comfort to your harte, Virginius be content" (lines 979, 992). Apius, the corrupt and lustful judge, is the one to suffer, not Virginius, who triumphs in the play's moral economy. The differences between Titus' and Virginius' situations are more significant than the parallels, and they all point towards the closeted model of Lucrece, Ovid's "matron of manly spirit" (*animi matrona virilis, Fasti* 2.847).[43] First of all, Titus knows that if his sorrows die with his daughter's shame, it is because his revenge guarantees his own death. In Titus' stoic suicide by proxy, Saturninus is the instrument by which Titus takes his own life. But if Titus claims to author his own death, his act depends on equating Lavinia with himself and reading her body as the text of his woes. Just as her raped and maimed body provided the text and authority for his vengeful identity as Procne, so her violated honor and death supply Titus with his final role, that of Lucrece.

If Titus gains sympathy at the play's end, it is paradoxically because he killed the daughter whom he called the "cordial of my age to glad my heart" (1. 1.169), a pun that came early enough in the play to emphasize identity rather than disjunction. But while it testifies to paternal devotion, it also anticipates Titus' terrible inability to distinguish between himself and his children. In killing Lavinia and casting himself as the violated Lucrece, Titus proves that his experiences in loss and injustice failed to change him from the father who killed his son for disobedience – for refusing to replicate Titus. Lavinia dies to re-establish Titus' identity, her final service in the Roman traffic in women and especially in upholding the Andronican sense of honor. In the first scene, Titus readily accedes when Saturninus claims her as his bride to "advance / [Titus'] name and honorable family" (1.1.242–3). When Bassianus seizes her in an act Saturninus terms "rape" (line 409), the two princes hotly debate whether the term means theft of property or the seizure of a woman against her will. Yet the most telling exchange which places Lavinia on a sliding scale between person and commodity takes place in her own family, between Titus and his son Lucius. When Titus disowns Lucius as a "traitor" and demands that he "restore Lavinia to the emperor," Lucius chillingly replies, "Dead if you will, but not to be his wife / That is another's lawful promised love" (1.1.302–3). It is no wonder that Lavinia, worth more dead than devalued as a token of men's honor, dies in the service of Titus' allegorical play.

The death of Vergil and the Elizabethan political inheritance

In the concluding move to restore order, the play calls on Vergil to perform the last rites. A Roman lord requests Lucius to address the Senate

as erst our ancestor,
When with his solemn tongue he did discourse
To love-sick Dido's sad-attending ear
The story of that baleful burning night,
When subtle Greeks surprised King Priam's Troy.
Tell us what Sinon hath bewitched our ears,
Or who hath brought the fatal engine in
That gives our Troy, our Rome, the civil wound.   (5.3.79–86)

Although the Senate places its hope in the healing powers of the *Aeneid*, master code of the Roman empire, Vergil can do no more than bandage the civil wound. The motivations and sources of authority – literary, political, ethical – have been hopelessly confused. Titus himself, a man more sinned against than sinning, nonetheless stands as a monument to the failings of the Roman imperial machine. No Sinon insinuated the "fatal engine" – Vergil's *fatalis machina* – into Rome, although that is the tale Lucius will gravely unfold.[44] As in the first scene of the play, when Titus sacrificed Tamora's and his own sons to the rigid code of *pietas*, Roman institutions and values are dramatically emptied of their original meaning. Vergil's noble rhetoric and values sound hollow; he reappears not to rejuvenate Rome, but to receive, like Titus' dead body, the last kiss of his sons. Vergil's vision of disordering emotional and political passions may be sacrificed or overlooked in the renaissance in order to gain an unambiguous champion of social order. Yet Shakespeare suggests that late imperial Rome made a fatally reductive icon of Vergil's poem and ignored the double meaning of the monument – not just a tribute, but a warning.

Given the disintegrative violence that the play inflicts on bodies and texts alike, it seems unlikely that the remaining Andronici can teach the Romans "how to knit again / This scattered corn into one mutual sheaf, / These broken limbs again into one body" (5.3.69–1). These lines, with their glimmer of hope, are uttered within a mere five lines of the deaths of Titus, Tamora, and Saturninus, and immediately after an invocation of the Vergilian storms which swept through the beginning of the play: such epic similes have lost their power to bind the "sad-faced men, people and sons of Rome, / By uproars severed, as a flight of fowl / Scattered by winds and high tempestuous gusts" (5.3.66–8) into a thriving community. Although some critics place their confidence in Lucius, who conquers Rome with an army of Goths, the young man can hardly camouflage his political *coup*, and relies on the play's enervated Vergilian rhetoric of order for its success. A play which insistently conflates various antagonistic models and ostensible opposites – e.g., piety and barbarousness, Romans and Goths, Vergil and Ovid – cannot confidently promote a vision of social order and providential design at its conclusion. The play derives its horrors from fragmenting and contaminating sources which knit scattered and broken bits of Roman authority into monstrous emblems.

In the milieu of the *translatio imperii*, Shakespeare's dismemberment of Roman imperial authority is astonishing. The strangest contaminations in his play portray Tamora as an over-lusty Dido, Dian with hot dreams, monstrous *Venus armata*, and whoring Astraea. His choice of Elizabeth's icons to disfigure hardly seems characteristic of the bard frequently assumed to rank among the more politically conservative Elizabethan dramatists. Frances Yates, for example, hopes that Lucius' return at the end of the play is an "apotheosis" which "perhaps represents the Return of the Virgin – the return of the just empire and the golden age."[45] She then notes that Shakespeare's

treatment of the Astraea image – so utterly surprising and unconventional, so remote in its passion and wildness, not only from the stock-in-trade Astraea of a Lord Mayor's pageant, but also from the more subtle Neoplatonic Virgo of a court poet – leaves him with the eternal question-mark still against his name. (p. 76)

Yates speculates that for Shakespeare, the "imperial theme" might have a religious, Dantesque dimension in addition to its national significance.

Shakespeare's "utterly surprising and unconventional" engagement of the literature and icons supporting the Tudor myth of national origins places the question-mark after his *political* stance. Like an unnerving response in an echo poem, the question of politics haunts even criticism that seeks social restoration through Lucius as Rome's champion of traditional values. In a dense paragraph of *Hero and Saint*, for example, Brower observes that "the saving of Rome by Lucius, traditionally first of the British kings and descended from their 'ancestor' Aeneas, or from his brother Brute, had a special meaning for Shakespeare's audience" (p. 194) and, following Yates, recalls the prophetic ending of the pageant play, *The Misfortunes of Arthur*:

> That virtuous Virgo born for Britain's bliss:
> That peerless branch of Brute: that sweet remain
> Of Priam's state: that hope of springing Troy:
> Which time to come, and many ages hence
> Shall of all wars compound eternal peace.

With the scene in which Titus shoots arrows at the Zodiac and quotes Ovid on Astraea's departure, Brower aptly juxtaposes a second Elizabethan image of the cosmos, an illustration to John Case's *Sphaera Civitatis* (1588, fig. 15): in it "Elizabeth as Virgo-Astraea, 'descended of the Trojan line,' is shown holding the universe (!), which in the 'sphere of

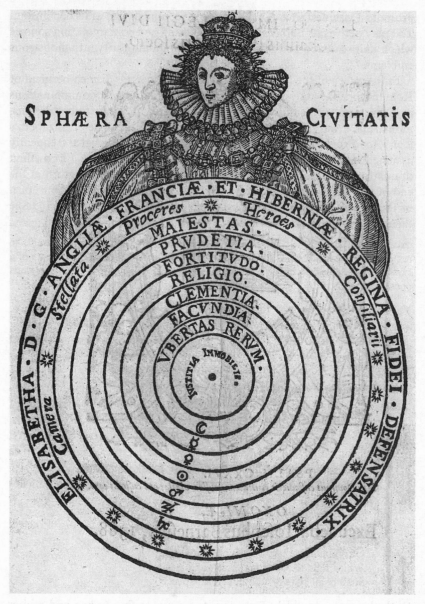

Figure 15. John Case, frontispiece to *Sphaera Civitatis* (London, 1588)

the fixed stars' are ranged the Star Chamber, Princes, and Heroes:
Camera Stellata-Proceres-Heroes" (p. 194). Even before cultural poetics
became a branch of literary criticism, critics like Brower felt that literate
audiences might understand *Titus Andronicus'* allusion to Elizabeth-
Astraea as an icon of "unchanging justice," and that "less learned
auditors would have seen the point in the restoration of peace and order
under Lucius, the 'first Christian king of England,' as he 'was presented'
in Foxe's *Book of Martyrs*" (p. 194). The continuity of political reading
in *Titus* criticism is surely more remarkable than the disagreements about
which of the figures in the play's political Zodiac – Augustus, Titus,
Lucius, Elizabeth I, and her Star Chamber – are suspect and which
unswervingly just.

(*NB*)

In fact, criticism of the play traces the question of Shakespeare's
political stance through debates about the political ethics of characters in
the play, namely Titus and Lucius. Of the major critics, Waith is most
celebratory of Titus' exemplarity, finding in him a "restorer of order"
that Lucius replicates when he is acclaimed emperor and "the ceremonial
order again prevails."[46] Dissenting from Waith's view of Titus, Brower
notes that the Goths help construct Lucius as a Roman hero through
epic diction: they promise to follow Lucius like "stinging bees in hottest
summer's day, / Led by their master to the flow'red fields" (5.1.14–15)
or, as Brower aptly puts it, like warrior bees in a Vergilian simile (p. 190).
Like Brower, Miola finds a principle of social order in Lucius in contrast
to Titus. A fair number of critics agree that Lucius is a chip off the old
block but, arguing that Lucius merely perpetuates Titus' "cruel irreligious piety," find him anything but socially restorative.[47] Since critics
agree that Shakespeare's Roman characters have a double life as
Elizabethan icons, the critical dissent about the political virtues and
injustices Shakespeare means to blazon in individual characters traces a
shadowy debate about Shakespeare's confidence in Elizabethan as well as
Roman justice.

✓

Titus Andronicus subjects icons of justice – Astraea, Saturn, Horace's
ode, and Elizabeth I's body iconographic – to the violent skepticism that
his exemplary characters endure. Shakespeare's play does not hold out
the promise of rejuvenation once Roman models make the quantum leap
to early modern England: instead, he challenges the capacity of privileged
classical models to translate political and literary authority from Troy to
imperial Rome and the Elizabethan court. His strenuous critique of
petrarchism, attached to Lavinia's body, serves indirectly to interrogate
the literature and iconography used to consolidate royal power in the
court. For reasons of censorship and reprisal, if not temperament, a
playwright had to keep a question-mark against his name. In his

theatrical translations of empire, Shakespeare travesties the icons of Elizabethan power rather than the queen herself: to the end of establishing his theater as an alternate sphere of cultural authority, Shakespeare kidnaps privileged political icons from their courtly abode and gives them new significances in the popular theater. Bradbrook suggests that the evocations of the myth of Troynovant in *King Lear* record "the moment when it was recognized that the miracle would *not* happen," and that Shakespeare's "open form" or avoidance of direct icon-to-prince correspondence is a theatrical virtue: "to set the audience debating meant full houses."[48] With its panoply of toppled authorities spread out on the stage, *Titus Andronicus* takes a radically disruptive position in the translation of empire and suggests that even before *Lear* and James I, Shakespeare was establishing the Troy legend as a ground for ideological contestation in the theater.

3   "Tricks we play on the dead": making history in *Troilus and Cressida*

The previous chapter argued that the gory, idiosyncratic *Titus Andronicus* inaugurates Shakespeare's career-long engagement of the translation of empire and that his aberrant reproductions of classical icons should be recognized as calculated assaults on the political program invested in transporting imperial authority from Rome to Elizabethan England. *Titus Andronicus'* eccentric rhetoric and dramaturgy raise questions about the successful transmission of imperial authority through classical myth and example, which the play gleefully strips of their competence. The legends, icons, and models that Titus once took to be reliable sources of cultural nourishment turn out to be enervated metaphors for values they have come not to betoken but betray. As signs pried loose from their original contexts, Astraea and such once-reputable exemplars as Virginius and Lucrece, Vergil and Horace no longer anchor the Romans to their civic origins and defining virtues. With long histories and impressive credentials, these exemplars are cultural giants and tower over *Titus Andronicus* as claimants to fame. Yet *Titus* reduces them to media and not sources of authority, mere allusions to a ghostly past and their earlier, more famous appearances. Shakespeare's next exploitation of the resources of combative imitations comes not in Rome but at the originary site of the *translatio imperii*: "In Troy, there lies the scene" (1.1.1).

Long before Shakespeare turned to the matter of Troy, poets and historians alike had voiced skepticism about the relationship of the Troy legend to political propaganda. In cantos 33–5 of the *Orlando furioso*, the knight Astolfo makes his extraordinary voyage to the moon, where he is taken on a tour of the lunar junkyard by none other than the Apostle John. There, Astolfo receives an astonishing lesson in history:[1]

> Non sì pietoso Enea, né forte Achille
> fu, come è fama, né sì fiero Ettorre;
> e ne son stati e mille a mille e mille
> che lor si puon con verità anteporre:
> ma i donati palazzi e le gran ville

dai descendenti lor, gli ha fatto porre
in questi senza fin sublimi onori
da l'onorate man degli scrittori.

Non fu sì santo né benigno Augusto
come la tuba di Virgilio suona.
L'aver avuto in poesia buon gusto
la proscrizion iniqua gli perdona . . .

Omero Agamennòn vittorioso,
e fe' i Troian parer vili ed inerti;
e che Penelopea fida al suo sposo
dai Prochi mille oltraggi avea sofferti.
E se tu vuoi che 'l ver non ti sia ascoso,
tutta al contrario l'istoria converti:
che i Greci rotti, e che Troia vittrice,
e che Penelopea fu meretrice.

Da l'altra parte odi che fama lascia
Elissa, ch'ebbe il cor tanto pudico;
che riputata viene una bagascia,
solo perché Maron non le fu amico.   (35.25, 27–8)

Aeneas was not as devoted, nor Achilles as strong as is rumored, nor was Hector so fierce. There have been thousands upon thousands upon thousands of men who could, in truth, supersede these men. But the palaces and large villas given by their descendants – these have granted such men boundless sublime honor from the honored hands of writers. / Augustus was not so holy or benign as Vergil's horn sounded. Having good taste in poetry excused his wicked proscription . . . / Homer made Agamemnon seem victorious, and the Trojans low-class and sluggish; he made Penelope faithful to her husband, and had her suffer thousands of insults from the suitors. If you wish the truth not to be concealed from you, invert the whole story: the Greeks were destroyed, Troy was victorious, and Penelope was a whore. / On the other hand, listen to what reputation Dido left behind, she who had such a chaste heart; she is reputed a tart only because Vergil was not her friend.

The Apostle then declares his affection for writers, stemming from his own authorship of the life of Christ. These were favorite stanzas of Voltaire, who may have had in mind Ariosto's analysis of the economics and politics motivating literary history as well as such historical frauds as the Donation of Constantine when he remarked that "history is tricks we play on the dead."

In England, the critique of the Troy legend and its political interests was pursued, without Ariosto's sublime blasphemy, in the skeptical questions that humanist scholars asked of Geoffrey of Monmouth's *History* and its untraceable source, the *vetustissimus liber*. Geoffrey's contemporaries, William of Newburgh and Gerald of Wales, derided the marvelous stories of Arthur's feats, which filled the void of early British history.[2] Gerald enjoyed his tale about devils fleeing when the gospel of St. John was placed on their familiar's chest and flocking back with reinforcements when the word of truth was replaced with Geoffrey's *History*, but he did not doubt Britain's Trojan origins. Not until the fifteenth century and the rise of humanists in Duke Humphrey's circle did the Brutan legend face antagonism and, for a brief moment, the threat of eclipse. What saved the Troy legend for continuance from Caxton's *Chronicles of England* (1480) to the popular works of Fabyan (1516), Grafton's edition of Hardyng (1543), and Grafton (1568), along with Holinshed and Harrison (1577) and Stow, was the ascent to the throne of the Welsh Henry Tudor in 1485.

The Tudors were willing to host the legend, as long as they were not required to give it credence. Elizabeth I listened to John Dee's earnest arguments that she had rights over Iceland based on Arthur's conquests, but she did not act on them. In her diplomacy and skepticism, she resembled her grandfather: when Henry VII named his first born son Arthur, he fed the Tudor propaganda mill – a christening admired by John Twyne, a great disbeliever in the legend – but Henry also hired Polydore Vergil, the Italian historian who dismantled the legend's historicity with gusto and without reprisal. The Welsh Tudor manifestly stood to gain by preserving the legends of Brute and Arthur, but had greater need for Polydore's defense of the Tudor claim in terms of more recent history: Polydore was better prepared to misattribute Richard II's problems to the lack of an heir than to favor Geoffrey's recreative history over Gildas and Roman histories. Polydore Vergil paradoxically destroyed the credibility of the Troy legend and guaranteed its ardent defense. Tudor supporters, influenced by Reformation sentiment, were less able than the king to stomach the efforts of a foreigner and papist to discredit England's legendary origins.

Leland attacked Polydore tirelessly and somewhat incoherently; John Bale traced Brutus' ancestry to the Bible; Henry Lyte (1592) – whose family motto was *Fuimus Troies* – and Richard Harvey defended the Brutan legend for its moral value; Sir John Price complimented Polydore's learning but demurred at his conclusions. Touchiness along the lines of Captain MacMorris' "What ish my nation? Who talks of my nation?" (*Henry V* 3.2.125) abounded. The Welsh Arthur Kelton and Humphrey Lhuyd vociferously promoted the Welsh claim to "an uninterrupted descent from the earliest inhabitants of the island" through Brutus[3] and lambasted Polydore, who, Lhuyd said, "doth in all places nippe and girde at the Britaynes," being "an infamous baggage-groome, ful fraught wt. Envie and hatred."[4] And when the Scottish George Buchanan expressed doubts about the Brutan legend, he was also accused of trying to cheapen England for Scotland's greater glory. Perhaps to forestall the abuse that skeptics learned to expect from zealous patriots, historians and poets responded to the legend with varying degrees of enthusiasm. While Rastell (*Pastyme of the People*, 1529), and Elyot, in the 1545 edition of his dictionary, were comfortable with skeptical references to the legend, later generations either glossed over it or applied strippers with the least toxins: Coke was not above citing the Brutan legend to establish the priority of England's common law over the Roman civil law; Camden gently but effectively separated the legend from acceptable historiography; and Selden tried to discourage Drayton from using Geoffrey as a creditable historian rather than a fanciful but inspiring muse.

Increased sophistication in historical methods both weakened the legend and made its continued viability an article of faith. Based on their awareness of its history of ideological manipulation in literature, poets such as Chaucer and Ariosto were making parallel discoveries of the legend's lack of authenticity. In the middle ages, the ranks of authorities, from Dares and Dictys to the more familiar Benoît (c.1160), Guido della Colonne (1287), Boccaccio, Chaucer, Henryson, Lydgate, Lefèvre (1464), Caxton (1474), and Lemaire (1509) – swelled to include a range of vested interests. Since each of these authorities negotiates the heroic and romance material to stamp different values on the legend and its characters, the legend's generic transformations reflect shifts in ethics, value, and nationalist ideology.[5] Even in antiquity, the causes and values of the Trojan war were disputed implicitly or directly in the texts of Homer, Vergil, and Ovid. In the *Metamorphoses*, Ovid pointedly reinterprets the motivations for combat: Aeneas and Turnus fight not for a kingdom in dowry, nor a father-in-law's scepter, nor Lavinia herself, but for conquest – *nec iam dotalia regna, / nec sceptrum soceri, nec te, Lavinia virgo, / sed vicisse petunt* (14.569–71). In his apostrophe to the *Aeneid*'s unfortunate cipher of a heroine, Ovid insists that the war was wholly about imperial claims legitimated by conquest alone and not, as Vergil suggested, by marriage and inheritance.

While Ovid and the medieval romances "debased" classical epic, the final step that the legendary figures at Troy took down the scale of genres led them into the literary productions of ballad-makers and satirists. There, distilled by time, tradition, and the reductive powers of those genres, they took essentialized forms as the wily Ulysses, blockish Ajax, petulant and destructive Achilles, whoring Cressida, foolish Troilus – Sir Trollelollie to Samuel Rowlands[6] – and pandar or bawd. Elizabethans held no uniform view of the divisive tradition, but could hardly escape skepticism when they had plentiful authorities to intimate that even the great Vergil, like Homer, twisted history to accommodate the interests of his prince, Augustus. Yet even the comforts of disbelief were hard to maintain: another complication for the Elizabethan evaluation of Troy came with Chapman's translation of Homer's *Iliades*, of which he had published seven books, dedicated to the Earl of Essex, by the time Shakespeare composed *Troilus and Cressida*. His translation suggested a return to the legend's origin in Homer, controverting the medieval opinion that Homer was a relative late-comer to the tradition. His work revitalized and politicized the epic ethos, however neoplatonized, in the Elizabethan consciousness of Troy. At the time of Shakespeare's play, the lovers and colossal warriors of the Troy legend stood variously prized, devalued, and redeemed.[7]

Genre, ideology, and the crisis of exemplarity

In *Troilus and Cressida*, Shakespeare exhibits and exhausts literary and historical authorities on the Troy legend. From the prologue in which time is "digested" and warriors "disgorged" from their ships to the epilogue in which Pandarus bequeaths us his syphilitic disease, the play satirically "digests" the highly privileged tradition only to cast it up, along with the play's women, as "relics," "scraps," and "greasy orts." This play entertains the spectral appearances of all *auctores* in the tradition – classical, medieval, and contemporary; epic, chronicle, romance, ballad, and satire. At Troy, the originary site of literary representation and political authority, Shakespeare sets imitations of the divisive tradition to battle out, on a synchronic stage, the question of the identities of Troy, its warriors, and its lovers. The result is a play bristling with anger and defenses, one whose competing ideologies are constantly staging their *aristeia* – the stepping forth of a warrior (or idea) to prove itself in battle. In such a history as that experienced by the Troy legend, authority and identity, national or characterological, do not accrue, stabilize, and deepen. *Troilus and Cressida* presents the tradition as driven by political and economic hunger to supersede, control, be recognized as a powerful, single essence. As a result of the nationalist and literary battles waged on its ground, however, it is fragmentary and inconsistent – a totality menaced by its various parts.

In *Troilus and Cressida*, Shakespeare refuses to privilege or adjudicate among versions of the Troy legend, but instead twists, disorders, and occasionally inverts versions of the Troy legend. Drawing attention to the narrative techniques – rhetoric, genre, and disposition – that stamp interpretive values on the legendary events and heroes at Troy, he exposes lack of authenticity in a legend which exists only to bequeath authoritative origins. Robert Kimbrough, remarks of the play's "experimental principle of discontinuity" that[8]

there is no handling of the Troy legend before Shakespeare's which does not try to point the story with some kind of moral or ethical observation. The sources may be responsible for the facts that make up the ending of *Troilus*, but the same sources emphasize that Shakespeare made no attempt to shape his material so that it would carry thematic reverberations outside the play.

To sharpen this observation, Shakespeare not only refuses to shape his material, but systematically subverts the narrative shapes into which the Troy legend had been cast, and does so to strip the legend of its power to influence the world outside its texts. In the play's very dramatic construction, Shakespeare reiterates Troilus' notorious query, "What's aught but as 'tis valued?" (2.2.53).

The question is jarring in part because it comes from Troilus, the sometime idealist who has acted his part so often that he has gained an actor's ability to stand apart from his role and consider the economic advantages of the philosophical position he is routinely asked to supply. The question is a version of the Cretan liar's paradox: as the trope for amorous idealism, Troilus cannot interrogate value without calling into question his own continued significance, as well as that of the play and the larger tradition he inhabits. It is a cruel irony that Troilus musters his most passionate commitment to undermine value and continue the war he abhors: "Helen must needs be fair," he says to Greeks and Trojans alike, "When with your blood you daily paint her thus" (1.1.90–1). His cynical question and paradoxically faithless commitment to the war can only come from a character aware of his own and his world's fatiguing repetitions, which are gradually eroding his marriage to fidelity: this is why Troilus dreams up his appalling analogy, beginning "I take today a wife" (2.2.62), often associated with his ambivalence about Cressida rather than his argument about the grounds for conquest based on the theft of a wife, Helen. Troilus can pose the question of value only in his Elizabethan incarnation, when timeless repetitions of idealistic love have made him both reflexively committed to his traditional position and cynically aware of its lack of authenticity.

The doubleness of Troilus relates to the hybrid character of *Troilus and Cressida* as a play stymied by its composition from mismatched parts in its long and varied tradition. Shakespeare endows the world of the play with partial awareness of the multiple sources that constitute the Troy legend as well as the politics and economics that underwrite the continual reproductions of its characters and events, and he presents this world as enraged at its own fragmentary, unauthentic, and exploited character. When critics diagnose pathology in the discordant and abrasive play itself rather than its characters,[9] they respond to the generic anomaly of a play born from the tradition's rarely acknowledged literary psychomachia. The rage mimicked and generated by the play has its roots in the disillusionments of the late Elizabethan period, following the spectacular fall of the earl of Essex, whose ambition and chivalric virtue find their reflection in Shakespeare's Achilles and Hector, respectively. The Troy legend presents Shakespeare with the means to philosophize and exacerbate that disillusionment: to seek out a critique of representation on the ground of Troy is to unsettle Western culture at its putative foundation. In inhabiting the myth of origins but defying its authority, the play enters into a paralyzing struggle with cultural needs for authoritative origin and purposeful direction. Psychological terms offer greater interpretive yield for a play like *Troilus and Cressida* than for *Titus Andronicus*: the play's characters have the misfortune of actually being the kinds of emblems and signs from which Titus is alienated and against which he ultimately takes arms.

Generic mutability governs *Troilus and Cressida*'s edgy defensiveness about the ambivalent nature it inherits from the Troy legend. Unlisted on the title page of the *Folio*, the play is slipped in between the histories and tragedies as if the editors were uncertain of its proper affiliation. The *Folio* title dubs it a tragedy, while the Epistle to the Quarto finds it "passing full of the palme comicall." Critical arguments advanced to settle questions of the play's genre often convincingly demonstrate the power of their genre of choice to inform the play's construction and effects.[10] Attempts to dismiss the claims of other genres, however, do not fare well. Critics must resort to textual emendation and even wholesale reconstruction on the lines of Dryden: so Nevill Coghill is obligated to do in support of his argument that *Troilus and Cressida* is a tragedy that can be recovered only when the distortions of the play's textual histories have been removed.[11] In fact, the play zealously exploits its various textual and generic resources with the goal of self-deformation. In this it resembles Ajax, a "very man *per se*" – the tautology reflects the slipperiness of heroic identity – who is thrown out of Aristotelian balance by partaking of too much. "This man"

hath robbed many beasts of their particular additions. He is as valiant as the lion, churlish as the bear, slow as the elephant: a man into whom nature hath so crowded humours that his valour is crushed into folly, his folly sauced with discretion. There is no man hath a virtue that he hath not a glimpse of, nor any man an attaint but that he carries some stain of it. He is melancholy against the hair; he hath the joints of everything, but everything so out of joint that he is a gouty Briareus, many hands and no use, or purblind Argus, all eyes and no sight. (1.2.15, 19–31)

Like a Polonian "tragical-comical-historical-pastoral" play or the fishy creature that Horace rejects at the outset of the *Ars Poetica*, Ajax is over-concocted and undone by the heroic epithets and additions that compound him.

Ajax is one of many characters who act as generic sign-posts for *Troilus and Cressida*. Critics often champion a representative character who can furnish a defining genre to secure an identity for the elusive play, and traditional favorites are the satirical Thersites or the politic Ulysses. Joel Altman also proposes the unfaithful heroine, Cressida, a felicitous choice in light of the play's defensive, changeful, and self-betraying nature.[12] This woman, who knows only "seems," prompts her uncle Pandarus to exclaim, "You are such a woman, a man knows not at what ward you lie." To this she responds,

> Upon my back, to defend my belly; upon my
> wit, to defend my wiles; upon my secrecy, to
> defend mine honesty; my mask, to defend my
> beauty; and you, to defend all these; and at all
> these wards I lie, at a thousand watches.   (1.2.265–9)

Troilus and Cressida, like its heroine and literary tradition that resist being known, gains its resilience and enigmatic character from an apparent readiness to surrender or betray itself to the certifiable meaning of some one of its historical authorities only to be, suddenly, elsewhere, being someone else's literary kind.[13] It exhibits an exasperating pleasure in rousing audience expectations based on an anticipated genre or text such as Chaucer's romance or Homer's epic, only to renege on "the promis'd largeness" and "ample proposition that hope makes / In all designs begun" (1.3.3–5) onstage. The play seeks its audience's confusion, and we are left to unperplex the interpretive and evaluative knot into which the play and characters are twisted.

To catalogue the play's subversions of genre and textual precedent would be a daunting task, calling for annotated summary of every frustrating scene and nuance. Admirably begun by Bradbrook, Colie, Donaldson, and Bradshaw, this work would begin with the parodically epic prologue, "Suited / In like condition as our argument" (lines 24–5), who signals the play's participation in ideological skirmishes from the war of the theaters to uses of the Troy legend: his defensive armor, speech, and tone introduce the play's juggling of familiar genres that should facilitate, not hinder, interpretation. The work would then laboriously plow through to the anti-closural conclusion, in which

Pandarus turns his diseases to commodities.[14] Disappointing scenes abound. Troilus first appears as a Chaucerian lover, but his cloying and perverse petrarchism replaces Chaucer's sympathetic touches. In the Greek camp, bombast topples the Greek commanders from the epic heights towards which they strive. In the Trojan council, Hector invokes Aristotelian virtue only to toss it aside blithely in favor of an arbitrarily assessed honor. If we search out lyric pleasures in the boudoir of Helen and Paris, we stumble into a bordello.

These scenes conspicuously fail to imitate famous scenes of petrarchan love, epic council, and lyric sweetness. Refining the art of swerving from precedent, *Troilus and Cressida* reverses Agamemnon's dictum: "Distinction, with a broad and powerful fan / Puffing at all, winnows the light away, / And what hath mass or matter by itself / Lies rich in virtue and unmingled" (1.3.27–30). Sorting through the tradition, Shakespeare selects the least reputable versions of characters and events and heightens their unsavory aspects. Ajax is far from Lydgate's hero, Achilles from Homer's, Troilus from Chaucer's, and Nestor from anybody's version of the experienced counselor. On the other hand, all that is obnoxious in Ovid's account of the Greeks is writ large in the dolts (Ajax), machiavellian politicians (Ulysses), and thugs (Achilles) of Shakespeare's stage. Shakespeare unerringly chooses compromising details from Chaucer to amplify. When Chaucer's Troilus writes his love letter, he laughs at the amorous protestations he cribs from Ovid, and later prefers the exchange of Criseyde for Antenor to elopement with her. In Shakespeare's aubade scene, these choices reappear in more discouraging forms: Troilus shares a knowing laugh with Pandarus – "ha, ha!" – at Cressida's expense, and scarcely conceals his urge to leave once he has eaten the "cake" for which he "tarried."

Conflating sources and genres similarly disrupts stable signification. The strangest contamination comes in the scene of Pandarus' "complimental assault" on Helen and Paris. As Rosalie Colie demonstrates, Pandarus establishes the sweet and fair terms fit for Helen of Troy, but parodies rather than imitates the sonneteer's stock attitude of idolatry:[15]

> Fair be you, my lord, and to all this fair company;
> fair desires in all fair measure fairly guide them –
> especially to you, fair queen: fair thoughts be
> your fair pillow! (3.1.42–5)

The wit he elicits from the "Sweet queen, sweet queen, that's a sweet queen, i' faith" (lines 69–70) recalls another "quean," Doll Tearsheet. Reduced to a "Nell," Helen of Troy teases Pandarus into singing a love song: "You shall not bob us out of our melody; if you do, our melancholy on your head" (lines 67–8). His ditty features the cries of sexual love from woe, to pleasure, to regret – "O ho, groans out for Ha, ha ha! – Heigh ho!" (line 121). His parody of orgasm strikes critics as an appropriate answer to Nell's fatuous cry, "this love will undo us all. O Cupid, Cupid, Cupid!" (lines 105–6). Although she gets no credit for it, Nell is grammatically right: the kind of love to which she and Paris are reduced in this play wholly "undoes" them as legendary figures.

Yet as soon as Pandarus leaves the stage, the famous lovers abruptly and inexplicably transcend the satiric genre:

> PARIS. They're come from the field: let us to Priam's hall
> To greet the warriors. Sweet Helen, I must woo you
> To help unarm our Hector. His stubborn buckles,
> With these your white enchanting fingers touch'd,
> Shall more obey than to the edge of steel
> Or force of Greekish sinews: you shall do more
> Than all the island kings – disarm great Hector.
> HELEN. 'Twill make us proud to be his servant, Paris,
> Yea, what he shall receive of us in duty
> Gives us more palm in beauty than we have,
> Yea, overshines ourself.
> PARIS. Sweet, above thought I love thee!   (lines 144–55)

In private, Helen and Paris break into verse which reasserts their characteristic ambiguity: self-centered but beautiful, they can almost explain away the Trojan war. No longer a bawdy Nell, this seductive Helen alone can disarm great Hector with her "white enchanting fingers." Her restored powers introject Homeric resonances into a scene of generic debasement.[16] Here is the romance in epic that the scene utterly denied to the lovers. Paris and Helen's fragile decorum and belief that their passion and beauty can redeem Trojan losses cannot withstand the urbane coarseness of later traditions represented by Pandarus. When he exits, the dominant genre of satire ceases to prevail and, simultaneously, critics cease to comment on the scene.[17] The moment of verse is oddly dislocated and static, like a nostalgic flashback to a time before Pandarus was granted his disillusioning role in the tradition. Through the substitution of genres, the play enacts the repression of an earlier historical period, to recall Jean-Joseph Goux's definition of neurosis.[18] Who remembers this fragile moment of dignity? And yet, who is not haunted by desire for the authenticity that this verse afterthought recalls through the residual lyric genre?

The scene typifies the way the play destabilizes generic, evaluative, and characterological categories. The consequence of over-representation is that *all* the legendary figures at Troy suffer from the "textual psychosis" that Carol Cook identifies in Cressida. Stressing the difficulties of psychologizing her, Cook expands on L. C. Knights' suggestive term for Cressida, "the wanton of tradition," and suggests that a "bizarre textual psychosis seems to voice itself through her; she is a creature of intertextuality, of Chaucer, Lydgate, Caxton, Henryson, and others . . . endowed with self-consciousness."[19] Cook further notes that "in revealing herself as the creation of a literary tradition, the effect of a textual operation, Cressida discloses the ideological tendentiousness of literary codes" (pp. 48–9). Cook's sense of character as simultaneously constituted and vitiated by conflicted textuality extends to the play's other characters and to the dream of cultural integrity that it translates from its earliest authorities.

If the play were to escape indeterminacy, it would have to subscribe to one genre or text, allowing an Achilles to emerge as conqueror on the battlefield of tradition. The play and the war cannot effectively end before their values have been defined. Yet at its end, the play offers no more than the hostile challenge issued by its armed prologue: "Like or find fault: do as your pleasures are: / Now good, or bad, 'tis but the chance of war" (lines 30–1). *Troilus and Cressida* allots no settlement to the creatures and events it exposes as dependent upon ideologically motivated genres for significance. In conclusion, Shakespeare's play systematically repudiates its predecessors:

1. Cressida does not "enter with the lepers" as she did in Henryson's "Testament of Cresseid" and the contemporary play by Chettle. Cressida does not shoulder full responsibility for the play's failures of value, and we are denied an edifying moral.

2. Hector turns down his role as hero to play the chivalric fool. He chases a suit of armor about the battlefield while Achilles' Myrmidons stalk and bushwhack the Trojan hero. Committing a crime against heroic epic, the "god-like" Achilles orders his men to keep themselves well-breathed until they find Hector, and then "Empale him with your weapons round about; / In fellest manner execute your arms" (5.7.5–6). When they slaughter the unarmed Hector, Achilles orders them to give him the credit: "On, Myrmidons, and cry you all amain / 'Achilles hath the mighty Hector slain'" (5.8.13–14). Dispatching epic, the play replaces heroic combat with a sordid, behind-the-scenes execution befitting an Elizabethan revenge drama. At its conclusion, *Troilus and Cressida* turns the great epic warrior to a political propagandist.

3. Troilus fights but fails to die. He never achieves the status of metonym for fallen Troy, as he does in kindlier sources. Instead, Hector dies in the ambush plotted, in Lydgate and Caxton, for Troilus.

Shakespeare denies the eleventh-hour efforts of tragedy to deliver the play from irresolution.[20]

4. Troilus delivers a ringing speech of choric closure: "Strike a free march to Troy! With comfort go: / Hope of revenge shall hide our inward woe" (5.10.30–31). At this moment, Pandarus rushes onto the stage to disrupt the tragic equilibrium Troilus momentarily achieves. Pandarus makes his anachronistic intrusion to complete the movement of the *translatio imperii* through time, geography, genre, textual variants, and ideology to Elizabethan England and the moment of performance. A play that systematically exhausts value and genre fittingly assigns its last word to Pandarus: he has throughout stood for a skeptical tradition grown weary of itself, and he stands at the last as an Elizabethan bawd appealing to the common bond he claims to share with the audience. We are "Good traders in the flesh" (5.10.46) and "Brethren and sisters of the hold-door trade" (line 52), and to us he bequeaths his ancient diseases.

How did we come to be on familiar terms with a pimp who trades in his niece's flesh? The answer depends on taking Pandarus as a personification of the cynical position he occupies in the tradition – a characterological reduction appropriate to the play's metatheatrical and tropical practices. Like Iago, who embodies and mobilizes the language of social hatreds, Pandarus both courts and resists characterological interpretation. *Troilus and Cressida* gathers no dramatic energy from the war or romance plots, for audiences can hardly suspend knowledge that the Trojans lost the war and that Cressida betrayed Troilus. Instead of trying to revitalize the tradition, the play stages the conversion of its characters into tropes and dead metaphors.[21] Wherever in their histories the warriors and lovers begin the play, at its end they are identical with Elizabethan by-words, including "merrygreek" and "base" or "honest Troyan," for bullies, whores, johns, and pimps. When we recognize and accept the "gross terms," we exchange their characterological potential for their verbal coinage. Like Prince Hal, we study the characters "Like a strange language, wherein, to gain the language, / 'Tis needful that the most immodest word / Be look'd upon and learnt; which once attain'd . . . comes to no further use / But to be known and hated" (*2 Henry IV*, 4.4.68–73). However much we would like to except ourselves from Pandarus' fraternity, we do, in fact, trade in the characters' flesh for their significance as "gross terms." Nor is it at all clear that we are as adept as Hal at purging ourselves of their contagion. Through Pandarus, the play finally insists upon the ideological purchase of tropes, figures of speech, and representation itself. Genre is both the stake and the agency of the representations that seek a narrative and correlative meaning under the auspices of epic, tragedy, satire, or history but fail to fictionalize coherent identities for the characters and events at Troy. Pandarus' epilogue constitutes the play's final defensive strategy: he looks to the audience and assumes its participation in a brokerage of representation.[22]

Troilus and Cressida earns its place between the genres of tragedy and history in the Folio, and its reputation as a play that was never clapper-clawed. It both unfixes distinctions and requires an explanatory text or genre to grant it and its legendary material the integrity necessary to establish its historical origin and nationalistic destination and to still its hyperactive oscillations up and down the scale of genres. By disassembling a tradition that usually feigns ignorance of its multiplicity and inconsistency, *Troilus and Cressida* demonstrates the need to commodify the legendary characters and events in order for them to yield socially usable meaning. The play's self-conscious mishandling of the Troy legend's cultural ambition cuts, perhaps, too deeply into the skins of late Elizabethan audiences, who may not have been willing to applaud a lively witness of their own diseased body politic, as the foreword complains.

"He pageants us": imitation in the Greek camp

The authenticity of a thing is the essence of all that is transmissible from its beginning, ranging from its substantive duration to its testimony to the history which it has experienced. Since the historical testimony rests on the authenticity, the former, too, is jeopardized by reproduction when substantive duration ceases to matter. What is really jeopardized when the historical testimony is affected is the authority of the object. – Walter Benjamin

The play, its characters, and action are subject to the assaults that brought *Titus Andronicus'* Roman exemplars to their knees. Those legendary icons lost their status as sources of cultural authority: condemned to the ghostly existence of signs, stripped from their original contexts, they came to signify alienation from securing origins. *Troilus and Cressida* is similarly stripped from the authority that ontological claims can offer an over-produced legend, and the characters feel the difference in their status. The play, as critics have noted, anticipates ideas in Benjamin's famous essay on the mechanical reproduction of a work of art: apposite to *Troilus and Cressida*'s status as a repetition are Benjamin's comments that the reproduction lacks "its presence in time and space, its unique existence at the place where it happens to be," and that "the presence of the original is the prerequisite to the concept of authenticity."[23] The characters of *Troilus and Cressida* have differing degrees of sensitivity to their existence in multiple forms and their scandalous reproducibility, and at times fret over their jeopardized authority. In *Troilus and Cressida*, Shakespeare poses a question that lies beyond his concerns in *Titus Andronicus*: what happens when subjects, in a textually aggravated version of Hamlet's sense of his slippage from his Hyperion-like father, perceive themselves as diminished and altered copies of a lost original?

The legendary figures are not, as were Titus' virtuous exemplars, merely allusions to earlier, stronger performances of themselves. Their peculiar histories of transformative imitation render them complex figures who frequently find themselves at odds with the interim temporality of *Troilus and Cressida*, which cannot settle in any one of the legend's historical eras. Besides Helen and Paris, who shift from Elizabethan satire to Homeric epic coordinates, and Pandarus, whose intrusion on the battlefield at the play's end reminds the audience of the Elizabethan end of the Trojan war, we might consider Hector's cavalier *volte face* in the Trojan council, where he intelligently questions the value of the war only to cast aside his doubts in the name of honor. Since he cites no motive for his change of heart, Hector has troubled critics who wish to preserve the fine reputation that Hector earned in the moralizing tradition after Homer.[24] The problem is that Hector cannot maintain his distinguished role as the ethical Trojan after he has been tempted by his equally attractive role as the chivalric one: in the Trojan council, he insists upon his ethics and even cites Aristotle on the subject – anachronism intended – and then, warming to Troilus' speeches on honor, formally exchanges one traditional role for the other and issues a highly romantic challenge to single combat.[25]

These cases of jointly textual and characterological instability seem, at times, to be the result of random mechanical tics of the play rather than willed acts on the part of the characters. There are, however, abundant signs that the characters are possessed by the need to assume definitive identities by choosing the strongest of their many versions. Troilus passionately desires to become the "authentic author" of truth for the citational purposes of love lyric. Nestor and Agamemnon are obsessed to the point of incoherence with the dignity and rhetoric they are accorded in epic and chronicle traditions: as if steeped in Lydgate's "depured rethoryke,"[26] their language is hyperbolic, horribly stuffed with epithets and similes, and Nestor is gratified to be termed a "good old chronicle" (4.5.201). The hope of being, not merely imitating, Achilles puffs up the traditionally respectful Ajax. It is true that the characters are often weary with their status as tropes. As John Bayley elegantly writes,

Ulysses is a charade of policy as Nestor is one of age, Troilus of fidelity, Cressida of faithlessness. "He must, he is, he cannot but be wise" is the ironic comment on Nestor. But all of them must, are and cannot but be voices imprisoned in role and argument, figures condemned to tread the mill of time without ever being free of it.[27]

But they are only so condemned while they inhabit Shakespeare's interim temporality, and they pursue, with determination, lasting and singular identities as tropes. They cast covetous glances at the annals in which they may be recorded as heroes without the Hamlet-like curse of "conscience," which tells them of the unstable ground on which they tread the mill of time and base their actions. Like Coriolanus, who wishes to be "author of himself" (5.3.35), the characters accept a model of identity that is constituted almost farcically in one's relationship to the many authoritative texts of ones' "future" historiographers.

(NB)

The characters' sensitivity to their reproducibility becomes epidemic in the Greek camp, where "Pale and bloodless emulation" mimics the larger problems of the much-imitated Troy legend. Shakespeare chooses to let the problem of "emulation" – *aemulatio* or rivalrous imitation – begin in the closet theater of Achilles, who delights in Patroclus' satirical "imitation" (1.3.150, 185) of the Greek commanders. "Having his ear full of his airy fame," Ulysses charges, Achilles "Grows dainty of his worth, and in his tent / Lies mocking our designs" (lines 144–6). This unsavory Achilles earns his declension from "the great Achilles" to "the large Achilles," "god Achilles," the "broad Achilles," and "Sir Valor." While the once great warrior lolls on his bed, Patroclus "Breaks scurril jests" and "pageants us" (lines 148, 151), a term that captures Ulysses' frustration with the politics of camp parody.[28] "Sometime, great Agamemnon," Ulysses continues, "Thy topless deputation he puts on, / And like a strutting player . . . acts thy greatness" (lines 151–3, 158) with bombast and "hyperboles" (line 161). To drive home his case against presumptuous imitations, Ulysses includes extempore character sketches of Patroclus playing Nestor preparing for an oration and answering a night alarm. The problem is one of unlicensed reproduction rather than "slanderous" inaccuracy. Agamemnon leaves little room for parody when he defines himself through inflated rhetoric: "checks and disasters / Grow in the veins of actions highest rear'd, / As knots, by the conflux of meeting sap, / Infects the sound pine and diverts his grain / Tortive and errant from his course of growth" (1.3.5–9). Nestor is harder on epic style: he issues an epic simile on "the ruffian Boreas" who enrages "gentle Thetis" so that one might "behold / The strong-ribb'd bark through liquid mountains cut, / Bounding between the two moist elements, / Like Perseus' horse" become a "toast for Neptune" (lines 38–45), i.e., a shipwreck in a storm.

It is symptomatic of the characters' thorough discomfort with their status as imitations of themselves that Ulysses alludes to no parody of himself, unless it is elided in the abstract reference to strategy: "plots, orders, preventions, / Excitements to the field, or speech for truce" are "stuff for these two to make paradoxes" (lines 181–4). Achilles and Patroclus "mock our designs" and call Ulysses' strategy "bed-work, mapp'ry, closet-war" (line 205). While Ulysses is ready to reproduce Patroclus' imitations of others and Achilles' merry applause, he cannot bring himself to duplicate his own caricature, although he inclusively stresses that the actor "pageants us" and makes "paradoxes" of "our abilities, gifts, natures, shapes" (line 179). What would be the reaction of his onstage viewers, one wonders, if he "boy'd" his own greatness, rendering himself a parody, paradox, parallel, and comparison to himself? Might Agamemnon and Nestor privately think, "Excellent! 'Tis Ulysses right?" To parody oneself is to isolate the mimetic in any self-representation, and for Ulysses to mimic the parody of him would put him "beside himself." Shakespeare is toying dangerously with the royal language of self-reference: the prince alone can be "like himself."

Imitations hurt because they publicize the fact that the characters inhabit a play in which no originals exist.[29] At no small risk to his own appearance as a stable model of policy, Ulysses takes revenge by outdoing the great Myrmidon in "emulation," and exposing Achilles as an accumulation of warriors: not the greatest warrior in Western civilization, after all, but only a set of copies. Ulysses begins by exploiting Ajax the Greek warrior who traditionally emulates Achilles: he introduces Ajax to a preferable version of himself, and leads him to believe that he might replace Achilles in the annals. For the two versions of Ajax, Shakespeare adopts the Oilean and Thelamonian Ajaxes from Lydgate. Shakespeare's Ajax plays the Oilean *miles gloriosus* to the hilt: he is "hye of stature and boysous in a press, / And of his speche rude and reckles. / Ful many worde in ydel him asterte." On the other hand, he in no way resembles Lydgate's Thelamonian Ajax, who is "descrete and vertuous, / Wonder fayre and semely to beholde"; has a talent for music (a harmony which sharply contrasts with the distinct lack of proportion in Shakespeare's warrior); and is "Nor desyrous for to have vyctorye, / Devoyde of pompe hatynge all vaynglorye, / All ydle laude spent and blose in vayn."[30] This man is the mirror that the Greek commanders hold up to their Oilean dupe. The "dull brainless Ajax," whom they "dress . . . up in voices" (1.3.381–2), neatly inverts his Thelamonian exemplar: "Why should a man be proud?" he asks, "How doth pride grow? I know not what pride is" (2.3.153–4). Ulysses calculates an act of socially constructing identity which, for the play's audiences, trades on versions of the warrior who goes by the name Ajax. Our recognition of the different

Ajaxes exploited to make the one onstage socially usable tends to empty him out characterologically, but deepens our understanding of identity construction in early modern England as a social practice and a theoretical proposition. The figures who have been "known" for centuries and should be self-evident are defamiliarized by their alienated relationships to their conventional representations and their constitution in divisive versions of themselves.

Ajax is an obvious candidate to manipulate: since he traditionally emulates Achilles, he might be said to have a comparatively tenuous hold over his own identity. We might hypothesize that the man Ajax emulates, the greatest of all warriors, will demonstrate greater self-possession. After all, Achilles challenged Agamemnon's right to cheapen his reputation, thus pitting personal merit against social rank. Tradition, however, does not secure Achilles in self-evident identity any more than it does Ajax. The defiant warrior undergoes the play's most elaborately staged identity crisis, one induced by social pressures and conducted in the specifically textual terms that characterize the divisiveness of the play and the tradition behind it. Ulysses instructs the Greek commanders to "pass strangely by [Achilles] / As if he were forgot." After they "Lay negligent and loose regard on him" – an eye-rolling smirk – Ulysses enters reading a book which holds out the promise of an answer to Achilles' question, "why such unplausive eyes are bent, why turn'd on him?" (3.3.39–43). Achilles knows the importance of eyes/ayes in preserving reputation: "greatness once fall'n out with fortune / Must fall out with men, too," he says, and the "declin'd" will "read [his fall] in the eyes of others" (lines 75–7). Yet he resists concluding that he has sustained material damage, adding that "Fortune and I are friends. I do enjoy / At ample point all that I did possess, / Save these men's looks, who do methinks find out / Some thing not worth in me such rich beholding / As they have often given" (lines 88–92). When Ulysses enters with his book, Achilles is already caught by the hook of analysis. Poised between confidence and anxiety, the warrior known for his independence is eager to theorize self-construction.

Their discourse on the material basis of epistemology comments slyly on the play's repeated jokes on how men know themselves and each other.[31] Ulysses muses over the "strange fellow" who writes that man "how dearly ever parted . . . Cannot make boast to have that which he hath, / Nor feel not what he owes, but by reflection" (lines 95, 98–9). Like Chiron in *Titus*, who learned Horace's great ode "in grammar long ago," Achilles has a schoolboy's memory of epistemology and phenomenology but no sense of how they bear on him:

                    This is not strange, Ulysses.
          The beauty that is borne here in the face
          The bearer knows not, but commends itself
          To others' eyes; nor doth the eye itself,
          That most pure spirit of sense, behold itself,
          Not going from itself; but eye to eye oppos'd,
          Salutes each other with each other's form;
          For speculation turns not to itself
          Till it hath travell'd and is mirror'd there
          Where it may see itself.   (lines 102–11)

Achilles is thinking of secret dignities in a man's life and character, for which he gains no credit until they are discovered by others, and does not acknowledge reputation as the "immortal part" of himself until Ulysses threatens Achilles' literary immortality: "no man is the lord of any thing," Ulysses comments, "Till he communicate his parts to others . . . and behold them formed in th' applause" (lines 115–18). A leader gains his stature as magnanimous only as a gift from the society for which he must actively perform, and the public's warm applause constitutes the promethean fire of a great man, for his "virtues, shining upon others, / Heat them, and they retort that heat again / To the first giver" (lines 100–2). To be informed that his reputation is the property of the Greeks is unsettling to the man defined by martial prowess and willful independence.[32] Then Ulysses ambushes his pupil with a surprise example to ground their discourse: the as yet "unknown Ajax."

    Up to this point in their quasi-Platonic dialogue, Ulysses essentially follows the plan he outlined in 1.3. Although his method is unexpectedly academic and text-bound, the audience is "in the know" about his goals until Achilles proudly reminds Ulysses that he has "strong reasons," which he takes as self-evident, for his "privacy," or withdrawal from the war for reasons of honor. Once Achilles speaks these Homeric words, Ulysses ambushes him – and the audience – with a strategically delayed disclosure concealed even from Nestor:

                    But 'gainst your privacy
          The reasons are more potent and heroical:
          'Tis known, Achilles, that you are in love
          With one of Priam's daughters.   (3.3.191–4)

An intense emotion, an unrehearsed anxiety never felt before in his literary history, grips Achilles: "Ha, known?" Halfway through the play, Achilles and the audience together discover that Achilles is "known" to be the lover from the medieval chroniclers and not Homer's "potent and heroical" warrior. Ulysses, head of the Greco-Elizabethan secret service, invades the "privacy" by which Achilles meant his proud withdrawal to his tent. The very appearance of the word instigates an attack on Achilles' right to the self-definition and "self-stabilization" that Lars Engle has found to be virtually impossible in the unstable and "deflationary market" of the playworld where there is no "private life" defined as "a distinct, to some extent idiosyncratic, market of value that each character partially insulates from public scrutiny" (p. 150). Ulysses translates "privacy" to mean the amorous and medieval identity Achilles kept in the closet and the murky inwardness, the simultaneously textual and sexual duplicity, that Shakespeare's warrior tried to conceal in Homeric armor.[33]

Under assault is Achilles' identity as a "potent and heroical" warrior – Ulysses tauntingly says, "And better would it fit Achilles much / To throw down Hector than Polyxena" (lines 206–7) – and a subject who constitutes himself partly in a shielded, uninterpretable space. Ulysses' strategy of spying and unmasking gives him the appearance of "knowing" Achilles when the great Myrmidon loses himself in the public exposure of his multiple histories. Ulysses makes a triumphant exit, having managed, to borrow Benjamin's words, "to pry an object from its shell, to destroy its aura, [which] is the mark of a perception whose 'sense of the universal equality of things' has increased to such a degree that it extracts it even from a unique object by means of reproduction" (p. 223). In short, Ulysses sets off a chain reaction that causes differing redactions of Achilles to come into abrupt and violent contact and – like the pit in *Titus Andronicus* – produce an excess of meanings that undo Achilles as a character and "Achilles" as a stable exemplary type.

Once set in motion, the mechanism by which Achilles becomes reproducible – simply, estrangement from the tradition – runs without the guidance of an operator. As Ulysses leaves, yet another copy of Achilles flickers into view onstage. Despite Achilles' exposure as his medieval, romanticized self, motivated by love for Polyxena, Patroclus unaccountably takes responsibility for Achilles' guilty "privacy," now understood as his sexuality as well as his withdrawal from the war. Patroclus urges the homosexual interpretation of their relationship that has dogged Achilles in the moralizing tradition:

> To this effect, Achilles, have I mov'd you.
> A woman impudent and mannish grown
> Is not more loath'd than an effeminate man
> In time of action. I stand condemn'd for this:
> They think my little stomach to the war
> And your great love to me restrains you thus.
> Sweet, rouse yourself, and the weak wanton Cupid
> Shall from your neck unloose his amorous fold,

And, like a dewdrop from the lion's mane,
Be shook to air.   (3.3.215–24)

 No longer the proud Homeric hero, but not exactly the medieval lover, Achilles undergoes severe disorientation by confronting too many versions of himself. Because his sexualities and sexual motivations to abstain from fighting are based on mutually exclusive versions of Achilles in literary history, his sexualities are rival and paralyze him: he is heterosexual and homosexual but not, paradoxically, bisexual. Achilles emerges as an indeterminate creature under erasure in the tradition if he does not satisfy the desires of the other Greeks.

The play provisionally translates Achilles into a contamination of textual and sexual forms which threaten his characterological integrity: the tradition's greatest hero suffers a nervous "breakdown" into his constituent versions. This scene threatens the coherence of the play as well: a notorious crux in traditional textual criticism, its narrative discontinuity is significant as an index of the play's constitution in a tradition that betrays its "matter" and leaves its characters and events as "fragments, scraps, the bits, and greasy relics of [an] o'er-eaten" (5.2.158–9) legend. The contamination of traditions creates an incoherent image of an Achilles who withdraws from war officially for reasons of honor but privately to negotiate with the enemy for a girl while he enjoys continued sexual dalliance with his ingle, the "boy" Patroclus (5.5.45). But what is conspicuously aberrant in the individual is standard procedure in this famous war, which justifies its wasteful economic, nationalistic, and virile interests in terms of the quintessentially seductive Helen of Troy.

In *Troilus and Cressida*, Helen is a "pearl / Whose price hath launch'd above a thousand ships, / And turn'd crown'd kings to merchants" (2.2.82–4).[34] A "theme of honor and renown, / A spur to valiant and magnanimous deeds" who will "canonize" the Trojans (2.2.200–3), she "must needs be fair" when the warriors of both sides "paint her thus" (1.1.90–1). As a commodity enabling the ideological and martial combat of the Trojans and Greeks, Helen of Troy is either a pearl or a whore of great price. Diomedes believes he is unmasking the real Helen when he excoriates her as a "flat tamed piece" and tells Paris, "For every false drop in her bawdy veins / A Grecian's life hath sunk . . . for every scruple / Of her contaminated carrion weight / A Troyan hath been slain" (4.1.70–3). Diomedes' scapegoating of Helen demonstrates that for good or ill, for epic expansion or satiric reduction, Helen measures and weighs out the value of men.[35] The play's interest in the traffic in women partly explains why Helen of Troy, so authoritative elsewhere, is aggressively vacant when she enters into a play in which economics dominate and interpret the action and language.

Achilles' textual breakdown and effeminization link him counter-intuitively to Helen of Troy, excoriated but universally accepted as the general equivalent of heroic products.[36] Ulysses provisionally acknowledges the arbitrariness of heroic virtue when he subjects the great warrior to an intense seminar in the contingency of his heroic masculinity. Unmasking the mechanics of self-constitution in one's relations to others and the sovereign state must be provisional: neither Achilles nor Ulysses could continue to function if they were always openly "unsecret to themselves." As a reminder, Ulysses' stratagem succeeds brilliantly, and Achilles is abruptly removed from the market of heroic exchange and left at his tent to engage only in literal homosexuality.

Achilles regains his heroic masculinity only by foisting his compromised or soiled identity on Hector. His characterological upheaval rouses an unusual desire:

> I have a woman's longing,
> An appetite that I am sick withal,
> To see great Hector in his weeds of peace,
> To talk with him, and to behold his visage
> Even to my full view.   (3.3.236–40)

When he meets Hector, he "speculates" on his enemy: "Now, Hector, I have fed mine eyes on thee; / I have with exact view perus'd thee, Hector, / And quoted joint by joint . . . I will the second time, / As I would buy thee, view thee limb by limb" (4.5.230–3, 237). What Achilles seeks to purchase is an image of his own integrated and valued self. Fixing an ambiguous gaze on the Trojan, he regards Hector as an animal destined for the butcher's block and Achilles' trencher and a catamite or a book he is perusing for purchase. To regain his own authority, Achilles reads Hector as Ulysses did him: "O, like a book of sport thou'lt read me o'er" (line 238) Hector observes. Achilles reinscribes his heroic virtue by interpreting Hector's body as a vulnerable text testifying to Achilles' definitive act, the slaying of Troy's greatest hero. His heroic reinscription of himself fully endorses the logic Ulysses used to entrap him earlier: Hector becomes the commodity affirming Achilles' worth to all who doubt it. Ulysses has taught him to understand, as Luce Irigaray puts it, that "in order to have a relative value, a commodity has to be confronted with another commodity that serves as its equivalent." The value of a commodity is "never found to lie within itself. And the fact that it is worth more or less is not its own doing, but comes from that to which it may be equivalent. Its value is transcendent to itself" (p. 176). The value of Achilles, mirrored in the doomed Hector, transcends the butcher who appears onstage.

Ulysses forces Achilles to look into himself, where he finds his "mind is troubled, like a fountain stirr'd, / And I myself see not the bottom of it" (3.3.306–7). He compares his troubled mind to a stirred fountain because he does not know his origin or source, standard meanings for *fons* or fountain. He cannot see through the depths of his literary accretions to his origin because it is impossible for him to know what author or even what genre is at the bottom of his identity. The case history of Achilles, like the plight of Lavinia in *Titus Andronicus*, is a textual contamination that ties Shakespeare's play transgressively to the translation of empire. The raped and mutilated Lavinia is transformed into a visual palimpsest of the textual struggles that reflect the loss of cultural integrity in an empire mythically founded on rape. Achilles similarly appears as a palimpsest of the differing versions of him in literary history, when the three accounts of his motivations for withdrawal from the war are issued in rapid succession, rather like critical glosses. These textual operations momentarily render him characterologically unsound, and permanently affect his status as heroic exemplar. Like Lavinia and like Cressida, whose plight is the subject of the next section, Achilles is transformed into an emblem of larger problems of representation in the play and the tradition.

The trope-plighting of Troilus and Cressida

When Troilus hears that Cressida is to be handed over to the Greeks, he exclaims, "How my achievements mock me!" and inadvertently confesses the extent to which he considers her to be a quite unromantic extension of himself. She is a sign of his labor and value, and Troilus is stunned to find that she has become part of larger negotiations that pre-empt his interests.[37] At the very center of the play, Troilus and Cressida act out what I call their "trope-plighting" scene: they swear to become the tropes for faithful and faithless lovers that are their literary destinies. Troilus wishes to become "truth's authentic author to be cited," declaring, " 'As true as Troilus' shall crown up the verse / And sanctify the numbers" (3.2.180–1). He achieves the illusion of self-authorization through Cressida, whose defection guarantees his own transcendence. Troilus is liberated from his indeterminate identity, however, only when Cressida enters the Greek camp to assume her tropical role. He is then able to read his superfluity and ambivalence in her and define himself as simple truth. The "speculations" that prevail in the Greek camp also dominate the romance plot, with the difference that Helen comes "between men" and Cressida mediates Troilus' relations with himself.

Troilus invents coherent interiority for himself by reading Cressida as a page on which he writes his lyric devotions.[38] The play reserves for Cressida enigmatic and compelling representations of selfhood and, simultaneously, strenuous insistence on scripted identity. She emerges as lively and self-possessed in her first appearance, when she bests Pandarus in skirmishes of wit, yet concludes that scene by instructing herself in her contingent worth:

> Women are angels, wooing:
> Things won are done; joy's soul lies in the doing.
> That she belov'd knows naught that knows not this:
> Men prize the thing ungain'd more than it is.
> That she was never yet that ever knew
> Love got so sweet as when desire did sue.
> Therefore this maxim out of love I teach:
> "Achievement is command; ungain'd, beseech."   (1.2.291–8)

Left to soliloquize, Cressida anticipates and personalizes Troilus' question about value: the illusion of an unknown and unachievable interior is functional, she claims, for it defers her inevitable exhaustion by another's desire.

Cressida realizes that she belongs to herself tenuously, at best. In a moment of tantalizing disclosure, she tells Troilus,

> I have a kind of self resides with you,
> But an unkind self, that itself will leave
> To be another's fool.   (3.2.146–8)

Her ambiguous words speak to her liminal state between past and present tenses, a closed and open book. On the one hand, her oracular words predict that she will abandon the self stamped by Troilus in favor of one marked by Diomed: they anticipate her conflation with Helen of Troy, the "contaminated carrion-weight" whose impure body bears the signatures of two men and two nations. Simultaneously – taking the second line as apposite to the first – she says that she must abandon herself and become generically "unkind" to herself in order to become Troilus' lover: she must exchange her interests for his. She fulfills this role in an unexpected fashion when she learns that she is to be traded for Antenor. Exhibiting desperate selflessness, she cries out:

> I have forgot my father;
> I know no touch of consanguinity,
> No kin, no love, no blood, no soul so near me
> As the sweet Troilus. O you gods divine,
> Make Cressid's name the very crown of falsehood,
> If ever she leave Troilus! Time, force, and death,

> Do to this body what extremes you can;
> But the strong base and building of my love
> Is as the very centre of the earth,
> Drawing all things to it.   (4.2.99–108)

In this petition, which recalls the one that prefaces her trope-plighting, Cressida enters fully into her role and appears determined to see Troilus' desires through to their completion. An uncannily perfect Elizabethan wife, she bases her internal coherence on Troilus and seeks to reproduce his will: her willingness to donate her name as a sign of falsehood testifies to the magnetic draw of her love and identity as Troilus' and the tradition's kind of self.[39] Cressida continues to pose problems of agency, because she *seeks* to copy Troilus' will and because the closer she comes to her tropical role, the more she displays an agency that "is, and is not" hers. The sense that she has deepened characterologically comes partly from a shift in her rhetoric: she has a phenomenological intuition, rather than an oracular knowledge, of her literary destiny.

Paradoxically, Cressida fulfills her vow of selfless devotion to Troilus when she enters the Greek camp and is "kiss'd in general" (4.5.21) by a receiving line of commanders. Cressida is silent while Agamemnon sets precedent for Nestor, Achilles, and Patroclus to step up, boast or insult his predecessor, take his kiss, and name himself. Their competition is so overt that Patroclus – by claiming to be Paris and interrupting Menelaus' kiss – jokingly suggests that the commanders are replaying the Trojan war with Cressida/Helen as the "theme of all our scorns" (line 30). When Cressida finally speaks, it is with a cool and pert familiarity that draws Ulysses' withering condemnation:

> Fie, fie upon her!
> There's language in her eye, her cheek, her lip –
> Nay, her foot speaks; her wanton spirits look out
> At every joint and motive of her body.
> O, these encounterers, so glib of tongue,
> That give accosting welcome ere it comes,
> And wide unclasp the tables of their thoughts
> To every ticklish reader. Set them down
> As sluttish spoils of opportunity
> And daughters of the game.   (4.5.54–63)

Ulysses' censure comes, appropriately, at the moment Cressida is consigned to tradition as its most frequently handled figure for wantonness. The role of a censor – he wants to snap shut the pornographic book's covers – may help Ulysses get the better of the discomfort she causes him. Her nonchalant management of the merry Greeks prompts him to describe her as a solicitous blazon[40] in which her wanton agenda appears in every term of her body – eye, cheek, lip, and unpetrarchan foot. Ulysses successfully depicts Cressida as an emblem of feminine incontinence, largely by presenting her as a gaudy poem that Puttenham might compare to the extravagant fashion statements made by upstart courtiers, or as a deliberate violation of the poetic decorum in which "the skinne, and coat" of language, as Jonson writes, ideally "rests in the well-joyning, cementing, and coagmentation of words; when as it is smooth, gentle, and sweet, like a Table, upon which you may runne your finger without rubs, and your nayle cannot find a joynt."[41] He less convincingly asserts Cressida's full responsibility, since it takes a "ticklish reader" to find so much solicitation in so many joints and rubs. The "motive" of her body – an exclusively Shakespearean usage of the word – expresses the complicated state of agency and instrumentality that distinguishes Cressida: are those "motives" inward promptings and impulses? Or over-interpreted joints?[42]

Cressida's textual conversion is characterologically impoverishing in a way that Achilles' textual breakdown is not. John Bayley notes that "Cressida *does* strike us as a real person, in spite of her role as a commonplace in the play's externalized and intellectual scheme" and "when Ulysses calls her a daughter of the game we may feel obscurely that he is wrong, and, if we feel so, it is at this moment that she gives some sort of impression of personality" (p. 205). Bayley's account rings true, despite the facts that Cressida has never been less comprehensible or coherent and that Ulysses' bitter summary of Cressida is unnervingly accurate: only moments ago, Cressida was a different woman. *Troilus and Cressida* displays the shocking lengths to which it will go to deliver its characters into the hands of a tradition whose final moves are to eradicate what Joel Fineman calls "subjectivity effects" and replace a characterological function with a rhetorical one.[43] When Cressida's character vanishes, a retrospective sense of her subjective possibilities emerges and is felt as loss.

Troilus himself paves the way for Cressida's conversion in the trope-plighting scene, in which he appears more eager for his own tropical resolution than for sexual consummation. Evidently yearning to be free of *Troilus and Cressida*'s epistemologically mired world, he indirectly requests that Cressida relieve him of his burden of doubt:

> O that I thought it could be in a woman –
> As, if it can, I will presume in you . . .
> Or that persuasion could but thus convince me
> That my integrity and truth to you
> Might be affronted with the match and weight
> Of such a winnowed purity in love –

> How were I then uplifted! but alas,
> I am as true as truth's simplicity,
> And simpler than the infancy of truth.   (3.2.156–7, 162–8)

Troilus is almost swept up, ungrammatically, in his hopes for release from his skepticism. This is the speech of a fallen idealist whose fears about his lover's reciprocation are overwhelmed by a greater anxiety over his incapacity for the faith that should "convince" and "uplift" him. Logically, when Troilus exclaims, "but alas," his dejected admission should be, "but I cannot believe." What he does instead is fall back on the very axiom that he is testing – his traditional simplicity – and redefine "truth's simplicity" as the failure to achieve the complex state of mind required for unverifiable faith in one's lover.

In the plighting of oaths, Troilus predicts his future as a trope for the amorous simplicity and integrity that he described as a consummation devoutly to be wished. In their "trope-plighting," Troilus and Cressida construct their future identities in the negative image of the other. Troilus swears that

> True swains in love shall, in the world to come,
> Approve their truth by Troilus; when their rhymes,
> Full of protest, of oath, and big compare,
> Wants similes, truth tir'd with iteration
> (As true as steel, as plantage to the moon,
> As sun to day, as turtle to her mate,
> As iron to adamant, as earth to th' centre)
> Yet, after all comparisons of truth,
> As truth's authentic author to be cited
> "As true as Troilus" shall crown up the verse
> And sanctify the numbers.   (3.2.171–81)

Troilus' speculations are fantasies of an integrated self which he jubilantly greets as his "ideal ego." He formally exchanges the weakness of infancy – his first complaint of the play – for the infancy of truth, the trope for original devotion. Anticipating his future value, Troilus constitutes himself as a source and author of truth and – by virtue of his status as a citation – a creature presumed to be an "authentic" self.[44]

Cressida assumes the negativity of the doubts Troilus casts off when he resolves to be the essence to which all positive lyrical comparisons will refer:

> If I be false, or swerve a hair from truth,
> When time is old and hath forgot itself,
> When water-drops have worn the stones of Troy,
> And blind oblivion swallow'd cities up,
> And mighty states characterless are grated

> To dusty nothing – yet let memory,
> From false to false, among false maids in love,
> Upbraid my falseness! When they've said "As false
> As air, as water, wind, or sandy earth,
> As fox to lamb, or wolf to heifer's calf,
> Pard to the hind, or step-dame to her son" –
> Yea, let them say, to stick the heart of falsehood,
> "As false as Cressid."   (lines 182–94)

Cressida's oath, conditional and subjunctive, differs from Troilus' predictive precedent. She utters an indirect command, a proleptic performative which fulfills Troilus' fantasy of fixed identity, if only as figures of speech.

To become "true as truth's simplicity," Troilus must await Cressida's entrance into the Greek camp. He implores Pandarus to be his "Charon / And give me swift transportance to those fields / Where I may wallow in the lily-beds / Propos'd for the deserver!" (3.2.9–12). Sexual achievement furnishes Troilus' first anxious steps towards his literary future but does not itself secure for him the integrity and simplicity that he seeks in passing over the river Styx. In the aubade scene, he is so desirous to be gone that his very tenderness menaces: "To bed, to bed. Sleep kill those pretty eyes / And give as soft attachment to thy senses / As infants empty of all thoughts" (4.2.4–6). Cressida laments his readiness to abandon her: "O foolish Cressid! I might have still held off, / And then you would have tarried" (lines 17–18). Lost to the amnesia of literature, this scene cannot enter the annals, where Troilus is to stand for truth. According to the play's mechanics of troping, however, he may assume exemplary fidelity only when Cressida enters the Greek camp.[45]

In the camp and in her father's tent during her meeting with Diomed, the divisions we have witnessed in Troilus are formally inscribed on Cressida:

> Troilus, farewell! one eye yet looks on thee,
> But with my heart the other eye doth see.
> Ah, poor our sex! this fault in us I find:
> The error of our eye directs our mind.
> What error leads must err; O then conclude,
> Minds sway'd by eyes are full of turpitude.   (5.2.106–11)

Her lines, which as Carol Cook aptly notes, sound "like an effect of ventriloquism" (p. 51), are so conclusive of her fault that one forgets, as the tradition will, that Troilus had stopped wanting to "tarry" once he had achieved the grinding, the bolting, and the leavening of the cake. The couplet form highlights the scriptedness of Cressida's last words, an effect further enhanced by the metaphor of printing that the men watching and reading her employ. Thersites comments that "A proof of strength she could not publish more, / Unless she said 'My mind is now turn'd whore'" (lines 112–13). Troilus himself lingers to "make a recordation to my soul / Of every syllable that here was spoke. / But if I tell how these two did co-act / Shall I not lie in publishing a truth?" (lines 115–18).

Troilus gives full voice to the "madness of discourse," as he names it in his notoriously opaque soliloquy:[46]

> This is, and is not, Cressid.
> Within my soul there doth conduce a fight
> Of this strange nature, that a thing inseparate
> Divides more wider than the sky and earth;
> And yet the spacious breadth of this division
> Admits no orifex for a point as subtle
> As Ariachne's broken woof to enter.
> Instance, O instance! strong as Pluto's gates:
> Cressid is mine, tied with the bonds of heaven.
> Instance, O instance! strong as heaven itself:
> The bonds of heaven are slipp'd, dissolv'd, and loos'd;
> And with another knot, five-finger-tied,
> The fractions of her faith, orts of her love,
> The fragments, scraps, the bits and greasy relics
> Of her o'er-eaten faith, are given to Diomed.   (5.2.145–59)

He maintains, if barely, his integrity by referring his internal chaos to spiraling epistemological doubts which he inscribes onto Cressida. He is later able to distill his characterological upheaval into a more concise linguistic theory: Cressida, who sends "Words, words, mere words, no matter from the heart" (5.3.108), signifies the fickleness of language. We never learn the contents of Cressida's letter. Troilus' condemnation rings with an authority that pre-empts any possibility that Cressida might pursue a narrative and characterological reversal. Such defiance of tradition would introduce intolerable and undermining complications. Cressida is necessarily a sign of fragmentation in the tradition and in Troilus. In *Troilus and Cressida*, no authority, origin, or integrity is allotted to the Troy legend or its eponymous hero, and Troilus' trauma serves as an extreme representation of the internal division of the tradition and the cultural legacy inherited by Elizabethan England.

The mystery in the soul of state: drama, politics, and treason

Ulysses spots a mutiny in the closet theater going on in Achilles' tent, and asserts that Patroclus' unlicensed theatrical imitations for his patron "take degree away," leaving hapless members of the commonwealth wondering "what plagues and what portents, what mutiny . . . Commotion in the winds, frights, changes, horrors, / Divert and crack, rend and deracinate / The unity and married calm of states / Quite from their fixture" (1.3.96–101). What cultural conditions prompt Shakespeare, in *Troilus and Cressida*, to multiply the damage caused by imitation and, taking representational disturbance much further than Patroclus, contaminate the Troy legend?

Explanations may begin with the appearance of Chapman's Homer and the fall of the Earl of Essex. For all the novelty of restoring a neoplatonized Homer to his privileged seat at the head of the Trojan banquet, Chapman anachronistically refeudalizes the power structures and the classical idioms that had come to proliferate in the London market of the late Elizabethan period.[47] *Troilus and Cressida*, in contrast, reflects a developing capitalist society which promoted social mobility and generated strong tensions among rivals for economic and cultural capital. Unlike Chapman's Homer, Shakespeare's play cheapens the coin of the realm by delivering it over to London merchants: the play is appropriate to a city in which a chapman could have a Homer of his own. When Meres sought for native equivalents for classical talents in *Palladis Tamia*, and Jonson announced his personal identification with Horace, they suggested that poetic authority was necessary to the establishment of England as a nation with an imperial destiny: poets are bearers of political authority rather than mere conduits for its passage to the crown and court. When Jonson dons his guise as Horace in *Poetaster*, his upgrading of the playwright's status is analogous to *Poetaster*'s politically transgressive Ovid, who usurps Augustus' identification as Jupiter at his profane dinner of the gods.[48]

The second occasion for Shakespeare's revaluation of the Troy legend is the rebellion and fall of the Earl of Essex, "an overmighty subject, a noble resistant to royalty and centralization, on the one hand, and to market evaluation, on the other," in Engle's words for Chapman's Achilles (p. 155). In Achilles' private theater Shakespeare places dramatic versions of the questions of feudal rights that Essex imprudently asked Egerton:

Dothe religion enforce me to serve? doth god require it? is it impietie not to doe it? why? cannot princes Erre? and can not subiectes receyve wronge? is an earthlie power an authoritie infinite? Pardon me, pardon me, my lorde, I can never subscribe to these Principles.[49]

Whereas Essex was condemned "to be drawn on a hurdle through London streets and so to the place of execution . . . [to] be hanged, bowelled, and quartered,"[50] Achilles strikes the set of his closet theater when he discovers the power of the state over its subjects' basic prerogatives. At the height of Achilles' identity crisis, Ulysses invokes the "providence that's in a watchful state":

> There is a mystery, with whom relation
> Durst never meddle, in the soul of state,
> Which hath an operation more divine
> Than breath or pen can give expressure to.
> All the commerce that you have had with Troy
> As perfectly is ours as yours, my lord . . .   (3.3.200–5)

Ulysses introduces a politically topical form of the speculations and eye metaphors involved in the constitution of social subjects: spying. The state gains a divine soul – its *arcana imperii* – when it uses intelligence agencies to search into, appropriate, and reform its citizens.

Shakespeare and Ulysses are punning, although to different effect, on the meanings of "mystery" as "profession" and something shielded from public view – what Hamlet calls the "heart of my mystery." Achilles' theater is impotent in the face of the "providential" knowledge that makes his commerce with Troy as "perfectly" known to the government as to himself; defeated, Achilles abandons his subversive theater and plays his part in the Trojan war. Shakespeare, however, does not capitulate to the specter of power in quite the obliging manner of his glorified thug. Instead, he comments on the censors, state officials, and delators who adopt theatrical tactics – disguise, plots, and entrapping dialogue – to keep citizens from overmighty lords to recusants, printers, players, or rogues and vagabonds from "meddling" with state practices. Taking Ulysses' lines as a point of departure, it is possible to see how *Troilus and Cressida* engages the aftermath of the Essex rebellion, suffered by the citizens of London as well as Essex himself.

Throughout Elizabeth's reign, direct assaults against state power with "breath" and "pen" tended to end in the speaker's and author's imprisonment, interrogation by the Star Chamber, and punishment. Speech and writing fell under Elizabethan treason laws, which included "compasses, imaginations, inventions, devices, or intentions" and sought out persons who "maliciously, advisedly, and directly publish, declare, hold opinion, affirm, or say by any speech express words or sayings" (p. 414) prejudicial to Elizabeth's sovereign authority.[51] On the issue of succession, Elizabethan treason laws extended to those who "set up in open place, publish, or spread any books or scrolls to that effect," or who attempted to "print, bind, or put to sale, or utter, or cause to be printed, bound, or put to sale, or uttered, any such book or writing wittingly" (p. 416). Rigorous and comprehensive, Elizabethan treason laws reversed the greater liberality of Edward VI and Mary Tudor, both of whom had begun their reigns by repealing Henry VIII's expansion of treason from deeds to speech and writing. At no time does Elizabeth's government express Mary Tudor's concern (for Catholic martyrs) that certain laws and statutes are made

whereby not only the ignorant and rude, unlearned people, but also learned and expert people minding honesty, are often and many times trapped and snared, yea, many times for words only, without other fact or deed done or perpetrated (p. 406)

or Edward VI's government's attempt to lighten treason laws:

as in tempest or winter one course and garment is convenient, in calm or warm weather a more liberal race or lighter garment both may and ought to be followed and used, so we have seen divers strait and sore laws made in one Parliament, the time so requiring, in a more calm and quiet reign of another Prince by like authority and Parliament repealed. (p. 401)

The political crises that led both Mary and Edward to rescind their clement policies[52] and the constant pressure of plots against the Protestant Queen taught Elizabeth I's government to word its treason laws severely.[53] Her government at all times found criminality in speech and writing as well as deeds. In a famous example, John Stubbs paid for his exposure of the "Gaping Gulf" threatening England with the hand that wrote his treatise. Yet what is striking about the range of treasonous activities under Elizabeth I is the inclusion of thoughts and unarticulated motives. With the rise of the secret service, the mystery that lent divinity to the "soul of state," the government fully undermined Sir Thomas More's claim that "God only . . . [is] the judge of our secret thoughts."[54] Many Londoners of the late Elizabethan reign may have agreed with Cressida that it was increasingly difficult not to be "unsecret to ourselves."

While Essex engaged in overt treason, Ulysses' surveillance and exposure of Achilles bear on those whose thoughts were not yet "perfectly" known to the state. The Essex rebellion led to a zealous searching out of further accomplices and sympathizers among London's inhabitants. In February 1601, Elizabeth I announced the arrest of Essex along with Rutland and Southampton in a proclamation that concluded with exhortations and warnings, admonishing her "good people" that the "open act" of rebellion[55]

cannot yet be thoroughly looked into how far it stretched and how many hearts it hath corrupted, but that it is to be presumed . . . that it was not without instruments and ministers dispersed in divers places to provoke the minds of our people to like of their attempts, with calumniating our government . . . that they shall do well (and so we charge them) to give diligent heed in all places to the conversation of persons not well known for their good behavior, and to the speeches of any that shall give out slanderous and undutiful words or rumors against us and our government; and they that be in authority to lay hold on such spreaders of rumors; and such as be not in authority to advertise those thereof that have authority to the end that by the apprehension of such dangerous instruments, both the drift and purpose of evil-minded persons may be discovered, their designs prevented . . .

Within a week, her government placed London vagabonds (once again) under Martial Law on the grounds that they, unlike "the loyal and true hearts and settled and unmoveable affections as well as the rest of our subjects as specially of our citizens of London," were more likely "to lie privily in corners and bad houses, listening after news and stirs, and spreading rumors and tales." On April 5, she issued a further proclamation

to signify to all manner of person and persons that whosoever shall in any sort either openly or secretly discover and make known to any of the lords or other of our Privy Council, or to the Lord Mayor of our said city, the name of any of *the authors, writers, or dispersers of any of the said libels*, whereby the offenders therin may be known and taken, shall presently have and receive for their pains therein the sum of £100 of current money paid and delivered unto him by the Lord Mayor . . .

One thinks of the unscrupulous courtier in John Donne's fourth satire, bent on exhibiting the court's dirty laundry: he recounts "More then ten Hollensheads, or Halls, or Stowes, / Of triviall houshold trash" until, Donne's speaker claims, "I . . . felt my selfe then / Becomming Traytor, and mee thought I saw / One of our Giant Statutes ope his jaw / To sucke me in" (lines 97–8, 130–3). Howard Erskine-Hill notes that an early manuscript mentions the treason-happy agent, Richard Topcliffe.[56] After Essex's rebellion cast London under a pall of suspicious and surveillance, Elizabethans grew eager for the next regime to restore the golden age lost in the queen's final years. Pressures from "foreign Enemies, Domestical Discontents" ultimately led Edward Phelips, the new Speaker of the House of Commons who addressed the newly crowned James I, implicitly to criticize Elizabeth I's cultivation of favorites who advanced by denouncing their rivals: "Virtue is now no Treason, nor no man wisheth the Reign of *Augustus*, nor speaketh of the first Times of *Tiberius*."[57]

Despite his brush with the Star Chamber over the Essex rebels' sponsorship of a new performance of the old play, *Richard II*, Shakespeare continued to test the political issues raised by the rebellion: the liberties of the subject and the sometime greater freedom of speech, writing, and private thought from relation, or delation, to the authorities. Shakespeare was fortunate to work unscathed by censorship and interrogation, unlike his colleague, Ben Jonson, imprisoned for his part in *The Isle of Dogs* and interrogated by Topcliffe. Jonson recalled the episode in conversation with Drummond:

jn the tyme of his close Imprisonment under Queen Elizabeth his judges could gett nothing of him to all yr demands bot I and No, they placed two damn'd Villans to catch advantage of him, wt him, but he was advertised by his Keeper.

For his revenge, "of the Spies he hath ane Epigramme."[58] He suffered interrogation again over *Sejanus his Fall*, for despite Jonson's efforts copiously to annotate and document his sources, ancient histories had become almost as suspect as modern ones.[59] Because Shakespeare had the forethought to produce Ulysses' toe-lining speech on degree, bedrock of the *Elizabethan World Picture*, or perhaps simply because *Troilus and Cressida* was never "clapper-clawed," Shakespeare himself did not face the interrogations endured by his fellow playwright or his character Achilles.

Yet his theater, where he filters his sociopolitical critiques through the literature supporting political iconography, warrants close scrutiny. By the end of *Troilus and Cressida*, the late Elizabethan audience should mortally fear that England has indeed inherited its national identity from the Troy legend. The diseased and leering Pandarus, with his "Winchester goose" of a syphilis sore, is altogether too close: at the play's end he stands in what Nashe called "this great Grandmother of Corporations, Madame Troynovant,"[60] and specifically in the Southwark brothels, situated on land that fell under the Bishop of Winchester's jurisdiction. The Troy legend made abundant surrogate authorities available for exploitation and analysis: Ulysses himself demonstrates the use of authoritative texts to bolster and mystify the sources and coercive effects of authority. Through surrogate authorities, it is possible to bring into view the institutional mechanisms cloaked by classical reference. Shakespeare investigates, with surprising vigor, the degree to which identity and thought are impinged on by politically authoritative codes ranging from statutes to hortatory norms. All citizens, like Achilles, may consider what it means for their identities to be as fragmentary and conflicted as the cultural codes that inform their social possibilities.

Shakespeare's political readers within his plays suggest that class does not determine the ability to decode the political content of classical signs. Shakespeare dishes up the events and exemplars of the Troy legend as "greasy orts" not "caviar to the general." His uses for the Vergilian-Marlovian line of classicizing dramaturgy do not require an elitist reader.

like Prince Hamlet: Ulysses and Thersites outperform Nestor, Agamemnon, and Ajax as interpreters and Tamora and Aaron are skilled in reading political significance in imperial Roman icons, texts, or performances, while Tamora's sons are failures. *Titus Andronicus'* unfortunate Clown is an unmistakable sign of the consequence of small Latin and worse political cryptography: hanging for treason.

Classical figures and events, moreover, were available to anyone hungry for a ballad or broadside: genre stamped the seal of class distinction on the social coordinates of Ajax, Cressida, Aeneas, or Dido ("A Jakes," "Cresset-light," "Any-ass" and "Die-doe" to the irreverent).[61] The sliding scale of class to which Trojans and Romans were susceptible does not mean that late Elizabethan purchasers of a broadside were unaware that upscale models were available in other venues of London. On the contrary, critics need to imagine the circumstances in which a classical allusion would inflame rather than glaze the eye: classics appealed to all because social and political values were at stake, as Chapman knew when he dedicated his *Iliades* to Essex and as Topcliffe knew when he questioned Jonson over *Sejanus*. Censors and secret service agents suspected the subversive power of staging events from the classical past, yet the very range of their available meanings rendered the figures and events of the *translatio imperii* a resilient mirror that Shakespeare might hold up to socially eclectic audiences. Should the need arise, the players might adapt their text or performance to suit the court, the Inns-of-Court, or audiences of the Globe. Yet in any venue, Shakespeare invites his audiences to be Hamlets, and to study, mull over, appropriate, and act on his play.

4   To earn a place in the story: resisting the *Aeneid* in *Antony and Cleopatra*

> Eros! – I come, my queen: – Eros! – Stay for me,
> Where souls do couch on flowers, we'll hand in hand,
> And with our sprightly port make the ghosts gaze:
> Dido, and her Aeneas, shall want troops,
> And all the haunt be ours. Come, Eros, Eros!   (4.14.50–4)[1]

Although *Antony and Cleopatra* manifestly concerns empire, it is not at once clear that this play "translates" empire with either the textual specificity or the eccentricity of *Titus Andronicus* and *Troilus and Cressida*. To be distinguished from other Roman plays as a translation of empire, *Antony and Cleopatra* would have to assume roughly combative relations with its sources, exploiting differences among textual authorities in order to take issue with their formal and evaluative choices. Source studies of the play, however, demonstrate that a far from disputatious Shakespeare plunders Plutarch's history with abandon, scarcely altering such passages as the description of Cleopatra on the barge. Unlike *Titus Andronicus* or *Troilus and Cressida*, moreover, the play employs multiple and contrasting images of Antony, Cleopatra, and even Octavius to enrich rather than undermine the characters and the values they espouse.[2] This view seems generally right, and so it comes as a surprise that Antony defends his value of erotic love and protects his heroic exemplarity by directly resisting the *Aeneid*. Traditional source criticism is at a loss to explain the political dimensions of *Antony and Cleopatra*'s relations to textual authority. As Antony's revision of the *Aeneid* indicates, the play's principal characters are intensely aware of their duties to promote or disrupt the stories in which their meanings will be recorded.

Like *Troilus and Cressida*'s legendary warriors and lovers, who struggle for their meanings on a literary battlefield, Antony and Cleopatra seek control over their representation and interpretation throughout the play and resist literary-political commodification by Octavius and his scribes. Even more powerful than Octavius' various reporters within the play is Vergil, whose shadowy and formidable presence is continually felt in the

119

efforts of Antony and Cleopatra to appropriate and revalue his story about them. Seizing the Vergilian conventions through which they are recognizable as the legendary Antony and Cleopatra, the pair resist the characterological exhaustion planned by Caesar.[3]

When Antony defines himself against Vergil's poem and its implicit condemnation of the historical Antony for his affair with Cleopatra, he at last finds the means to conquer the self-doubts and anxieties that unshape him. His stunning revision of Vergil is matched by the reputation Cleopatra crafts for herself. Even Enobarbus sets aside his cynicism to celebrate Cleopatra's inexhaustible vitality: "Age cannot wither her, nor custom stale / Her infinite variety" (2.2.235–6). This lyrical commemoration of Cleopatra's charms comes from doubly unexpected sources in the play's great cynic and in Vergil's bitter summary of femininity: *varium et mutabile semper / femina* (*Aeneid* 4.569–70). Variously condemned as a "witch," "charm," and "spell," Cleopatra is nonetheless best known for an "infinite variety" that forms an indirect polemic against the stinging evaluation of Cleopatra's prototype as a "thing ever varying and changeful."[4] The line that precipitates Aeneas' departure from Carthage and Dido becomes the quality that binds Shakespeare's Antony to his Cleopatra, who can exact praise even from the most ideologically charged line in the *Aeneid*. "Vilest things / Become themselves in her" (2.2. 238–9) because Cleopatra wrests control over the interpretive contexts for her representations and displaces the censorious meanings they normally produce. Although Antony and Cleopatra lose the battle over empire, the histories and fictions that Shakespeare cites and adapts bear paradoxical witness to the characters' strategic differences from their constitutive authorities.

Pitiful love and imperial glory: social protest in Rome

For Antony and Cleopatra, defamation is the dreaded consequence of military defeat. Cleopatra memorably contemplates the Roman craftsmen who will carouse at her public display in Caesar's triumph:

> mechanic slaves
> With greasy aprons, rules, and hammers shall
> Uplift us to the view. In their thick breaths,
> Rank of gross diet, shall we be enclouded,
> And forc'd to drink in their vapor . . .
>   saucy lictors
> Will catch at us like strumpets, and scald rhymers
> Ballad us out o' tune. The quick comedians
> Extemporally will stage us, and present

Our Alexandrian revels: Antony
Shall be brought drunken forth, and I shall see
Some squeaking Cleopatra boy my greatness
I' the posture of a whore.   (5.2.208–19)

Roman mechanics will build the theatrical scaffolding, and Roman politicians with ideological hammers and rules will reconstruct her "i' th' posture of a whore." The mechanic slaves, rhymers, and lively comedians will place her in low genres all the more humiliating because they travesty Cleopatra's transgressive gender politics. In Caesar's triumph, she will be subjected to the Roman version of herself and obliged to confirm it when she appears as chief spectator and spectacle mocking her showy and erotic political style. As Cleopatra knows, Caesar's triumph will launch an entire tradition of representing history: those saucy lictors, rhymers, and comedians are low-class analogues to the Augustan poets and historians who square her by their Roman rule.

In defiance of Caesar's triumphant version of his victory, Cleopatra and Antony take full and creative advantage of the limited means to contest the interpretive conventions presented in the play as imminent but not yet fully installed. Set before the establishment of the empire under Augustus Caesar, the play historicizes the Augustan record, revealing how the ideologically charged narrative of Antony and Cleopatra's defeat is cast as the cornerstone of the new Roman state. The imminence of the empire seems inexorable as Vergilian fate when the Soothsayer tells Antony that his auspicious star will always droop in Caesar's presence and again when the soldiers interpret the mysterious underground music as Hercules' abandonment of Antony. The officially sanctioned interpretation of Antony and Cleopatra, however, is inadequate to the task of describing the politics of a given scene, much less the characters themselves: examples include Philo and Demetrius' commentary on the first scene; Enobarbus' desertion of Antony, his "aging lion" of a master; and Antony's anguished acceptance of the Augustan view that he unmanned himself at the battle of Actium. Caesar, above all, knows that control over interpretation is as essential to political achievement as military success. He carefully documents for public satisfaction his honorable role in the wars, insisting that the Romans understand his innocence of Antony's death:

Go with me to my tent, where you shall see
How hardly I was drawn into this war,
How calm and gentle I proceeded still
In all my writings. Go with me, and see
What I can show in this.   (5.1.73–77)

When Proculeius prevents Cleopatra's suicide attempt, he thinks of Caesar's reputation:

> Do not abuse my master's bounty, by
> The undoing of yourself: let the world see
> His nobleness well acted, which your death
> Will never let come forth.   (5.2.43–6)

Caesar's nobleness will be "well acted" in the official interpretation of the Alexandrian pair and the battle of Actium. Shakespeare does not, however, follow a pro-Augustan presentation of the historical events. Evidently aware that Actium was central in Caesar's propaganda but of relatively small historical importance, Shakespeare has Antony fight Caesar again and come "smiling from / The world's great snare uncaught" (4.8.17–18).

Because Antony and Cleopatra successfully modify the historical record, Caesar must consequently use romance instead of travesty in his official interpretation of his opponents. At the end of the play, he orders that Cleopatra

> be buried by her Antony.
> No grave upon the earth shall clip in it
> A pair so famous: high events as these
> Strike those that make them: and their story is
> No less in pity than his glory which
> Brought them to be lamented. Our army shall
> In solemn show attend this funeral,
> And then to Rome. Come, Dolabella, see
> High order, in this great solemnity.   (5.2.356–64)

Critics tend to divide between the transcendent reading, in which Antony and Cleopatra achieve a "higher" victory over the worldly Caesar's, and the skeptical reading, which stresses Caesar's mastery over Cleopatra's myth-making. Carol Thomas Neely notes that their "deaths are framed and distanced by Caesar, whose commentary reduces the lovers from myth to stereotype and exploits it to enhance his power" (p. 137), a point Linda Charnes amplifies:[5]

Octavius understands immediately the political uses to which he can put a mythologized "Antony and Cleopatra" . . . He swiftly translates them from rebellious figures who escaped his control and punishment into legendary lovers . . . [who,] once Octavius has full control of the machinery of reproduction . . . can be put to historiographic use . . . While many critics have observed that Octavius' historiography "officially" wins in the end, most tend to assume that Antony and Cleopatra have triumphed on "other" grounds that are not, finally, Caesar's. But such an assumption occludes the fact that it is Octavius *himself* who legitimates, and hypostatizes into frozen monumentality, this ground. (pp. 144–5)

Charnes stresses Caesar's canny appropriation of the love story, welcomed as a monument to his achievement on the more impressive ground of empire. At the play's end, Caesar attempts to classify the erotic displays that Antony and Cleopatra use towards political ends as private acts and elegiac motifs in his imperial epic. His lyricization of his Alexandrian opponents may remind Shakespeare's audiences of familiar stories – some generous to Cleopatra and hostile to Aeneas, like Chaucer's *Legend of Good Women* – which confirm Caesar's "glory" by the "pity" that the lovers' failure inspires. Because this account is essentially Augustan, it unsurprisingly touts Caesar's mastery in the game of warring fictions and suggests that Caesar concedes nothing and that he knits every loose end into a pro-Augustan fabric. Yet Caesar must adopt a story he went to great lengths to avoid: having failed to lead Antony and Cleopatra in triumph as a conquered libertine with his Egyptian whore, he must incorporate a positive appraisal of his opponents' erotic values into the official account of his victory.

When Antony and Cleopatra prise loose the cornerstone of contempt from Caesar's legend of imperial authority, they reground Caesar's triumph in the historical complexity recorded in the writings of Vergil, Horace, and Ovid, whose works should not be stripped of the tensions and skepticism that all three, in varying degrees, pit against their resounding praise of Augustus.[6] From Vergil and Horace, who are equally sincere in praise and in query, and from Ovid, whose tongue is firmly in his cheek when he most extravagantly praises Augustus, Shakespeare draws his interrogation of Caesar's triumph. When Caesar settles for compassion and regret as acceptable measures of his glory, he articulates the compromised terms of empire in the *Aeneid,* where Aeneas explains to Dido that he must go to Rome, for *hic amor, haec patria est.* Aeneas' words may sound a pro-imperial note, but they also record a historical yearning for a Rome that does not require the subordination of erotic desire.

This longing, evident in Roman poetry and the widespread resistance of Roman aristocrats to Caesar's unpopular morality and marriage laws, was one of Caesar's greatest political obstacles, and reason enough to suspect that Caesar deals unsuccessfully with the alternate view of Antony and Cleopatra. The literary and historical evidence indicates that Antony and Cleopatra will be monuments of the continuing problems Augustus Caesar faces in Rome, not of lamentable but salutary sacrifices made to preserve Rome from Alexandrian invasion. When Aeneas admits that he is leaving Dido and startlingly equates *patria* and *amor*, annotators at times invoke the patriotic sublime, partly based on the Roman enthusiasm for the anagrammatical relationship of *amor* to Rome. Yet there should be a shiver, at least, when Aeneas invents an identity between love and nation where schism had previously been assumed in the narrative. There is pathos in Aeneas' need to conflate the claims of Roman nationalism with his sexuality, which is increasingly co-opted by empire as he moves from Troy to Carthage and to Rome, and from Creusa to Dido and to Lavinia. But Vergil refuses to enhance the pathos by emphasizing Aeneas' inner turmoil. The lover is replaced by the defense lawyer: *hic amor, haec patria est* comes in the middle of a legalistic oration prefaced with the crisp words, "Let me say a few words on the subject" (*pro re pauca loquar*, line 337). In the speech, Aeneas is careful to point out the absence of law in binding him to Dido: "I never held the torches of a bridegroom," he says, "or entered into that bond" (*nec coniugis umquam / praetendi taedas aut haec in foedere veni*). Vergil is under no obligation to make Aeneas appeal to legalities rather than to conflicting moral obligations. Vergil risks discrediting not only Aeneas, but the kind of law Aeneas relies on to escape his common law marriage to Dido.

/ Vergil's poem loses its characteristic ambiguity when the text explicitly but extralegally inculpates Dido for calling her liaison with Aeneas marriage. The scene Vergil creates for the consummation intriguingly justifies, then condemns, Dido's understanding of her bond to Aeneas as marriage. The goddess of marriage rouses the portentous storm, yet Vergil assures his readers of Dido's guilt: "Dido no longer contemplated a secret love: she called it marriage and cloaked her guilt beneath that name" (*nec iam furtivum Dido meditatur amorem: / coniugium vocat, hoc praetexit nomine culpam*, 4.171–2). Although her guilt may be traced to her failure to honor the memory of her dead husband, Dido appears to be charged with more than a technical fault, indisputable albeit emotionally comprehensible. There are problems, moreover, with relying heavily on the *univira* ("one-man woman") virtue of old Rome in the service of a pro-imperial argument: Augustus had to be argued into allowing widows a three-year breathing spell before assuming new marital responsibilities. Nor can the *univira* value be considered peculiar to Vergil, who does not hold even Andromache to the same standard of devotion to a dead husband. What criminalizes Dido is the validity of her marriage to Aeneas, which poses legal and ethical obstacles to his Roman destiny. At the end of Book 4, Vergil discloses that her death was undeserved (*immerita*) and, in controverting the text's earlier certainty of her guilt, he acknowledges that she and the value of married love are imperial compromises.

Augustus Caesar strongly promoted a new morality among the
Roman aristocracy and eventually succeeded in passing laws governing
marriage. Suetonius reports in *The Historie of Octavius Caesar Augustus*
34 that Augustus "revised and corrected" some "lawes made before
time."[7] The earlier laws were enacted by Julius Caesar, who, Suetonius
reports in *Caius Julius Caesar* 42, rewarded men with more than three
children and prevented private citizens between twenty and forty years of
age from living outside of Italy for more than three years. Augustus' laws
or Sumptuaria bore on moral issues,

as touching expenses at the bord: of Adulteries and unnaturall filthinesse
committed with the male kind: of indirect suite for offices: of the mutual mariages
of Senatours and Gentlemen with Commoners. This act last named, when he had
amended and reformed somewhat more precisely and with greater severitie then
the rest, he could not carie cleerely and go through with, for the tumult of those
that refused so to do, but that part of the penalties at length was quite taken
away or els mitigated; an immunity also and toleration (of widow-head) graunted
for 3 yeeres, and the rewards [for three or more children] besides augmented.

When the senators and equestrians mounted their resistance "stifly and
stoutly," Augustus displayed for their chastisement Germanicus, bearing
some of his children in his arms and standing beside other of his children,
who bore their younger siblings in their arms. Suetonius continues,[8]

Moreover perceiving that the force and vigor of that Law was dallied with, and
avoided by the immaturity of young espoused wives, as also by often changing of
mariages: he brought into a narrower compasse the time of wedding and having
such spouses, and also limited divorcements.

During the time that Vergil was composing the *Aeneid*, Augustus
appears to have sought to legislate sexuality in the interests of developing
a more politically useful family unit. One of Propertius' love poems
suggests a violent response to an early attempt of Augustus to pass
morality and marriage laws at some time before 23 BC (possibly 27 or 28
BC). In Propertius 2.7, the poet appears to comment on a marriage law
and the rebellious place of sexuality and love lyrics within the emergent
Roman morality:[9]

> You were happy, my Cynthia, that the law was withdrawn
> which made us both weep long when it was issued.
> We feared it might separate us, although not even Jupiter himself
> is able to make two lovers part against their will.
> "But Caesar is great." Certainly, Caesar is great in war:
> but defeated nations count nothing in love.
> I would sooner let my head be cut from my neck
> than be able to waste my passion in love for some wife,
> or (I, a husband!) pass by your door,

looking back with moist eyes at the threshold I betrayed . . .
Why should I offer sons for the country's triumphs?
There will be no soldier from our blood.

The poem explicitly rejects the values espoused by an orthodox reading of the *Aeneid*. Propertius' Jupiter cannot separate lovers – even though Vergil's god easily parted Aeneas from Dido – and Augustus Caesar will be no more successful: Propertius will face execution before submitting to laws designed to produce politically useful families and more Roman soldiers. Under such legal circumstances, commitment to passionate sexuality may be viewed as resolutely political in the emergent Rome of Augustus.

Vergil confines his one unstinting piece of Augustan propaganda to the circumference of Aeneas' shield, where he largely defines Caesar's virtues by the negative image of his Alexandrian opponents:

> hinc ope barbarica variisque Antonius armis,
> victor ab Aurorae populis et litore rubro,
> Aegyptum virisque Orientis et ultima secum
> Bactra vehit, sequiturque (nefas) Aegyptia coniunx.   (8.685–88)

here Antonius – with barbaric wealth and varied arms, a victor from the peoples of the Dawn and the Red Sea – led the forces of the East and Egypt, along with the furthest Bactra, and (lawless) his Egyptian wife follows.

The shield presents an imperial ideology that opposes East and West, disorder and order, sickly wealth and disciplined austerity, female and male. As David Quint notes, in a valuable account of the shield's binary oppositions,[10]

The Western armies are portrayed as ethnically homogeneous, disciplined, and united; the forces of the East are a loose aggregate of nationalities prone to internal discord and fragmentation. The West, in fact, comes to embody the principle of coherence; the East, that of disorder. The struggle between the two acquires cosmic implications . . .

Quint is careful to emphasize, however, that the imperial ideology encoded on the shield is not "identical to the 'meaning' of the *Aeneid*, which devotes a considerable part of its energy to criticizing and complicating what it holds up as the official party line" (p. 23). The *Aeneid* is not coterminous with the derisive image of Antony and Cleopatra on the shield or with the "pitiful" version of their history that Shakespeare's Caesar promotes. That Dido dies undeserving of her role in Augustan propaganda inspires, beyond pity, reflection on the political expedience of imperial Rome's shifting sexual and marital mores. The censorious gasp heard in the word *nefas*, the parenthetical comment on

Antony's Egyptian marriage, should be interpreted in the context of the marriage Dido believes she has entered into in *Aeneid* 4.

What Vergil implies, Ovid confirms when he refers to the divorce of Dido's husband (*Metamorphoses* 14.79) and to Aeneas' deceit in a narrative abridged and distilled to the legal terms that Aeneas explicitly denies and the moral issues Vergil scrupulously avoids. Like Propertius' poem, Ovid's passage highlights the extent to which the *Aeneid*'s representation of the faultiness in its famous love affair bristles with problems of law. As these accounts suggest, there is no efficient discursive machinery for Shakespeare's Caesar to master. Historically, Caesar gained what Janet Adelman calls "the conflicts of opinion which are built into the traditional accounts" (p. 53) of Antony and Cleopatra; in Shakespeare's fiction, he shoulders the ideologically untidy and burdensome version of history because his opponents intervene and successfully modify his political myths.

Antony's visible shapes and the politics of historical representation

> Egypt, thou knew'st too well,
> My heart was to thy rudder tied by the strings,
> And thou shouldst tow me after. O'er my spirit
> Thy full supremacy thou knew'st, and that
> Thy beck might from the bidding of the gods
> Command me.   (3.11.56–61)

Of Caesar's competitors for empire, Antony faces the greater challenge in resisting the emergent Augustan ideology. To embrace eros as heroically self-defining, Antony must reject a form of heroic masculinity that powerfully appeals to him: the rugged Roman who, despite cultivation in Roman arts, has never lost his essential link to Rome's hypermasculine forebears. Antony's career defines him as the Herculean Roman, as Caesar himself recalls:

> Antony,
> Leave thy lascivious wassails. When thou once
> Was beaten from Modena, where thou slew'st
> Hirtius and Pansa, consuls, at the heel
> Did famine follow, whom thou fought'st against,
> Though daintily brought up, with patience more
> Than savages could suffer. Thou didst drink
> The stale of horses, and the gilded puddle
> Which beasts would cough at: thy palate then did deign
> The roughest berry, on the rudest hedge;
> Yea, like the stag, when snow the pasture sheets,
> The barks of trees thou browsed. On the Alps

> It is reported thou didst eat strange flesh,
> Which some did die to look on: and all this –
> It wounds thine honour that I speak it now –
> Was borne so like a soldier, that thy cheek
> So much as lank'd not.   (1.4.55–71)

Janet Adelman comments incisively on the "landscape of absolute deprivation" that here "serves as the test of Antony's heroic masculinity."[11] Caesar's landscape for heroic deprivation comes from hard pastoral, the genre that has nurtured great Roman heroes with the "roughest berry, on the rudest hedge" since Romulus and Remus. Antony's ability to thrive where men "browse" like stags on the barks of trees proves that rugged ancestral masculinity had not been domesticated out of Antony. Although "daintily brought up," he endured starvation as well as eating "strange flesh."

Caesar's portrait is flattering but politically canny: because he recalls Antony's heroic masculinity through the prized Roman genres of hard pastoral, georgic, and epic, Caesar establishes an ideal that paradoxically undoes Antony as a viable leader for Rome's imperial future. Caesar damagingly constructs his remembrance of the heroic Antony from fresher images of Antony's divergence from it. Antony's "lascivious wassails" and easy exchange of gender roles with Cleopatra cause Caesar to assert that Antony is "not more manlike / Than Cleopatra; nor the queen of Ptolemy / More womanly than he" (1.4.5–7), and, after the bitter defeat at Actium, Antony's own men to exclaim, "our leader's led, / And we are women's men" (3.7.69–70).[12] Antony's heroism is set up in generic and ideological terms that he cannot fail to violate in a "most unnoble swerving" (3.11.50). But more subtly, even if Antony were to maintain the heroic figure born of Rome's myths of rugged origins, he would become an anachronism in the emerging bureaucracy of the Roman empire. Caesar may value nostalgia for the primary genres of empire-building, but the exemplar who personifies them belongs to the mythic past and to Julius Caesar's failed experiment in strong personal rule.

When Antony accepts that he has lost control of his own self-representation, he experiences his failure as radical anamorphosis into empty "signs" indefinitely subject to refiguration by the artful viewer:

> Sometime we see a cloud that's dragonish,
> A vapour sometime, like a bear, or lion,
> A tower'd citadel, a pendent rock,
> A forked mountain, or blue promontory
> With trees upon 't, that nod unto the world,
> And mock our eyes with air. Thou hast seen these signs,

They are black vesper's pageants . . .
That which is now a horse, even with a thought
The rack dislimns, and makes it indistinct
As water is in water . . .
                  now thy captain is
Even such a body: here I am Antony,
Yet cannot hold this visible shape . . .   (4.14.2–14)

Antony is unshaped only when he fully accepts the Augustan view of
himself as the Roman hero emasculated by a foreign enchantress. In fact,
he precipitates his figurative undoing by rousing and manipulating his
own nebulous anxieties[13] – themselves produced by the imminence of his
political and ideological defeat by Caesar – until he generates enough
unmotivated rage against Cleopatra to cast her off as a "triple-turn'd
whore" (4.12.13). Overcome by the "Roman thoughts" that have dogged
him since the battle of Actium – Scarus asserts that he "never saw an
action of such shame; / Experience, manhood, honour, ne'er before / Did
violate so itself" (3.10.22–4) – Antony censures her for her affairs with
Pompey the Great and Julius Caesar.

Antony is scarcely kinder to himself, as he recoils from his nonchalant
willingness to let Cleopatra drink him under the table and then strap on
Philippan[14] – the sword with which he defeated Julius Caesar's assassins
– while she dresses him in her "tires and mantles" (2.5.22–3). He is far
from the state of mind that encouraged a playful identification with
Cleopatra's eunuchs: when Antony first enters the play he is anticipated
as the "bellows and fan / To cool a gipsy's lust" (1.1.9–10), and then
appears, as if to ratify the image, in the company of her ladies,
attendants, and "Eunuchs fanning her." He appears to accept the view of
himself and Cleopatra canonized by Vergil's derisive comment on
Aeneas, dandied up in Dido's wealthy attire, as a *semivir* or "half-man,"
and Horace's more lurid vision of Cleopatra plotting against the empire
with her contaminated herd of half-men (*imperio parabat / contaminato
cum grege turpium / morbo virorum*, 1.37.8–10). Above all, Antony
acknowledges the Roman myth most often invoked to summarize his
failings: Hercules unmanned by Omphale, humiliatingly discovered in
her clothes. In the spirit of self-indictment, Antony rouses his anxieties to
the highest pitch and unleashes them with specific reference to the
unflattering precedent of Hercules *furens*, moralized by Seneca as a figure
of ungoverned wrath:[15]

                        Eros, ho!
    The shirt of Nessus is upon me, teach me,
    Alcides, thou mine ancestor, thy rage.
    Let me lodge Lichas on the horns o' the moon,

> And with those hands that grasp'd the heaviest club,
> Subdue my worthiest self. The witch shall die . . .   (4.12.42–7)

It is no coincidence that Antony comes to act out the very roles he fears will come to define him and Cleopatra in the Augustan future of Rome: his crisis of identity anticipates the ideological accounts already setting in to construe his reputation in political and literary history. The course of Roman political history forbids him characterological integrity: Antony is doomed "sometimes, when he is not Antony," to come "too short of that great property / Which still should go with Antony" (1.1.57–9). He recognizes that literary-political history will continually unshape and dislimn him until he is as "indistinct / As water is in water." The literary future is all the more painful to him because it interprets the inconsistencies of his life all too persuasively.

Although both Caesar and Cleopatra are more deeply and pragmatically aware of their reliance on the historical record, Antony has intuitions of his vulnerability to future literary-historical accounts. He tells Cleopatra, "I and my sword will earn our chronicle," when he "appear[s] in blood" to "kiss these lips" (3.13.174–5), and pulls together his heroic image by revising the *Aeneid*, the epic that condemns him and his choice of eros:

> Eros! – I come, my queen: – Eros! – Stay for me,
> Where souls do couch on flowers, we'll hand in hand,
> And, with our sprightly port make the ghosts gaze:
> Dido, and her Aeneas, shall want troops,
> And all the haunt be ours. Come, Eros, Eros!   (4.14.50–4)

To readers and audiences even remotely familiar with the *Aeneid*, these lines jarringly defy the *Aeneid*'s firm refusal of a satisfying reunion for Dido and Aeneas in the Underworld. The problem is that Antony is not inventing a rival meeting of Dido and Aeneas in the Underworld. Instead, his fantasy recalls the painful encounter in which Vergil's Dido rejects Aeneas' attempt at reconciliation in the Fields of Mourning.

What Antony means to accomplish by invoking and altering the *Aeneid* has troubled critics. Ronald McDonald rejects the idea of "an Antony so ignorant of the *Aeneid* that he envisions Dido and her Aeneas united in death" and explains the curious revision in terms of chronology:[16]

Antony speaks his lines on the field of Actium in 31 BC. He cannot very well be misinterpreting a poem that never saw the light of day until the author's death in 19 BC. Antony, it would seem, is creating independently a version of a story that, from a strictly chronological point of view, has not yet been fixed in the canonical form we are familiar with from Vergil's *Aeneid*.

Of the two attractions offered by this account, historical accuracy and an Antony who resists the emergent Augustan ideology, only the second is palpably Shakespearean. The Antony I favor is iconoclastic and anachronistic: partly aware of his presence on the Jacobean stage and distinctly aware that literary history will deform and fragment him, Antony defines ✓ himself against the *Aeneid*. Anticipating Vergil's critique of his political and sexual choices, Shakespeare's Antony believes that if he cannot be author of himself, he can nonetheless influence the ways in which readers respond to his distorted image in Vergil's fiction. When they resist its pro-Augustan version of events, they may come to a more favorable evaluation of the historical Antony. This moment has a theatrical disruptiveness equal to Cleopatra's famous resistance to the day some "squeaking Cleopatra" will "boy" her greatness. Like Cleopatra, Antony challenges us to recognize the seam between historical person and theatrical representer and to wonder what thoughts and motives are being translated from history to the stage. Urgently and ventriloquistically, the historical Antony speaks through the fictional Antony and the actor onstage.

Antony's counter-fiction recalls the moment that Aeneas acknowledges his vulnerability to Dido's judgment of his choice of the Roman future. At the exact center of Book 6, Aeneas glimpses Dido with her wound still fresh, wandering in the great forest – an image that recalls both the simile of Dido to a wounded doe and her death upon Aeneas' sword (*Phoenissa recens a vulnere Dido | errabat silva in magna*, 6.450–1). It is to Antony's advantage that the passage presents Aeneas at the lone moment that he expresses the regrets he denied, stoically or cruelly, in his final encounter with Dido in *Aeneid* 4. Vergil conveys Aeneas' longing in the simile used to describe Aeneas' recognition of Dido's indistinct form amidst the shadows, "just as one, in the beginning of the month, sees or thinks he sees the moon rise through the clouds" (*qualem primo qui surgere mense | aut videt aut vidisse putat per nubila lunam*, 6.453–4). When the weeping Aeneas speaks to her in *dulci amore,* his first words express pained acceptance that the report of her death was true and anxiety that he was the cause: '*infelix Dido, verus mihi nuntius ergo | venerat exstinctam ferroque extrema secutam? | funeris heu tibi causa fui?'* (6.456–8). His questions suggest why Aeneas knew her so quickly and why her appearance is like a new moon rising obscurely and menacingly through the clouds: he feared such a confrontation with the facts and consequences of his actions.

When Aeneas expresses unprecedented and deep regrets, he fails to soften (*lenibat,* 6.468) Dido:

per sidera iuro,
per superos et si qua fides tellure sub ima est,
invitus, regina, tuo de litore cessi.
sed me iussa deum, quae nunc has ire per umbras,
per loca senta situ cogunt noctemque profundam,
imperiis egere suis; nec credere quivi
hunc tantum tibi me discessu ferre dolorem.
siste gradum teque aspectu ne subtrahe nostro.
quem fugis? extremum fato quod te adloquor hoc est.   (6.458–66)

"I swear by the stars, by the gods, and by whatever faith there is in the underworld, unwillingly, queen, I left your shores. But the gods' commands, which now force me to go through these shades, through rough and rotten places and through deep night, drove me with their bidding. Nor could I believe I brought such pain to you by my departure. Hold your step and do not withdraw from my sight. Whom do you flee? By fate this is the last that I speak to you."

Unlike Antony, Aeneas followed "the bidding of the gods" (3.11.60). For denying Dido's claim on his heart in Carthage, he suffers her utter rejection in the Underworld: her eyes and expression fixed, the flinty, "marble-constant" Dido is unyielding to Aeneas' appeal (*nec magis incepto vultum sermone movetur | quam si dura silex aut stet Marpesia cautes*, lines 470–1). Against this image of the guilty, regretful, and lonely Aeneas, Antony scripts his own identity and future reception: he and Cleopatra will royally display their "sprightly port" and the affection Aeneas longs for as Dido leaves the scene with Sychaeus, who responds to her in mutual love (*aequat amorem*, line 474).[17]

More than a counter-Underworld, Antony's Elysium represents the romantic narratives in which love takes precedence over the Roman empire. Long after Rome has melted in the Tiber and the wide arch of the ranged empire has fallen, Antony and Cleopatra will preside in fiction and in the Jacobean theater over the Augustan Aeneas. Antony's choice to marry his queen and walk with her "hand in hand" will, he claims, affect the way "Dido, and her Aeneas" exist in the imaginations of future readers.[18] The story of Dido will dominate the story of empire-building for many readers, including Hamlet, Tamora, and Imogen in addition to troops of Vergilian imitators and translators and troops of real medieval and early modern readers such as St. Augustine (who claims he wept more for Dido than for his own soul), Chaucer, Shakespeare. Histori-

cally, readers favor the fantasy of "Dido, and her Aeneas" that remains unrealized until Antony and Cleopatra, in Shakespeare's play, satisfy that desire and simultaneously defeat Vergil's official portrait of the pair in *Aeneid* 8, where Antony is surrounded by wealth and wildness, and flanked by his unlawful Egyptian wife. Shakespeare's Antony takes credit for influencing readers' perspectives on Dido and Aeneas, the fictions Vergil shaped to criticize the historical Cleopatra and Antony. By taking a stand against the ideological dimension of the literature that will "transport" him to future generations, to use Puttenham's word for metaphor, Antony seeks "to deny and defeat the reductive currents of time and policy."[19]

When Antony calls on Eros to help him to an Elysium in which he and Cleopatra, royally attended by "troops" of followers, may successfully compete with Dido and Aeneas, he invents a politically rivalrous fiction.　✓ In fact, Antony's vision is continuous with the aggressive display of the political alternative to Caesar's emergent Rome that he and Cleopatra present from Alexandria. At the beginning of 3.6, a scene which falls in the play's center, an outraged Caesar recounts the spectacle in which Cleopatra, dressed as Isis and surrounded by her children, receives kingdoms from Antony:

> I' the marketplace on a tribunal silver'd,
> Cleopatra and himself in chairs of gold
> Were publicly enthron'd; at the feet sat
> Caesarion, whom they call my father's son,
> And all the unlawful issue that their lust
> Since then hath made between them. Unto her
> He gave the stablishment of Egypt, made her
> Of lower Syria, Cyprus, Lydia,
> Absolute queen.
> MÆCENAS.　　　　　　This in the public eye?
> CÆSAR.　I' the common showplace, where they exercise.
> His sons he there proclaim'd the kings of kings:
> Great Media, Parthia, and Armenia
> He gave to Alexander; to Ptolemy he assign'd
> Syria, Cilicia, and Phoenicia: she
> In the habiliments of the goddess Isis
> That day appear'd, and oft before gave audience,
> As 'tis reported, so.　　　　　　　　　　(3.6.3–19)

Caesar is at most peripherally mindful of moral violations – "the unlawful issue of their lust" that they display in the "common show-place" – whose only use is to poison Antony's reputation in Rome. When Antony publicly declares himself married to Cleopatra and bestows on her children and friends kingdoms not his to give, he is serving his political ends, not his pleasures. Caesar himself provoked this theater of bounty: taking advantage of Antony's assassination of Pompey, Caesar seized Pompey's goods and refused to send any proceeds to Antony and, adding insult to injury, he deposed Lepidus and "detain[ed] / All his revenue" (3.6. 29–30). Antony's Alexandrian theater presents an alternate center of power to the public, and may even remind Jacobean audiences of the public ceremonies through which princes more ingratiating than Caesar – or James I – might allegorically act out "a concept of government" that "emphasized the reciprocal character of the bonds" between monarch and subjects.[20] Caesar recognizes Antony's extravagant and public generosity as a challenge to Caesar's markedly different imperial style: when Antony and Cleopatra "publicly enthrone" themselves on golden chairs placed on a silver tribunal, they theatrically imitate Rome, whose centrality and austerity they challenge.

Cleopatra is every inch the politician that Antony is. At their feet they prominently display "Caesarion, whom they call my father's son," Caesar reports with revulsion. Cleopatra's child by Julius Caesar is the centerpiece of the family's royal display because he constitutes their best claim to inheritance of the Roman empire. An astute reader of Antony and Cleopatra's royal iconography, Octavius questions Caesarion's legitimacy, aware that the pair seek to override his own claims as the adoptive son of Julius Caesar. Octavius understands that Antony and Cleopatra are staging a family portrait to suggest that they constitute the surer link to great Caesar; Antony assumes Julius' place at the side of Cleopatra and adopts his son, pointedly named Caesarion. Antony and Cleopatra intend their audience of admirers and detractors to translate the politically ambitious family emblem into words and purvey the rhetorical description through all parts of the empire. Their formal self-presentation counters the distracted image on Aeneas' shield and promises wealth, patronage, art, religious dominion, and popular access to the elite in their Alexandrian world. By implicit contrast, Caesar is stingy of his less-than-divine presence as well as his appropriated wealth and offices.

Cleopatra appears, moreover, in the "habiliments of the goddess Isis," a guise in which she "oft before gave audience." There is no mistaking the royal and political force of her choice to impersonate this goddess. To play-act Venus on the river Cydnus, as she did when she first met Antony, might be explained as erotic frivolousness; but to put on the dress of Isis is to appropriate the iconography of a powerful, many-named goddess whose religious jurisdiction extends beyond Rome. As Plutarch describes her in the *Moralia*,[21]

Isis is the feminine part of nature, apt to receive all generation, upon which occasion called she is by Plato the nurse and Pandeches, that is to say, capable of all. Yea and the common sort name her Myrionymus, which is as much to say, as having an infinite number of names, for that she receiveth all formes and shapes, according as it pleaseth that first reason to convert and turne her. Moreover, there is imprinted in her naturally a love of the first and principall essense, which is nothing else but soveraigne good, and it she desireth, seeketh, and pursueth after. (p. 1309)

Rome is a mere province to the ancient, multi-formed goddess, as readers of Plutarch and Apuleius know. Isis' place in Cleopatra's royal icono-graphy is not lost on Caesar, who bitterly stresses that even before the marketplace display, she often "gave audience," presumably in her capacity as the judge and queen entitled to sit upon the silver tribunal and gold throne. She appears in an analogous position to queen Dido when Aeneas first sees her, giving laws to men, assigning tasks, and administering justice. When Vergil introduces her in a simile to Diana, the choice of the virgin goddess resounds with historical as well as tragic irony, for the historical Dido never met Aeneas. The chaste and powerful Dido makes a brief appearance in Vergil's poem before undergoing her metamorphosis into the tragic lover Vergil uses, among other things, to trivialize the political choices of the historical Antony and Cleopatra. Shakespeare's Cleopatra's choice of Isis affirms that her sexuality informs her political powers. "The holy priests / Bless her, when she is riggish" (2.2.239–40) because they interpret her sexuality as divine, like that of Isis:

(NB)

according to the old tales, Isis was alwaies inamoured, and having pursued after it untill she enjoied the same, she afterwards became replenished with all goodnesse and beautie that here may be engendered. (p. 1318)

Beggaring description: the politics of petrarchan display

It is difficult for Antony to take a stand against the Roman conventions and attitudes, canonized in the *Aeneid*, that subtly changed to his disadvantage when the republic became irrecoverably an institution of the past. Change itself came to mean something pejorative in the emergent Augustan Rome, as is clear from the ideological scene embla-zoned on Aeneas' shield in *Aeneid* 8, where Vergil maintains the fiction that Caesar takes a stand against change: he represents a fixed point of stable values, anchoring the Roman present to her past, while Antony and the East stand for hectic variety and raucous, threatening change. It is difficult for Antony to defy familiar but transmuted values. He tends to have a Vergilian experience of *varietas*, which is to say a fluctuating, uncertain mind, torn between impulses and unsure of the rational grounds for action. Change or transformation and variety, so discom-fiting in the *Aeneid*, are the provenance of Ovid's *Metamorphoses*, in which changed bodies are the avowed topic of Ovid's *carmen perpetuum*.

Whereas Antony often experiences a self-defeatingly Vergilian anxiety about the changes in his reputation and body – such as those greying hairs[22] – Cleopatra is a creature summed up in quintessentially Ovidian terms when Enobarbus praises her for her "Infinite variety." In the *Metamorphoses*, *varietas*, used of Circe, Daedalus, and Orpheus, characterizes artistry rather than ethical or psychic distress.

More consistently than Antony, Cleopatra exploits the conventions that customarily would disempower her. She pitches an Ovidian version of variety and change against Vergil's generally negative representations of the opulence, instability, and distraction he associates with *varietas*.[23] As in *Titus Andronicus*, where Lavinia is "trimmed" in Ovidian and Petrarchan poetry, Shakespeare links the styles of Ovid and Petrarch, who records the history of his love for Laura in *vario stile* (1.5). Like Lavinia, Shakespeare's Cleopatra is elaborately presented in terms of the petrarchan heritage that emanates from Ovid. Unlike Lavinia, Cleopatra gains agency in the poetic transactions, revising the petrarchan poetics which reduced Lavinia to a political and rhetorical emblem. Cleopatra's disruptive power gains in force, paradoxically, because she herself is pervasively defined as a consummate work of craft: an enchanting queen, great fairy, Thetis, witch, gypsy, a charm, and a spell to Antony and her audiences alike, she is a quintessential woman and a quintessential work of artifice.[24] A supremely artificial creature, she seems virtually to define womankind as artful and proclaim herself a legendary source, not a mere instance, of literary temptresses. Cleopatra becomes a trope for feminine "infinite variety" that can be quantified as artistic, rhetorical, and sexual *copia*. To argue that Cleopatra profits by these associations is at first counter-intuitive: it is not immediately clear that Cleopatra disrupts her commodification as a trope any more successfully than do Lavinia or Cressida. As queen and a legend, however, she exploits artistry, spectacle, and theatricality as self-representational materials in the exercise of her royal power.

Cleopatra is aligned, often unflatteringly, with artifice. Near the beginning of the play, Enobarbus describes her to the uneasy Antony as magnificent artwork. When Antony claims she is "cunning past man's thought," Enobarbus engages in mock defense:

> Alack, sir, no, her passions are made of nothing but the finest part of pure love. We cannot call her winds and waters sighs and tears; they are greater storms and tempests than almanacs can report. This cannot be cunning in her; if it be, she makes a shower of rain as well as Jove. (1.2.144–9)

"Tear-floods" and "sigh-tempests" are petrarchan and their debt to convention denotes Cleopatra's artificiality: her emotional hyperboles

are insincere and visually pleasureful. As Enobarbus parodically represents Cleopatra's petrarchan mimicry, her displays eliminate subjective
depth. He implies, and Antony affirms, that she models desire for her
beholders to interpret and internalize, but that her displays have little to
do with "pure love."

Enobarbus complicates his picture of feminine artifice by comparing
Cleopatra's seductive cunning to the arts of that divine philanderer, Jove,
who seduced Danäe in an artful and amorous shower of gold. Interpreted
by St. Augustine as a figure for the lure of rhetoric, the tale appears at
the close of Petrarch's *canzone delle metamorfosi*, song 23. After
imagining himself successively metamorphosing into various figures from
Ovid's *Metamorphoses,* Petrarch at last invokes Jove's shower as the
success he cannot hope to emulate.[25] Enobarbus, on the other hand,
testifies to Cleopatra's ability to inhabit and reproduce the Ovidian
world of change, myth, and flamboyant rhetoric: Cleopatra can make "a
show'r of rain as well as Jove" and emerge as a petrarchan poet and
persuasive poem. At the last, Enobarbus furnishes a turn in his prose
anti-sonnet: she is, he tells Antony, a "wonderful piece of work, which
not to have been blest withal, would have discredited your travel"
(1.2.151–3). She is redeemed by the artifice to which she is simultaneously reduced.

Cleopatra is not, however, equivalent to the artistic conventions
through which the play's men recognize her as Cleopatra. In his great
set-piece, Enobarbus supplies the play's most sustained description and
analysis of Cleopatra's paradoxical relationship to artwork:

> The barge she sat in, like a burnish'd throne
> Burn'd on the water: the poop was beaten gold;
> Purple the sails, and so perfumed that
> The winds were love-sick with them; the oars were silver,
> Which to the tune of flutes kept stroke, and made
> The water which they beat to follow faster,
> As amorous of their strokes. For her own person,
> It beggar'd all description: she did lie
> In her pavillion – cloth of gold, of tissue –
> O'erpicturing that Venus where we see
> The fancy outwork nature. On each side her,
> Stood pretty dimpled boys, like smiling Cupids,
> With divers-colour'd fans, whose wind did seem
> To glow the delicate cheeks which they did cool,
> And what they undid, did . . .
> Her gentlewomen, like the Nereides,
> So many mermaids, tended her i' the eyes,
> And made their bends adornings. At the helm

A seeming mermaid steers: the silken tackle
Swell with the touches of those flower-soft hands,
That yarely frame the office. From the barge
A strange invisible perfume hits the sense
Of the adjacent wharfs. The city cast
Her people out upon her; and Antony,
Enthron'd i' the marketplace, did sit alone,
Whistling to the air; which, but for vacancy,
Had gone to gaze on Cleopatra too,
And made a gap in nature.   (2.2.191–218)

This rhetorical description – a virtual ecphrasis – sets up expectations that Cleopatra will be portrayed as a decorative object further embellished by the desiring gaze. In fact, the description, especially where Shakespeare diverges from North's Plutarch, reveals her to be a royal artisan who compels admiration and desire from beholders as part of her politics of display.[26]

This equivocally petrarchan description is a study in paradox. Enobarbus' rhetoric courts petrarchan techniques of representing feminine beauty, but deflects them from Cleopatra herself: although the production around her elicits singular eloquence, her body bereaves her viewers and Enobarbus of words. The first lines blazon the abundant royalty surrounding her in the barge that imitates a "burnish'd throne," the poop of beaten gold, the silver oars, the sails of royal purple, and the flutes that accompany her triumphal progress. Cleopatra's person, next on Enobarbus' inventory, "beggar[s] all description," a phrase adapting Narcissus' recognition of the devastating powers of his jointly rhetorical and physical excellence: *inopem me copia fecit*. After a conventional pause on the ineffability topos, Enobarbus ought to shift from Cleopatra's splendid wealth to her equally resplendent beauties. But he furnishes no elaborate description of the exotic Egyptian queen in a head-to-toe *descriptio* or blazon. Enobarbus is that unusual poet who literally means that a beautiful woman "beggars description."

Cleopatra's spectacle generates a surplus of desire in the viewers, who, if they look to fix and ballast love, find abundant means in dimples, smiles, delicate cheeks, eyes, and flower-soft hands. Yet these features expressly decline to constitute a blazon: although standard petrarchan items, they either do not belong to Cleopatra or, in the case of the cheeks and the eyes, frustrate the rules of the blazon. Although Cleopatra "o'erpictures" Venus, we hear a great deal more of the boy actors who play smiling Cupids and the gentlewomen who perform the parts of Nereides or mermaids. The cheeks belong to Cleopatra, but misleadingly appear in the midst of a detailed account of the smiling and prettily dimpled boys who fan those "delicate cheeks." Once we have begun to visualize their smiles and dimples, we are more likely to flesh out our picture with the plump and ruddy cheeks of Cupids or *putti* than we are to start afresh with the cheeks of the elusive Cleopatra.[27]

Although eyes should be the centerpiece of a traditional description, the eyes Enobarbus mentions create a stumbling block to aesthetic reconstruction: "Her gentlewomen, like the Nereides, / So many mermaids, tended her i' the eyes, / And made their bends adornings" (lines 206–8). The scenario in North's Plutarch presents no difficulties:[28]

Her ladies and gentlewomen also, the fairest of them were appareled like the nymphs Nereides (which are the mermaids of the waters) and like the Graces, some steering the helm, others tending the tackle and ropes of the barge . . .

Shakespeare obscures North's visual and rhetorical clarity by adding eyes that are curiously discontinuous with the spectacle and cause syntactic awkwardness. Unornamented, "nothing like the sun," or anti-petrarchan, these eyes are not "gemlike qualities the reader can string together into an idealized unity."[29] Cleopatra's eyes are doing something unimaginable in a conventional inventory, where Laura and her English descendants do not assume the assertive postures available to the petrarchan lady on other occasions: they are watching. Her unblinding eyes dislocate Cleopatra from a petrarchan context and resituate her in a political one. As the Arden editor explains, Cleopatra's gentlewomen "waited in her sight, i.e., were not just a group of attendants in the background." When Shakespeare alters the duties of Cleopatra's attendants – North's gentlewomen "tend the tackle and ropes" while Shakespeare's more obscurely "tend her i' the eyes" – he foregrounds the Egyptian queen's eyes and, consequently, Cleopatra's status as royal spectator.

The alteration serves to distract attention from the persons and objects described in Cleopatra's theatrical display and to highlight the under-described Cleopatra and her distanced role as an observer. The shift is puzzling only if Cleopatra is taken to be the central object in an artistic display in which the viewer's experience is privileged. Shakespeare's Cleopatra, who watches the performance of her attendants' duties, is the central spectator of a masque-like display – equipped with musical, olfactory, and above all visual, enticements. In other words, Cleopatra on the barge functions like King James I at court performances of masques. As Stephen Orgel has shown, James I assumed a privileged position to gaze upon the masques:[30]

In a theater employing perspective, there is only one focal point, one perfect place in the hall from which the illusion achieves its fullest effect. At court performances this is where the king sat, and the audience around him at once became a living emblem of the structure of the court . . .

Not only did James' position furnish the best view of the spectacle, it also put his royal figure on display: James I was the chief spectator who, in turn, drew admiring gazes to himself. Similarly, the artifice surrounding Cleopatra does not render her an artifact whose value is measured by such wealth, but instead testifies to her royal authority.

It is Cleopatra's royal status that makes her a paradoxically absent and omnipresent figure in her own masque. The success of her display depends on the audience's misrecognition of its basis in political strategy: if her politics of display are to match Stuart practices, her appearance should be perceived as a quasi-divine manifestation and interpreted in light of the divine right to rule. In fact, according to Enobarbus, the paradoxes of her display – which emanate from her equivocal appearance as a consumable object and a pre-eminent subject – generate a near violation of the laws of physics. The air itself, "but for vacancy / Had gone to gaze on Cleopatra too, / And made a gap in nature" (lines 216–18). Her power, not her individual beauties, compels the desiring gaze. Cleopatra is a political artisan who shapes the petrarchan gaze of her audience to reinforce her authority: she subjects her observers to the petrarchan gaze, but refuses to be the satisfying petrarchan object. She alone of all women "makes hungry where most she satisfies," another version of Narcissus' motto, *inopem me copia fecit*, because she has harnessed the energies of petrarchan narcissism for her political advantage.

Although Enobarbus casts the description generally in the form of an anecdote about Cleopatra as an exotic sexual spectacle, he nonetheless supplies the material for a political analysis of her royal display. At the end of the speech, Enobarbus reveals that Cleopatra achieves a political conquest and that Antony is her trophy. Her politics of display are indebted to the quite different strategies of the Elizabethan and Jacobean courts. Her display on the barge and her oblique use of petrarchan conceits recall the political techniques of Elizabeth I, who sailed on the Thames in ceremonial pageants[31] and who found in the language of petrarchan desire an effective means to represent her authority and to control ambitious statesmen. In the barge scene's masque-like properties and its representation of her political apotheosis, however, Cleopatra's political strategies resemble those of James I rather than the more modest Elizabeth I. Elizabeth's art of wooing and James' absolutism inform the odd duality of the barge scene, which represents Cleopatra's powers of seduction and subjugation. Enobarbus' speech concludes in the admission that the sexual and theatrical display is largely political and that in the competition of Egyptian and Roman powers, Cleopatra triumphs. Reclining in her burnished throne, Cleopatra overcomes Antony, "Enthron'd i' the market-place." She stages majesty to compete with Rome or at least defer being annexed to it. The barge speech perspectivally depicts Cleopatra one way as a feminine artifact, the other way a woman whose power and interiority are more compelling than her attractive outside.[32]

To test this reading of Cleopatra's politics of display, we might turn from Elizabethan and Jacobean court practices to evidence within the play itself. The most promising representations of her, and responses to her, are mostly to be found among the censorious but fascinated Romans who repeatedly solicit and narrate stories about her. Cleopatra poses a notorious problem of response and political utility to the Romans. The latter point is worth stressing, because the Romans themselves find it imperative to treat Cleopatra as a sexual rather than a political threat. Pompey, for example, grows lyrical over Cleopatra's beauty only under specific conditions. In an apostrophe to the aging temptress, Pompey conjures those attractions he hopes will detain Antony in Egypt long enough for his own forces to gain control in Rome:

> all the charms of love,
> Salt Cleopatra, soften thy wan'd lip!
> Let witchcraft join with beauty, lust with both,
> Tie up the libertine in a field of feasts,
> Keep his brain fuming . . .   (2.1.20–4)

Invoking her fascinations only under heavy guard, he casts Cleopatra as the romance enchantress closeting up Antony from the political world and insists upon his own skepticism about those beauties age is supposed to wither. But Pompey is not always so guarded about his interest in the legendary Cleopatra. Later, in the company of Antony and his men, he fishes for one of the most famous stories about her. "I have heard Apollodorus carried –" he begins, and Enobarbus completes his sentence, "A certain queen to Caesar in a mattress" (2.6.68–70). Pompey's responses to these legends reveal the extent to which Romans identify Cleopatra's attractions with the imaginative faculties themselves; they also suggest that Romans can only understand her sexuality as distracting and, therefore, as the siren call from Roman duty. Pompey's views do not, of course, constitute proof that Cleopatra's seductiveness is antithetical to political power: we are not obliged to privilege the assumption of a man who proves to be a far from canny politician.

Pompey is not the only Roman to seek out ample descriptions of

Cleopatra. Even Octavius Caesar's men prod for detailed accounts of the Egyptian queen: Maecenas and Agrippa solicit Enobarbus for information immediately after Agrippa has negotiated the marriage of Antony to Octavia. With studied casualness, Maecenas observes that Cleopatra is "a most triumphant lady, if report be square to her" (2.2.184–5). When Enobarbus obligingly mentions Antony's first meeting with Cleopatra on the river Cydnus, Agrippa pounces. He confirms the location – "There she appeared indeed" – and coyly hints for a more elaborate account of that spectacle: "or my reporter devised well for her" (lines 188–9). These men have listened to gossip and the reports of their political informers, but when Enobarbus holds forth in the famous barge speech, they greedily devour his rhetoric for pleasure, not moralistic reproof. Enobarbus completes his luxurious account, and Agrippa enthusiastically bursts out with a rare Roman commendation for Cleopatra's prodigious sexuality and generativity: "Royal wench! / She made great Caesar lay his sword to bed; / He plowed her, and she cropped" (2.2.226–8). Octavius Caesar's right-hand man can hardly contain his complex response to Cleopatra. His outburst is no locker room joke: he is ready, at this moment, to interpret Cleopatra's sexual and generative powers as a triumph over Roman militarism and, more astoundingly, to conceive of her sexuality as a complement to the warlike powers of "great Caesar." Compelling Caesar to turn his sword into a peaceful plow does not emasculate Rome's greatest commander. Moreover, she is not defeated by pregnancy – Caesar's child is the harvest she made out of the Roman instrument of devastation. Even Agrippa removes Cleopatra from the restraints of the temptress scenario. He recognizes, albeit obliquely, that she has power over Caesar as an explicitly "royal wench" who can combat and overcome Roman militarism. Her sexuality and generativity are versions of royal power, not disabling signs of feminine weakness.

Cleopatra establishes her political identity by subverting and exploiting the artistic conventions through which she is recognized and ideologically reconstructed by the Romans and Shakespeare's audiences alike. She greets as theatrical challenges the ideological institutions that define her, whether they are the triumphs of Caesar, fictions of Vergil, or conventions of petrarchism. The marketplace scene, perhaps, offers the clearest evidence that Cleopatra's self-displays are decidedly political. Although the scene recalls Enobarbus' famous description of Cleopatra on the barge, the Romans are unable to privatize and eroticize her spectacular display of her royal person. There is no way to exclaim of the marketplace display, "O rare for Antony!" (2.2.205) – Agrippa's response to Enobarbus' description of Cleopatra's devastatingly erotic appearance –

and thus use a man's amorous response to neutralize Cleopatra's royal appearance as Isis. Although the Romans recognize the political dimensions of Cleopatra's display, they may nonetheless assimilate Enobarbus' description to the legend of Cleopatra, foreign temptress. The second episode, however, resolutely identifies theatrical spectacle, the use of the marketplace, and Cleopatra's sexuality as politically efficient strategies. Caesar himself recognizes the challenge, as we learn in the next scene when Cleopatra asks Enobarbus, "If not denounc'd against us, why should not we / Be there in person?" (3.7.5–6): Caesar recognizes her political authority and declares war on Cleopatra as well as Antony.

Caesar recognizes that gender ranks in the forefront of Cleopatra's politically subversive performances. He perceives the danger in a queen who can act more "manlike" than Antony and can stage herself as the goddesses Venus and Isis. Gender, the Egyptian queen insists, is a performance affirming or subverting political agendas: she can perform either as the goddess of love or as "the president of my kingdom" who can "Appear there [in battle] for a man" (3.5.17–18). Cleopatra asserts her right to "appear . . . for a man" in the face of Enobarbus' Roman-inflected gender anxiety: "'tis said in Rome / That Photinus, an eunuch, and your maids / *Man*age this war" (lines 13–15). Judith Butler's analysis of gender construction and its vulnerability to subversion is useful to an understanding of Cleopatra's sense of gender as a performance and a political strategy:

gender is an identity tenuously constituted in time, instituted in an exterior space through a *stylized repetition of acts*. The effect of gender is produced through the stylization of the body and, hence, must be understood as the mundane way in which bodily gestures, movements, and styles of various kinds constitute the illusion of an abiding gendered self . . . That gender reality is created through sustained social performances means that the very notions of an essential sex and a true or abiding masculinity or femininity are also constituted as part of the strategy that conceals gender's performative character and the performative possibilities for proliferating gender configurations outside the restricting frames of masculinist domination and compulsory heterosexuality.[33]

Butler's approach to gender illuminates the political strategy of Cleopatra's performances as "Cleopater," as the Egyptian queen is sometimes called when asserting her manly authority, and Cleopatra, who is skilled in the public performance of femininity in the extreme forms of Venus and Isis in order to consolidate her political authority. In the battle of Actium, however, her attempt to switch from a politics of display to military action proves to be a fatal error. A female prince had better "Appear . . . for a man" only in show, as Elizabeth did before her troops at Tilbury in 1588.

Cleopatra's dream

Shakespeare grants Antony five magnificent lines of resistance to Caesar's ideological appropriation of him. Cleopatra, on the other hand, requires an entire act to fashion her alternate myths of selfhood. If Caesar attempts to reduce her to a puppet in his triumph, Cleopatra uses myth to escape. Myth, however, is not the unadulterated triumph it is sometimes thought to be: mythological greatness is Cleopatra's compromise for failing to achieve imperial command. Of her complex fictions, her dream of Antony stands out. In her reverie, she tells Dolabella:

> I dreamt there was an Emperor Antony.
> O such another sleep, that I might see
> But such another man!
> DOLABELLA.   If it might please ye, –
> CLEOPATRA. His face was as the heavens, and therein stuck
> A sun and moon, which kept their course, and lighted
> The little O, the earth.
> DOLABELLA.   Most sovereign creature, –
> CLEOPATRA. His legs bestrid the ocean, his rear'd arm
> Crested the world: his voice was propertied
> As all the tuned spheres, and that to friends:
> But when he meant to quail, and shake the orb,
> He was as rattling thunder. For his bounty,
> There was no winter in't: an autumn 'twas
> That grew the more by reaping: his delights
> Were dolphin-like, they show'd his back above
> The elements they lived in: in his livery
> Walk'd crowns and crownets: realms and islands were
> As plates dropp'd from his pocket.
> DOLABELLA.   Cleopatra!
> CLEOPATRA. Think you there was, or might be such a man
> As this I dreamt of?
> DOLABELLA.   Gentle madam, no.
> CLEOPATRA. You lie up to the hearing of the gods.
> But if there be, or ever were one such,
> It's past the size of dreaming: nature wants stuff
> To vie strange forms with fancy, yet to imagine
> An Antony were nature's piece, 'gainst fancy,
> Condemning shadows quite.   (5.2.76–100)

In her dream, one of Cleopatra's greatest moments in the play, she assumes and adapts the role of the desiring poet for the final time. She seems to remember specifically Antony's extraordinary generosity and political defiance in the Alexandrian marketplace. Dolabella proves to be an ideal audience: although he claims not to believe in the hyperbolic portrait of the emperor Antony, he betrays Octavius' plans to exhibit the Egyptian queen in his triumph. His choice of loyalties discloses his astonishing investment in Cleopatra's fiction. An entranced reader, Dolabella falls in love with the Antony she creates and with the Cleopatra who can create "such a man."

To recompose the heroic Antony, Cleopatra uses the petrarchan blazon, which should at this point in the play stand out as a convention more honored in the distortion than the observance. On only one occasion, when Cleopatra requires the messenger to return with a list of Octavia's individual traits, does the blazon contain the threat to female power by fragmenting her body: "bid him / Report the feature of Octavia; her years, / Her inclination, let him not leave out / The colour of her hair" (2.5.112–15), Cleopatra cries, momentarily exposing her own body's vulnerability to catalogue and comparison. When representing her own royal person, Cleopatra avoids being itemized for visual and ideological purchase: Enobarbus' ecphrasis of Cleopatra on the barge reproduces the structure of a blazon while repudiating its conventional function, and Cleopatra wields power by subjecting her beholders to a petrarchan gaze of desire for which she refuses to be the petrarchan object. In her dream, when she employs and revises the blazon, singling out for admiration Antony's face, eyes, legs, "rear'd arm," and voice, she uses the blazon to recall her imperial lover's extraordinary "bounty," out of which she reconstructs the heroic masculinity of an Antony whose identity has been fragmented and scattered by Roman opinion. In her dream of the emperor Antony, Cleopatra once more enacts the role of Isis, this time as the goddess recomposed the scattered limbs of her husband, Osiris. "Wandering heere and there," Isis set herself to "gathering together the dismembered pieces" of Osiris' body, torn and mangled by his jealous brother Typhon. "The report goes," Plutarch tells us, "that Isis found all other parts of Osiris body but only his privy member . . . In sted of that natural part, she made a counterfet one, called Phallus, which she consecrated."[34] Through her cosmic blazon, Cleopatra restores Antony: in death he finally becomes the integrated, magnanimous hero who is spectrally present in the memories of others and in rare moments of self-possession.[35]

Readings which celebrate Cleopatra's successes in promoting her myths in the last act rarely address the counter-evidence, which is variously taken to be hypocrisy (if one takes the Seleucus episode at face value), delusion (if Cleopatra believes it is paltry to be Caesar when one can die impressively), or tragic failure. The reading of Cleopatra as an anti-feminist stereotype is of limited interest to a study of Shakespeare's and,

Cleopatra's powerful revisions of negative conventions: it illuminates what Caesar thinks it means to be a woman. This chapter has emphasized Cleopatra's extraordinary self-advancement through strategically revising unlikely and even hostile traditions. Cleopatra does not achieve transcendence from a historical Egyptian queen to a myth escaping the belittling contingencies of history and politics – although this is her ploy against Caesar's ideological rewriting of her as a whore and political travesty. Her modest triumph is transcendence over the artistic, petrarchan, and ideological codes designed to objectify or depersonalize her literarily, and to disempower her politically. Given this argument, it is necessary to come to terms with Cleopatra's formal rejection of the very qualities that make her compelling, vital, and powerful:

> My resolution's placed, and I have nothing
> Of woman in me: now from head to foot
> I am marble-constant: now the fleeting moon
> No planet is of mine.   (5.2.237–40)

With these words, Cleopatra rejects her femininity, her association with Isis and the moon, and her "infinite variety."[36]

Although Cleopatra claims to reject the moon and, by extension, the iconography of Isis, she nonetheless dies with the asp placed to suck on her breast, a monument to, and of, Isis. And although Cleopatra declares there is "nothing / Of woman" in her, she characterizes death as a marriage: "Husband, I come" (5.2.286). Her next lines help explain the contradictory descriptions that Cleopatra offers of herself: "Now to that name, my courage prove my title! / I am fire, and air; my other elements / I give to baser life" (lines 287–8). She bequeaths the feminine elements of water and earth to life, which she is trying with difficulty to regard as "baser" than death, which, in a magnificently ambivalent celebration of fixedness, "shackles accidents, and bolts up change" (5.2.6). Imagining herself as fire and air, the masculine elements that rise up impatiently from worldly matters, she is able to interpret death as transcendence. Cleopatra borrows the Aristotelian binarisms – the same that undergird the oppositions on Aeneas' shield – that denigrate femininity, moisture, variety, and change, and uses them to steel herself to the suicide she fears only slightly less than being led in Caesar's triumph. In Caesar's words, she manages, perhaps barely, to foil the wish Caesar states when he sends Proculeius to watch Cleopatra, "Lest, in her greatness, by some mortal stroke / She do defeat us. For her life in Rome / Would be eternal in our triumph" (5.1.64–6). In a victory limited to her afterlife as a sign, Shakespeare's Cleopatra manages to turn herself into an icon critical of imperial Rome. She succeeds in representing, if not quite being, the

Cleopatra at the end of Horace's Ode: the queen who, through suicide, scorned to be humbled and led as a private citizen in a proud triumph: *scilicet invidens | privata deduci supero | non humilis mulier triumpho* (1.37.30–2).

Redefining the court and theater in Jacobean London

The temptations to speculate on *Antony and Cleopatra*'s political stance are strong, even if one is more likely to meet with rebuttal or frustration than in similar speculations on *Titus Andronicus* and *Troilus and Cressida*. The appeal and the risk may be greater because Shakespeare, writing for a new prince and as the chief playwright of the King's Men, blurs the lines between the provenance of the theater and that of the court. As a translation of empire, *Antony and Cleopatra* bears as least as much on the theater as it does on the political world of Jacobean England. Critics have noted various ways in which the play is specifically Jacobean: it engages the ambivalent Jacobean response to its former queen, Elizabeth I (Jankowski); reflections on the debauchery that distinguished the visit of Christian of Denmark (Davies); the decline of the Jacobean military (Dollimore); and the play's investment of James' self-representation both in Caesar as the austere moralist and architect of peace and in Antony and Cleopatra, whose public indulgence of their sexuality may recall similar displays in James I's own court (Kernan).[37] *Antony and Cleopatra* provides a hospitable environment for topical readings, which only falter when a critic insists on their pre-emptive relevance.[38]

The range of persuasive topical readings suggests that the play encourages political readings but avoids hierarchical ranking. As a translation of empire, *Antony and Cleopatra* eludes frontal disputes of the kind that incur censorship and reprisal but bristles with political and social meanings. The changes that Shakespeare introduces in North's Plutarch's description of Cleopatra's progress down the river Cydnus, for example, suggest that he imaginatively adopts a position along the shore from which he and his audiences might view their own ship of state, once helmed by a popular, petrarchan, and maternal queen, now governed by a paternal and absolutist Stuart prince. In writing *Antony and Cleopatra* under a new prince and as a King's man, Shakespeare may well have become conscious of his translations of empire as an aggregate or even a genre; the play's increased metatheatricality, along with its characters' distinctive use of textual authorities, suggests Shakespeare's growing awareness of the theater's potential to respond playfully or polemically to social and political preoccupations and to do so through textual surrogates for political powers.

Antony and Cleopatra exhibits an intense curiosity about the new roles of the theater and the King's Men under the relatively new prince. Shakespeare's mind seems arrested by the possibilities for a theater that performed for both popular and courtly audiences, acquisitive of the cultural authority available to him through his relations with the new court, and inquisitive about his newly-acquired powers and their boundaries. *Antony and Cleopatra* suggests a Shakespeare testing the possibility that his theater might become annexed to the court: "Perform't, or else we damn thee" (1.1.24), Cleopatra says to discourage Antony from responding to Caesar's messengers. The taunt comes close to suggesting the kind of instrumental agency that Kernan sees in Shakespeare's courtly theater when he remarks that "the Stuart monopolization of theater was a characteristic move, putting a powerful propaganda medium in James' hands" (p. 10) and that Charnes sees in the Augustan literature she terms a "monumental machinery of language . . . at [Caesar's] disposal" (p. 108).

I propose that in *Antony and Cleopatra* Shakespeare begins to dream of the theater as the space of cultural play that he only relinquishes in *The Tempest,* when he foresees that his revels along with his dreams of empire are ended. In this play, Shakespeare calls on his audiences to join him in *imagining* the theater rather than merely attending it – to join in inventing the theater's cultural place. In *Antony and Cleopatra,* Shakespeare's theater is engrossed by the notion of playing to a court that is itself increasingly mimicking the theater, in masques or in the sometimes farcical scenes performed in court and then purveyed about and beyond the environs of London when courtiers and diplomats took to their pens and paper and described debauched scenes. The play and its cultural moment suggest options for the theater, positions for it to occupy: to be co-opted, to collude playfully, to rival, or to oppose.

The theater is in some ways aligned with the liminal and flamboyant Alexandrian world, staged in the cultural marketplace, where roles and genders may be provisionally exchanged and social duties suspended, questioned, and resisted. By corollary, in some ways Caesar and his Rome relate to James I and his court. Contemporaries given to "Roman thoughts" might agree: "The players do not forbear to present upon their stage the whole course of the present time, not sparing either Church or King, with such freedom that any would be afraid to hear them," remarked Samuel Calvert,[39] and the Venetian ambassador in 1620 concurred: "In this country . . . the comedians have absolute liberty to say whatever they wish against any one."[40] Yet there are no guidelines to determine how the transgressive character of the Alexandrian world translates to the Jacobean stage. In fact, given the stand-off between the

Alexandrian theatrical values and the crabbed, censorious ones articulated by Caesar, the leader of Rome's empire relates more persuasively to the puritans attempting to close down the London theaters than he does to London's king.

The elusive but tantalizing relations that *Antony and Cleopatra* proposes among history, the Jacobean political world, and the theater come into brief focus on the occasions that Antony and Cleopatra independently confront the prospect of their future on the stage: these are moments of historical "ventriloquism," when the theatrical moment is estranged from the historical moment dramatized. In the most celebrated episode, the boy actor playing Cleopatra upstages the historical character with self-reference to the "squeaking Cleopatra" who "boys" her greatness. By usurping Cleopatra's derisive line and cockily hauling onto the stage the pederastic in-jokes that yoke together the theater and the court, the boy actor suggests that Cleopatra will donate her erotic politics to the Jacobean theater or, more to the point, that theatrical camp will trace its lineage to the historical Cleopatra. Artistically, it is a showy moment in which Shakespeare, at no little risk to his heroine, flaunts the theater and his art, and scores a good theatrical and courtly in-joke.[41]

Yet the relationship of historical person to actor is not always tilted to favor the actor and the theater. When Antony revises the *Aeneid,* he becomes momentarily an anachronistic figure, aware that he is revising the text that will indict him through Dido and Aeneas and aware that he is onstage because he will succeed in altering his literary-political reception, Shakespeare's dramaturgy releases an aggressive energy that seems to come from the historical character dramatized and not from the player. When Lavinia chases the copy of the *Metamorphoses* to explain the meaning of her "martyr'd signs," when Achilles beholds a book and breaks down into his constituent texts, and when Antony revises the *Aeneid,* Shakespeare uses the actor's body as a prop on which larger cultural issues in the play converge. Antony momentarily estranges himself from the actor's body in order to assert his priority in authoring his own identity and significance. Antony claims the actor's body as a cultural palimpsest from which he scrapes Caesar's meanings and impresses his own. While the body testifies to the vulnerability of political icons, Antony insists that more history enter into signs whose meanings have been narrowed for ideological purposes.

When Antony estranges the signs from their dominant political meanings and leaves his own mark on them, Shakespeare is the shadowy figure behind him. In this iconoclastic moment, the theater presents a political emblem and stages its ideological analysis or breakdown and susceptibility to reconstruction. In this way, *Antony and Cleopatra* develops the pattern established by *Titus Andronicus* and *Troilus and Cressida* of questioning the ideologically settled nature of political iconography or representation through self-authorizing signs and stories. Antony and Cleopatra's habit of appropriating myths is analogous to Shakespeare's own imitative practice: Shakespeare returns to the books that normally lend authority, historical precedent, and iconographic material to the court, and uses them as sources to diverge from the dominant political usage.

5   *Cymbeline*'s mingle-mangle: Britain's Roman histories

Souldiers call for Tragedies, their obiect is bloud; Courtiers for Comme-
dies, their subiect is loue; Countriemen for Pastoralles . . . Trafficke and
trauell hath wouen the nature of all Nations into ours, and made this
land like Arras, full of deuise, which was Broade-cloth, full of worke-
manshippe. Time hath confounded our mindes, our mindes the matter;
but all commeth to this passe, that what hertofore hath beene serued in
seuerall dishes for a feaste, is now minced in a charger for a Gallimau-
frey. If wee present a mingle-mangle, our fault is to be excused, because
the whole worlde is become an Hodge-podge.

(John Lyly, prologue to *Midas*)

Enfranchising the mangled law: Britain and the sword of Caesar

Cymbeline relies upon overblown romance to resolve its awkward
mixtures of sources, genres, and chronology. Set simultaneously in the
times of Augustus Caesar and early modern Europe, its disparate sources
and generic conventions include epic, history, and pastoral, as well as
romance, novella, and courtly behavior manual in addition to dream
vision and fairy tale. The play's constituent sources range from Vergil
and Ovid, Livy and Plutarch, to Boccaccio, Mantuan, and Holinshed:
ancient originals mingle with contemporary innovations which either
sensationalize the classical texts or purge them of their paganism. These
sources, each clearly stamped with specific and at times contrary values,
forge a hesitant treaty to blend amicably and aesthetically into the play's
conclusion, a romance solvent of its various conflicts. Like all of the
translations of empire that precede it, *Cymbeline* finds strength in
awkward inconsistency: its chronological, generic, and textual idiosyn-
crasies address the play's dominant preoccupation, which is the status of
Britain's emergent nationhood, particularly as it relates to classical
Roman authorities and their roguish early modern Italian descendants.

Cymbeline suspends its emblems of cultural authority between fusion
and fragmentation. The play's insistent puzzles include the peculiar
anachronism which allows Iachimo, the degenerate modern Italian, to

151

rub elbows with Romans under Augustus and Britons under Cymbeline; Cymbeline's voluntary payment of tribute to the defeated Romans; Posthumus' worthiness to be Imogen's husband and to sum up British masculine virtue; and Imogen's bizarre encounter with the headless body of Cloten, which she mistakes for her husband's corpse. In *Cymbeline*, Shakespeare exploits these enigmas to test and trouble models of authority generally used to translate empire from imperial Rome to early Britain. Linked by their strictly ambiguous character, the enigmas both synthesize the disparate elements of the play in a nationalistic project and blazon the inconsistencies that threaten the goals of uniting Cymbeline's family and forging his nation. Through its unstable "mingle-mangle" of sources and historical periods, *Cymbeline* threatens to dissolve rather than ratify the emergent British nation along with its Jacobean political iconography.

In *Cymbeline*, Shakespeare presents Jacobean Britain as a nation born of historical accidents and in need of retrospective self-fashioning to gird up its political and ethical foundations. Here we might consider the presentation of British patriotism, which varies from Imogen's quiet enthusiasm for the self-sufficient isle to the Queen and Cloten's insular baiting of the Roman emissary Lucius. Shakespeare uses his theater to "delve Britain to its roots," much as antiquarians and legal historians were doing in their descriptions and reports.[1] For Shakespeare, as for many of his contemporaries, a nation must be defined not by a territorial attitude or a casually imported political theory but in terms of the laws, customs, and ethics established through its history. Without a clear historical methodology to construct it, the image of the nation will inevitably disintegrate into the kind figured in Cymbeline's discontented court as well as his dispersed family, warriors, and royal composure. Even Posthumus' degrading jealousies reflect the threat of cultural disintegration: as we will see, they culminate in the terrible image of Imogen as she laments over the headless body and cites the *Aeneid* on the fall of the Trojan civilization. In short, the potential for precipitous ("headless") action in defining the British nation jeopardizes the glorious peace promised in the play by Jupiter; simultaneously, it questions the terms of nationhood in the early modern England of James I, the self-styled "peace-maker" and royal absolutist who wished to import not only the Augustan *pax Romana* but also the deified and central status of the nation's ruler.

In early Britain's troubled relations with Rome, *Cymbeline* offers a useful fiction to test what it means to define a nation in terms of an absolute authority: the struggle between imperial Rome and the emergent British nation runs roughly parallel to that of James I and his

Parliamentary opponents over the disposition and grounds of political power in England. In the war for British independence, the Britons defeat the Roman forces and then, paradoxically, agree to pay voluntarily the tribute that they would not allow Augustus Caesar to force from them. The tricky balance of power that Britain seeks in its relations with Rome is condensed in the twice-interpreted vision of the westbound eagle who disappears into the sun. An image of the *translatio imperii*, the vision ambiguously distributes power between the rival authorities of the Roman eagle and the western sun. A Roman Soothsayer first interprets the vision as an omen favorable to the Romans:

> Last night the very gods show'd me a vision . . .
> I saw Jove's bird, the Roman eagle, wing'd
> From the spongy south to this part of the west,
> There vanish'd in the sunbeams, which portends . . .
> Success to th' Roman host.   (4.2.346–52)

The Soothsayer assumes that the westward flight of the eagle, the bird of Jupiter and Augustus Caesar, prefigures the extension of Augustus' power over Britain: under a new imperial rubric, Augustus is to continue the command over Britain established by his adoptive father, Julius Caesar. The Soothsayer seems unaware that cultural change has taken place in England as well as Rome, for the British are no longer rustic sources of laughter. As Posthumus points out, Philario's "great Augustus" will have to face Britons better prepared than when "Julius Caesar / Smil'd at their lack of skill, but found their courage / Worthy his frowning at" (2.4.21–3).

It does not occur to the Soothsayer that Jupiter may extend his favor to Cymbeline's burgeoning nation. In a perceptive comment on the prophecy, G. Wilson Knight brings into focus its mix of nationalism and anachronism:[2]

The word "spongy" suggests softness and also, perhaps, an enervating, clammy heat, as though the imperial eagle were leaving a soft, effete, decaying land for one more virile. It underlines the precise relation within our drama of Renaissance Italy to ancient Rome, whilst indicating why their synchronization was forced: as the Roman virtue sinks to the level of Iachimo, the heritage of ancient Rome falls on Britain.

What is invisible to an Augustan Soothsayer is that Rome will come to produce "effete" and decadent men like Iachimo, and that Roman authority will move, like the eagle, and take up residence in "virile" Britons like Cymbeline's two sons and Posthumus himself, all closely associated with eagles in the play. The prophecy, as Knight says, "symbolize[s] a certain transference of virtue from Rome to Britain"

(p. 166), but is deliberately vague about whether the transference is a matter of Rome's expansion or her eclipse by Britain.

Generally presented as the play's vacant center, Cymbeline saves his strenuous thinking for questions about the constitution of his authority[3] and publicly worries about his contractual relations with Rome. The effort of "the injurious Romans" to "extort / This tribute from us" (3.1.49–50) violates British "liberties" (line 76): "we were free" (line 50), he says, before Julius Caesar's conquest, and the honors bestowed by Augustus, while attractive, affirm the British "yoke" (line 53): "Thy Caesar knighted me," he tells Lucius, "my youth I spent / Much under him; of him I gather'd honour, / Which he to seek of me again, perforce, / Behoves me keep at utterance" (lines 71–4). Trained and rewarded at the Roman court, Cymbeline regards his honor as a gift of Caesar, but not his royal authority. He appears not to confuse the appealing *dative* honor he received from Augustus with his less illustrious but more potent *native* honor as the descendant of British kings.[4] Drawing on British precedents, Cymbeline articulates the constitutional basis for his liberty from Roman force:

> Our ancestor was that Mulmutius which
> Ordain'd our laws, whose use the sword of Caesar
> Hath too much mangled; whose repair, and franchise,
> Shall (by the power we hold) be our good deed,
> Though Rome be therefore angry. Mulmutius made our laws,
> Who was the first of Britain which did put
> His brows within a golden crown, and call'd
> Himself a king.   (3.1.56–63)

When Cymbeline favors Britain's history over his own courtly experience, he discovers that customary law demands his resistance to Roman supremacy. By preferring Mulmutius to Caesar as his political father, he affirms that imperial Rome merely dignifies the pre-existing authority rooted in Britain's own history. Augustus' attempt to revive the terms of Julius Caesar's conquest causes Cymbeline to reinvest in Britain's pre-Roman institutions, which he declares he will repair and enfranchise.

Even when he cedes the tribute to Rome at the end of the play, Cymbeline makes the apparently gratuitous move to claim equality with Rome and to link native British rule to the Augustan paradigm:

> My peace we will begin: and Caius Lucius,
> Although the victor, we submit to Caesar,
> And to the Roman empire; promising
> To pay our wonted tribute.   (5.5.460–3)

Although he blames his "wicked queen" for his former rebelliousness, Cymbeline prides himself on the independent terms of "his" peace. He is prepared to pay the "wonted" tribute so long as he may explain it as a matter of British custom and his prerogative. Since his warlike country defied Augustus' effort to second Julius "Caesar's ambition, / Which swell'd so much that it did almost stretch / The sides o' th' world" (3.1.50–2), Cymbeline is ready to proclaim Augustan Rome as his country's mentor.

His intuitive sense that Britain has eclipsed imperial Rome no doubt encourages Cymbeline's gallantry. The anachronistic, or telescopic, transferral of power becomes clear when the Soothsayer, at last identified as one Philarmonus, emends his interpretation of the westering eagle:

> For the Roman eagle,
> From south to west on wing soaring aloft,
> Lessen'd herself and in the beams o' the sun
> So vanish'd; which foreshadow'd our princely eagle,
> Th' imperial Caesar, should again unite
> His favour with the radiant Cymbeline,
> Which shines here in the west.   (5.5.471–7)

Philarmonus' happy gloss politely overlooks the crippling of Roman power in the merger. The Roman eagle is startlingly diminished: first feminized and lessened, she finally vanishes in Cymbeline's radiant glory. Shakespeare does not stage the harmonious balance of power between Caesar and the British nation, although that is what Philarmonus tries to celebrate. Instead, he presents the invention of political myths that negotiate complicated power struggles and camouflage disruptions in the constitution of cultural authority.

The struggle for cultural authority dominates the play's themes: Shakespeare sets the action of his play against the backdrop of the ancient feud between imperial Rome and early Britain, which itself suggests the royal and Parliamentary arguments beginning in Jacobean England over the source of political power – in the king's person or in the laws of the land. In the peace Cymbeline establishes with Augustan Rome, following his battle against the terms of Julius Caesar's conquest, playgoers from the Inns-of-Court might see a reflection of the constitutional insistence for mixed monarchy over royal absolutism. The play's end, when Cymbeline joyously proclaims his peace and co-opts the more famous Augustan *pax Romana*, falls into the pattern of Fortescue's appropriation of Augustan empire to serve as the precursor of England's mixed monarchy, in sharp contrast with Julius Caesar's tyranny.[5]

Like Cymbeline, only more dexterous, Shakespeare develops fictions to delve British authority to its root. *Cymbeline* stages the possibility of Britain's failure to fulfill the prophetic union: the emergent nation may instead leap headlong from its rugged origins to "spongy" or effeminate ends. The identity of Britain lies suspended between original valor, represented in Augustan Rome and Cymbeline's lost sons, and cultural malaise, concentrated in the modern Italian Iachimo and in Cloten, who is almost advanced to the throne by the Queen's Italianate poisons and machinations.[6] Britain's national identity, as it hesitates between classical and modern Italies, is played out on characterological and textual levels: first, in the crisis of identity that Posthumus faces when he succumbs to Iachimo's lurid narrations and convicts his wife of adultery; second, in the classical and roughly contemporary texts Shakespeare uses to figure and refigure the identities of both Britain and the exemplary characters implicated in British succession – Posthumus, Imogen, and Cymbeline's sons. The resources of Vergil, Plutarch, Livy, and Holinshed form the proper lineal descent from Augustan Rome to Troynovant, or London; and those of Ovid and his Boccaccian descendants compose the "debased" classical heritage that sensualized Italy. At the pivotal moment of Britain's national formation, the Ovidian line of cultural heritage threatens to pervert Posthumus and to thwart the passage of the Vergilian tradition from Rome to Britain.

Delving Posthumus to the root

The image of Imogen lamenting over the body of Cloten, whom she mistakes for Posthumus, is crucial to the translation of empire. The bizarre spectacle is *Cymbeline*'s fatal Cleopatra, or semiotic matrix which confuses differences among sources, characters, and historical moments and generates more meanings than it can authorize and contain. Like the pit in *Titus Andronicus*, *Cymbeline*'s central image makes full sense only in terms of the *translatio imperii* and specifically the problematic aspects of the classical heritage that Britain may not want to incorporate.[7] Why and how is it that Posthumus comes to be a spectral and headless presence in the arms of his blood-smeared wife, when he is supposed to represent "the best of British masculinity" according to Knight and the finally humbled Iachimo? Through no good deed known to Iachimo, the young Briton who earned his scorn early in the play becomes "the good Posthumus / (What should I say? he was too good to be / Where ill men were, and was the best of all / Amongst the rar'st of good ones)" (5.5.157–60).[8] The image of corporeal fragmentation will be the point of departure and return in an analysis of the play's unusual handling of textual authorities and the primary issue they engage: the joint constructions of national identity and heroic identity.

Posthumus' path to the play's threatening image of his annihilation in a faceless corpse begins with the first lines of *Cymbeline*. An admiring lord explains the British court's recent disruptions over Posthumus, a man who,

> to seek through the regions of the earth
> For one his like; there would be something failing
> In him that should compare. I do not think
> So fair an outward, and such stuff within
> Endows a man, but he.   (1.1.20–4)

In the courtier's view, Posthumus' rival is not worth the breath it takes to describe him: Cloten is "a thing / Too bad for bad report" (lines 16–17) while Posthumus defies description. The courtier can only "extend him . . . within himself, / Crush him together, rather than unfold / His measure duly" (lines 25–7). He mentions the rhetorical techniques fit to depict a man's worth, but finds his amplification and comparison insufficient to the task. He also reveals why the young man stands in need of eloquent praise: an orphan adopted by Cymbeline, Posthumus secretly married the king's daughter. The marriage, unsanctioned by Cymbeline, aggravates Posthumus' already uncertain social status: although his family performed brave services for Britain, their origins are resolutely mysterious, and the courtier describing Posthumus admits that he cannot "delve him to the root" (line 28).[9] Posthumus' scandalous marriage effectively removes him from comparison with other men, and since his royal wife is the root and guarantor of his manly worth, the ineffability topos becomes the only rhetorical device suitable to describe him:

> To his mistress,
> (For whom he now is banish'd) her price
> Proclaims how she esteem'd him; and his virtue
> By her election may be truly read
> What kind of man he is.   (1.1.50–4)

Posthumus' reliance on Imogen's esteem ultimately undermines the self-evident and incomparable worth that the courtier wants to invest in him. His dependence on Imogen's "election" for his worth places an unusual burden on her motivations in choosing him: for Posthumus it is indispensable, albeit disagreeable in other ways, that dispassionate judgment and not sexual desire inspired her choice of a husband.

His virtue is subjected to more formal interrogation in Rome, where that skeptical and salacious reader of people, Iachimo, interprets the young Briton according to the sophisticated conventions of renaissance Italy. Iachimo sneers that when he last saw the young man, Posthumus appeared of "crescent note," worth his "name," but nonetheless, "I could then have look'd on him without the help of admiration, though the catalogue of his endowments had been tabled by his side and I to peruse him by items" (1.5.4–7). Like Achilles reading Hector as a book of sport and testimony to his own martial reputation, Iachimo peruses Posthumus as a malleable text that smugly measures British virtue against Italian sophistication. Fastening on Posthumus' insecure reputation, he insinuates social-climbing into that "crescent note": "This matter of his marrying his king's daughter, wherein he must be weighed rather by her value than his own, words him (I doubt not) a great deal from the matter" (lines 14–17). Posthumus' upwardly mobile and clandestine marriage offers considerable potential for rewriting the promising young Briton – along the lines Iago used to fashion Othello for Brabantio – and Iachimo immediately begins to test the possibilities.

These innuendoes, tempting to discredit because of their speaker, are oddly borne out in *Cymbeline*'s central image, when Imogen fails to distinguish the corpse of the ambitious Cloten from the body of her husband. She mistakes a puttock for an eagle (1.2.70–1), and raises questions about how the two men come to be confused, even conflated. At the beginning of the play, their similarities are purely superficial. The two men are rivals for Imogen and for Cymbeline's approval in addition, it would seem, to his throne. For their social worth, both men depend on powerful women who advance them towards the throne, aggressively in the Queen's case and somewhat reluctantly in Imogen's. Despite their clear structural affinities, the play takes pains to differentiate between the two men. We are invited to credit Posthumus with great innate worth and a strongly developed interiority in contrast with Cloten's comical superficiality. When the Queen's son harps on social status, he draws to himself the stigma of social climbing that threatens to discredit Posthumus.

To parody his superficiality, the play relentlessly associates Cloten with clothing. Imogen, irritated by his insults to the low-born Posthumus, declares

> His mean'st garment,
> That ever hath but clipp'd his body, is dearer
> In my respect, than all the hairs above thee,
> Were they all made such men.   (3.3.134–7)

From this moment, Cloten can hardly be induced to speak of anything else. " 'His garment!' " he blusters twice, as he works up to the full elitism of her remark: " 'His *meanest* garment!' " From this insult, which he minds more than Imogen's assertion that he is not good enough to be the under-hangman to Posthumus' kingdom, Cloten spins a plan of revenge whose violence jars with his generic coordinates in comedy:

She said upon a time (the bitterness of it I now belch from my heart) that she held the very garment of Posthumus in more respect than my noble and natural person; together with the adornment of my qualities. With that suit upon my back, will I ravish her: first kill him, and in her eyes; there shall she see my valour, which will then be a torment to her contempt. He on the ground, my speech of insultment ended on his dead body, and when my lust hath dined (which, as I say, to vex her I will execute in the clothes that she so prais'd) to the court I'll knock her back, foot her home again. (3.5. 136–49)

With a hearty belch, Cloten makes it clear that social frustrations are the source of his dangerously comical imagination. The dinner attire, table manners, and corporeal table he hopes to use in his meal of revenge suggest how vulnerably he is constructed from behavior manuals and "civilizing processes" which discriminate between low-class boors and the elite.[10] Imogen could not have found a more devastating insult than to compare his studied qualities with Posthumus' meanest garment, and Cloten contemplates revenge in sundering Posthumus' head from his shoulders after forcing him to watch his "garments cut to pieces before [his] face" (4.1.19–20). The Queen's son seems to have read *Il Cortegiano* and let Castiglione's metaphors for true courtiership "word him from the matter" of courtliness: his insistence on clothing, in fact, prompts one to wonder if the word followed the pattern of "nothing-noting" and thus sound like "Cloten," a relentless characterological reduction. When death comes to Cloten, it is because he mistakes the outward appearance of gentility for its substance: "Know'st me not by my clothes?" he asks the unadorned and exasperated prince Guiderius, who chops off "Cloten's clot-poll" (4.2.184).

Cloten is the model of cultural degeneration that the play offers first as Posthumus' foil and double. In the face of Iachimo's lurid narrations, Posthumus vulgarly dismisses all doubt about Imogen's guilt: "She hath bought the name of whore, thus dearly" (2.4.128), he begins, "she hath been colted by him" (line 133). Setting the precedent for Cloten's later obsession, Posthumus whets his anger and need for certainty. He moves precipitously from paranoid sarcasm – "Spare your arithmetic, never count the turns: / Once, and a million!" (lines 141–2) – to the insane threat, "I will kill thee if thou dost deny / Thou hast made me cuckold" (lines 145–6). His rage culminates in a fantasy of revenge parallel to the one that Cloten later amplifies and attempts to execute: "O that I had her here, to tear her limb-meal! / I will go there and do't, i' th' court, before / Her father" (lines 147–9). Strikingly, Cloten amplifies Posthumus' fantasy of violating Imogen before her father: he picks up where Posthumus left off, and winds up as the headless emblem of Posthumus' internal state.

Through Cloten as his double, it becomes clear that ambition complicates Posthumus' state of mind and feelings for his wife. Imogen comments that while Posthumus was in Britain, "He did incline to sadness, and oft-times / Not knowing why" (1.7.62–3). His lack of family surely contributes to his melancholy – Jupiter himself points to the joint psychological and genealogical confusion of the "lion's whelp," *leonatus*, who is "to himself unknown" (5.1.138–9). But class-related frustrations are the most common cause of melancholy on the Jacobean stage, and Posthumus is not free from the social discontents associated with the malady. Britain weighs on Posthumus' mind while he is in exile, and he asks the newly returned Iachimo about the diplomatic affairs between Rome and Britain: "I do believe / (Statist though I am none, nor like to be) / That this will prove a war" (2.4.15–17). Might there be more chagrin than self-deprecating irony in his parenthetical remark? Cymbeline reacts to Posthumus' social presumption by banishing Posthumus as "poison to my blood" (1.2.59) and accusing Imogen: "Thou took'st a beggar, wouldst have made my throne / A seat for baseness" (lines 72–3). *Cymbeline* goes to extreme lengths to protect Posthumus from the charge of marrying for status, but simultaneously harps on the fact that Imogen is "fasten'd to an empery / Would make the great'st king double" (1.7.120–1). Posthumus, moreover, never seconds Imogen's wish that she were a "neatherd's daughter, and my Leonatus / Our neighborshepherd's son" (1.2.80–1). But it is Cloten who supplies the primary means to implicate Posthumus in social ambitions that he, unlike his loutish double, cannot entertain directly. Cloten is no foolish pawn in his mother's schemes: the Queen angles for "the placing of the British crown" (3.5.66) and attempts to poison Cymbeline and work her son "into th' adoption of the crown" (5.5.56), but Cloten too desires the marriage: if he "could get this foolish Imogen," he "should have gold enough" to gamble (2.3.7–8).

At the crisis of the play, Posthumus and Cloten become ethically indistinguishable, a homology the play represents visually when Cloten dresses in the maddened Posthumus' clothes and attempts to carry out the fantasy of revenge he shares with Posthumus. Unlike Posthumus, who is allowed to redeem himself, Cloten winds up as a headless corpse and emblem of Posthumus' internal condition. With the spectacle of Cloten's truncated body onstage, Posthumus' identity hangs in suspension: in the wane is his identity as the best of British masculinity and on the rise is his identification with Cloten. The tension between his potential selves increases when Imogen mistakes the corpse for her husband and her laments run from tragic to bathetic:

A headless man? The garments of Posthumus?
I know the shape of's leg: this is his hand:
His foot Mercurial: his Martial thigh:
The brawns of Hercules: but his Jovial face –
Murder in heaven! How? – 'Tis gone. Pisanio,
All curses madded Hecuba gave the Greeks,
And mine to boot, be darted on thee! Thou,
Conspir'd with that irregulous devil, Cloten
Hast here cut off my lord. To write, and read
Be henceforth treacherous!   (4.2.308–17)

Because Imogen is cradling a headless body and the wrong one at that, her Olympian blazon of Posthumus bizarrely revises the dream in which Cleopatra recreates Antony as a colossus. Whereas Cleopatra successfully pulls together and re-animates the scattered Antony, Imogen inadvertently widens the gap the audience perceives between Posthumus' sublime potential and his present debasement. He is both the eagle and the puttock she sought to avoid.

Posthumus' conflation with Cloten marks his unworthiness to be joined to Imogen and be a "statist," much less a royal heir, but the political dimensions of the scene are considerably more precise than the account has so far indicated. At the moment Posthumus is identified with the headless Cloten, Shakespeare introduces into the play the great authority on empire, Vergil. The translation of empire, as Patricia Parker has discovered, appears in a spectacular citation of cultural decline from the *Aeneid*: Imogen joins her curses to those of the "madded Hecuba," the Trojan queen forced to watch the slaughter of her husband and the fall of Troy. When Imogen, like Hamlet, recalls Vergil on the death of Priam, she ties Posthumus' imperiled heroic identity to the scheme of the *translatio imperii*.[11] Stabbed in the side by Achilles' son Pyrrhus, Priam is transformed into a symbol of his civilization's fall:

haec finis Priami fatorum, hic exitus illum
sorte tulit Troiam incensam et prolapsa videntem
Pergama, tot quondam populis terrisque superbum
regnatorem Asiae. iacet ingens litore truncus,
avulsumque umeris caput et sine nomine corpus.   (2.554–8)

This was the end of Priam's fates; this was the death that fell to his lot: to see Troy burning and Pergamum fallen, he who was the proud ruler of so many peoples and lands, the monarch of Asia. He lies a huge trunk on the shore, his head severed from his shoulders and a corpse without a name.

Vergil amplifies the uncanny effects of this extraordinary image through narrative discontinuity: how does Priam wind up headless, on the shore, when he was stabbed in the side within the inner sanctum of Troy? The image powerfully evokes the fall of the Asian empire against which Rome will define her more severe Western values; with equal power, it alludes to Rome's civil wars and the struggle that ended in Pompey's decapitation on the Egyptian shore. *Cymbeline* translates the image of the decapitated Priam, monument to the fall of Troy, to comment on the imperiled state of Britain. The man compared to Priam/Pompey is Posthumus, although Cloten's body is used as the prop on which cultural decline is inscribed. The contamination of Priam and Cloten serves as a stage emblem for Posthumus' great failure. Posthumus' ambition and mindless, vengeful jealousy take on national consequences: his failure metonymically stands for the fall of an entire civilization. As Priam became a nameless and headless corpse, Posthumus signals Britain's potential to collapse precipitously from its vigorous origins to a dismal end. The Queen's earlier words accurately sum up Posthumus' state: "His fortunes all lie speechless, and his name / Is at last gasp" (1.6.52–3).

In Vergil's epic, Aeneas himself is subject to a similar superimposition onto Priam's corpse. Dido prays to Jupiter that if Aeneas must succeed in establishing his kingdom, he may nonetheless derive no personal pleasure from his accomplishment, and finally, "fall before his time and lie unburied in the sands," *cadat ante diem mediaque inhumatus harena* (4.620). Aeneas shall lie unburied on the sand as a sign of Rome's compromised success, just as Priam lies beheaded on the shore as a sign of Troy's absolute ruin. When Imogen confuses Cloten's headless body with Posthumus, Britain's fated emergence as a nation, backed by the combined authority of Troy and Augustan Rome, hangs in perilous suspension. Britain's young hero is on the verge of failing before he has properly begun to build the nation.

Headless Posthumus: repeating and undoing the *Aeneid*

At this point in the play, the major connection between Aeneas and Posthumus is, uninspiringly, that both men abandon their royal lovers, Dido and Imogen. The difference is that emotional betrayal confirms the project of empire-building for Aeneas but jeopardizes Posthumus' prospects. Britain's fate hinges on a dramatic revision of the *Aeneid*: Posthumus must lay the foundations of British character without Aeneas' emotional compromise. Posthumus embarks on a Vergilian career, in fact, exclusively to atone for ordering his wife's murder. Although elements of Aeneas' tale saturate his heroic narrative, Shakespeare formally identifies Posthumus with Vergil's hero at the moment that

Aeneas abandons Dido and brings her curse down on the Roman nation. Learning that Posthumus has ordered her death, Imogen cries,

> Men's vows are women's traitors! All good seeming,
> By thy revolt, O husband, shall be thought
> Put on for villainy; not born where't grows,
> But worn a bait for ladies . . .
> True honest men, being heard like false Aeneas,
> Were in his time thought false: and Sinon's weeping
> Did scandal many a holy tear, took pity
> From most true wretchedness: so thou, Posthumus,
> Wilt lay the leaven on all proper men;
> Goodly and gallant shall be false and perjur'd
> From thy great fail. (3.4.53–64)

Seeking a precedent for Posthumus' failure and its consequences for the credibility of all men, Imogen thinks of Aeneas. Although a Sinon-like Aeneas betrayed Troy to the Greeks in a medieval tradition, Imogen's Aeneas is not a traitor on political grounds. Her treacherous Aeneas suggests a strong reading of Aeneas' behavior to Dido in the *Aeneid*: despite presenting himself to Dido as Sinon's opposite, Vergil's hero plays the role of the artful Greek who persuaded the Trojans to take the fatal horse into the city walls. Imogen re-interprets the complicated ethics of Vergil's love story in light of the medieval Aeneas' overt treason: like Ovid's, her Aeneas betrays the vows of love and marriage and effectively sentences Dido to death.

When Imogen invokes her vividly interpreted Aeneas, she condenses the moral of Shakespeare's subsequent narrative: Posthumus must amend the emotional betrayal he shares with Vergil's hero and redeem himself through roughly Vergilian rites of passage. These rites begin when Posthumus battles the Romans and intensify when he is thrown into an underground prison. There, he descends into conscience, entering a quasi-Vergilian Underworld where he sees the shade of his father, hears a prophecy, and at last gains a national identity. As Patricia Parker convincingly argues, the ghosts of his family plead for Posthumus in Vergilian terms: presenting his battles and emotional hardship as moral *labor*, they finally persuade Jupiter to descend and preside over Posthumus' fate.[12]

As his mother Venus emphasizes in her imploring speeches to Jupiter in *Aeneid* 1 and 10, the pious Aeneas suffers in spite of his merits. The ghosts of Posthumus' father, mother, and two brothers similarly beg Jupiter to spare the virtuous Posthumus from continued miseries. Echoing Venus' complaint, his mother pleads, "Since, Jupiter, our son is good, / take off his miseries" (5.4.84–5). One brother notes that both brothers,

> striking in our country's cause,
> fell bravely and were slain,
> Our fealty and Tenantius' right
> with honour to maintain.   (5.4.71–4)

The second brother carries out the implicit argument about honorable toil:

> Like hardiment Posthumus hath
> to Cymbeline perform'd,
> Then, Jupiter, thou king of gods,
> why hast thou thus adjourn'd
> The graces for his merits due,
> being all to dolours turn'd?   (lines 75–80)

The brothers do not object to their deaths in battle, because their honorable sacrifice established them as national heroes. Posthumus, on the other hand, is disinherited from "Leonati seat," "With marriage . . . mock'd," and "exil'd" (lines 58–60). Worse, he is catapulted from classical epic and into an ignominious Italian novella, where he plays the vengeful cuckold to the hilt:

> Why did you suffer Iachimo,
> slight thing of Italy,
> To taint his nobler heart and brain
> with needless jealousy;
> And to become the geck and scorn
> o' th' other's villainy?   (lines 63–8)

The brothers argue that they were fortunate to die heroically in battle while Posthumus has suffered without redemption or honor: uprooted from family, cast out of his marriage, and exiled from his country, the youngest Leonatus has fallen precipitously or anachronistically into the villainous schemes of a latter-day Italian. Their claim refigures the cry of Aeneas, plagued by the storm Juno roused to thwart him: *o terque quaterque beati, / quis ante ora patrum Troiae sub moenibus altis / contigit oppetere*, "O three or four times blest were those who met death before their fathers' eyes beneath the high walls of Troy!" (1.94–6). With his first words in the epic, Aeneas expresses a submerged death wish and a diplomatic reminder that his mission is national – he is destined to found the high walls of Rome, as the seventh line of the poem announces. Posthumus' father, Sicilius, seconds the view that punishing Posthumus and the Leonati amounts to afflicting the British nation itself:

> Thy crystal window ope; look out;
> no longer exercise
> Upon a valiant race thy harsh
> and potent injuries.   (lines 81–4)

Sicilius implores Jupiter to look out and, like Vergil's Jupiter surveying the damages from Juno's storm, witness the injuries brought on by national jealousy.

Cymbeline's testy Jupiter follows Vergil's in answering family prayers with prophecies of national and personal peace. Vergil's father of the gods provides the closest thing to a conclusion in the epic when he assures Venus that Aeneas' trials will culminate in Roman glory and the *pax Romana*. In *Cymbeline*, Jupiter "descends in thunder and lightning, sitting upon an eagle: he throws a thunderbolt. The Ghosts fall on their knees." This irascible authoritarian proceeds to insult the "petty spirits of region low" and "Poor shadows of Elysium," and charges them no more to "Offend our hearing" and "Accuse the thunderer" (lines 93–5). When he softens his approach, telling them to go "rest / Upon your never-withering banks of flowers" in Vergil's Underworld and "be not with mortal accidents opprest," he echoes Aeneas' tragic bewilderment about the terrible desire of certain shades to leave the banks of Elysium and return to mortal bodies and the caprice of life (6.719–21).

Jupiter goes on to point out that inflicting trials upon Posthumus is the divine way of expressing care:

> No care of yours it is, you know 'tis ours.
> Whom best I love I cross; to make my gift,
> The more delay'd, delighted. Be content,
> Your low-laid son our godhead will uplift:
> His comforts thrive, his trials well are spent:
> Our Jovial star reign'd at his birth, and in
> Our temple was he married. Rise, and fade.
> He shall be lord of lady Imogen,
> And happier much by his affliction made.   (lines 100–8)

Vergil's Jupiter tells Venus to spare her fears (*parce metu*, 1.157), for he is mindful of her care (*cura*, 1.261): Aeneas will achieve the city and the "promised walls of Lavinium" (lines 258–9). *Cymbeline*'s Jupiter grants Posthumus a considerably more rewarding marital life than Aeneas' with his Latin bride, Lavinia, whose identity is absorbed by the city walls that take her name: Imogen, in fact, represents the full heights to which this "low-laid son" will be "uplifted." When Jupiter says that Posthumus will be "happier much by his affliction made" and asserts, "Whom best I love I cross; to make my gift, / The more delay'd, delighted," his words remind the reader of the *Aeneid* that Rome's greatness was measured by the afflictions and delays endured by its founder. The immediate difference between the fates allotted to the two men is personal "delight," which Jupiter never promises Aeneas. Aeneas, bravely lying through his teeth, is the one to express tentative optimism when he encourages his harassed companions to take a long view of their suffering: *forsan et haec olim meminisse iuvabit* ("Perhaps it will be a pleasure someday to recall even these events," 1.203). The tablet Jupiter leaves with Posthumus implies that the youth's happiness will correspond to the larger peace of the British nation. Aeneas will be "uplifted" to the stars and Rome will find peace and empire without end; Posthumus will "end his miseries, and Britain [will] be fortunate and flourish in peace and plenty" (5.4.143–4).

Posthumus' Vergilian itinerary differs significantly from the heroic course suggested by his family, who refuses to see Posthumus as the agent of his miseries. Blame has been the focus of several critical studies of *Cymbeline*, which attempt to settle the problem of Posthumus' violent jealousies in terms of genre. As Homer Swander points out, Shakespeare's protagonist is responsible for living up to a more complex characterological and ethical standard than the type known as the "blameless hero."[13] And yet, there is something to the Leonati's attempt to spare Posthumus from exclusive blame, for the young man falls headfirst into a misogynistic cultural convention with ancient roots. In Shakespeare's time-traveling fiction, Posthumus' derangement owes much to Italian genres and, less predictably, to Aeneas' latent gynephobia, for which Posthumus shoulders responsibility. This state of affairs controverts the old critical argument that Posthumus is blameless yet complicates the play's model of personal agency.

Cymbeline contests the imperial view of Aeneas' desertion of Dido: obliged by fate and divine command to observe a higher code of loyalty to the Roman family and empire of the Augustan future, Aeneas must repudiate Dido and, by extension, the treacherous changefulness that nature gives in too full a measure to women. At a turning point in book 4, Aeneas receives a visitation from a figure "like" Mercury, who whips up Aeneas' fears about the woman "hatching plots," and concludes with the famous dictum that Shakespeare reappraised in *Antony and Cleopatra*: *varium et mutabile semper / femina*, "woman is an ever changing and mutable thing." If the speaker is Mercury, then the sentiment is presumably unimpeachable, but it is probable that Aeneas' imagination has called up a simulacrum of Mercury to voice his own hysterical anxieties about Dido's plans to detain him or retaliate. Shakespeare settles on this axiom and amplifies both the topos and the paranoia:

                                    Could I find out
The woman's part in me – for there's no motion
That tends to vice in man, but I affirm
It is the woman's part: be it lying, note it,
The woman's: flattering, hers: deceiving, hers:
Lust, and rank thoughts, hers, hers: revenges, hers:
Ambitions, covetings, change of prides, disdain,
Nice longing, slanders, mutability;
All faults that name, nay, that hell knows, why, hers
In part, or all: but rather all. For even to vice
They are not constant, but are changing still. (2.4.171–81)

As rhetorical *amplificatio*, Posthumus' insane speech is exemplary. For all its variations, it never loses sight of its source in Vergil's claim that "the woman's part is still varying and changing still."[14] It is an obvious truth of Shakespeare's play that Posthumus must overcome his irrational suspicions in order to reintegrate his fragmented identity. It has become less obvious to audiences unfamiliar with the *Aeneid* that the play trains a relentless eye on the greatest fissure in the *Aeneid*'s commemoration of imperial Rome – Aeneas' abandonment of Dido – and uses it to propose a radical critique of Roman values.

Cymbeline reopens the question of how nationhood relates to love and sexuality that Aeneas settled when he declared that Rome, and not Dido, possessed his heart: *hic amor, haec patria est*. If Posthumus is to be worthy of rule, he must master not only his passions but also his fears in marriage, a challenge that lies beyond the epic parameters of the *Aeneid:* for Posthumus to become the British Aeneas, he must reverse the epic itinerary that took Aeneas from love in Carthage, to the transitional Underworld, and finally to Rome. Posthumus is "low-laid" when he sinks to the emotional and ideological depths of the fantasy which elaborates Aeneas' patriotic belief that women are changeful but an empire is without end. For both men, the phobia of dependence upon a woman leads to a descent into an Underworld – Posthumus' underground prison – and a prophecy of marriage and national peace. Posthumus' experiences, however, are rites of passage back into the marriage he violated.

Aeneas faces his greatest crisis of identity in Carthage, when he is identified primarily by his amorous association with Dido. Derisively termed a *semivir* by the native prince Iarbas, Aeneas is caught enjoying his luxurious ignominy when Mercury descends from the heavens to deliver Jupiter's rousing message. The god eyes Aeneas, *fundantem arces ac tecta novantem:*

> atque illi stellatus iaspide fulva
> ensis erat Tyrioque ardebat murice laena

demissa ex umeris, dives quae munera Dido
fecerat, et tenui telas discreverat auro.   (4.261–4)

His sword was starred with yellow jasper, and the cloak hanging from his shoulders blazed with Tyrian purple – a gift that wealthy Dido had made, and interwove the threads with cloth-of-gold.

Mercury's disdainful gaze writes shame over the image of Aeneas, draped in Dido's glittering wealth: the rugged masculinity Romans admired in their origins is threatened with feminine diminution. Aeneas recovers fully only when, in the Underworld, he is officially translated from a luxurious Trojan to a proto-Roman: there, his father calls him *Romane* for the first time and instructs him in the distinctively Roman imperatives to establish laws, spare the humble, and battle down the proud.

Like Aeneas, torn among Trojan, Carthaginian, and Roman identities, Posthumus suffers a crisis of national identity that he attempts to address when he battles as a British peasant and surrenders as a Roman. Yet stable identity is asymmetrically conferred on Aeneas and Posthumus. As Mercury's scornful Roman gaze reminds readers, Aeneas is hardly a man if he is not a Roman. Posthumus, on the other hand, earns the right to represent British masculinity only when he finds his identity through union with Imogen rather than over against his wife and, in fact, all womankind. Aeneas' crisis of national identity is sensationalized and gendered; Posthumus suffers an emotional and marital crisis that has national consequences. In *Cymbeline*, the order of politics owes concessions to the domestic sphere because, in the move from Augustan Rome to Britain, national identity is shifting its focus to the family and household.

Posthumus designs rites of contrition to undo his social identity, for he recognizes that he blamed the "woman's part" for social obstacles which frustrated him in Cymbeline's court: lying, flattering, deceiving, lust, rank thoughts, revenges, ambitions, covetings, change of prides, disdain, nice longing, slanders, mutability. He determines not to fight against Britain but to

> disrobe me
> Of these Italian weeds, and suit myself
> As does a Briton peasant: so I'll fight
> Against the part I come with: so I'll die
> For thee, O Imogen, even for whom my life
> Is, every breath, a death: and thus, unknown,
> Pitied, nor hated, to the face of peril
> Myself I'll dedicate. Let me make men know
> More valour in me than my habits show.
> Gods, put the strength o' th' Leonati in me!

To shame the guise o' th' world, I will begin,
The fashion less without, more within.   (5.1.22–33)

Posthumus adopts the guise of a lowly Briton, the most socially
disgraceful possibility of his unknown roots. In so doing, he addresses his
anxieties about the public contingency of his personal worth on Imogen.
He does not merely scale down or mystify his social claims, as grieving
knights do in romance fiction. Instead of playing the Arcadian game to
advantage, he attempts to invert the very purpose of courtly guises
themselves. By establishing the "fashion less without, more within," he
symbolically strips Britain of its courtly garb, down to its rugged
originary self. With the same gesture, he purges himself of his association
with the "tailor-made" Cloten. The manner in which Posthumus returns
to native virtue aligns him with Cymbeline's sons, whose mountaineers'
attire and habits accentuate their manly and royal worth. In purging
himself of cultured guises, Posthumus finds a role and a system of values
he can represent with conviction. The play fans Jacobean complacence
further in the knowledge that Italian courtly fashion is as effeminate as
Aeneas' Carthaginian luxury: the *translatio imperii* is advancing surely on
its westering course to Milford Haven – the site of Henry Tudor's
landing in England – and from this auspicious place it will march in
triumph with Cymbeline's family to "Lud's town."

In the next scene, Posthumus defeats Iachimo in a skirmish that leaves
the jaded Italian wondering how "could this carl, / A very drudge of
Nature's, have subdued me / In my profession?" Humiliated by a "lout,"
Iachimo gratifyingly moralizes his defeat as personal emasculation and
national inadequacy:

> The heaviness and guilt within my bosom
> Takes off my manhood: I have belied a lady,
> The princess of this country; and the air on't
> Revengingly enfeebles me . . .   (5.2.1–4)

When Posthumus is restored to manly virtue in gratifying proportion to
Iachimo's loss of it, the whole of Britain partakes of his new-found
integrity.

Posthumus' trials effectively rewrite his past in order to ensure a
happier future. In the play's final scene, he is rewritten as the "descended
god" he clearly was not. Iachimo dramatizes "the good Posthumus /
(What should I say? he was too good to be / Where ill men were, and was
the best of all / Amongst the rar'st of good ones)," and sets the youth on
a tragic stage:

> Upon a time, unhappy was the clock
> That struck the hour: it was in Rome, accurst

The mansion where: 'twas at a feast, O, would
Our viands had been poison'd (or at least
Those which I heaved to head).   (5.5.153–7)

This Posthumus is an image of patient self-containment damned by Machiavellian "practice."

If an audience is obliging enough to emend the memory of a volatile Posthumus grasping at vulgar straws to condemn Imogen – "I will kill thee if thou dost deny / Thou 'st made me cuckold" (2.4.145–6) – it is not because Iachimo has himself submitted to the "religion" he once found ridiculous in Posthumus. If an audience allows Posthumus to be rewritten as a continent man and blameless victim of Italian ingenuity, it is because the young man has cracked the rigid episteme of the jealous cuckold, the role prescribed to him by Iachimo's generic coordinates. Bernabò, Shakespeare's Boccaccian source, is embarrassed by the town's disapproval; the slightly more reflective Ambrose of *Frederick of Jennen* regrets "that he spake not with her before that he caused her to be put to death, to examyne her, wherfore John of Florence had the Jewels" (Arden, p. 205). Posthumus unveils his originality when he receives the bloody handkerchief as proof of Imogen's death:

Yea, bloody cloth, I'll keep thee: for I wish'd
Thou shouldst be colour'd thus. You married ones,
If each of you should take this course, how many
Must murder wives much better than themselves
For wrying but a little? O Pisanio,
Every good servant does not all commands:
No bond, but to do just ones. Gods, if you
Should have ta'en vengeance on my faults, I never
Had liv'd to put on this: so had you saved
The noble Imogen, to repent, and struck
Me, wretch, more worth your vengeance. But alack,
You snatch some hence for little faults; that's love,
To have them fall no more: you some permit
To second ills with ills, each elder worse . . .   (5.1.1–14)

While Ambrose wonders, momentarily, about his enemy's reliability and his own credulity, Posthumus astonishingly indicts his, and all men's, reliance on absolute judgment. His perspective is unthinkable for the men in *Much Ado about Nothing* and *Othello*, since it can imagine that so admirable a creature as the "noble Imogen" may "wry" without losing her value.[15]

Posthumus suggests that cultural understanding of the grounds for marriage and self-construction is due for a change: he voices a tough-minded epistemological position considered both culturally emergent and extraordinarily difficult to maintain. The position allows doubt to occupy space with admiration. A famous example is John Donne's poem, "The Good-Morrow," in which wonder is at once speculative, doubtful, and admiring: "I wonder, by my troth, what thou and I did, til we loved?" The poem and the epistemological state it depicts broach the union of wills and not the assimilation of the woman's will to the man's, a collapse that was a cornerstone in Tudor marriage doctrine.[16] The point was often stated in homilies, such as "An Homily of the State of Marriage" and "A Homily against Disobedience and Willful Rebellion," both contained in the two books of homilies that were mandatory reading in the Elizabethan Church. And it is the triumphant conclusion to Thomas Overbury's popular poem, "A Wife":[17]

> As *good* and *wise*; so be she *fit* for me,
> That is, to *will*, and *not to will* the same:
> My *wife* is my *adopted selfe*, and she
> As me, so what I love, to love must frame:
> For when by mariage both in one concurre,
> Woman converts to man, not man to her.

Overbury's distillation of conventional but hardly uncontested wisdom about proper marital relations helps bring into focus problems with James I's hotly argued point that the state is subordinate to him as a body to a head and a wife to a husband.[18] When James insisted that his relationship to the kingdom was like a marriage, and when, as Leah Marcus notes, he issued a coin inscribed, "*Quae Deus conjunxit nemo separet*, 'Those whom God hath joined together let no man put asunder,'" he reminded Parliament of his "headship" and its "subjection."[19] Important as the engagement of courtly preoccupations is to *Cymbeline*, there is a larger social and philosophical project that Shakespeare launches through scrutiny of the terms of marriage: the cuckold theme signals the need to change the structure of belief rather than be mastered by the will to absolute knowledge.[20] The epistemological directions of Posthumus' encounter with sexual doubt and misogyny prove to be of utmost importance to Shakespeare's thinking about British nationhood: they help explain why Shakespeare proposes Posthumus as a second Aeneas and an empire-builder only to rescind this contract at the play's end.

Imogen and the woman's part

The image of the truncated corpse bears on the interpretation of Imogen as well as Posthumus. The play makes a troubling spectacle of its heroine as she hovers over the body and mistakes Cloten for Posthumus in the minute details of his hand, his "foot Mercurial, his Martial thigh, / The brawns of Hercules" – all "but his Jovial face" (4.2.309–11). *Cymbeline* courts revulsion or ridicule from its audiences, moreover, when Imogen melodramatically smears her face with Cloten's blood: "O, / Give colour to my pale cheek with thy blood, / That we the horrider may seem to those / Which chance to find us. O my lord, my lord!" With these words, she falls upon the body, where she remains until the Roman commander Lucius finds her "dead, or sleeping . . . on [her] bloody pillow" (lines 355, 363). Imogen seems even "horrider" when Lucius points out that "nature doth abhor to make his bed / With the defunct, or sleep upon the dead" (lines 357–8). The spectacle uncomfortably mixes violence and comedy. It treats lightly the death of Cloten and, with less justification, presents Imogen's shock and grief over her husband as grotesque or post-tragic. The imperial significances of the image are reserved for the Cloten/Posthumus figure, the fallen Priam or "ruin [which] speaks that sometime / It was a worthy building" (lines 355–6). Less generous to Imogen, the scene punishes and dismisses her through blithe violence to her dignity.

The image, which functions similarly to the pit in *Titus Andronicus*, confounds distinct figures, roles, and genres: Posthumus and Cloten; Aeneas and Priam; imperial origins and decline; early Britain, imperial Rome, and early modern Italy; comedy and tragedy. It confounds these distinctions, moreover, at the very moment that it conjures the specter of a powerful but degenerate female sexuality. To call the scene bathetic is to take a defensive measure against a more threatening impression that the image generates with apparent irrelevance: her face smeared with the blood of the corpse over which she hovers, Imogen appears to have haled off the head of the man whose body she praises and strokes.[21]

Although she compares herself to Hecuba, she does not physically resemble Vergil's ancient Trojan queen lamenting the death of her husband. More immediate mythological precedents for Imogen are Ovid's bacchantes, such as Pentheus' mother Agave. Maddened by the powers of Dionysus, she fails to recognize her own son when he intrudes upon her bacchanalian rites. Mistaking him for a wild boar (perhaps a "full-acorn'd" one), Agave calls on her sisters to dismember her son. Pentheus' aunts each tear off an arm and, when Pentheus tries to plead with the arms that have been "lopped from his trunk," Agave howls and tears off Pentheus' head.

> non citius frondes autumni frigore tactas
> iamque male haerentes alta rapit arbore ventus,
> quam sunt membra viri manibus direpta nefandis.   (3.729–31)

The wind does not more quickly seize from the lofty tree its leaves, barely clinging, when they are touched by the cold of autumn, than are Pentheus' limbs ripped from him by those impious hands.

Posthumus/Cloten, too, is compared to a "trunk . . . Without his top" (4.2.353–4) and is guilty of the presumptuous skepticism that leads him to intrude upon the realm of female sexuality, despite an initial foreboding characterized as "religion." Like Pentheus' dismemberment, Imogen's blazon begins with a hand and ends with the head. As noted earlier, her blazon in which she lovingly identifies Posthumus' Mercurial foot, Martial thigh, Herculean chest, and murdered Jovial face resembles the blazon Cleopatra used to remember and reintegrate Antony on the transcendent plane of myth. But when Imogen parcels her beloved's body, she symbolically re-enacts the fragmentation of Posthumus' identity.

With the interpretive model of Agave and Pentheus in mind, Imogen provisionally doubles for Cymbeline's wicked queen. The queen, who dies in a frenzy over her lost son, is instrumental in producing Cloten's villainous character, and her malicious agency is answered by Guiderius, who sends "Cloten's clotpoll down the stream / In embassy to his mother" (4.2.184–5). The queen and Cloten, however, cannot absorb the full force of the allusion to Agave and Pentheus. The stubborn and counter-intuitive fact remains that Imogen is implicitly likened to a mother who dismembers and decapitates the son she fails to recognize. To criminalize Imogen, however, would be to join Posthumus in his paranoid distortion of Imogen's social and sexual power to make and unmake Posthumus. It is not Imogen's will but Posthumus' fears that turn her into a destructive mother.

Orpheus is the other mythological figure evoked by the spectacle of Imogen as a bacchante apparently in the act of dismembering a man. Critics note in Cloten's fate an allusion to Orpheus, whose tongue went babbling down a river after the poet was torn apart by enraged bacchant women. *Cymbeline* makes cheeky use of details of Orpheus' death other than his conveyance down the river. Cloten is an obscene poet who wants to "penetrate" Imogen with his "fingering" and if that is insufficient, he says, "we'll try the tongue too" (2.3.14–15). Since Cloten is decapitated and not dismembered, Orpheus' death is farmed out to the comic fate Cloten wishes on Posthumus and his clothes: "Posthumus," he declares in apostrophe, "thy head (which now is growing upon thy shoulders) shall within this hour be off . . . [and] thy garments cut to pieces before thy face" (4.1.17–20).

Although his death is unlamented, the allusions to Orpheus seem to dignify Cloten quite without desert. Cymbeline's sons, in fact, explicitly ask why the villainous oaf deserves royal burial rites. One answer is that dignifying Cloten might serve the conservatism of the play, which makes transgressive proposals only to foreclose on the possibilities. Although the play approaches *Troilus and Cressida* in its suspicion of the arbitrary and socially constructed value bestowed on men, it also confirms Cloten's social status at the last: Belarius comments that the "foe was princely, / And though you took his life as being our foe, / Yet bury him as a prince" (4.2.249–51). Yet no one thinks the better of Cloten for receiving comparison with Orpheus. Possibly, then, upgrading Cloten attempts to undo some of the damage done to Posthumus' reputation for sinking to the depths of the queen's son.[22] Although the options are worth pursuing, particularly in view of *Cymbeline*'s habit of generating enigmas, it is unlikely that Orpheus dignifies either man. On the contrary, their conspicuous failings indict the great poet for a signal weakness for which he is rarely condemned in the twentieth century. Shakespeare was one of the early modern readers of Ovid who considered the poet's death by dismemberment a punishment for misogyny.[23] The bacchantes dismember the poet who chose to "sing of boys chosen by the gods and girls struck by lawless desires and the punishment they have earned for their lust" (*puerosque canamus / dilectos superis inconcessisque puellas / ignibus attonitas meruisse libidine poenam*, 10.152–4) or, in the words of Posthumus, to "write against them, / Detest them, curse them" (2.4.183–4). Misogyny is the emotional derangement that causes Posthumus figuratively to lose his head.

The violent and compromising image of Imogen relates primarily to Posthumus' peculiar breakdown into constituent but warring roles – imperial founder (Aeneas) and bearer of cultural degeneration (Priam, Cloten), mythical colossus and dismembered body. Brought on by his deranging sexual and social doubts, the image transforms Imogen into a kind of perspective painting: one way she's painted like a menacing specter of sexual voracity, the other way she's a pathetic emblem of feminine weakness. The emblem of Imogen radicalizes the division and amplification that Iachimo develops to describe her sexual power for Posthumus. Iachimo reads and reinscribes Imogen as a renaissance Italian text in the line of Ovid. As in *Titus Andronicus*, Ovid's narrative techniques alienate a Vergilian precedent from its proper ideological context. The rhetorical and narrative methods of Ovid and his Italian literary descendants wrench Posthumus from his simple faith and positive associations with Aeneas.

To bifurcate Imogen on sexual grounds, Iachimo adopts the figure of the *Venus armata*, drawn from *Aeneid* 1, which was the renaissance's favorite image for chaste eroticism. Tucked in his trunk in Imogen's bedroom, a latter-day Sinon with his Trojan horse, Iachimo arises to imagine himself as Tarquin out to rape Lucrece. He marks Imogen's body inconsistently with conventional signs of both sexuality and virginity: "Cytherea, / How bravely thou becom'st thy bed! fresh lily!" (2.2.13–14). The exclamation that initially identifies her as Venus concludes with a celebration of her as a virginal lily. A gifted erotic poet, Iachimo dwells on her lips and eyes in an ornamental blazon:

> But kiss, one kiss! Rubies unparagon'd,
> How dearly they do't: 'tis her breathing that
> Perfumes the chamber thus: the flames o' th' taper
> Bows toward her, and would under-peep her lids,
> To see th' enclosed lights, now canopied
> Under these windows, white and azure lac'd
> With blue of heaven's own tinct.   (2.2.17–23)

Although he excels in this kind of description, Iachimo knows how to defer rhetorical *amplificatio* for its proper occasion. Despite a momentary stir to imitate Tarquin's rape, he has come to read Imogen's body:

> But to my design.
> To note the chamber: I will write all down:
> Such, and such pictures: there the windows, such
> Th' adornment of her bed; the arras, figures,
> Why, such, and such; and the contents o' th' story.
> Ah, but some natural notes about her body
> Above ten thousand meaner moveables
> Would testify, t' enrich mine inventory.   (lines 23–30)

Iachimo is preparing two overlapping narrative activities: his Ovidian erotic poem and his defense against the charge of rape. Subscribing to the view that rape is not theft of property but a matter of consent, he prepares his "notes" to furnish a narrative of willing seduction. The bedroom's elaborate decor furnishes him with circumstantial evidence. For harder proof, he forces Imogen's body to supply "natural notes" to "testify" that he is not, he later tells Posthumus, "the wronger / Of her or you, having proceeded but / By both your wills" (2.4.554–6). Imogen's body serves also as the chief adornment of his erotic epyllion, and Iachimo pretends, as Ulysses said of Cressida, to "wide unclasp the tables of [her] thoughts / To every ticklish reader" (4.5.60–1) in his rhetorical "inventory." The bookishness of the scene contrasts painfully with the immediate threat of rape that Iachimo presents as he pores over Imogen's sleeping body and teaches the audience to read her vulnerable body with rapacious eyes. Shakespeare is careful to credit the classical authority Iachimo will employ to transform those opaque deictics – "Why, such, and such" – into lurid detail: Iachimo picks up the book Imogen was reading when she fell asleep, and finds that it is the "tale of Tereus, here the leaf's turn'd down / Where Philomel gave up" (lines 45–6). Ovid is the *locus classicus* for narratives of inflamed desires and jealousies, and as his Italian descendant, Iachimo offers to refine Ovidian technique.[24]

Iachimo's technical innovation is to expand and polarize the chaste eroticism he perceived in Imogen, the Cytherea and chaste lily. His success is measured by Posthumus' acknowledgment that Imogen's synthesis of cold chastity and warm sexuality is precisely what gives her unnerving power:

> Me of my lawful pleasure she restrain'd,
> And pray'd me oft forbearance: did it with
> A pudency so rosy, the sweet view on't
> Might well have warm'd old Saturn; that I thought her
> As chaste as unsunn'd snow.   (2.4.161–5)

Iachimo seeks to break into inconsistent halves the synthesis of chastity and eros symbolized by Vergil's *Venus armata*. He criminalizes sexuality and chastity alike by describing Imogen's artwork as solicitation. The first is a tapestry of Cleopatra, herself a consummate work of art:

> her bedchamber,
> (Where I confess I slept not, but profess
> Had that was well worth watching) it was hang'd
> With tapestry of silk and silver, the story
> Proud Cleopatra, when she met her Roman,
> And Cydnus swell'd above the banks, or for
> The press of boats, or pride. A piece of work
> So bravely done, so rich, that it did strive
> In workmanship and value; which I wonder'd
> Could be so rarely and exactly wrought,
> Since the true life on't was –   (2.4.66–76)

Posthumus dismisses Iachimo's detailed knowledge of the tapestry, pointing out that the Italian could have heard it described by Posthumus himself, "Or by some other" (line 78). Yet he might well wish he were the only man able to recite such an intimate engagement with the tapestry, for Iachimo takes pains to stress the solicitation in the craftsmanship and its female subject alike. Had Posthumus not interrupted Iachimo's description, enriched with eroticism displaced from Imogen, the Italian might have gone on to claim that the "true life on't was" its replication of Imogen's proud sexuality.

The second work of art Iachimo describes as a mirror of Imogen features Diana, the goddess opposed to the seductiveness summed up in Cleopatra:

> the chimney-piece,
> Chaste Dian, bathing: never saw I figures
> So likely to report themselves; the cutter
> Was as another Nature, dumb; outwent her,
> Motion and breath left out.   (lines 81–5)

No one is more likely than this chaste Diana to "report" herself as she bathes. In Iachimo's account, it is abundantly clear that the artist transformed his subject's source, which is Ovid's tale of Diana and Actaeon: this Diana *wants* to be viewed, and Ovid's Actaeon is nowhere to be seen. Ovid's Diana sought to hide her naked body and transformed Actaeon into a stag with the words, *nunc tibi me posito visam velamine narres, / sit poteris narrare, licet!* (3.192-3), which Golding renders, "Now make thy vaunt among thy Mates, thou sawste *Diana* bare, / Tell if thou can: I give thee leave: tell heardly: do not spare." The Diana represented in the plastic arts and described in the *Golden Ass*, Iachimo points out, can hardly be kept from describing herself. Actaeon's place is left vacant so that it may be occupied by the viewer. Iachimo, who usurps Posthumus' pleasure in gazing on Imogen, takes on the role of an Actaeon ravished by the spectacle. He indulges in the role of an Actaeon privileged to see and tell so that he may induce Posthumus, too, to see with Actaeon's eyes. Imogen's husband is placed in the intolerable position of gazing on his wife as narratively described by a supposed seducer: he instantaneously feels the burden of Actaeon's punishment, loses his identity, and acquires the horns of a cuckold.

The common terms in the images of Cleopatra and Diana are seductive narratives, female erotic power, and voyeurism. Classical in origin, the texts are received as early modern productions and placed in the service of a plot from Boccaccio, the great Italian inheritor of Ovid. Since Antony is not represented in Iachimo's reweaving of classical texts, Cleopatra might meet *any* Roman, such as Iachimo. His narrative techniques bring about Posthumus' crisis, a psychological fragmentation that is later figured in the theme of dismemberment that haunts both Cloten and Posthumus. Although Actaeon found a new identity as a cuckold in poetry and on the Jacobean stage, Shakespeare follows Ovid in moving from internal alienation to physical dismemberment.

Cymbeline delights in having things both ways, so it is unsurprising that the radical conclusion of Posthumus' trials in his acceptance of sexual doubts runs counter to the play's conservative impulses satisfied by its simplification of Imogen.[25] Posthumus learns to wedge open his experience of wonder to admit doubt, even in the extreme case of sexual jealousy – extreme because the Other seems too powerfully constitutive of one's own identity. Yet *Cymbeline* does not require the same harrowing experience of its audience. There is never a shred of doubt about Imogen's innocence. Furthermore, the play goes out of its way to reduce the powerful threat she poses to her husband socially and iconographically. Only when Imogen hovers emblematically over Posthumus' corpse is the audience invited to grapple with her significations. Classical allusions again serve to complicate the audience's understanding of Imogen when Iachimo rewrites her chaste and erotic duality as duplicity in his descriptions of Cleopatra and a "Dian [who] has hot dreams." Through the texts and myths adduced to interpret Imogen, the audience and Posthumus both confront powerful and enigmatic images of the British princess.

Pisanio's plot for Imogen to dress as a boy and serve the Roman commander Lucius promises to strengthen the assertiveness characteristic of the *Venus armata*. The ulterior motive of her travels and cross-dressing – to keep an eye on Posthumus – invites comparison with Britomart and her quest to find her future husband. *Cymbeline* prepares for such a transformation of Imogen into a lady knight of romance epic when Pisanio proposes that she

> forget to be a woman: change
> Command into obedience: fear, and niceness
> (The handmaids of all women, or more truly,
> Woman it pretty self) into a waggish courage,
> Ready in gibes, quick-answer'd, saucy, and
> As quarrelous as the weasel . . .   (3.4.155–60)

Imogen answers that she can "see into thy end, and am almost / A man already" (lines 168–9), and asserts, "This attempt / I am soldier to, and will abide it with / A prince's courage" (lines 183–5). As a boy, however, Imogen becomes a weak and feeble woman without the heart and stomach of a king. She collapses into the "nice" creature Pisanio calls "Woman it pretty self," although she was self-assertive in woman's garb. The crossed-gender motifs and the powerfully figured sexuality iconographically expressed in the *Venus armata* image are undone by Imogen's appearance as a boy. Instead of feeling exhilarated like Rosalind, she becomes a sickly, frightened thing who inspires pity and protectiveness in every man she meets – her rough brothers, Lucius, and her father, as well as admiring critics.[26] The play progressively unsettles her strength and integrity. Its central image provides an extreme representation of her discomposure: she is not constituted but ~~undone~~ by rival interpretive conventions.

Grass roots: Britain's Romulus and Remus and the resources of pastoral

So far, the mingle-mangle of models adduced to construct national and characterological identity confirms *Cymbeline* in a diffident and erratic relationship to its principal theme of authority. Its representatives of cultural authority are by no means stable. To summarize: the offstage Augustus Caesar and his newly-established empire must cede to Cymbeline's Britain their claim to originary virtue; Vergil's Aeneas finds a spiritual descendant in Posthumus, but, dishearteningly, mostly because the young Briton emulates him in abandoning his Dido; and Cymbeline himself exhibits his authority primarily in its abuse, his tyranny over Imogen, and reliance on the counsel of his Queen, whose evil is transparent to all save the king. The atmosphere of Cymbeline's uneasy and gossipy court recalls that of James I. Malcolm Smuts observes that

The lapses in decorum within the court . . . the mounting costs of the royal household, and James's own surliness in public all tarnished the monarchy's prestige, inhibiting spontaneous public support. There are no Jacobean parallels to the *Faerie Queen[e]*, *the Book of Martyrs*, or the profusion of loyal ballads produced in the 1580s and 1590s. In an age when Englishmen were writing and gossiping about politics more than ever before, their ruler had ceased to be an effective symbol of national aspirations.[27]

Like James, "Cymbeline is less a man than a centre of tensions due to his royal office; persuaded, attacked, tugged asunder and finally re-established by the various themes and persons" (p. 130), as Knight astutely remarks in a less-than-reverent account that makes sense of the play's skewed relationship to symbolic centers of authority.[28]

The greatest display of authority in *Cymbeline* – possibly the most absolute in all of Shakespeare – shades into awkward hyperbole. In Posthumus' vision, "Jupiter descends in thunder and lightning, sitting upon an eagle: he throws a thunderbolt. The Ghosts fall on their knees." Jupiter inspires an awe in the Leonati's ghosts that he is unlikely to achieve in an audience. It is enough to ask an actor to keep his balance on the descending mechanical eagle while he hurls his thunderbolt; it is too much to require him to manage his props with Olympian aplomb. The play's strongest assertion of authority, from none other than the father of the gods, is also its clumsiest theatrical display.[29] Jupiter's prophecy, moreover, barely meets classical requirements:

When as a lion's whelp shall, to himself unknown, without seeking find, and be embrac'd by a piece of tender air: and when from a stately cedar shall be lopp'd branches, which, being dead many years, shall after revive, be jointed to the old stock, and freshly grow, then shall Posthumus end his miseries, Britain be fortunate, and flourish in peace and plenty. (5.4.138–45)

The prophecy's syntax has a greater potential to mislead than its facile puns. Its status as prophecy suggests a causal relation between the constituent elements of the temporal clause – Posthumus' self-discovery, his reunion with Imogen, the recovery of Cymbeline's sons – and the result clause, in which Posthumus ends his miseries and Britain flourishes. In fact, the prophecy indiscriminately mixes two distinct narrative strands, one marital and the other imperial. In a restricted sense, Jupiter's prophecy is literally incoherent: it can be translated into Latin and back into English so that Leonatus finds himself and his wife, Cymbeline his sons, and Britain its prosperity, but there is no joining the distinct family plots, which diverge into private and public spheres. Any sense that Posthumus' epistemological and psychological discoveries will facilitate the imperial prosperity of Britain is illusory.

Cymbeline advances Posthumus as the inheritor of Aeneas, but retracts his corresponding dynastic function when the missing princes are restored to court. Posthumus, it turns out, takes on the *Aeneid* to revise the epic's ideological stance on domestic, erotic, and subjective matters but not to modify the imperial directions of Aeneas. Posthumus' anti-Vergilian goals are the epistemological opening of the British mind and amorous, not dynastic, union in marriage. His reward is to become a heroic husband. *Cymbeline* promotes domestic and epistemological concerns through Posthumus but, more explicitly than the *Aeneid*, divorces the domestic from the imperial. Politically, Posthumus declines from heir apparent to the heirs' brother-in-law. The place of privilege is occupied by Cymbeline's hyper-masculine sons, who appear to be wholly free of the "woman's part" with which Posthumus bravely comes to terms only to be barred from epic and imperial exemplarity.

Unlike Posthumus, the boys seamlessly relate to the *translatio imperii*. Primarily through Posthumus and Imogen, *Cymbeline* scatters authority and exploits the potential divisions among the literary and political exemplars that must concur if they are to transmit authority. *Cymbeline* pitches its divisive contaminations against a stable authority that must be reintegrated if the play is to produce a singular and politically usable discourse on the *translatio imperii*. The reintegration comes in the secondary plot, in which the king's lost sons – unlike Posthumus, who flirts with Italian degeneracy – mingle sources and times with unambiguous valor. Britain's deliverance comes mainly from these sons, restored at the last to their father. In contrast to the renaissance Italianisms of Iachimo and the British court, they are marked by a blend of native and Roman qualities, English chronicle and Roman mythology. Holinshed's *Chronicles* have long been recognized as the source for the wondrous event at the lane, which Posthumus describes first heroically and then reduces to an angry riddle, "Two boys, an old man twice a boy, a lane, / Preserv'd the Britons, was the Romans' bane" (5.3.57–8). Posthumus is enraged that the British lord reacts to his stirring heroic narrative as if it took no tough native valor to seize the day, only a "strange chance: / A narrow lane, an old man, and two boys" (lines 51–2). Whether he is gathering samples of native wit suited for Camden's *Remains of Britaine*, or material for a ballad or broadside that he might "vent . . . for a mock'ry" (line 56), the lord is unresponsive to the techniques of heroic narrative – the speeches, hyperbole, epic similes, and catalogues.

Epic and chronicle devices establish the manly virtue of Cymbeline's sons: at last tested in battle after years of rustic training, the boys prove that Britain's great chronicle history supplies their generic and textual roots. The episode from Holinshed features a Scottish farmer, Haie, and his two sons, who come to the aid of the Scots in a battle against the Danes.[30] When the Scots arrived at the point of defeat, it happened that there

was in the next field at the same time an husbandman, with two of his sons busie about his worke, named Haie, a man strong and stiffe in making and shape of his bodie, but indued with a valiant courage. This Haie beholding the king with the most part of the nobles, fighting with great valiancie in the middle ward, now destitute of the wings, and in great danger to be oppressed by the great violence of his enimies, caught a plow-beame in his hand, and with the same exhorting his sonnes to doo the like, hasted towards the battell, there to die rather amongst other in defense of his countrie, than to remaine alive after the discomfiture in miserable thraldome and bondage of the cruell and most unmercifull enimies. There was neere to the place of the battell, a long lane fensed on the sides with ditches and walles made of turfe, through the which the Scots which fled were beaten downe by the enimies on heapes. Here Haie with his sonnes, supposing they might best staie the flight, placed themselves overthwart the lane, beat them backe whome they met fleeing, and spared neither friend nor fo: but downe they went all such as came within their reach, wherwith diverse hardie personages cried unto their fellowes to returne backe unto the battell, for there was a new power of Scotishmen come to their succours, by whose aid the victorie might be easilie obtained of their most cruell adversaries the Danes: therefore might they choose whether they would be slaine of their owne fellowes comming to their aid, or to returne againe to the fight with the enimies. The Danes being here staied in the lane by the great valiancie of the father and sonnes, thought verely there had beene some great succors of Scots come to the aid of their king . . .

Haie, who in such wise (as is before mentioned) staied them that fled, causing them to returne againe to the field, deserued immortall fame and commendation: for by his means chieflie was the victorie atchiued.

Cymbeline closely follows the illustrious and home-bred model. According to Posthumus, who adopts the sequence and specific vocabulary of Holinshed's narrative, "the king himself / Of his wings destitute, the army broken, / And but the backs of Britons seen; all flying / Through a strait lane," where the enemy struck them down until "the strait pass was damm'd / With dead men" (5.3.4–7, 9–12). At the lane, which was "Close by the battle, ditch'd, and wall'd with turf," an "ancient soldier . . . with two striplings" took their stand and "cried to those who fled" (lines 19–23) commands to fight the Romans or die at their hands.

In other respects, Posthumus diverges from the chronicle. Holinshed makes much of Haie and very little of his sons, while Posthumus lavishes more attention on the fair youths than on Belarius, who is simply not the hero that Haie is. When he recommends flight higher in the mountains and fears death, he earns Guiderius' reproof: "This is, sir, a doubt / In such a time nothing becoming you, / Nor satisfying us" (4.4.14–16). The boys rally the old man into battle – a scenario reversing the one in Holinshed – and they do so despite the threat to Guiderius, who killed Cloten and refuses to hide the fact.

Posthumus also adds rousing epic diction to Holinshed. He employs compound epithets, from start to finish, and from "the enemy full-hearted" (line 7) to each Briton, finally transformed into "the slaughter-man of twenty" (line 49). As he hurtles into the pitch of heroic description, Posthumus' epic similes run thick: the three inspired others "to look / The way that they did, and to grin like lions / Upon the pikes of hunters" (lines 37–9) and the enemy soldiers "fly / Chickens, the way which they stoop'd eagles" (lines 41–2). Another modification is the direct report of speech, a conventional feature of both classical epic and history. Whereas Holinshed reports that the men turned back by Haie and sons "cried unto their fellowes to returne backe unto the battell, for there was a new power of Scotishmen come to their succours," Belarius and Cymbeline's sons are "Three thousand confident, in act as many" (line 29), and do not rely on deception. They are also the ones who "cried unto those that fled," and Posthumus furnishes the exact words:

> "Our Britain's harts die flying, not our men:
> To darkness fleet souls that fly backwards; stand,
> Or we are Romans, and will give you that
> Like beasts which you shun beastly, and may save
> But to look back in frown: stand, stand!"   (lines 24–8)

The differences in both narrative detail and technique do not obscure the battle's source in Holinshed, the native chronicle. Instead, they set the British story on a template of classical Roman epic and history.

Cymbeline adapts Holinshed as a native British source for exemplary masculinity; the Scottish derivation would please James I all the more. The classical Roman motifs absent from Holinshed suggest that the British source is actually the upper layer of a cultural palimpsest which, if the pages of Holinshed's chronicle were turned back, would reveal an imperial Roman base. Although the Arden editor notes that for "the story of Belarius and the kidnapped princes . . . nothing that can really be termed a source has, as yet, been identified" (pp. xvii–xviii), there is a famous model for the theft of princely sons who later come to the aid of their kingly relation: the story of Romulus and Remus, as told by both Livy and Plutarch. Perhaps critics concerned with sources have so well understood the importance of the specifically British heritage of *Cymbeline* that the classical Roman model has been rendered invisible, like the buried portion of a palimpsest. Cymbeline's sons, however, are fortified by Roman precedents which – paradoxically, were it not for the translation of empire – reinforce their thoroughly British character. The battle represents their coming of age and their entrance into their British imperial destiny. Were they unable to "gild" the Britons' "pale looks" and make men out of "harts," then Cymbeline's sons might literally have chosen to be Romans aligned with Augustus Caesar: "stand, / Or we are Romans" (5.3.25–6).

Plutarch tells us of the strife between two brothers, descendants of Aeneas, over the succession. Amulius usurped Numitor's right by forcing his daughter, Ilia, to become a vestal virgin, thus cutting off the succession. The plan went awry when Ilia was raped by Mars and gave birth to twins, Romulus and Remus. Amulius then "commounded one of his men to take the two children, and throwe them awaye, and destroye them. Some say that this servants name was Faustulus: other thincke it was he that brought them up" (p. 34).[31] This Faustulus, who was the "chief neatherd to Amulius" (p. 36), raised the boys with his wife. Romulus and Remus stood apart from the rustic and pastoral context of their upbringing, and "wholy gave them selves to all gentlemanly exercises and trades, thincking to live idely and at ease without travell, was neither comly nor convenient: but to exercise and harden their bodyes with hunting, running, pursuing murderers and theeves, and to helpe those which were oppressed with wronge and violence, shoulde be credit and commendation to them" (p. 37). Even Cloten's scurrilous accusation that Guiderius is "a robber, / A law-breaker, a villain" (4.2.74–5) bears upon a passage in Livy, who describes the youthful days of Rome's founders, who as[32] grown boys . . . began to go hunting in the woods; their strength grew with their resolution, until not content only with the chase they took to atacking robbers and sharing their stolen goods with their friends the shepherds. (I.5)

In both accounts, Remus is seized by the robbers and taken to Numitor for justice. At this point, the history of Romulus and Remus grows strikingly close to the last scene of *Cymbeline*. According to Plutarch, Faustulus,

hearing that Remus was prisoner . . . went to pray Romulus to helpe him, and tolde him whose children they were: for before he had never opened it to them but in darcke speaches, and glawnsingwise . . . So Faustulus taking the troughe [in which he had found the twins] with him at that time, whent unto Numitor in great haste, as marveilously affrayed for the present daunger he thought Remus in. (p. 39)

Having discovered their true parentage and their royal identities, Romulus and Remus help their grandfather Numitor overthrow the tyrant Amulius.

Belarius, Cymbeline's man though no neatheard, marries the boys' nurse for her aid in stealing them. He heads to the wilds of Wales and raises them on hard pastoral. When we meet the boys, they are darting up mountains to hunt. Their hard physical activities figure in their every scene as matters of custom and competition: their putative father "train'd [them] up" (5.5.338) by making a daily contest of their hunting. Belarius confesses the boys' heritage and his theft only when he sees that Guiderius' life is in danger for killing Cloten. To verify his testimony, he produces the "most curious mantle" in which Arviragus was "lapp'd" at the time of the kidnapping (lines 361–2). The primary difference between their stories is that Romulus and Remus aid their grandfather after they discover their heritage and kinship, while Arviragus and Guiderius assist their father before the discovery.

In both the Roman and British cases, the discovery of sons whose valor is all the greater for their rugged upbringing promises a new era for the nation. Romulus founded the walls of Rome; his authority, vested in Guiderius, passes to Lud's town at the end of *Cymbeline*, when the king orders "A Roman, and a British ensign [to] wave / Friendly together" and the Romans and Britons to ratify a peace in "the temple of great Jupiter" (5.5.483) in Lud's town. The "harmony of this peace" (line 468) is reflected in the seamless blending of Roman and British sources to body forth Guiderius and Arviragus. Their contamination of models represents an integration of traditions, a fulfillment of the *translatio imperii*.

The decision to negotiate with the Romans establishes more than the

Britons' ethical inheritance of Roman *virtus*, for they are able to moderate the fiercer effects of Roman emulation. Guiderius' decapitation of Cloten – as well as his verbal bravery – inspires an honest admission of envy in his brother:

> would I had done't;
> So the revenge alone pursued me! Polydore,
> I love thee brotherly, but envy much
> Thou hast robb'd me of this deed.   (4.2.156–9)

Romulus, on the other hand, slew his brother for his insulting leap over the growing walls of Romulus' city. The British Romulus and Remus, in fact, fulfill the prophecy of Jupiter in Book 1 of the *Aeneid* better than the Roman originals. Jupiter foretells that "Romulus, taking pleasure in the tawny hide of his nurse, the wolf, will take up the people and found the walls of Mars, and he will call them Romans after his own name" (*lupae fulvo nutricis tegmine laetus | Romulus excipiet gentem et Mavortia condet | moenia Romanosque suo de nomine dicet*, 1.275–7). He then adds a detail which jars with history: "Romulus with his brother Remus will give laws" (*Remo cum fratre Quirinus | iura dabunt*, lines 292–3). Like Romulus and Remus, Cymbeline's sons were trained up in a hard pastoral world, an ethical and physical boot camp. Under Belarius' tedious tutelage, Mantuan didacticism permeates the rugged Welsh landscape and foregrounds the moral lessons, evidently to the boys' advantage. Like Duke Senior, Belarius finds sermons and social criticism in every rock and tree. The deliberate educational program, in which the boys are weaned on moralized pastoral and georgic genres, enables them to moderate the divisive character of rivalry for which Romulus and Remus are notorious. Their fraternal rivalry sewed the seeds of civic restiveness in Rome's future, and the civil wars were only put to rest with the rise of Augustus Caesar. When Cymbeline's sons engage in epic battle for their father, they bring about national peace. And that battle, as *Cymbeline* takes pains to stress, takes place near Milford Haven, where Henry Tudor landed to put an end to the War of the Roses.[33]

Jacobean Cymbeline

Cymbeline engages the double form of romance epic, in which the romance wanderings of narrative and the male protagonist's imagination are finally brought under restraint by the epic machinery of closure.[34] Unlike romance epic, however, resolution is not achieved through dynastic marriage: Posthumus recovers his integrity and enjoys a reunion with Imogen, but he does not fulfill the imperial and dynastic promise implicit in Jupiter's prophecy. The play misleadingly uses the powers of allusion to mark his failure and subsequent recovery as stages in an imperial epic itinerary, for Posthumus is Priam at his lowest point and Aeneas as he begins his steady ascent from a Vergilian nadir. Despite his precedents, Posthumus is only accidentally linked to the flourishing of Britain. In *Cymbeline*, Shakespeare introduces romance epic conventions but curiously rejects the genre's final means of justifying its blend of romance and epic, which is to treat romance wanderings in epistemology and the subjective experience of desire as an extended moment of suspension and a stage preparatory to the hero's transcendent assumption of political responsibility. *Cymbeline* effectively bifurcates romance epic into separate genres and worlds of experience: the domestic and subjective realms do not find fulfillment in dynastic service.

The play reiterates these generic issues at the level of characterological construction: why, when Posthumus suffers from textual contamination, do Cymbeline's sons enjoy an undisturbed line of descent from Rome to Britain and from classical to early modern sources? The boys reinvent Roman virtues and neatly synthesize Livy, Plutarch, and Holinshed, while Posthumus is a psychologically and textually distracted character. It seems that Posthumus is proposed as a dynastic and imperial hero primarily to dramatize his removal from the line of royal authority and relegation to a purely domestic and characterological function. At the center of the play, Posthumus vacillates between representing British origins and his nation's potential dissolution in Italianate decadence. At the play's end, however, we find that if his experiences in epistemological doubt have any bearing on his final social position, they have disqualified him from serious political consideration. If he is indeed a "descended god," in Iachimo's hyperbole, his destiny is to be a courtly ornament, a courtier who continues to feel that he will never achieve the coveted role of a "statist."

The radical element in Posthumus' experiences and Cymbeline's court is the role played by the "woman's part," which has divergent effects on the young man's characterological and political identities. At the end of the play, the Queen dies in madness and Imogen joyfully cedes her place in the succession to her brothers. In this way, *Cymbeline* neutralizes the power of the "woman's part" to disrupt masculine authority and transfers it from the political to the domestic stage. When female power is safely dismantled, so is the political promise in Posthumus: his claim to succession depended entirely on Imogen and his dramatic function was to confront the sexual and social doubts that he summed up as the "woman's part." Furthermore, Posthumus is at the center of the romance plot which unleashed the transgressive meanings of allusion.

Romance, women, doubt, subversion: all are subordinated to the epic simplicity of the play's political conclusions, in which Cymbeline's hyper-masculine and characterologically underdeveloped sons are restored to their father and the British court.

On the other hand, the "woman's part" allows Posthumus to gain in interiority what he loses in imperial promise. The young Briton began the play as a cipher, his virtues describable only by the ineffability topos. He is not, however, merely translated from one generic stereotype to another, or from the orphan of heroic narrative to jealous cuckold to dynastic progenitor. He has a complex relationship to his history and to the versions of himself which might, in a characterologically simpler man, simply be stages in the itinerary of a master genre. The character-ological status of Cymbeline's sons, for example, is wholly governed by imperial exigencies. Their education in the rigors of hard pastoral and georgic do not promote a complex interiority; on the contrary, they empty the boys of stray and ungovernable distinctions that might interfere with their epic exemplarity. Although Posthumus' textual complications finally bar him from the throne, there is no reason to assume that his characterological deepening renders Posthumus politi-cally insignificant. It might, on the other hand, broaden the sphere of politics in Cymbeline's Britain and on the Jacobean stage: his asymme- trical relation to the dominant British power might suggest models of political agency that complement or counter royal power. It is not clear that Shakespeare endorses James I's view that political authority was reducible to his royal power and that the throne was the center from which all cultural power should exfoliate.

This chapter, mainly concerned with the uses of generic and textual forms to engage political issues and place them on the Jacobean stage, leads to the conclusion that Shakespeare's contaminations promote a sense of national identity that is considerably broader than the restricted authority James I passionately and stridently sought to establish. Since critics have discussed amply the ways in which *Cymbeline* ambiguously adopts James I's political rhetoric, that argument needs little elaboration here. James' speeches, in which domestic and corporeal union figure as tropes of his own absolute authority, feature images of corporal and marital union that are of considerable interest to *Cymbeline*.[35] Speaking of the possible union of Scotland and Britain, James wished to "discourse more particularly of the benefits that doe arise of that Union which is made in my blood, being a matter that most properly belongeth to me to speak of, as the head wherein that great Body is united."[36] He continues to base his arguments for union on his absolute authority and the integrity of his natural body:

What God hath conioyned then, let no man separate. I am the Husband, and all the whole Isle is my flocke: I hope therefore no man will be so unreasonable as to thinke that I am a Christian King under the Gospel, should be a Polygamist and husband to two wives; that I being the Head, should have a divided and monstrous body . . . (p. 273)

In *Cymbeline*, absolutist rhetoric echoes in the unflattering spectacle of the headless corpse which sums up marital division and national collapse.

Cymbeline treads a fine line between affirmation and parody of James I's absolutist claims. If *Cymbeline* endorses the political rhetoric which appropriates domestic and corporal images to affirm James' singular royal authority, then the play would have to subordinate familial organization to politics narrowly defined as royal. This is exactly the ideological move that *Cymbeline* refuses to make. Demoting Posthumus from a potential prince to a husband would seem to confirm James' stance. Yet to rest assured in this ideologically straitened view requires us to dismiss the interests in epistemology that *Cymbeline* has promoted as culturally emergent. Bearing in mind this positive appraisal of open rather than closed sites of agency, the play's affirmation of conventional authority appears mechanical – like Cymbeline's sons and Jupiter as he descends on his eagle. Like Cymbeline's disgruntled court at the beginning of the play, Shakespeare's carefully poised conclusion may affirm James' ideology loudly to his face while muttering critical asides. The national identity developing in London's theaters had, to judge by *Cymbeline*, broader interests than strictly royalist, parliamentary, or civic ones. *Cymbeline* offers evidence that London's theaters were aware of ways in which the court was moving away from vital sites of social change: as the "Head" of state began to quarrel ever more polemically with its "body," James I's political imagery and *Cymbeline*'s central image alike become, in hindsight, weirdly proleptic of Charles I's fate.[37]

6 "How came that widow in?": allusion, politics, and the theater in *The Tempest*

> Knowing I loved my books, he furnished me
> From mine own library with volumes that
> I prize above my dukedom.   (1.2.166–8)[1]

Shakespeare secured considerable legitimacy for the theater by the time he approached retirement, and one measure of his success is the number of his plays – at least six – included in the court performances to celebrate the wedding of the Princess Elizabeth to the Elector Palatine in 1612. One of *The Tempest*'s compelling questions is whether cultural legitimacy may coexist with autonomy or whether Shakespeare's immersion in the courtly system of patronage means that he, chief playwright of the King's Men, must treat his theater as an instrument of royal authority. The last of Shakespeare's translations of empire, *The Tempest* reflects on the collusion of theater with the courtly representation that it brashly interrogated in earlier forays. If the play is conceived as a humanistic *institutio principi* or, more panegyrically, a compliment to King James – and Prospero's paternal authority, love of playing Cupid, disguises, magic, and masque all bear lightly on the figure and pastimes of James I – then the play emerges as a royal address to which other audiences are imagined as second affirmers of royal prerogative. There is no evidence that Shakespeare expressly ingratiates himself to James I in the epilogue, although the final scene has been imagined in just this way,[2] and good reason to suppose that he is well aware of potential tensions among his audiences in the court and the Globe or Blackfriars.

When Prospero looks out at a popular audience and asks for approval, he relinquishes a dream of immediate access to the highest levels of cultural influence. Within the dramatic action of the play, Prospero always aimed his educational spectacles at courtiers; only at the play's end does he reawaken the mariners, an action that prepares somewhat for his final and surprising re-entrance to humble himself to a theater-going assembly including their social equivalents. If Shakespeare is imagined as turning his eyes with anything like Prospero's reluctance

189

from the king to the people, then he appears as a failed theatrical equivalent of the courtly poet in Sidney's *Defence of Poesie*, who effects social change by appealing to the court and monarch. Sidney could defend the golden world of poetic ideals by appealing to the ideal reader, the next princely Cyrus. In poetry circulated among courtiers, it is possible to imagine that imitation might create "so true a lover as *Theagenes*, so constant a friend as *Pylades*, so valiant a man as *Orlando*, so right a prince as *Xenophon's Cyrus*, so excellent a man every way as *Vergils Aeneas*" – or the legendary Sidney. Sidney's poet delivers an excellent political idea that

is not wholly imaginative, as we are wont to say by them that build Castles in the aire: but so farre substancially it worketh, not only to make a *Cyrus* . . . but to bestow a *Cyrus* upon the world to make many *Cyrusses*, if they will learne aright, why and how that maker made him.[3]

The playwright and common player, however, had better stick to building less gorgeous structures in the air: the humanistic model of political influence behind the efforts of Spenser to gain the ear of Elizabeth I in *The Faerie Queene* and Jonson to gain James I's in his masques unpersuasively accounts for plays designed for performance outside of the court. With a mixed society installed as a cumbersome audience for educative and political dreams, the playwright can expect no magical transition from the idea to social practice.

In his final translation of empire, Shakespeare develops an equivocal figure of authority in Prospero, the duke who loses political powers in his pursuit of magical ones and, after twelve years of exile, puts his art to the supreme test of effecting political change. It is clear to Prospero himself that he risks his most ambitious ideals by attempting to realize them through an ambiguous form of magic that seems to have less to do with the necromantic arts of a Faustus, Cornelius Agrippa, or John Dee than with political coercion and Shakespeare's own theatrical medium. As if to draw attention to the questionable union and function of political and theatrical manipulations in Prospero's project, Shakespeare's magician employs Vergilian resources to body forth his personal translation of empire, which ambivalently vacillates between a revenge play and a divine comedy. Even as the play announces its adaptation of New World marvels and commonplaces,[4] Prospero himself refers his interventions in the Italian courtiers' adventures and minds to Vergil's *Aeneid*: Strachey's storm in the "still-vexed Bermudas" meets the epic storm from *Aeneid* 1, Peter Martyr's inarticulate harpies speak with the voice of Vergil's Celaeno from *Aeneid* 3, and what has been termed "Shakespeare's Virginian Masque," in celebration of the "temperance" and "fruitfulness" of the Jamestown colony, might be subtitled "Prospero's Vergilian

Masque," which breaks down because Prospero doubts that either art or institutions may successfully temper rebellious and erotic passions.[5]

The form of government: utopia, liberties, and absolute command

what hath a more adamantive power to draw unto it the consent and attraction of the idle, untoward, and wretched number of the many, then liberty, and fulnesse and sensuality? . . .

If I should be examined from whence, and by what occasion, all these disasters, and afflictions descended upon our people, I can only referre you . . . to the Booke, which the Adventurers have sent hither . . . wherein the ground and causes have beene produced, not excusing likewise the forme of government of some errour, which was not powerfull enough among so headie a multitude . . . [Yet] the better authoritie and government [are] now changed into an absolute command. – Strachey[6]

Before making a case for topical or literary specificity in *The Tempest*, whether classical or Virginian, it is a good idea to account for the play's reluctance to settle its topoi anywhere at all. Geographically situated somewhere between Tunis and Italy and temporally bounded by Dido's Carthage and the new Troys of early modern Europe, Shakespeare's island is a conceptual site for testing grounds for dominion and forms of government in general and examining in particular growing differences between England's traditional theories of the commonwealth and its changing sociopolitical practices. Its discursive companions are constitutional tracts and utopias, both of which aim to establish institutional means, in the words of J. C. Davis, to "enable government to proceed without personal dependence in a world of deficient actors," whose ignorance, idleness, and self-service interfere with the well-being of the commonwealth. But whereas constitutionalism seeks to safeguard politics so that "policies may be chosen, adapted or abandoned in pursuit of the common good," utopianism – such as Prospero's – aims to make its "constitutional engineering . . . so complete that there is no longer any need for policy."[7]

Both constitutionalists and utopianists take a warmer view of liberties than William Strachey, author of the *True Repertory of the Wracke*, whose account of the storm, shipwreck, and subsequent rebellions faced by the Virginia Company under Sir Thomas Gates spurred Shakespeare's interest in the idea of a political storm of uprisings against inadequately constituted authority. After seeing the émigrés to Virginia fall into disease, famine, and faction, and dwindle from 900 to 60, Strachey spent time between 1609 and 1611 editing new rules that Sir Thomas Gates, Thomas West, and Sir Thomas Dale developed for the Virginia Colony.

His *Lawes Divine, Morall, and Martiall* suggested that the Virginia Company authorities gained the "absolute command" necessary to reduce their willful men to order: impiety, blasphemy, and insubordination earned capital punishment and worship, along with property, trade, and prices, was closely monitored.[8]

While the Virginia Company rhetoric denigrated liberties and promoted absolutism in the New World, the evaluation of these terms was reversed in the struggle gathering to a head in the House of Commons. In 1610 the House renewed its attempt, begun with the Humble Apology of 1604, to persuade King James to respect its ancient liberties, furnished by English constitutional thought.[9] In response, James I lectured Parliament on the divine nature of kings:[10]

Kings are iustly called Gods, for that they exercise a manner or resemblance of Diuine power vpon earth . . . God hath power to create, or destroy, make, or vnmake at his pleasure, to giue life, or send death, to iudge all, and to be iudged nor accomptable to none: To raise low things, and to make high things low at his pleasure . . . And the like power haue Kings; they make and vnmake their subiects: they haue power of raising, and casting downe; of life, and of death: Iudges ouer all their subiects, and in all causes, and yet accomptable to none but God onely.

More troubling to Parliament, James fulminated against their right even to discuss the constitutional basis of his prerogative: "it is sedition in Subiects, to dispute what a King may do in the height of his power . . . I wil not be content that my power be disputed vpon" (p. 310). Legal historians were quick to question his political theory, and Thomas Wentworth responded that "if we shall once say that we may not dispute the prerogative, let us be sold for slaves."[11] It is no wonder that Shakespeare's island, placed in the tradition of commonwealth treatises and housing hotly disputed issues of the day, both invites specific comparison with England, the New World, and the Old World and simultaneously resists reduction to any one of them.

The play begins with the wreck of the ship of state followed by the breakdown of the traditional household.[12] Under pressure from change in the social relations of the estates without a corresponding change in their theoretical articulation, the paternalistic and hierarchical model of state and family had become a contested rather than an assumed authority by the early seventeenth century, and it emerges as such in *The Tempest*. When the ship of state splinters – an episode discussed in the next section – the play turns to the troubled history of Prospero's household. Not only did Prospero, negligent of his princely duties in Milan, alienate his officers and abandon his loving commons, but his experiment of good governance on the island evidently failed as well. The governing estate's most attractive relationship with the governed in the play is not Prospero's with Ariel, who turns out to require a monthly chiding to resume his labors without "grumblings" (1.2.249). The ideal relationship emerges, with pointed irony, from the mutual recriminations that Prospero and Caliban fling at each other after Ariel has left the stage. When Prospero summons Caliban to the stage for the first time with defining insults, the "poisonous slave, got by the devil himself / Upon [his] wicked dam" (1.2.319–20) responds with imaginative curses for which Prospero decrees a punishment of cramps, side-stitches, and pinches. Prospero, Miranda, and Caliban then reconstruct their familial history from grievances inflamed by memories of their halcyon days:

> CALIBAN.   When thou cam'st first,
> Thou strok'st me and made much of me; wouldst give me
> Water with berries in't, and teach me how
> To name the bigger light and how the less,
> That burn by day and night; and then I loved thee,
> And showed thee all the qualities o' th' isle,
> The fresh springs, brine pits, barren place and fertile –
> Cursed be I that did so! . . .
> here you sty me
> In this hard rock, whiles you do keep from me
> The rest o' th' island.
> PROSPERO.   Thou most lying slave,
> Whom stripes may move, not kindness, I have used thee –
> Filth as thou art – with humane care, and lodged thee
> In mine own cell, till thou didst seek to violate
> The honour of my child . . .
> MIRANDA.   . . . I pitied thee,
> Took pains to make thee speak, taught thee each hour
> One thing or other. When thou didst not, savage,
> Know thine own meaning, but wouldst gabble like
> A thing most brutish, I endowed thy purposes
> With words that made them known. But thy vile race –
> Though thou didst learn – had that in't which good natures
> Could not abide to be with; therefore wast thou
> Deservedly confined into this rock,
> Who hadst deserved more than a prison.   (lines 332–61)

Behind the accusations of betrayal and bad faith is an old dream of harmonious and gratifying familial relations between those who govern and those who obey. Prospero, Miranda, and Caliban sentimentalize, as a fallen ideal, a household held together by the traditional patriarchal bonds between those who "provide governance, employment, and hospitality" and those who "respond with obedience, hard work, and gratitude."[13] The ideal recalled, the same one celebrated by Cheke, Crowley, and Smith in early Tudor representations of the commonwealth, is doubly jeopardized because Shakespeare presents it as doomed from the start to the failure that continues to shock and anger Prospero and Miranda.

The attempted rape that shattered Prospero's household was no stray act of lust, but a deliberate act of conquest, a consequence of the political theory Caliban learned along with the names of master and servant: "O ho, O ho! Would't had been done! . . . I had peopled else / This isle with Calibans" (1.2.348–50). Prospero invited Caliban into his home, Miranda nurtured and educated him as an underprivileged dependent, and Caliban reciprocated with love and obedience. Yet Caliban insists that his very education taught him villainous discontent. He learned his social identity as a laborer in whom any lapse in gratitude would undo him as a dissident; he learned about self-sovereignty when he lost it; he understood property when Prospero enclosed the land Caliban customarily enjoyed. At some point in Caliban's education as the grateful servant in a paternalistic Tudor household, he asked himself something like the angry question posed by a Somerset rioter in 1549: "Why should one man have all and another nothing?"[14] Since Caliban was educated into knowledge of his losses, his only "profit on't," he points out, "Is I know how to curse" (1.2.362–3).[15]

Shakespeare's point is not to sentimentalize Caliban – a laborer would presumably not feel gratified to hear his concerns voiced through Caliban – but to cast the trio in a political dialogue of mutual complaint, such as Robert Crowley's "The Waie to Wealth" (1550), in which the commons and the gentry accuse each other of being the cause of sedition. The "greedy cormorants" complain that the poor laborers[16]

know not themselves, they know no obedience, they regard no laws, they would have no gentlemen, they would have all men like themselves, they would have all things common! They would not have us masters of that which is our own! . . . These are jolly fellows! They will cast down our parks, and lay our pastures open! They will have the law in their own hands! They will play the king!

Designed to inhabit the tensions in the idea of the "masterless man," Caliban cannot imagine existence without a master and cannot cease longing for the imagined time when he was "mine own king" (1.2.342). Prospero, who winds up looking hypocritical about the work ethic,[17] subjects Caliban to imprisonment and labor, the institutional replacements for hospitality and personal bequests developed by a changing society. As David Underdown puts it, [18]

the deserving (the aged and impotent) were now to be taken care of by the regular provisions of statute, the rest disciplined and put to work. The victims constituted a vast, disorganized reservoir of discontent, as well as a source of guilt for those who ignored or coerced them. A tendency to look for scapegoats among the vulnerable – to indulge in accusations of witchcraft, for example – was a natural result. There were other methods of imposing social discipline, but for the vagrant the whip, the stocks, and the House of Correction were the preferred solution.

For Prospero to conclude that Caliban can be moved only by "stripes" rather than "kindness" puts him in an awkward position between conceptual models of good governance. The bad faith that Harry Berger perceived in a Prospero who dislikes the "good clean manual labor"[19] he supervises is the conflict of rivaling ideas about the relationship of social classes: Prospero is divided by his loyalty to the traditional model, characterized by inflexible verticality, paternalistic care from masters, and grateful obedience from servants, and the reformist mission of his project, which is indebted to the early seventeenth-century Protestants' social focus on moral reformation, the work ethic, and personal responsibility. Prospero would appear a less ambivalent and vulnerable figure of authority if he did not prefer to exchange kindness for the thankful cooperation of his servants instead of stripes for grudging labor. His reluctance to embrace the ethic of reform in place of the ideal of harmonious reciprocity is felt in his inability to find a political explanation for his Milanese subjects' defection. Faltering over the issue of their agency, he stumbles on the idea of metamorphosis three times in his search for the just verb: his brother must have "new created / The creatures that were mine, I say: or changed 'em, / Or else new formed 'em" (1.2.81–3).

Caliban, an extreme representation of the social misfit, is not *The Tempest*'s only dissident voice from England's domestic front. The play takes pains to bring social classes into tense contact, especially in its first and final scenes – the boatswain and crew unnecessarily reappear onstage to mingle with the courtiers after Miranda has dubbed it a "brave new world / That has such people in't" (5.1.183–4). The range of social types caught up in its discursive web is considerably wider than the boatswain, Stephano the butler, and Trinculo the clown. The play is filled with references to dead Indians and monsters suited for exhibition in English marketplaces; Sycorax, whose social history only complicates Prospero's story; the scolding Kate disliked by the sailors; the leaky wench of a ship; and the "widow" unflatteringly attached to Dido as a reminder of the propertied, demanding widows of English stereotype. Even Miranda, in a rare moment, appears as a seditious upstart in Prospero's government: "My foot my tutor?" (1.2.470), Prospero exlaims in mock outrage. With these dissident voices comes an even wider range of ideas about how to respond institutionally to their intransigence.

Stray remarks about Sycorax suggest that Prospero's orthodox view of her lurid history is only one possible inference that might be drawn about her: her pregnancy and trial for witchcraft – "for one thing she did / They would not take her life" (1.2.269–70) – are more likely to recall Reginald Scot's skeptical *Discoverie of Witchcraft* than James I's convinced *Daemonologie*. Prospero's extravagant praise of Miranda, whom he educated, loved, and tenderly regards as "a third of mine own life, / Or that for which I live" (4.1.3–4), joins his bullying remarks to her in further contribution to the *querelle des femmes* that threads its way through the play. Masters and laborers variously inspire sympathy or outrage, depending on the passages emphasized. Traditional pastimes appear seditious yet festive, when Caliban declares a holiday from building dams, fetching firewood, and washing dishes, and uses his "freedom" to persuade his Lord of Misrule, Stephano, to brain Prospero. Resounding with the clashing imperatives of absolute command and liberty, *The Tempest* casts a net wide enough to encompass the domestic concerns of sour apprentices and the House of Commons.

The social questions that permeate *The Tempest* furnish the context for evaluating Prospero's Vergilian project: is it the cure or merely another symptom of the social ill that proceeds from placing one's "particular weal" above the "common weal," as Cardinal Pole expressed it in Thomas Starkey's *Dialogue between Pole and Lupset*?[20] Vergil's prominence in Prospero's project – he donates material for Prospero's storm, harpy, and masque – betokens Prospero's need for objective authority in his efforts to administer justice, reform moral character, and restore social order. Although the *Aeneid* appears as a master text to assuage and suppress the problems of authority and sedition raised in the Virginia Company tracts, the theatrical uses to which Prospero puts Vergil ultimately betray Prospero's exercise of authority as coercive and, worse, effectless.

Prospero's Books: Vergil in the New World

Particularly when Prospero is on the stage, *The Tempest* reveals the alienated presence of Vergil in a New World topography. Since there is a strong tradition in travel literature of finding Vergilian and Ovidian patterns in New World adventures, it is tempting to find harmonious relations between the Vergilian episodes that Prospero cites and dramatizes and the New World motifs they suggest without the help of Prospero's guiding hand. Like old veneer sprung loose from the unlike wood beneath it, however, the *Aeneid* continually separates from the travel literature and merchant-venturers' tracts, although both offer material for the play's emphases on discovery, amazement and wonder, authority and sedition, the labor of colonizing, and the stigma of idleness. The most spectacular example of the strained yoking together of the *Aeneid* and travel literature is the trivial dialogue which the courtiers strike up shortly after their arrival on Prospero's island. Adrian describes the island as a "desert . . . Uninhabitable, and almost inaccessible," but also "of subtle, tender and delicate temperance" (2.1.36, 39, 43–4). While he and Gonzalo find the island's air sweet-smelling and its grass "lush and lusty" (line 53), Sebastian and Antonio smell air wafting from rotten lungs or a fen and falling on dead grass: the idealizing and cynical portraits, as John Gillies argues, mirror the Virginia Company's propaganda and the grim reports of sickness in the colonies and infertility in the land with which colonizers who abandoned the project in Jamestown returned to England.[21]

After firmly establishing both the New World milieu in which the castaways discover themselves and the divergence of opinion surrounding New World topoi, the conversation takes a brief historical turn, when Gonzalo explains that present-day Tunis was once Carthage, and embarks on what has been called "a series of apparently trivial allusions to the theme of Dido and Aeneas."[22] The six references to "widow Dido," which take place within twenty-five lines, cause almost as much annoyance in critics as in Antonio:

GONZALO. Methinks our garments are now as fresh as when we put them on first in Afric, at the marriage of the King's fair daughter Claribel to the King of Tunis.

SEBASTIAN. 'Twas a sweet marriage, and we prosper well in our return.

ADRIAN. Tunis was never graced before with such a paragon to their Queen.

GONZALO. Not since widow Dido's time.

ANTONIO. Widow? A pox o' that! How came that widow in? widow Dido! you take it!

ADRIAN. "Widow Dido," said you? You make me study of that. She was of Carthage, not of Tunis.

GONZALO. This Tunis, sir, was Carthage.

ADRIAN. Carthage?

GONZALO. I assure you, Carthage.

ANTONIO. His word is more than the miraculous harp.

SEBASTIAN. He hath raised the wall, and houses too.

ANTONIO. What impossible matter will he make easy next?. . .

GONZALO. Sir, we were talking that our garments seem now as fresh as when we were at Tunis at the marriage of your daughter, who is now queen.

ANTONIO. And the rarest that e'er came there.

SEBASTIAN. Bate, I beseech you, widow Dido.

ANTONIO. O, widow Dido? Ay, widow Dido.   (2.1.66–85, 92–7)

Jan Kott, one of the first critics to consider at length the relation of Shakespeare's play to Vergil's epic, rightly asks if "Shakespeare repeat[s] and at the same time negate[s] the Vergilian myths of purification of men and history through suffering and of civilizations lost and won?"[23] Yet his important question is too general to arise from the obnoxious allusions to "widow Dido," whose story is by no means synecdoche for the imperial epic. The quirky allusion puzzles and provokes the audience into contemplating not only general Vergilian themes but the haunting and menacing presence of Dido, the victim of passion and empire and, like Carthage, the implacable enemy of the future Roman empire. When the play formally invokes its authority on empire, it harps on the epic's greatest compromise and in so doing, sets adrift the very authority that Vergil's epic is supposed to convey from Augustan Rome to early modern England.

Gonzalo means to praise Claribel by comparing her to the triumphant queen displaced in Africa – perhaps distributing tasks and laws to her growing city, as she does in *Aeneid* 1 – yet he instigates a struggle over how to evaluate Dido or, in Falstaff's lewd phrase for Mistress Quickly, "where to have her."[24] Antonio's response is harder to gauge. Although eternally disgruntled, he loses his equanimity only once in the play, and that is when he bursts out, "Widow! a pox o' that! how came that widow in? widow Dido!" Only Sebastian's timely introduction of the "widower Aeneas" allays Antonio's irritation. Passion is the stuff of their easy jokes, and ridicule offers refuge from contemplating the death it takes to make a widow: Sebastian and Antonio blame Alonso for leaving Naples and Milan with "mo widows in them of this business' making / Than we bring men to comfort them" (2.1.130–1). The aristocratic malcontents displace their anxieties in derisive jokes about Gonzalo's naive view of the *Aeneid* and Dido's career, but they only prompt the indefatigable Gonzalo to comfort his king with silver linings like Aeneas' famous line to his men, after the storm, that someday it will be a pleasure to remember these distresses (*forsan et haec olim meminisse iuvabit*, 1.203). The dialogue unleashes a derisive and bawdy revision of the *Aeneid* and a traditionally optimistic reading of Vergil's epic, the island, and the court's prospects for survival. The passage refuses to disclose how that widow came in and expands Antonio's question into an interrogation of the bases for interpreting the epic that launches the translation of empire.

An explanation for the aggressive and under-motivated allusions does not come immediately or directly,[25] and the dialogue instead returns to New World concerns in Gonzalo's utopian commonwealth. Invented as a "castle in the air" to amuse and distract his king,[26] his dream is proved

hopeless in the speaking by its allusions to the 1609 disaster that befell
the Virginia Company expedition. The seditious and idle voyagers shipwrecked in the Bermudas actually attempted to create their own "plantation of [the] isle" (2.1.139) without the "name of magistrate . . . use of
service, none; contract, succession, / Bourne, bound of land, tilth,
vineyard, none . . . No occupation," and above all, "No sovereignty"
(2.1.139–52). When Gonzalo swears he would have "all men idle, all,"
his golden-age fantasy overlaps with Strachey's grim reports of the sea-
men who used "false baits" to hook the land-men:[27]

The Angles wherewith chiefly they thus hooked in these disquieted Pooles, were,
how that in Virginia, nothing but wretchednesse and labour must be expected,
with many wants, and a churlish intreaty, there being neither that Fish, Flesh,
nor Fowle, which here (without wasting on the one part, or watching on theirs, or
any threatning, and aire of authority) at ease, and pleasure might be injoyed . . .
This . . . begat such a murmur, and such a discontent, and disunion of hearts and
hands from this labour, and forwarding the meanes of redeeming us from hence,
as each one wrought with his Mate how to diverse him from the same.

These are the "knaves" Antonio finds in Gonzalo's utopia, as desperate
as Caliban to "attempt the innovating of the [governor] . . . or forme of
government," and as poor in judging their new leaders as Caliban finally
proclaims himself: "What a thrice-double ass / Was I to take this
drunkard for a god, / And worship this dull fool!" (5.1.295–7).

The annoying jokes about the "widow Dido" juxtapose an ancient
problem with empire and a new problem in the Virginia Colony: political
and sexual restiveness in Vergil's *furor* and the social "fury" and
"tempest of dissention" stressed in the *True Repertory of the Wracke* and
the *True Declaration*. Revenge, rebellion, and sexuality are the passions
increasingly identified with *The Tempest* and passion is what Prospero
seeks to chasten in others and ultimately in himself. Cited in a context of
interpretive debate, the *Aeneid* is susceptible to idealizing and cynical,
pious and dissident uses. Like manipulations of the Bible by malcontents
under Sir Thomas Gates, the multiple readings of Vergil suggest that
authority is up for grabs. Stephano makes the point comically when he
extends his makeshift bottle of sack to his new man, Caliban, and
exclaims, "Kiss the book" (2.2.124, 136).

A compelling reason to favor the Virginian over the Vergilian context
is that Prospero, like the beleaguered Sir Thomas Gates, deals with a
rapid sequence of rebellions, while Aeneas faces little in the way of
sedition. Unlike Aeneas' epic descendant, Goffredo of *Gerusalemme
liberata*, Aeneas does not have to struggle against mutinous impulses in
his own men. Even when the Trojan women in his party, agitated by Iris,
burn several ships and opt to stay in colony on Sicily, Aeneas benefits:

the women keep the old, tired men with them and free the vigorous Trojan men to follow their leader's example and intermarry with the Latins. Nonetheless, the famous storm which begins the *Aeneid* sports the personification and the imagery of mutiny that characterize the "roarers" – winds and roaring boys – that Shakespeare's boatswain asserts discount "the name of king." Strachey, on the other hand, neither significantly personifies the storm nor allegorizes it as the source of the subsequent political afflictions:

the cloudes gathering thicke upon us, and the windes singing, and whistling most unusually . . . a dreadfull storme and hideous began to blow from out the North-east, which swelling, and roaring as it were by fits . . . at length did beat all light from heaven; which like an hell of darkenesse turned blacke upon us; so much the more fuller of horror, as in such cases horror and feare use to overrunne the troubled, and overmastered sences of all which (taken up with amazement) the eares lay so sensible to the terrible cries, and murmurs of the windes, and distraction of our Company, as who was most armed, and best prepared, was not a little shaken.

. . . we could not apprehend in our imaginations any possibility of greater violence, yet did we still finde it, not onely more terrible, but more constant, fury added to fury, and one storme urging a second more outragious than the former . . . nothing heard that could give comfort, nothing seene that might incourage hope . . . the glut of water (as if throatling the winde ere while) was no sooner a little emptie and qualified, but instantly the windes (as having gotten their mouthes now free, and at liberty) spake more loud, and grew more tumultuous, and malignant . . . Windes and Seas were as mad, as fury and rage could make them . . .

Curiously, Strachey's description of the storm influences the experiences of Shakespeare's courtiers on the island, under the direct influence of Prospero's magic, more than during the storm itself. Its counterparts in *The Tempest* are the mad distraction into which Prospero casts his enemies and Alonso's agonized reception of the harpy's judgment:

> O, it is monstrous, monstrous!
> Methought the billows spoke and told me of it,
> The winds did sing it to me; and the thunder,
> That deep and dreadful organ-pipe, pronounced
> The name of Prosper: it did base my trespass.   (3.3. 95–9)

Dispersed throughout the play, the effects of the 1609 storm appear as the theatrical effects of Prospero's harrowing rituals.

The interplay of authority and mutiny in a personified storm comes from the *Aeneid* rather than Strachey. Reading the storm as a disruption of social order, an act of aggression by the unruly laboring class – pieties familiar in colonialist writing – the courtiers charge the mariners with insubordination. When Gonzalo rebukes the boatswain for verbal rebellion – "What cares these roarers for the name of King?" – he rejoins,

You are a councillor; if you can command these elements to silence, and work the peace of the present, we will not hand a rope more – use your authority. If you cannot, give thanks you have lived so long, and make yourself ready in your cabin for the mischance of the hour, if it so hap. (1.1.20–5)

Mocking the courtier's diplomatic arts and the notion that courtly rhetoric has any weight outside of its own element, the "blasphemous" (1.1.40, 5.1.218) boatswain proposes a class-oriented version of Troilus' question, "What's aught but as 'tis valu'd?" It is also a specific allusion to Vergil's first epic simile of Neptune, who calms the waves and separates the elements of sky and earth, to a man of such civic authority that his mere appearance and words can quell civic rebellion or, in the boatswain's words, "command these elements to silence, and work the peace of the present":

> ac veluti magno in populo cum saepe coorta est
> seditio saevitque animis ignobile vulgus,
> iamque faces et saxa volant, furor arma ministrat;
> tum, pietate gravem ac meritis si forte virum quem
> conspexere, silent arrectisque auribus astant;
> ille regit dictis animos et pectora mulcet:
> sic cunctus pelagi cecidet fragor . . .   (1.148–54)

As when sedition has risen in a great nation, and the common mob rage angrily, and now torches and rocks fly – passion supplies weapons – then, if by chance they see a man dignified by his patriotic duty and service, they fall silent and stand with attentive ears; he rules their spirits with words and softens their hearts. Just so, all the roar of the ocean sank . . .

The boatswain is fittingly created to mock Vergil's simile, which Shakespeare used in *Titus Andronicus* as well as his contribution to *Sir Thomas More*. Perhaps ready to join the "common mob" in hurling rocks and torches, the boatswain is unlikely to drop them and prick up his ears at the command of an official like Gonzalo. Sure that such a rogue is ordained to hang for treason, Gonzalo hopes for survival: "I have great comfort from this fellow. Methinks he hath no drowning mark upon him – his complexion is perfect gallows. Stand fast, good Fate, to his hanging" (1.1. 28–30).

The anti-Vergilian boatswain, chief actor in *The Tempest* 1.1, introduces the overdetermined character of the storm's commentary on sedition. While the boatswain seems right to resist the courtiers' political applications, the storm nonetheless proves to be far from innocent of allegorical readings, as his inadvertent anchor to Vergil's simile and themes suggests. The storm, as the next scene indicates, constitutes Prospero's commentary on the collapsing ship of state (fig. 16), a theme that recurs even in the antics of Stephano and Trinculo, who drink so much that their "state totters" (3.2.6). Yet Prospero's tempest has a double edge, for it also glosses Prospero himself as a governor scarcely able to weather his own passions. In the following scene with Miranda, Prospero offers assurance that the court and crew came safely through the tempest, but is careful only to justify his past and future actions rather than to explain them: Miranda has evidently long wished to know her history,[28] and responds gratifyingly to Prospero's tale, but what is "beating in [her] mind" throughout the dialogue is the desire to know Prospero's "reason / For raising this sea-storm" (1.2.176–7). Prospero reveals his emotional incontinence in his slippery syntax, repetition, and dependence on Miranda's wholly compassionate response to his tale: when he bids her, "ope thine ear" (1.2.37), and narrates his tale, a tragedy laced with epic, he stops just short of imagining her as a Dido with "her sad-attending ear" listening to his tale of the joint betrayal of him and his Troy-like Milan, whose gates "one midnight / Fated to the purpose did Antonio open" and admit his "treacherous army" (lines 128–30).

Prospero regains the appearance of mastery when he turns to art that touches him less personally. Asked if he has "Perform'd to point the tempest that I bade thee?" (1.2.194), Ariel rhetorically recreates the storm:

> To every article.
> I boarded the king's ship; now on the beak,
> Now in the waist, the deck, in every cabin,
> I flamed amazement. Sometime I'd divide,
> And burn in many places; on the topmast,
> The yards and bowsprit would I flame distinctly,
> Then meet and join. Jove's lightning, the precursors
> O' th' dreadful thunder-claps, more momentary
> And sight-outrunning were not: the fire and cracks
> Of sulphurous roaring the most mighty Neptune
> Seem to besiege, and make his bold waves tremble,
> Yea, his dread trident shake.   (1.2.195–206)

Using epic classicism, Ariel's battle imagery invites specific comparison with Vergil, whose "roarers" line up like military columns, and his personifications of the lightning and ocean as Jupiter and Neptune recall the calming presences of those gods on Vergil's storm. His visually brilliant and immediate rhetoric rouses an "amazement" featured in both Vergil and Strachey.[29] Yet Vergilian ornamentation comes late to *The Tempest*'s storm, originally presented as natural and, in fact, anti-Vergilian.

INNVMERIS *agitur Reſpublica noſtra procellis,*
Et ſpes venturæ ſola ſalutis adeſt:
Non ſecus ac nauis medio circum æquore, venti
Quam rapiunt; ſalſis iamq̃ˌ fatiſcit aquis.
Quòd ſi Helenæ adueniant lucentia ſidera fratres:
Amiſſos animos ſpes bona reſtituit.

Figure 16. Ship of state. Andrea Alciati, *Emblemata* (Antwerp, 1577)

Ariel's recreation of the storm in Prospero's closet theater becomes more Virginian when he describes his effect on the crew and court. In his performance as St. Elmo's fire, Ariel enacts the Virginia Company's encounter with "an apparition of a little round light, like a faint Starre, trembling and streaming along with a sparkeling blaze, halfe the height upon the Maine Mast, and shooting sometimes from Shroud to Shroud, tempting to settle, as it were upon any of the foure Shrouds . . . running sometimes along the Maine-yard to the very end, and then returning":

> Not a soul
> But felt a fever of the mad and played
> Some tricks of desperation. All but mariners
> Plunged in the foaming brine and quit the vessel,
> Then all afire with me: the King's son Ferdinand,
> With hair up-staring – then like reeds, not hair –
> Was the first man that leapt, cried "Hell is empty,
> And all the devils are here!"   (1.2.208–15)

The second half of Ariel's account tends to denaturalize the earlier Vergilian and epic touches and raises questions about what function, other than aesthetics, they serve for Prospero, who ordered Ariel's performance "to point." Prospero will specifically recall "Jove's lightning" and "the most mighty Neptune" when he rejects his magic.

Prospero's allusions cloak his intentions and provide channels for motives he may not wish to encourage or acknowledge. The question about Prospero's purpose that beats in Miranda's mind arises again in the masque-like banquet offered to the court, exhausted and despondent from treading a "maze" (3.3.2) through the island in search of Ferdinand:

Solemn and strange music, and Prosper on the top, invisible. Enter several strange shapes bringing in a banquet, and dance about it with gentle actions of salutations; and inviting the King, etc., to eat, they depart.

The spectacle amazes the court and completes physical in epistemological wanderings. It jars even the typically cynical Sebastian and Antonio into professing belief in travelers' tales, the unicorn, and the phoenix. Gonzalo admires the gentle manners of the monstrously shaped "islanders," a response typical in travel literature. Confident in the truth of tales – even those of "mountaineers / Dew-lapped like bulls, whose throats had hanging at 'em / Wallets of flesh," and "men, / Whose heads stood in their breasts" (lines 44–47) – the aristocrats help themselves to the feast.

Here they commit a mistake of genre, for their wanderings do not retrace the steps of fortunate travelers but, instead, those of the exiled

Aeneas and his men in *Aeneid* 3, where, harassed and scattered by yet
another storm, they are left "wandering" and blind in the ocean (*caecis
erramus in undis*, line 200), until they land on the island of the harpies,
presume to eat their food, and receive judgment by Celaeno, oldest of the
Furies. Like Aeneas' men, Alonso and his court encounter "Thunder and
lightning," then

> *Enter Ariel, like a harpy, claps his wings upon the table, and, with a quaint
> device the banquet vanishes.*
> ARIEL. You are three men of sin, whom Destiny
> That hath to instrument this lower world
> And what is in't, the never-surfeited sea
> Hath caused to belch up you, and on this island,
> Where man doth not inhabit – you 'mongst men
> Being most unfit to live. I have made you mad;
> And even with such-like valour men hang and drown
> Their proper selves.
>   *Alonso, Sebastian, etc., draw their swords.*
>   You fools! I and my fellows
> Are ministers of Fate – the elements,
> Of whom your swords are tempered may as well
> Wound the loud winds, or with bemocked-at stabs
> Kill the still-closing waters, as diminish
> One dowl that's in my plume. My fellow ministers
> Are like invulnerable . . .   (3.3.53–66)

Ariel echoes Celaeno's taunts when Aeneas and his men fail to harm so
much as a feather with the swords they raise against the harpies (*sed
neque vim plumis ullam . . . accipiunt*, lines 242–3). Also like Celaeno, the
dira vates who reveals a portion of Jupiter's designs and curses the
Trojans for their crime, Ariel announces the terrible wrath of heaven
(*tristis denuntiat iras*, line 367):

>   you three
> From Milan did supplant good Prospero,
> Exposed unto the sea, which hath requit it,
> Him and his innocent child; for which foul deed
> The powers delaying, not forgetting, have
> Incensed the seas and shores, yea, all the creatures,
> Against your peace. Thee of thy son, Alonso,
> They have bereft; and do pronounce by me
> Ling'ring perdition, worse than any death
> Can be at once, shall step by step attend
> You and your ways . . .   (lines 69–79)

Ariel "vanishes in thunder; then, to soft music, enter the Shapes again,
and dance with mocks and mows, and carrying out the table." Prospero's

prophetic harpy has little to do with Peter Martyr's bats or "harpies," but traces its lineage securely to Vergil's, and proclaims that "Fate" and "Destiny" guide the courtiers' adventures on the island.

If the episode's ties to the New World are loose, those to the *Aeneid* and Prospero become constricting.[30] That Prospero has scripted the allegorical scene is clear:

> Bravely the figure of this harpy hast thou
> Performed, my Ariel; a grace it had, devouring:
> Of my instruction hast thou nothing bated
> In what thou hadst to say.   (lines 83–6)

The dramatic role he casts for himself is less clear. Ariel's emphasis on powers that delay but do not forget recalls the *Aeneid*'s general pattern of destiny over which Jupiter presides. In *Cymbeline* and the *Aeneid*, Jupiter delays in order to delight, crosses those he best loves. There is a distant hope that Prospero, too, intends blessings to follow trials, but he does not say so. Instead, the vanishing banquet prophesies further reprisals and, using more thunder and lightning for special effects, confirms that the present judgment began with the storm, at last unveiled as divinely ordained.

Prospero, who relies heavily on Vergil's female agents of revenge, curiously exposes that he is no paternal god from the *Aeneid* but a kind of fury himself. Juno is the divine power who, "not forgetting" the wrong done her, delays the Trojans "step by step": she incenses the seas, shores, and native Italians against Aeneas and threatens the "peace of the present" as well as the future peace in Rome's empire under Augustus. Celaeno's "ling'ring perdition" and assertion that Alonso has paid for his crime with the life of his son recall the words of Dido, who wishes she had killed Ascanius and curses Aeneas and his Romans with a fate worse than death. He unwarily condenses the vindictive rage of Celaeno, Juno, and Dido in the figure of his spiteful harpy, then weaves their passions into generalized Vergilian themes, such as the father's tragic loss of his son and the gods' strategy of deferring justice. An abstract as much as an imitation of Vergil, the episode compacts more anger and more vengeful female models than it can order and direct towards the fulfillment of the Vergilian ideal of temperance.

Prospero's supreme display of Vergilian temperance is his masque, the "vanity of [his] art" he creates to celebrate the engagement of Ferdinand and Miranda. The couple's brief but exciting courtship, stage-managed by Prospero, is a study in tempering the lusts of political ambition and sexual desire. It begins when Prospero forces Miranda to confront Caliban – who obligingly presents himself as the epitome of sedition and rape – and then leads her to meet Ferdinand and conjures a response in her: "The fringéd curtains of thine eye advance, / And say what thou seest yond" (1.2.409–10). Kermode notes "the formal language and rhythm as of a magician about to 'raise' " a 'spirit' " (p. 36), and what Prospero means to rouse are his daughter's desires. Pygmalion-like, he formally awakens her from pre-sexual existence when she advances the "fringed curtains" of her eyes and, like Ovid's ivory maid who opens her eyes upon her lover and the heavens (*ad lumina lumen / attolens pariter cum caelo vidit amantem*, 10.293–4), sees a man she "might call. . . A thing divine" (418–19). Perhaps because Prospero is working on a tight schedule, he insists on Miranda's disobedience and entry into the conventions of new comedy, in which she and Ferdinand play rebellious lovers to his tyrannical father: for Miranda as well as Ferdinand, Prospero finds "this swift business / I must uneasy make lest too light winning / Make the prize light" (1.2.451–3).

Prospero selects a different passion to rouse and quell in Ferdinand: ambition. Part of the comedy of his early scenes with the youths is that Ferdinand craves exactly what Prospero wants to give – Miranda's hand in marriage – but Prospero insists on disciplining Ferdinand's apparently non-existent passion for conquest. He repeatedly accuses Ferdinand of wanting to usurp his island: "Put thy sword up , traitor, / Who mak'st a show but dar'st not strike, thy conscience / Is so possessed with guilt" (1.2.470–2). Prospero's choice to interpret Ferdinand's inquiries about his daughter's availability and virginity as acts of political aggression recalls the eroticization of conquest typical in New World rhetoric, from the cheeky cry in *Eastward Ho!* (1605), "Come, boys, Virginia longs til we share the rest of her maidenhead" (3.3.14–15),[31] to Ralegh's claims in the *Discoverie of Guiana* that "*Guiana* is a Country that hath yet her Maydenhead, never sackt, turned, nor wrought" and that he, unlike the rapacious Spaniards, has willingly "lost the sacke of one or two townes (although they might haue been very profitable) then to haue defaced or endaungered the future hope of so many millions, and the great good, and rich trade which England maie bee possessed off thereby."[32]

Prospero casts and molds Ferdinand's amorous expressions of admiration for Miranda as a prince wrangling for kingdoms by mercantile courtship or amorous bargaining rather than by conquest. The distinction in erotic styles is thrown into relief by the deliberately unjust comparison that Prospero sets up between Ferdinand and Caliban. "To th' most of men this is a Caliban, / And they to him are angels" (1.2.481–2), he tells Miranda before he actually substitutes Ferdinand for Caliban and threatens to "manacle [his] neck and feet together" (line 462).[33] For the love of his divine mistress, the prince cheerfully hauls wood and thrives on the insults, food, and labor that Prospero inflicts on his original traitor and "[im]patient log-man" (3.1.67), Caliban. The allusion is wasted on Ferdinand, if not Miranda, who well knows that Caliban attempted to rape her. Reminded of his attempt, Caliban laughs seditiously,

> O ho, O ho! Would't had been done!
> Thou didst prevent me – I had peopled else
> This isle with Calibans.   (1.2.348–50)

Stephen Orgel persuasively explains the attempted rape and its political context: Caliban, who has been brought to understand notions of mastery, property, and usurpation, has also learned that empire is founded on rape in authoritative myths of national origin. Inserting himself into the paradigm initiated by Romulus, who commanded the rape of the Sabine women,[34] Caliban celebrates his attempt at rape as the closest he ever got to overthrowing his tyrant and freeing himself from being, as he puts it to Prospero, "all the subjects that you have, / Which was first mine own king" (1.2.341–2). At the end of Prospero's rituals, Ferdinand has "strangely stood the test" (4.1.7) of seditious lusts, and is at last found in Prospero's cell playing chess with Miranda:

> MIRANDA. Sweet lord, you play me false.
> FERDINAND.   No, my dearest love,
>   I would not for the world.
> MIRANDA. Yes, for a score of kingdoms you should wrangle,
>   And I would call it fair play.   (5.1.172–5)

The dialogue itself defiantly hovers between the pastimes of flirtation and conquest on which Miranda lovingly and shrewdly comments. The pair no longer breathe the air of pure new comedy, where Prospero confined them during the two hours of their courtship. Here they are found in an anti-Vergilian cell, playfully negotiating the passions and politics of their marriage.[35]

Prospero's Vergilian masque seems designed to appeal to the young prince who, at his first sight of Miranda, bursts out with a translation of Aeneas' address to Venus, *o dea certe*: "Most sure, the goddess / On whom these airs attend!" (1.2.422–3). The masque, which turns on the formal banishment of the widow Dido, is a work in progress that reveals a great deal about the ever-widening gap between desires and their idealized representations. As soon as Iris promises a decorous representation of natural bounty,

> most bounteous lady, thy rich leas
> Of wheat, rye, barley, vetches, oats, and peas;

> Thy turfy mountains, where live nibbling sheep,
> And flat meads thatched with stover, them to keep   (4.1.60–3)

Prospero adapts and increases the astringency of Mantuan pastoral traditions[36] in an effort to contain even so reserved a natural store as Ceres'

> banks with pionèd and twillèd brims,
> Which spongy April at thy hest betrims
> To make cold nymphs chaste crowns; and thy broom groves,
> Whose shadow the dismissèd bachelor loves,
> Being lass-lorn; thy poll-clipped vineyard;
> And thy sea-marge sterile and rocky-hard.   (lines 64–9)

Placed amidst anaphrodisiac flowers and nymphs, Prospero's bachelor is no Corydon fretting for his Alexis, or Colin Clout for his Rosalind, but a swain content with petrarchan displacement: he loves a shadow in place of his diffident beloved.

Unripened desires soon break down into irreconcilable opposites of sexuality and temperance. This nature is too fragile to sustain the powerful urges ushered in by the goddess of generation, *alma Venus*. The Lucretian Venus, who pacifies raging storms with her smiles, causes the daedal earth to yield its abundant fruits, and brings, as Spenser puts it, "salvage beasts" to play, frisk, and rebellow.[37] Prospero's masque seeks to banish the goddess who inspires in Spenser's beasts

> To come where thou doest draw them with desire:
> So all things else, that nourish vitall blood,
> Soone as with fury thou doest them inspire,
> In generation seeke to quench their inward fire.   (4.10.44–6)

Such fury can only destroy the hymeneal masque, as it does when Prospero remembers Caliban and acknowledges the impossibility of banishing desires as easily as he dismisses the classical gods who represent them. Prospero's Ceres, goddess of plenty, hesitates to come to Juno, goddess of marriage, until she hears that Venus and her son Cupid were last seen

> Cutting the clouds towards Paphos, and her son
> Dove-drawn with her. Here thought they to have done
> Some wanton charm upon this man and maid,
> Whose vows are that no bed-right shall be paid
> Till Hymen's torch be lighted; but in vain.
> Mars's hot minion is returned again;
> Her waspish-headed son has broke his arrows,
> Swears he will shoot no more, but play with sparrows,
> And be a boy right out.   (lines 93–101)

No Spenserian "root of all that ioyous is," Prospero's Venus is a frustrated and rebuked version of Vergil's goddess, who contrived with Juno to cast a "wanton charm" on Dido with the help of her son Cupid. Prospero designs his wedding masque to expel Vergil's Venus and Cupid, chasten his Juno – her one point in common with Vergil's goddess is her regal gait[38] – and omit Dido's fatal error.

The passions and corporeality excluded from the idealized vision of love erupt, perhaps, because Prospero has begun to bowdlerize Vergil. The final dance between "properly habited" reapers and nymphs grinds to a heavy halt, "to a strange, hollow, and confused noise." Passions, formally banished in the forms of Venus, Cupid, and the spectral Dido, disturb Prospero himself, who is "in some passion / That works him strongly" (lines 143–4) and "distempered" (line 145) in contrast to his "temperate" nymphs (line 132) when he recalls

> that foul conspiracy
> Of the beast Caliban and his confederates
> Against my life. The minute of their plot
> Is almost come.   (4.1.139–42)

Prospero's educational spectacle, which he deprecatingly calls "Some vanity of mine art" (line 41), cannot tolerate the memory of Caliban as "a devil, a born devil, on whose nature / Nurture can never stick" (4.1.188–9). Prospero is never fully to recover from his traumatic recognition that his theatrical arts cannot coerce his subjects into compliance with Vergilian ideals.

Distopic Intruders: Ovid and the impertinent allusion

Prospero's faith in his own dream was always precarious, and the spectral centrality of the widow Dido to his masque paved the way for Caliban's intrusion. Not only a pathetic figure of sacrifice, Dido is also a terrifyingly vindictive antagonist: she imaginatively embodies Fortune, who can make dreams prosper, as she does when Aeneas arrives desperate in Carthage, or blight them with her curse, as she does when Aeneas abandons her empire for one of his own. Prospero banishes the widow Dido from his masque because he wishes to exclude the seditious and sexual passions that can poison social contracts – marriages and commonwealths – with "barren hate, / Sour-eyed disdain" (4.1.19–20). His failure to repress Dido is unsurprising, first because he has produced only a wish-fulfillment and not an institutional means for regulating such destructive passions, and second because Prospero himself relies on his own governed fury to advance his ideal of Vergilian temperance.

Ovid offers Prospero the model for the vengeful project that threatens to displace his officially benign Vergilian design. At the moment his masque breaks down, Prospero confronts the darker purpose of his project – the motive of fury which he disguised with Vergilian personifications and themes. When his utopian masque falters, Prospero steps into an antithetically Ovidian mode of revenge and adopts an explicit identification with Ovid's vindictive and powerful Diana and Medea. The rage that always threatens to disrupt the pacific surface of his project breaks through in an adaptation of a scene from the *Metamorphoses*. Borrowing the tale of Actaeon, he punishes the rebels:

> *A noise of hunters heard. Enter divers spirits in shape of dogs and hounds,*
> *hunting them about, Prospero and Ariel setting them on.*
> PROSPERO. Hey, Mountain, hey!
> ARIEL. Silver! There it goes, Silver!
> PROSPERO. Fury, Fury! there, Tyrant, there! Hark, hark!
> *Caliban, Stephano, and Trinculo are driven out*
> Go charge my goblins that they grind their joints
> With dry convulsions, shorten up their sinews
> With agèd cramps; and more pinch-spotted make them
> Than pard or cat o' mountain.
> ARIEL.   Hark, they roar!
> PROSPERO. Let them be hunted soundly.   (4.1.255–62)

Like Ovid's epic catalogue of hunting hounds, Prospero's pack of spirits issues forth, then tracks down and plagues the rabble while Prospero himself fantasizes that their physical afflictions will effect a bestial metamorphosis: he will shorten their sinews with cramps, make their hides more "pinch-spotted" than a mountain cat's and "plague them all, / Even to roaring" (4.1.192–3), metamorphic hints confirmed in Caliban's anxiety that "From toe to crown he'll fill our skins with pinches, / Make us strange stuff" (4.1.233–4).

Prospero's Ovidian identification at the moment of crisis in his Vergilian translations traces his characterological breakdown to the textual terms familiar in Shakespeare's translations of empire. While Prospero does not adopt exemplary Vergilian and vengeful Ovidian roles with the deliberation of Titus, he becomes, at the crisis of the play, a microcosm of warring identifications that are equally relevant to his sense of himself. Constituted and undone by incompatible textual authorities, he embodies the conflict of interpretation that hounds Vergil in *The Tempest*, a crisis intensified by the conversion of the play and protagonist to an Ovidian mode that interrogates Vergilian authority. Ovid's tale of Diana and Actaeon authorizes Prospero's metamorphic revenge: Caliban attempted to rape Miranda, a transgression parallel to

Actaeon's intrusion into the naked goddess' grove. Yet it is Prospero, not Miranda, who assumes the role of Diana and threatens Caliban with metamorphosis and dismemberment by hounds. Casting himself as the virgin goddess, Prospero exacts punishment for a transgression against his own inviolate purity. Prospero's austere masque grinds to a heavy halt at the memory of Caliban, his plot, and the unredeemable nature for which he stands. The rebellion and stubborn existence of Caliban intrude upon Prospero's sacred ground, the cold pastoral that is Prospero's vulnerable display of his mind and art. Caliban inevitably disrupts Prospero's utopia when the ideal of desire sweetly restrained by marriage shades into a fantasy of eradicated passions. For Prospero, the intrusion constitutes a repeat offense of attempted rape.

The tale of Actaeon simultaneously indicts Prospero himself as a magician who tampers with human fates and conscience – Prospero administers a spiritual physic to the aristocrats of "inward pinches" to stimulate "remorse."[39] Transgressing into the divine realm, Prospero, too, is threatened with the alienated, fragmented identity that is Actaeon's fate. Were he to persist in the metamorphic and vengeful Ovidian identity he momentarily adopts, he would write himself into a tragedy of revenge and self-destruction along the lines of *Titus Andronicus*. Prospero's impulsive slip into the tale of Actaeon and Diana indicates that he resists knowledge of his attempt to seize divine authority. His use of Ovid's tale precipitates the climactic rejection of revenge and magic necessary if he wishes to remain known to himself as a Vergilian, creative force of order.

Prospero uses the Ovidian tale of Diana and Actaeon spontaneously and without overt citation, a condition which does not necessarily weaken its status as an allusion. The fact that Prospero does not control it deliberately, as he did the harpy, may grant the tale a power to represent aspects of Prospero's project and consciousness that he himself does not fully acknowledge. He may glimpse himself in the mirror of his Ovidian improvisation, a possibility strengthened by his choice of Ovid's witch, Medea, to govern his recantation:

> Ye Charmes and Witchcrafts, and thou Earth which both with herbe and weed
> Of mightie working furnishest the Wizards at their neede:
> Ye Ayres and windes: ye Elves of Hilles, of Brookes, of Woods alone,
> Of standing Lakes, and of the Night aproche ye everychone.
> Through helpe of whom (the crooked bankes much wondring at the thing)
> I have compelled streames to run cleane backward to their spring.
> By charmes I make the calme Seas rough, and make the rough Seas plaine

And cover all the Skie with Cloudes, and chase them thence againe.
By charmes I rayse and lay the windes, and burst the Vipers jaw,
And from the bowels of the Earth both stones and trees doe drawe.
Whole woods and Forestes I remove: I make the Mountaines shake,
And even the Earth it selfe to grone and fearfully to quake.
I call up dead men from their graves: and thee O lightsome Moone
I darken oft, though beaten brasse abate thy perill soone
Our Sorcerie dimmes the Morning faire, and darkes the Sun
    at Noone.   (7.263–77)

With these words, as Golding translates them, Medea celebrates her
control over nature. In a curious mingling of self-recognition and
indictment, Prospero draws on her spell formally to renounce his own
magic:

Ye elves of hills, brooks, standing lakes, and groves,
And ye that on the sands with printless foot
Do chase the ebbing Neptune, and do fly him
When he comes back; you demi-puppets that
By moonshine do the green sour ringlets make,
Whereof the ewe not bites; and you whose pastime
Is to make midnight mushrooms, that rejoice
To hear the solemn curfew; by whose aid –
Weak masters though ye be – I have bedimmed
The noontide sun, called forth the mutinous winds,
And 'twixt the green sea and the azured vault
Set roaring war; to the dread rattling thunder
Have I given fire, and rifted Jove's stout oak
With his own bolt; the strong-based promontory
Have I made shake, and by the spurs plucked up
The pine and cedar. Graves at my command
Have waked their sleepers, oped, and let 'em forth
By my so potent art. But this rough magic
I here abjure.   (5.1.33–51)

Prospero closely follows Medea's incantation, altering her words only to
weave his own magical displays more tightly to her words.

What Prospero uses to conform the words of Ovid's Medea to his
dilemma are the Vergilian elements of his storm scene. To Medea's
rehearsal of magical powers, he imports Jove and Neptune – the gods
who allay Vergil's storm – from Ariel's ornamental recitation of the
tempest. When he employs for the first time the epic language of political
revolt to describe the storm, claiming he "called forth the mutinous
winds, / And 'twixt the green sea and the azured vault / Set roaring war,"
Prospero re-enacts the course of Aeolus, who cracks open the hollow
mountain containing the mutinous winds which dim the noontide sun
and rouse the seas to roaring war against the heavens:

cavum conversa cuspide montem
impulit in latus; ac venti, velut agmine facto,
qua data porta, ruunt et terras turbine perflant . . .
eripiunt subito nubes caelumque diemque
Teucrorum ex oculis; ponto nox incubat atra . . .
Interea magno misceri murmure pontum
emissamque hiemem sensit Neptunus et imis
stagna refusa vadis, graviter commotus; et alto
prospiciens summa placidum caput extulit unda.
. . . videt . . . caelique ruina.   (1.81–3, 88–9, 124–9)

Turning his spear, he struck the side of the hollow mountain; the winds, as if in armed array . . . rush forth and blow through the lands in a hurricane . . . Suddenly, the clouds snatch away the sky and day from the Trojans' eyes; black night broods over the ocean . . . Meanwhile, Neptune felt the waters stirred up in a great uproar, the storm let loose, and the still waters heaved up from the deepest ocean, and he was deeply disturbed. Looking out over the deep, he raised his peaceful head above the waters, and saw the fall of the heavens.

He chooses, at the moment of renunciation, structurally to fill the position of the Ovidian sorceress who commands the metamorphic powers that oppose his Vergilian ideal of integrity and order. The Vergilian mage who governed storms and harpies in magnificent theatrical productions does not match the Circean shape-changer who can transform Caliban, Stephano, and Trinculo "to barnacles, or to apes / With foreheads villainous low" (4.1.248–9). When Prospero contaminates Vergil's epic storm with the incantation of Ovid's Medea, he marks the collapse of distinctions between Vergilian authority and subversive Ovidian metamorphoses.

Despite the evidence of Prospero's Circean powers, critics question Shakespeare's choice for Prospero's renunciation, stressing that his magician does not practice the black magic of Medea, and that Shakespeare literally goes too far in his translation of Medea's speech. The unsavory, dangerous, black magic it takes to raise the dead may suit Sycorax, but not Prospero. Of the ghoulish climax of Prospero's speech, Kermode asserts that "there seems to be no occasion for this; all other magic feats Prospero has performed, or could have performed, save this one" (p. 115). Although Shakespeare blundered,

the story of Medea, a witch, stood in little need of allegorizing; it was quite intelligible in the light of contemporary doctrine and controversy. Thus her methods generally resemble those of contemporary witches, and Shakespeare went to Ovid as to a *locus classicus*.

As a standard authority, the logic runs, Ovid's witch does not complicate or even contribute to the interpretive issues:

there is no reason to doubt that Shakespeare's audience was quite capable of the degree of discrimination required to perceive that there were two opposed kinds of magic in *The Tempest*, and that their opposition provided an important structural tension. (p. 150)

The necessity to discriminate apparently calls for us to disavow the tensions introduced when Shakespeare translates too much.

There is, of course, every reason to assume an antithetical relationship between Prospero's art and Sycorax's magic *until* Prospero cites Medea's words. Here, he employs the moon and tidal imagery that he later ties specifically to the diabolical Sycorax: "His mother was a witch: and one so strong / That could control the moon, make flows and ebbs, / And deal in her command, without her power" (5.1.269–71). The critic who resists Prospero's provisional association of himself with Ovid's Medea and, by extension, Sycorax, joins Prospero prematurely in his ultimate denial of the problem. Prospero, however, strategically identifies the magical arts he relinquishes with powerful female witches: the momentary acceptance of an Ovidian taint effectively purges him of black magic, Ovidian changeability, and the "woman's part." These are the changeful, metamorphic, passionate forces that Prospero wishes to subdue to "nobler reason" when, moved by Ariel, he repudiates the revenge tragedy welling up within him:

> Though with their high wrongs I am struck to th' quick,
> Yet with my nobler reason 'gainst my fury
> Do I take part. The rarer action is
> In virtue than in vengeance. They being penitent,
> The sole drift of my purpose doth extend
> Not a frown further.   (5.1.25–30)

Attempting to master his own self-division, Prospero recognizes his vulnerability to being "struck to th' quick" with passion, fury, and vengefulness: he cannot successfully externalize and control them in tempests and prophetic harpies. Dividing his confused motivations between reason and fury, he associates "nobler reason" with human nature and tropes Vergilian "fury" as the magic he must give up when he restores his enemies to their reason. His success in divorcing himself from "fury" is witnessed by the critical choice to deny Prospero authority over the words of his own renunciation.

(NB)

Vergilian displays of power cloak the metamorphic character of Prospero's magic and present it as divine and natural. The tempest, the harpy, and the masque – all Vergilian in heritage – have little in common with other accounts of Prospero's art. Caliban complains that the spirits "For every trifle are . . . set upon me; / Sometime like apes, that mow and chatter at me, / And after bite me; then hedgehogs, which / Lie tumbling in my barefoot way, and mount / Their pricks at my footfall; sometime am I / All wound with adders, who with cloven tongues / Do hiss me into madness" (2.2.8–14). Caliban's deep fears of metamorphosis, however comical, appear justified in light of Prospero's decision to reject his magic. His recognition that he must abjure – legislate against – his "rough magic" brings into focus the play's sustained juxtaposition of Prospero and Sycorax. Not until Prospero rejects his magic does the threat of identity with Sycorax predominate. Here, in order to disown their part in him, Prospero momentarily aligns himself with the powerful women who work metamorphic magic for their own interests and oppose the selfless Vergilian ethic. For this moment alone, as he intones Medea's words and contaminates them with prized elements of Vergil, Prospero destabilizes those Vergilian distinctions he tried carefully to maintain throughout the play: there is no absolute difference between reformation and revenge, Jupiter and Juno, Prospero and Sycorax, Prospero and Caliban, or the aspirations of reason and will. In Sidney's words, "our erected wit maketh us know what perfection is, and yet our infected wil keepeth us from reaching unto it" (p. 9)

The theater and political consent

One of the curiosities of *The Tempest* is that the play furnishes the structure of a redemptive plot without supplying the grounds for believing in the social rejuvenation claimed by Gonzalo when he says it should be "set down / With gold on lasting pillars" that Claribel found a husband, Ferdinand a wife, "Prospero his dukedom / In a poor isle, and all of us ourselves / When no man was his own" (5.1.208–13). While the play points toward a salutary goal, it pulls its audiences towards skepticism, stopping just short of producing, anamorphically, an ideal and cynical version.[40] Instead, the play aborts Prospero's reformative project, much as Prospero himself frustrates the courtiers of the banquet, Stephano and Trinculo of the rich apparel, and himself of his idealistic masque. Prospero identifies the uneasy alliance of revenge and reformation that causes him to abort his entire plan. At the moment that he has all his enemies in his power, Prospero takes stock of the pivotal moment supplied by "bountiful Fortune," whom he must "court" lest his "fortunes . . . ever after droop" (1.2.178–84):

> Now does my project gather to a head:
> My charms crack not; my spirits obey; and time
> Goes upright with his carriage.   (5.1.1–3)

The alchemical significance of the metaphor, to "gather to a head," noted by both Kermode and Orgel, is fully appropriate to Prospero's magic and the redemptive thrust of the play. Yet – as the reader of Orgel's introduction to *The Tempest* would expect – Prospero's heightened agitation and rage are hard to sublimate in an alchemical process. Familiar as a metaphor for military uprising, to "make" or "raise head" is a favorite expression for pulling together armies, and "to gather head" adds bodily corruption to rebellion: "The time shall not be many hours of age, / More than it is ere foul sin, gathering head, / Shall break into corruption" (*Richard II*, 5.1.57–9 and *2Henry IV*, 3.1.76–7). Not yet persuaded by Ariel to forgive, Prospero understands his project as something that erupts and corrupts: the pressures of his "beating mind" (4.1.163) gather together for a violent uprising.

Precisely why Prospero interrupts his project remains a question, although moral grounds supply motivating factors. One of the play's most persuasive readers, Stephen Greenblatt, argues that Prospero deliberately "puts himself through the paralyzing uneasiness with which he has afflicted others," and suggests first that "we are witnessing the practice of salutary anxiety operating at the center of the play's world, in the consciousness of Prospero himself, magician, artist, and prince" and second that "as a further exemplification of the salutary nature of anxiety, . . . reconciliation and pardon can issue forth."[41] It may be that Prospero rouses his fears and frustrations in the expectation of purging them and remaking his "inner life" (p. 146). If so, the technique, which fails to change Antonio and Caliban, goes badly awry with Prospero, who requires Ariel's intervention to reconcile him to his victims and, although he chooses rational virtue over fury, nonetheless finds himself depleted physically and spiritually: his fortunes appear to "droop" (1.2.184), and he expects to retire to Milan "where / Every third thought shall be my grave" (5.1.310–11). Prospero's decision not to resume his princely duties or to instill his political ideas in the minds of his loving subjects suggests, as he confirms in his epilogue, that what Prospero experiences in his interrupted masque is a negative epiphany. The few clues Prospero leaves behind to explain his distemper are to be found in the theatrics that his "beating mind" produces before Ariel counsels forgiveness.

In his parable of the glistering attire, Prospero reveals what he thinks of the ambition in his own theatrical project. Stephano and Trinculo, parodies of ruthless conquerors, confess their humble status as revelers in Misrule when they are stopped in their tracks by a tree decked with gorgeous apparel:

TRINCULO. O King Stephano! O peer! O worthy Stephano
– look what a wardrobe here is for thee!
CALIBAN. Let it alone, thou fool, it is but trash.
TRINCULO. O ho, monster! We know what belongs to a frippery.
He takes a robe from the tree and puts it on
O King Stephano!
STEPHANO. Put off that gown, Trinculo. (*Reaches for it*)
By this hand, I'll have that gown
TRINCULO. Thy grace shall have it. . .
we steal by line and level, an't like your grace.
STEPHANO. I thank thee for that jest: here's a garment for't.
He takes another garment and gives it to him
Wit shall not go unrewarded while I am king of the country. . .
Monster, lay to your fingers. Help to bear this away where my
hogshead of wine is, or I'll turn you out of my kingdom. Go to, carry
this.
TRINCULO. And this.
STEPHANO. Ay, and this.
They give Caliban the remaining garments. (4.1.221–8, 239–3, 251–5)

When Prospero harasses them with spirits in the shape of hounds,
Stephano and Trinculo are roundly punished for presumption. They
prove themselves satisfied with the theatrical trappings and suits of
power, but do not leave Prospero to claim that within which passes
show. To conclude that this is Prospero's moral, tempting as it is, misses
the scope and direction of his anger, which is not aimed at Stephano's
insignificant challenge to his power.

When Stephano and Trinculo encounter the rich attire, they fail a
parodic romance test. In this temptation scene, unlike the interrupted
banquet, Stephano and Trinculo are justified when they ignore Caliban's
insistence that the clothing is "trash" and stock up on what are undeni-
able emblems of social worth, sure to be coveted by many in the play's
audience. What they stumble upon is no illusory temptation but the
wardrobe of a theater's tiring-house: as Trinculo points out, they know
the difference between such magnificence and the cast-offs sold in a
frippery where, one gathers, Trinculo has had his closest encounters with
finery. A theater company's stock of such clothing was its most valuable
property, and if Stephano and Trinculo encounter anything like Alleyn's
eighty-three item inventory that Andrew Gurr reprints in *The Shakespearean Stage*, they are pilfering sumptuous, colorful, and expensive
properties.[42] Gurr notes that Alleyn paid "£20 10s. 6d. for a 'black velvet
cloak with sleeves embroidered all with silver and gold,' more than a
third of Shakespeare's price for a house in Stratford" (p. 194).

Stephano and Trinculo's choice proclaims them theatrical impostors:

comedians, as Thomas Platter remarked in 1599, "are very expensively and elegantly costumed, since it is usual in England, when important gentlemen or knights die, for their finest clothes to be bequeathed to their servants, and since it is not proper for them to wear such clothes, instead they subsequently give them to the comedians to purchase." A play representing royalty might be, in Orgel's seminal phrase, "a mere fiction, but its trappings were paradoxically the real thing."[43] What makes Prospero's satire so successful is that inadvertently Stephano and Trinculo expose deep social tensions when they set out to attempt a political coup and are intercepted by the theater. Prospero's jest is bitter, for he proves that the clowns are no more contemptibly foolish for valuing theatrical clothing than is Prospero himself. Frustrated by his art's inefficacy, Prospero uses Stephano and Trinculo to mock his own trust in the theatrical medium to effect social transformation. Like Titus assaulting the empty authority of Horace's ode or the Zodiac, Prospero confronts the "vanity" of the theatrical arts he loves.

The clothing parable exposes Stephano as an actor, a disclosure to which Prospero himself is equally vulnerable, and develops the strong anti-theatrical thrust that Prospero began in the revels speech that ends his dearest vision. Exhorting Ferdinand to be "cheerful," presumably in the way that Stoics face death or a bracing encounter with a *memento mori*, Prospero delivers himself of his most compelling artistic production, his explanation of the vanity of his art:

> Our revels now are ended. These our actors,
> As I foretold you, were all spirits, and
> Are melted into air, into thin air,
> And, like the baseless fabric of this vision,
> The cloud-capped towers, the gorgeous palaces,
> The solemn temples, the great globe itself,
> Yea, all which it inherit, shall dissolve,
> And, like this insubstantial pageant faded,
> Leave not a rack behind. We are such stuff
> As dreams are made on; and our little life
> Is rounded with a sleep. Sir, I am vexed;
> Bear with my weakness; my old brain is troubled:
> Be not disturbed with my infirmity.   (4.1.148–60)

The play's greatest speech elegiacally summarizes the concerns with empire-building, reformation, and theater that pervade the play and make Prospero's project a translation of empire. Like Henry V's prayer on the eve of the battle of Agincourt, when he admits his anxiety about the "idol ceremony" that generates his royal charisma, Prospero's despairing synthesis – or collapse – of the theater, the world, and majesty allows a shiver to run through the backbone of the play. His crisis of mimesis is also one of faith in the values his representations are meant not merely to affirm but institute. Those towers, palaces, and temples which commemorate aspiration and power are as ephemeral as Prospero's art, the "miraculous harp" which raises the walls of his utopia. Remembrance of the stubborn nature which rebels against good nurture ushers Prospero into despair over the capacities of his art to effect change at all, and like a Sidneian poet-maker discouraged that his *poesis* has no relation to *praxis*, that his ideals are so many "Castles in the aire," and that his "infected wil" has defeated his "erected wit," Prospero falls from his poet's "golden" world back into the "brasen" (*Defense of Poesie*, pp. 24–5). He imagines the apocalypse of civilized forms, and with it comes the collapse of his internal architecture, leaving Prospero an uncanny mirror of the very distempered passions he seeks alternately to subjugate, banish, and nurture out of others.

Prospero's interrupted masque does not inoculate him against anxieties, if that is its purpose, nor does it ultimately affirm social order. Unlike Henry V's speech on ceremony, Prospero's shattered masque ushers him into a despair from which royal charisma cannot save him. Shakespeare's Jacobean play does not culminate in an affirmation of the prince's absolute command, despite the welcome that such a message would receive from James, who had been instructing his House of Commons not to dispute his prerogative. Absolutism is not the message of the play, nor is a play judged an appropriate medium for the absolutist position. Obviously vulnerable for the first time in the play, Prospero steps forward at its end to plead for the audience's applause and approval:

> Now my charms are all o'erthrown,
> And what strength I have's mine own,
> Which is most faint. Now 'tis true,
> I must be here confined by you,
> Or sent to Naples. Let me not,
> Since I have my dukedom got,
> And pardon'd the deceiver, dwell
> In this bare island by your spell,
> But release me from my bands
> With the help of your good hands.
> Gentle breath of yours my sails
> Must fill, or else my project fails,
> Which was to please. Now I want
> Spirits to enforce, art to enchant;
> And my ending is despair
> Unless I be relieved by prayer . . .   (5.1.319–34)

Prospero's final lines, which stir critics to debate their success, may be "profoundly satisfactory Shakespearian octosyllabics" (p. 134) as Kermode calls them in defense against E. E. Stoll's interrogation of their authenticity, but it is likely that the lines are objectionable not as verse but petition. The plea to the audience, which Stoll dismisses as irrelevant to Shakespeare's position, Orgel explains as Prospero's desire for "the freedom to continue his history beyond the limits of the stage and the text" (p. 204).

Prospero explicitly does not repeat his suggestion in the revels speech that there is no substance to his art or, in the words Puck used to excuse his audacity, "If we shadows have offended, / Think but this and all is mended, / That you have but slumber'd here / While these visions did appear" (*Dream* 5.1.423–6). Instead, he acknowledges that he has relinquished his powers and depends wholly on the audience's acquiescence to restore potency to his project and save it from failure. Shakespeare's protagonist reappears, surprisingly and to many disappointingly, to confess his weakness and deliver the power of ratification over to the audience. At the end of a play torn between liberties and absolute command, in which Prospero aborts his own project out of anxiety that his manipulations impaired the humanity of his enemies and himself alike, Shakespeare's magician, artist, and prince acknowledges to his audiences that his authority derives from their consent. Shakespeare's firmly and, to some, noxiously humble stand delicately proposes an answer to the question raised in *The Tempest* about the theater's relationships to royal authority and popular audiences. Emphatically not seditious in its themes, the play nonetheless aligns the theater with constitutional theory that derives the royal authority from the people, who technically have the right to withdraw their consent and leave the prince stranded on a desert island.

Notes

INTRODUCTION: SHAKESPEARE'S FATAL CLEOPATRA

1 A recent exception is Lawrence Manley's valuable *The Literature and Culture of Early Modern London* (Cambridge University Press, 1995), which studies an exhaustive range of the artistic forms and social ideologies that went into the fashioning of London.

2 The classic study of imitation is Thomas M. Greene, *The Light In Troy: Imitation and Discovery in Renaissance Poetry* (New Haven and London: Yale University Press, 1982). Greene has little interest in "exploitative" and "eclectic" contaminations (p. 39), perhaps because his argument about the disruptive force of historical anachronism in dialogical imitations leads him to isolate interpretive differences between a fairly monolithic classical period and the renaissance rather than among available classical authorities. I am presently working on *Literary Contamination*, a study of the political and poetic uses to which early modern writers put the black sheep of the imitation family.

3 Quoted from Lawrence Manley, *London in the Age of Shakespeare* (University Park and London: Pennsylvania State University Press, 1986), pp. 277–8.

4 I borrow Maynard Mack's wonderful observation of *Hamlet,* rpt. in the Signet Classic edition by Edward Hubler (1963), gen. ed. Sylvan Barnet, p. 237.

5 *Johnson on Shakespeare*, ed. Walter Raleigh (Oxford University Press, 1908, rpt. 1957), pp. 23–4.

6 Johnson also alludes to Atalanta, who turned from her career to chase the golden apple of Aphrodite. The story, which Ovid tells in *Metamorphoses* 10, presents a female Hercules at the crossroads suited to Johnson's Shakespeare *in bivio*.

7 I quote from *Paradise Lost*, ed. Alastair Fowler (London: Longman, 1971), p. 475.

8 George Puttenham describes the indiscriminate use of different languages as a "mingle-mangle" in *The Arte of English Poesie*, ed. Gladys Doidge Willcock and Alice Walker (Folcroft, Pa.: The Folcroft Press, 1936, rpt. 1969), p. 252 and John Lyly uses the term apologetically to describe mixed genres in the prologue to *Midas*, in *The Complete Works of John Lyly*, vol. 3, ed. R. Warwick Bond (Oxford: Clarendon Press, 1902), p. 115.

I SHAKESPEARE AND THE TROY LEGEND

1 I quote Jonson's poem from *The Riverside Shakespeare*, G. Blakemore Evans, textual editor (Boston: Houghton Mifflin Co., 1974). All references to Shakespeare's plays, other than the ones primarily studied here, are to this edition.

2 All references to Vergil's *Aeneid* are from the edition by R. D. Williams, 2 vols. (New York: St. Martin's Press, 1972). All references to Ovid's *Metamorphoses* are from the Loeb edition of Frank Justus Miller, 2 vols. (Cambridge, Ma.: Harvard University Press, 1916). Unless otherwise specified, all Latin translations are my own.

3 I cite from *Horace: Odes and Epodes*, ed. Paul Shorey and Gordon J. Laing (Benj. H. Sanborn & Co., 1919; rpt. University of Pittsburgh Press, 1960).

4 Considering Jonson's ardent desire to be Britain's Horace, his choice to imitate Horace 2.20 on Shakespeare's behalf is a gift Jonson would not make if he meant by "small Latine, and lesse Greeke" what Charles Martindale means, condescendingly, in *Shakespeare and the Uses of Antiquity* (London: Routledge, 1990). See Vergil K. Whitaker, *Shakespeare's Use of Learning: An Inquiry into the Growth of his Mind and Art* (San Marino, California: The Huntington Library, 1964). On the subject of education in general, see David Cressy's valuable *Education in Tudor and Stuart England* (London: Edward Arnold, 1975), Joan Simon, *Education and Society in Tudor England* (Cambridge University Press, 1966), and Craig R. Thompson, *Schools in Tudor England* (Washington: Folger Library, 1958), who remarks that Jonson's line is often misinterpreted, since "every Elizabethan who completed grammar school, even the most inconspicuous country grammar school, had studied Latin for seven years and studied it more than anything else" (p. 24). For a judicious reading of the poem and its relationship to Horace, see Richard S. Peterson, *Imitation and Praise in the Poems of Ben Jonson* (New Haven: Yale University Press, 1981).

5 Generations of classicists have censured the ungainly transformation. Hermann Fraenkel, *Horace* (Oxford University Press, 1957), sanctions only the words, *non ego quem vocas, delecte Maecenas,* in an otherwise "disappointing" ode (p. 300). Shorey and Laing refer to the "somewhat artificial poetic frenzy" and "bad taste" of the details of Horace's metamorphosis. Matthew S. Santirocco, *Unity and Design in Horace's Odes* (Chapel Hill: University of North Carolina Press, 1986), wonders if Horace is still under the influence of Bacchus, inspirer in the previous poem. In *Horace's Poetic Journey: A Reading of Odes 1–3* (Princeton University Press, 1987), David H. Porter explains the poem's "occasional absurdities" and "grotesque transformation" in terms of Icarus and concludes that "we can only wonder somewhat incredulously at this Horatian swan, at the soaring presumption of its reckless surge, the total absence of ... hesitations and inhibitions" (pp. 146–7). None of the commentaries interprets Horace's focus on colonies facing defeat by Rome or notices the connection between the fiction of poetic immortality and the spread of empire. David Armstrong, however, in his excellent introduction to the poet, *Horace* (New Haven and London: Yale University Press, 1989), implicitly connects "the dizzying heights of immor-

tality" in 2.20 to "the map of the empire and the rest of the known world of 23 BC." Armstrong discusses the poem in terms of map making and geography, which were "high-priority items supported by government-paid research. It was one of Agrippa's long-term projects to set up as a public monument a colossal map of the known world" (p. 73).

6 Jonson's swans suggest that Shakespeare's appearances on the Thames compliment civic rather than exclusively royal power. The Thames was famous for its swans, which figure prominently in encomiastic poetry such as John Leland's *Cygnea Cantio* (1542) and Spenser's "Prothalamion." See Lawrence Manley, *London in the Age of Shakespeare: An Anthology* (University Park and London: Pennsylvania State University Press, 1986).

7 *The Place of the Stage: License, Play, and Power in Renaissance England* (University of Chicago Press, 1988), pp. 8, 30. Given Mullaney's emphasis on the "alienation" of the theater, his boundary between the city and its liberties is less permeable than Jonson's apppears to be. Drawing on Glynne Wickham, *Early English Stages, 1300–1600,* 3 vols. (London: Routledge & Kegan Paul, 1959–80), Mullaney engages the ideological aspects of the physical sites of the playhouses. He avoids the Marxist views of Michael D. Bristol, *Carnival and Theater: Plebeian Culture and the Structure of Authority in Renaissance England* (New York and London: Methuen, 1985) and Robert Weimann, *Shakespeare and the Popular Tradition in the Theater*, ed. Robert Schwartz (Baltimore and London: The Johns Hopkins University Press, 1978), yet modifies the new historicist axiom that authority always recuperates subversion when he links the rise of the public playhouses to the erosion of traditional hierarchies and argues that plays and playhouses were not "contained by the customary antitheses of rule and misrule, order and disorder" (p. 49). In *Shakespearean Negotiations: The Circulation of Social Energy in Renaissance England* (Berkeley and Los Angeles: University of California Press, 1988), Stephen Greenblatt similarly remarks that it is "important to resist the integration of all images and expressions into a single master discourse" (pp. 2–3). The present study addresses the formal means by which Shakespeare engages a literary-political tradition that is both highly privileged and contested in order to pose his own challenge to the notion of "a single master discourse" about power.

8 Benedict Anderson, *Imagined Communities: Reflections on the Origin and Spread of Nationalism* (London and New York: Verso, rev. edn., 1991), emphasizes the role of print in forming the idea of nationality in a fashion that Ben Jonson might support. His remark that imagined communities may be " 'realized' (as in stagecraft)" is suggestive. For discussions of Jonson's efforts to invent himself as an author and the conditions of publication under treason laws – signs of official recognition of the role of print – see Joseph F. Loewenstein, "Legal Proofs and Corrected Readings: Press-Agency and the New Bibliography," *The Production of English Renaissance Culture*, ed. David Lee Miller, Sharon O'Dair, and Harold Weber (Ithaca and London: Cornell University Press, 1994), pp. 93–122.

9 *Ben Jonson*, ed. C. H. Herford, Percy Simpson, and Evelyn Simpson, 11 vols. (Oxford: Clarendon Press, 1925–52). All references to Jonson are from this edition, hereafter cited as Herford and Simpson.

10 Jonson's discussion of English orators confirms Richard Helgerson's argument, in *Forms of Nationhood: The Elizabethan Writing of England* (University of Chicago Press, 1992), that a generation of Elizabethans was trying to transform the English language and literature into an imperial "form." For a reading of English diffidence towards imperial identity, see Jeffrey Knapp, *An Empire Nowhere: England, America, and Literature from Utopia to The Tempest* (Berkeley and Los Angeles: University of California Press, 1992).

11 For the pre-Vergilian history of the myth of Trojan origins, used to find a non-Greek origin for Rome, see Erich S. Gruen, *Culture and National Identity in Republican Rome* (Ithaca: Cornell University Press, 1992), ch. 1. See also Howard Erskine-Hill's discussion of Octavius and his literary and cultural afterlife in England in *The Augustan Idea in English Literature* (London: E. Arnold, 1983).

12 *Epic and Empire: Politics and Generic Form from Vergil to Milton* (Princeton University Press, 1993), p. 8.

13 Thomas Lodge, *Reply to Gosson's Schoole of Abuse,* quoted from *Complete Works* (New York: Russell & Russell, 1963), vol. 1, pp. 20–1. Lodge assumes that Ovid's banishment from Rome is an act of censorship and reprisal, not punishment for adultery with Julia.

14 The classic study of Geoffrey of Monmouth is J. S. P. Tatlock, *The Legendary History of Britain: Geoffrey of Monmouth's Historia Regum Britanniae and its Early Vernacular Versions* (Berkeley: University of California Press, 1950). The following studies include useful discussions of the Troy legend: Richard Waswo, "The History that Literature Makes," *New Literary History* 10 (1988), 541–64; Graham Parry, *The Golden Age Restor'd: The Culture of the Stuart Court, 1603–42* (New York: St. Martin's Press, 1981); Arthur B. Ferguson, *Clio Unbound: Perception of the Social and Cultural Past in Renaissance England* (Durham, North Carolina: Duke University Press, 1979); May McKisack, *Medieval History in the Tudor Age* (Oxford: Clarendon Press, 1971); F. J. Levy, *Tudor Historical Thought* (San Marino, California: The Huntington Library, 1967); Robert Hanning, *The Vision of History in Early Britain: From Gildas to Geoffrey of Monmouth* (New York: Columbia University Press, 1966); T. D. Kendrick, *British Antiquity* (New York: Barnes and Noble, and London: Methuen, 1950); and S. K. Heninger, "The Tudor Myth of Troy-novant," *South Atlantic Quarterly* 61 (1962), 378–87. For Stuart historical thought, see D. R. Woolf, *The Idea of History in Early Stuart England: Erudition, Ideology, and 'The Light of Truth' from the Accession of James I to the Civil War* (University of Toronto Press, 1990). For a psychoanalytic interpretation of the Troy tradition, see Elizabeth J. Bellamy, *Translations of Power: Narcissism and the Unconscious in Epic History* (Ithaca and London: Cornell University Press, 1992).

15 *Astraea: The Imperial Theme in the Sixteenth Century* (London: Routledge, 1975), pp. 29–87. Roy Strong develops Yates' work in *The Cult of Elizabeth: Elizabethan Portraiture and Pageantry* (Berkeley and Los Angeles: University of California Press, 1977). In *Of Chastity and Power: Elizabethan Literature and the Unmarried Queen* (New York: Routledge, Chapman and Hall, 1989), pp. 61–82, Philippa Berry criticizes Yates and Strong's focus on "images of national unity and of political consensus" (p. 67). For the political use of

Augustan imperial mythology in the courts of Charles V and Philip II, see Yates, *Astraea*, Strong, *Splendour at Court: Renaissance Spectacle and Illusion* (London: Weidenfield & Nicolson, 1973), and Marie Tanner, *The Last Descendant of Aeneas: The Hapsburgs and the Mythic Image of the Emperor* (New Haven and London: Yale University Press, 1993).

16 Thomas Heywood, *The Life of Merlin, sirnamed Ambrosius. His prophecies, and Predictions Interpreted; and their truth made good by our English Annales. Being a Chronographical History of all the Kings, and memorable passages of this kingdome, from BRUTE to the Reigne of our Royall Soveraigne King Charles* (London: J. Okes, 1641), p. 349.

17 Quoted from David M. Bergeron, *Elizabethan Civic Pageantry, 1558–1642* (Edward Arnold, 1971), p. 58.

18 The emblems to the "Aprill" eclogue are taken from Aeneas' words to Venus, disguised as a Spartan huntress. The *Venus armata* prepares for Dido's entrance, compared to Diana leading her nymphs. E. K.'s notes on the phrases, *o quam te memorem virgo?* and *o dea certa* elaborate the relation of this image to Elizabeth. See Louis Adrian Montrose, "'Eliza, Queene of Shepheardes,' and the Pastoral of Power," *Renaissance Humanism: Selections from "English Literary Renaissance,"* ed. Arthur F. Kenney and Dan S. Collins (Amherst: University of Massachusetts Press, 1987), pp. 34–63.

19 Quoted from Winfried Schleiner, "Divina Virago: Queen Elizabeth as an Amazon," *Studies in Philology* 75 (1978), 163–80, p. 180. Camden mentions a painting of the Spanish navy "in confusion with a fired Ship approaching, adding to Her Honour out of Vergil, "Dux Fæmina facti," *Remains Concerning Britain* (London: John Russell Smith, 1870), pp. 383–4. In *Puzzling Shakespeare: Local Reading and Its Discontents* (Berkeley and Los Angeles: University of California Press, 1988), pp. 67–105, Leah S. Marcus discusses the medal in an eye-opening reading of the Astraea imagery in the *Henry VI* plays.

20 The entire speech appears in *Cabala, Mysteries of State and Government: in Letters of Illustrious Persons and Great Ministers of State* (London: G. Bedel and T. Collins, 1654), pp. 372–4.

21 Thomas Dekker, *The Dramatic Works of Thomas Dekker*, ed. Fredson Bowers (Cambridge University Press, 1964–70), p. 298. Thomas Middleton, *Works of Middleton*, ed. A. H. Bullen (New York: AMS Press, 1964), pp. 224–5.

22 A pithy account of James' inheritance of Elizabeth's political, economic, and ideological legacy appears in Malcolm Smuts, "The Stuarts and the Elizabethan Legend," *Court Culture and the Origins of a Royalist Tradition in Early Stuart England* (Philadelphia: University of Pennsylvania Press, 1987), pp. 15–50.

23 *The Living Monument: Shakespeare and the Theater of his Time* (Cambridge University Press, 1976), p. 113.

24 Dekker, *Dramatic Works*, p. 292.

25 Herford and Simpson, vol. 7 (1941), p. 107. For James I's self-characterization as the *novus Augustus*, see Jonathan Goldberg, "Authorities," *James I and the Politics of Literature: Jonson, Shakespeare, Donne, and Their Contemporaries* (Baltimore and London: The Johns Hopkins Press, 1983), pp. 28–54.

26 Herford and Simpson, vol. 7, p. 256.

27 The proscriptions were infamous: shortly after Shakespeare's Antony delivers his speech over the body of Julius Caesar, he, Octavius, and Lepidus enter the stage and blithely discuss the list of "names [that] are prick'd" (4.1.1). This is Falstaff's word for his ghastly conscription of men as "food for powder." For a useful account of how Romans responded to the civil wars and to Augustus himself, see Gary B. Miles and Archibald W. Allen, "Vergil and the Augustan Experience," *Vergil at 2000: Commemorative Essays on the Poet and his Influence*, ed. John D. Bernard (New York: AMS Press, 1986), pp. 13–42.

28 *The Dramatic Works of Thomas Heywood*, ed. A. B. Grosart (New York: Russell & Russell, rpt. 1964).

29 Sir John Fortescue, *De Natura Legis Naturae*, Part I, ed. David S. Berkowitz and Samuel E. Thorne (New York and London: Garland Publishing, Inc., 1980), p. 206.

30 This point is noted by Jonathan Bate, *Shakespeare and Ovid* (Oxford University Press, 1993), pp. 139–40.

31 All references to Chaucer are from *The Riverside Chaucer*, 3rd edn., Larry D. Benson, gen. ed. (Boston: Houghton Mifflin Company, 1987).

32 See David Quint, *Epic and Empire*, ch. 1 for a detailed discussion of the art and ideology represented on Aeneas' shield. Philip Hardie, *Vergil's Aeneid: Cosmos and Imperium* (Oxford University Press, 1986), offers an interpretively rich discussion of the conservative view of the *Aeneid*. Although I seek to qualify, perhaps radically, the view of Vergil's political and artistic conservatism, I have no interest in opposing the traditional reading of Vergil with the so-called "Harvard" view, defined by W. R. Johnson's *Darkness Visible: A Study of Vergil's Aeneid* (Berkeley, Los Angeles, and London: University of California Press, 1976). Adam Parry productively describes the bifurcation of voices in the *Aeneid*, which he calls "public" and "private" in "The Two Voices of Vergil's *Aeneid*" (1963), *Vergil: A Collection of Critical Essays*, ed. Steele Commager (Englewood Cliffs, N. J.: Prentice-Hall, 1966), pp. 107–23.

33 This is the elegant translation of Robert Fitzgerald, *The Aeneid of Vergil* (New York: Random House, 1983). I thank Nancy Ciccone for drawing my attention to the linguistic ambiguity of Vergil's pervasive formula, *si qua gloria est*.

34 In *The Frenzy of Renown: Fame and its History* (Oxford University Press, 1986), pp. 55–149, Leo Braudy presents a compelling and informed meditation on the centrality of fame to Rome's military and literary preoccupations; his reading of Vergil's Fame and Ovid's general position within Augustan culture largely concur with my own, although he is not concerned with the ways in which Ovid interrogatively engages Vergil's poem.

35 Stephen Orgel, *The Tempest* (Oxford University Press, 1987), p. 42.

36 When Fitzgerald, stoically resisting the romantic enticements of the language, translates the phrase, "how they reveled all the winter long" (p. 102), he transposes the scene of love from a private experience of "warming the winter" to a public spectacle of revelry.

37 Caroline Dinshaw, *Chaucer's Sexual Poetics* (Madison: University of Wisconsin Press, 1989), pp. 136–7.

38 Daniel Javitch describes Ovid's revision of Vergil in "The Imitation of Imitations in *Orlando Furioso*," *Renaissance Quarterly* 38 (1985), 215–39.

39 In a seminal article, Michael C. J. Putnam, "*Aeneid* 7 and the *Aeneid*," in *Essays on Latin Lyric, Elegy, and Epic* (Princeton University Press, 1982), pp. 288–310, focuses on the metamorphoses that unexpectedly proliferate in Book 7.

40 I follow the Loeb translation except where Miller's version works hard to inculpate Dido rather than Aeneas, to the distress of the Latin. He translates *discidium* and *maritus* as "departure" and "lord," when their common meanings are "divorce" and "husband." Moreover, *decipio* means "deceive," not "disappoint."

41 As A. C. Hamilton notes, the satyr who "Nine times" came "aloft ere day" (x.48.5) "imitates Ovid who took Corinna nine times in one short night," as Ovid boasts in *Amores* 3.7.25–6 (London and New York: Longman, 1977).

42 Geoffrey Bullough, *Narrative and Dramatic Sources of Shakespeare* (London: Routledge & Kegan Paul and New York: Columbia University Press, 1964–75). It should be clear by now that I dispute the view, expressed in Steven Mullaney, *The Place of the Stage*, that when source study takes up "two highly problematic and historically determined texts . . . [it] necessarily strips them of their particular cultural contexts to establish a strictly linear and narrowly literary relationship between them" (p. 90). Such a stripping of text from history happens commonly enough, but not necessarily.

43 Timothy Hampton, *Writing From History: The Rhetoric of Exemplarity in Renaissance Literature* (Ithaca and London: Cornell University Press, 1990), pp. 26–7.

44 Shakespeare's tragic heroes characteristically confront their own inconsistencies, which they stigmatize as feminine, but Hamlet, Lear, Othello, and Macbeth do not pose the trauma as a conflict of texts. Othello comes closest to a textually inflected crisis of identity because of his habit of narratively presenting himself to the Venetian community. His autobiographical speech, moreover, recalls Aeneas' heroic tale which won Dido's compassion and heart much as Othello's wins Desdemona's "pity."

45 *The Machiavellian Moment: Florentine Political Thought and the Atlantic Republican Tradition* (Princeton University Press, 1975), p. 37. See also Hanna Fenichel Pitkin, *Fortune Is a Woman: Gender and Politics in the Thought of Niccolò Machiavelli* (Berkeley: University of California Press, 1982). The distinction between male virtue and female fortune is similarly important to the compelling reading of *Antony and Cleopatra* in Lars Engle, *Shakespeare's Pragmatism: Market of His Time* (University of Chicago Press, 1993), which quotes Pocock's discussion (pp. 200–1).

46 In a very different reading of the theater's operation under the aegis of femininity, Laura Levine, *Men In Women's Clothing: Anti-theatricality and Effeminization, 1579–1642* (Cambridge University Press, 1994), suggests that Shakespeare's theater envisions the effeminized world that the anti-theatricalists feared. The most comprehensive study of anti-theatricality is Jonas Barish's admirable *The Anti-theatrical Prejudice* (Berkeley and London: University of California Press, 1981). See also Jean E. Howard, *The Stage and Social Struggle in Early Modern England* (London and New York: Routledge,

1994). Levine's notion that theatrical spectacle is meant to generate anger seems to me compatible with the Senecan strand of Shakespearean dramaturgy; see Gordon Braden, *Renaissance Tragedy and the Senecan Tradition: Anger's Privilege* (New Haven and London: Yale University Press, 1985).

47 For Sidney's discussion of the power of poetry to create the necessary desire to move from γνωσις to πραξις, I refer to *Defence of Poesie, The Prose Works of Sir Philip Sidney*, vol. 3, ed. Albert Feuillerat (Cambridge University Press, 1963), p. 19.

48 Muriel Bradbrook, *The Living Monument* (Cambridge University Press, 1974), p. 42.

49 Essex's slight, quoted from Mervyn James, *Society, Politics and Culture: Studies in Early Modern England* (Cambridge University Press, 1986), p. 423, is addressed to Sir Robert Sidney at the surrender of Essex House: "Judge you . . . whether it can be grief to a man descended as I am, to be trodden underfoot by such base upstarts," whom he scorns as cowards since "they keep aloof from danger, and dare not approach me." As James notes, "Essex saw himself as chosen, both by lineage, and by his tenure of the office of earl marshal, to be the natural leader of a community of honour, 'the flower of the nobility and gentry of England'" – in the phrase of one follower describing Essex's aristocratic rebels.

50 Quoted from A. R. Braunmuller, ed., *A Seventeenth Century Letter-Book* (Newark: University of Delaware Press and Associated University Presses, 1983), pp. 66–7.

51 Annabel Patterson, *Shakespeare and the Popular Voice* (Oxford: Basil Blackwell, 1989), pp. 88–92, discusses the rhetorical models used to negotiate interactions between the monarch and a rough-spoken commoner and shows that Shakespeare sides with the common soldier. For some critics – and certainly for Kenneth Branagh's production of *Henry V* – the episode successfully engages what Victor Turner defines as the dialectical tension between "structure," which "holds people apart, defines their differences and constrains their actions," and "communitas," which expresses "the desire for a total, unmediated relationship between person and person, a relationship which nevertheless does not submerge one in the other but safeguards their uniqueness in the very act of realizing their commonness," *Dramas, Fields and Metaphors* (Ithaca: Cornell University Press, 1974), p. 274. Henry succeeds if Williams appreciatively accepts the glove stuffed with coins.

52 Garland publishes the two volumes together in its series, *Classics of English Legal History in the Modern Era*, selected by David S. Berkowitz and Samuel E. Thorne (New York and London: Garland Publishing Inc., 1979). For the growing sense in Tudor England that counsel was important even from the commoner, see Arthur B. Ferguson, *The Articulate Citizen and the English Renaissance* (Durham: Duke University Press, 1965), esp. pp. 133–61.

53 See Elizabeth Fowler, "The Failure of Moral Philosophy in the Work of Edmund Spenser," *Representations* 51 (Summer 1995), esp. p. 55.

54 "Versions of Imitation in the Renaissance," *Renaissance Quarterly* 33 (1980), 1–32.

55 See "Classical Culture and Moral Reform," *Court Culture*, pp. 73–116, especially p. 111. The annoyed tone is uncharacteristic of the fair-minded

Smuts, who himself furnishes subtle political readings of, for example, Cavalier poetry (pp. 183–243). For the Tudor culture of allusion-hunting, see David Bevington, *Tudor Drama and Politics: A Critical Approach to Topical Meaning* (Cambridge: Harvard University Press, 1968), pp. 1–26.

56 Smuts' sympathies for the critical study of censorship, politics, and allusion broaden to include guarded admiration for Annabel Patterson, *Censorship and Interpretation: The Conditions of Writing and Reading in Early Modern England* (Madison: University of Wisconsin Press, 1984), before constricting into nettled impatience with Martin Butler, *Theatre and Crisis: 1632–1642* (Cambridge University Press, 1984). It is unclear whether Smuts is annoyed because Butler gives "inadequate attention to this [methodological] problem" (p. 111) or because he draws strong and risky distinctions between parliamentary and courtly audiences repugnant to Smuts, who argues that early Stuart court satire is self-critical rather than oppositional and anti-monarchical. For Smuts' criticism of Butler's distinctions between parliamentary and courtly audiences, see p. 71n.

57 See H. S. Bennett's engaging and valuable *English Books and Readers 1558 to 1603* (Cambridge University Press, 1965). W. W. Greg, *London Publishing Between 1550 and 1650* (Oxford: Clarendon Press, 1956), discusses the institutions governing publication.

58 I follow Alfred Harbage, *Shakespeare and the Rival Traditions* (Bloomington and London: Indiana University Press, 1952) – although his emphasis on coterie drama is generally acknowledged as misleading – and Muriel Bradbrook, *The Rise of the Common Player: A Study of Actor and Society in Shakespeare's England* (Cambridge, Mass.: Harvard University Press, 1962) and *The Living Monument*. See also E. K. Chambers, *The Elizabethan Stage*, 4 vols. (Oxford: Clarendon, 1923), Andrew Gurr, *The Shakespearean Stage*, 3rd edn. (Cambridge University Press, 1992), and *Playgoing in Shakespeare's London* (Cambridge University Press, 1987). Since the Troy legend's history of political appropriation was available in a range of venues in London, only more detailed allusions might be "caviar to the general." My audience differs from that claimed by Ann Jennalie Cook in *The Privileged Playgoers of Shakespeare's London, 1576–1642* (Princeton University Press, 1981).

59 For education's bearing on Shakespeare's dramatic heritage, see Bate, *Shakespeare and Ovid*, pp. 1–47, Joel B. Altman, *The Tudor Play of Mind: Rhetorical Inquiry and the Development of Elizabethan Drama* (Berkeley: University of California Press, 1978), and Madeleine Doran, *Endeavors of Art: A Study of Form in Elizabethan Drama* (Madison: University of Wisconsin Press, 1954), pp. 24–46. For the use of drama to promote Protestant ideas, see Paul Whitfield White, *Theatre and Reformation: Protestantism, Patronage, and Playing in Tudor England* (Cambridge University Press, 1993), pp. 100–29.

60 Standing before the city, Henry swears he will "not leave the half-achieved Harfleur / Till in her ashes she lies buried," and warns her citizens that "the flesh'd soldier, rough and hard of heart . . . mowing like grass / Your fresh fair virgins and your flow'ring infants" (3.3.8–14). The rhetoric for sacking cities reappears in his courtship of Katherine. In conversation, Paul Whitworth, an RSC actor performing the part of Henry V for Shakespeare Santa

Cruz, told me he played the scene before Harfleur as his "rape scene," and confided his disappointment that audiences "fell in love with him" every night after his scene with Katherine, which Whitworth considered to be his repeat attempt.

61 Robert Miola, "Vergil in Shakespeare: From Allusion to Imitation," *Vergil at 2000*, ed. John D. Bernard (New York: AMS Press, 1986), pp. 241–58, p. 242.

2 BLAZONING INJUSTICES: MUTILATING TITUS ANDRONICUS, VERGIL AND ROME

1 All references are to the Arden edition by Jonathan Bate (London and New York: Routledge, 1995), whose excellent edition of the play inspired me to make the substitution for J. C. Maxwell's earlier Arden edition (London: Methuen, 1953, rpt., 1968), which I used to compose my argument and whose notes I use extensively. Bate generously shared portions of his edition with me in advance of publication and our conversations about the play were a source of pleasure. Since he extends act 1 through the scene that most editors designate as 2.1, I include two references where appropriate. I thank Eugene Waith, whose work on the play's relationship to Ovid prompted further critical interest in citation, for his cheerful skepticism, which brought me to advance my arguments with greater caution and, I hope, persuasiveness. I do not use his edition (Oxford University Press, 1984) in order to avoid an unprofitable catalogue of differences in our visions of the play's aesthetic and ideological dimensions: the value he places on harmony softens the strategic disjunctions which are of strict interest to the present study. See my discussion of the Oath of Revenge below.

2 In *Shakespeare's Ghost Writers: Literature as Uncanny Causality* (New York and London: Methuen, 1987), pp. 23–5, Marjorie Garber points out how persistently critics fall upon the infelicitous use of corporeal metaphors, such as head and hand, to describe facets of the play and Shakespeare's authorship. She notes that critics are merely following Shakespeare's lead: this is the playwright who talks about "headless Rome" (1.1.190) before bringing literal heads onstage, and has the play's protagonist exclaim, "O handle not the theme, to talk of hands" (3.2.29). Since failure seems inevitable if one tries to avoid the play's linguistic pitfalls, and since repudiating the pun indicates insensitivity to their function in the play, it seems preferable to leap headlong into them.

3 Shakespeare practices more brash forms of *aemulatio* and *digestio* than Ben Jonson happily contemplates as literary practices in *Discoveries* 3, where he remarks that the poet who excels in imitation is not like the "creature that swallows what it takes in crude, raw, or undigested; but that feeds with an appetite, and hath a stomach to concoct, divide, and turn all into nourishment," Herford and Simpson, vol. 8, p. 638.

4 These memorable words come from Edward Ravenscroft, the seventeenth-century playwright who refurbished *Titus Andronicus* for the stage. See his preface to *Titus Andronicus, or the Rape of Lavinia* (London, 1687). In the battle of quips, Ravenscroft prevails over T. S. Eliot, who calls Titus "one of the stupidest and most uninspired plays ever written" in "Seneca and

Elizabethan Tragedy," *Selected Essays*, new edn. (New York: Harcourt and Brace, 1950), p. 67, and Dover Wilson, who smugly likens the play to a "broken-down cart, laden with bleeding corpses from an Elizabethan scaffold," *The Complete Works of William Shakespeare* (Cambridge 1948, p. xii): Ravenscroft's "heap of Rubbish" – the bounteous compost of Latin tags which inform the play's structure – has the distinction of referring critically to the play.

5 Literary history slights both Ovid's poetry and Shakespeare's play. The self-proclaimed lasciviousness of the *magister amoris* has kept educators from seeing more than skin deep into Ovid's works; and *Titus Andronicus* has so long been regarded as merely sensational that a popular student edition of the play calls it both ahistorical and apolitical: the Signet edition of *Titus Andronicus* includes Germaine Greer's assertion that the play "found its way into the Stratford Roman series [of 1972] under false pretenses [it] is no more a play about history or politics than *Measure for Measure* is a play about Vienna," ed. Sylvan Barnet (1963, 1989), p. 175. In *The Scholemaster*, Elyot suggests avoiding the *Ars Amatoria* and *Metamorphoses*, a decision whose prurience is reflected in the *Metamorphoses*' late appearance in the Oxford and Teubner editions.

6 The association of rape and conquest in history and literature influenced by Rome has been discussed in various early modern contexts: see, for example, Stephen Orgel, Introduction to *The Tempest* (Oxford University Press, 1987); Nancy J. Vickers, "This Heraldry in Lucrece' Face," *The Female Body in Western Literature*, ed. Susan Rubin Suleiman (Cambridge: Harvard University Press, 1986), pp. 209–22; Catharine R. Stimpson, "Shakespeare and the Soil of Rape," *The Woman's Part: Feminist Criticism of Shakespeare*, eds. Carolyn Ruth Swift Lenz, Gayle Greene, and Carol Thomas Neely (Urbana: University of Illinois Press, 1980, rpt. 1983), pp. 56–64; Juliana Schiesari, "Libidinal Economies: Machiavelli and Fortune's Rape," *Desire in the Renaissance: Psychoanalysis and Literature*, ed. Valeria Finucci and Regina Schwartz (Princeton University Press, 1994), pp. 169–83; and Engle, *Shakespeare's Pragmatism*, pp. 199–207, for an account of rape imagery in Marvell's "Horatian Ode." See also Leo Curran's indispensable "Rape and Rape Victims in the *Metamorphoses*," *Arethusa* 11 (1978), 213–39.

Vergil's epic eventually opens itself to the charge of glorifying a second Trojan war based on rape when Turnus contests the Trojans' rhetoric of divine fate:

> sat fatis Venerique datum, tetigere quod arva
> fertilis Ausoniae Troes. sunt et mea contra
> fata mihi, ferro sceleratam exscindere gentem
> coniuge praerepta; nec solos tangit Atridas
> iste dolor, solisque licet capere arma Mycenis.   (9.135–9)

Enough has been granted to the "fates" and to Venus, since the Trojans touched the lands of fertile Ausonia. I have my fate to oppose theirs: since my bride was stolen, it is to destroy this wicked race with my sword. This sorrow does not touch the sons of Atreus alone, and to seize arms is not only allowed to Mycenae.

All Latin translations are mine, except where I use Arthur Golding's translations, quoted from *"Shakespeare's Ovid": Arthur Golding's Translation of the Metamorphoses*, ed. W. H. D. Rouse, Centaur Classics (Carbondale: Southern Illinois University Press, 1961).

7 I refer to the overlapping causes Vergil assigns to Dido's growing passion: Venus disguises her son Cupid as Aeneas' son, and while he enjoys Dido's maternal attentions, the god of love secretly pricks her with his arrow; while Dido listens to Aeneas' heroic narration, her "wound" silently grows. To detain Aeneas in Carthage with Dido, Juno later joins forces with Venus. The responsible agents are, then, the gods of love, Dido's feminine compassion and maternal weakness, Aeneas' eloquence and heroic masculinity (*viri virtus*, 4.3), and Juno's bungling interference. While Dido is paradoxically guilty and undeserving of her fate, Aeneas, overprotected from the consequences of his choice to love and leave Dido, remains conspicuously free from narrative responsibility. Shakespeare's interest in Dido as she listens to Aeneas' tale stretches from *Hamlet* to *The Tempest*.

8 "Empire without end" is Jupiter's gift to the Romans, promised early in the *Aeneid* (1. 279). Vergil and Aeneas, however, do not share Jupiter's supreme confidence in *Roma aeterna*. In the *Georgics*, the prior layer of his literary and cultural palimpsest, Vergil envies the happy man untouched by "the affairs of Rome and kingdoms doomed to fall" (*non res Romanae perituraque regna*, 2.498). Vergil's Rome, which was undergoing violent political changes, appears as both an inexorable colonizing force and another kingdom doomed to fall. Such anxieties and doubts permeate the *Aeneid*.

9 In "'Wresting the Alphabet': Oratory and Action in *Titus Andronicus*," *Criticism* 21 (1979), 106–18, C. Clark Hulse, generally concerned with the ways in which characters are converted into signifying spectacles, similarly describes Lavinia "as a tableau vivant, her mutilation recast in formal and mythological terms" (p. 111). See also Ann Haaker, "Non sine causa: The Use of Emblematic Method in the Thematic Structure of *Titus Andronicus*," *Research Opportunities in Renaissance Drama* 13–14 (1970–71), 143–68.

10 Daphne implores her father to destroy her too pleasureful *figura*: *"fer, pater,"* inquit *"opem! si flumina numen habetis, | qua nimium placui, mutando perde figuram!"* (1.546–7). Apollo finds greater satisfaction in the trope than the originally desired female body: the god of poetry finds language neither fleeting nor recalcitrant.

11 Thomas M. Greene, for example, adopts Apollo's perspective when he asserts that "the nymph's stubborn virginity is presented as a little deviant, but her plea for transformation is granted by [her father, the god of] the Peneus [river] and Apollo accepts it, according her a kind of affectionate apotheosis as his adopted emblem to which the laurel in its turn assents with a formal inclination of its leafy top." See *The Light in Troy*, p. 129.

12 Even Aaron's race taints Tamora more than Aaron. The displacement can be traced through puns on "raven," as "black," "plunder," or "eat ravenously," and comes from the Latin *rapere*, to rape. Aaron is Tamora's "raven-coloured love" (2.3.183), a pun on his blackness and Tamora's avid sexuality that Shakespeare toys with throughout 2.3. The play thoroughly contaminates racial difference and female sexuality: Aaron leaves the stamp of his race on the pit when he tells Titus' sons he has seen a black panther at its bottom;

before the men take their uncanny plunge, the pit transforms into a grotesque metaphor for Tamora's sexually voracious body; and the product of Aaron and Tamora's monstrous contamination in that pit is the black baby she bears in the fourth act.

13 A powerful Roman precedent for gendering as female and foreign problems internal to Roman society is Horace's Cleopatra Ode, 1.37, which celebrates the defeat of the Egyptian queen who "plotted the destruction to the empire with her contaminated crew of men" and finally imagines her refusal to be led in Caesar's proud triumph, *superbo / non humilis mulier triumpho* (31–2). Shakespeare's interest in the highly sexual, fertile, and proud queen of *Antony and Cleopatra* is anticipated by Tamora, who might be seen as Cleopatra's demonized double along the lines of the *fatale monstrum* in Horace's ode (1.37.21).

14 For the iconographic use of royal female bodies, see Marie Axton's *The Queen's Two Bodies: Drama and the Elizabethan Succession* (London: Royal Historical Society, 1977) and Philippa Berry, *Of Chastity and Power*.

15 Daniel Tuvill, *Essays Politic and Moral* (1608), ed. John L. Lievsay (University Press of Virginia and the Folger Shakespeare Library, 1971), p. 8. As the echoes of Vergil's storm and simile indicate, Shakespeare has no uniform practice of allusion, even when he treats the same piece of text: the scene from *Sir Thomas More* enacts the structure of the simile without citing it; the boatswain in *The Tempest* mockingly deploys it, while Titus personally acts out the simile. His method is caught by the figure of Lavinia as she leafs through the *Metamorphoses* in search of the tale of Philomela and "quotes the leaves" (4.1.50). In *The Gods Made Flesh: Metamorphosis and the Pursuit of Paganism* (New Haven and London: Yale University Press, 1986), Leonard Barkan explains that "to quote is to examine, at least in Elizabethan English, but it is also our quote, to reproduce – here, however, not verbatim, not using verbum at all, but as a dramatic image" (p. 246).

16 For the role of the family tomb in religious and political order, see Fustel de Coulanges, *The Ancient City: a Study on the Religion, Laws, and Institutions of Greece and Rome*, 12th edn., trans. Willard Small (Boston: Lothrop, Lee & Shepard Co., 1901), pp. 15–48.

17 T. J. B. Spencer remarks that *Titus Andronicus* conflates all forms of Roman government in "Shakespeare and the Elizabethan Romans," *Shakespeare Survey* 10 (Cambridge University Press, 1969), pp. 27–38. Although the play's anachronisms amuse Spencer, he astutely notes that Titus determines which Roman institutions will predominate.

18 Sir John Fortescue, whose popular *De laudibus legum Angliae* was first printed in 1537 and translated into English thirty years later, held, as J. P. Sommerville puts it, that "the king ruled as a constitutional monarch. The English system of government was an amalgam of monarchical and populist elements – a *regimen politicum et regale*. This implied no slur upon the king, for the monarch who ruled over free and prosperous subjects was likely to be both wealthier and more powerful than such a ruler as the king of France, who governed downtrodden, impoverished slaves" – in other words, a political order reminiscent of the late imperial Roman Senate as Tacitus depicted it: slavish and gutted of its ancient liberties. See J. P. Sommerville,

Politics and Ideology in England 1603–1640 (London and New York: Longman, 1986), p. 88.

19 When he kills Mutius for his infraction against filial duty, Titus recalls Rome's most uncompromising father, Manlius Torquatus: while consul in 340 BC, this exacting Roman executed his own son for disobeying orders not to engage the enemy forces. As usual, Titus has a precedent for his violent acts of justice, as he thinks of it. Of all critics since Reuben A. Brower, whose work on *Titus Andronicus* in *Hero and Saint: Shakespeare and the Graeco-Roman Heroic Tradition* (Oxford University Press, 1971) has quietly influenced many a study of the play's Roman heritage, Robert S. Miola has done most to remind critics of the centrality of Vergil's *Aeneid* in the construction of Titus' character and Rome as a failing institution. In *Shakespeare's Rome* (Cambridge University Press, 1983), Miola shows how Vergilian allusions present Titus initially as an embodiment of *Romanitas* "defined as a military code of honor that encompasses the virtues of pride, courage, constancy, integrity, discipline, service, and self-sacrifice" (p. 46) but, with the murder of his son, undermines *pietas* itself. For Miola, Rome is the protagonist and Lucius the "future hope of Rome" (p. 57), because his fraternal loyalty proves that for him family is the essential building block of the city.

20 In a useful article on the Elizabethan perception of the Romans and Goths, and their place in the *translatio imperii*, Ronald Broude points to the Elizabethans' consciousness of human sacrifice in the Aeneid: "From the description of Pallas' funeral in the eleventh book of the *Aeneid* as well as from other sources, the Renaissance had gained familiarity with the pagan belief that the spirits of the violently slain need to be appeased with the blood of their slayers lest they return to haunt their relatives who had been remiss in performing their duties" (p. 30). He then notes that "Shakespeare is careful to explain the sacrifice of Alarbus in these terms," citing Lucius' excuse, "ad manes fratrum" (1.1.101). See "Romans and Goths in *Titus Andronicus*," *Shakespeare Studies* 6 (1970), 27–34.

21 Miola, *Shakespeare's Rome*, remarks that "the rape of Lavinia by the new Roman princes parodies her Vergilian namesake's courtship and marriage by Aeneas" (pp. 54–5). Shakespeare's Lavinia even shares a famous blush with Vergil's: when her uncle describes her bloodied cheeks as "red as Titan's face / Blushing to be encountered with a cloud" (2.3/4.31–2), the chaste, erotic, and indecipherable image recalls the ambiguous blush of Vergil's dynastic bride. The allusive blush reinforces her disqualification, by rape, from the dynastic role of her predecessor. The allusion to Dido as a doe is one of a host of the play's reminiscences of the *Aeneid* noted by Reuben A. Brower (*Hero and Saint*, p. 182).

22 Robert Miola, "Vergil in Shakespeare: From Allusion to Imitation," *Vergil at 2000*, ed. John D. Bernard (New York: AMS Press, 1986), p. 243.

23 The classic discussion of the *Venus armata* – which recurs in *The Tempest*, where Ferdinand translates *o dea, certe* as "Most sure the goddess" (1.2.424) – is found in Edgar Wind, *Pagan Mysteries in the Renaissance*, rev. edn. (New York: W. W. Norton & Company, 1958, 1968).

24 Puttenham, *The Arte of English Poesie*, p. 177.

25 The allusion to Pyramus' "maiden blood" recalls the substitutive relationship

of sex and death in Ovid's tale of Pyramus and Thisbe. The allusion is a casual instance of substitution, which emerges as the mechanism structuring the play's revenge plot. Tamora substitutes the rape of Lavinia and the deaths of Titus' sons for her own sexual pleasure; the uncanny fall of Titus' sons into the pit substitutes for Lavinia's rape; Titus attempts to trade his hand for the lives of his sons and receives their heads in lieu of their whole selves; at the beginning of the play he substitutes the textual authority on *pietas* for piety itself, and later trades that text, the *Aeneid*, for Ovid's tale of Philomela. For the insight that Aaron devises an act of synecdoche by returning the heads of Martius and Quintus rather than the live sons, see Albert H. Tricomi, "The Aesthetics of Mutilation in *Titus Andronicus*," *Shakespeare Survey* 27 (Cambridge University Press, 1974), pp. 11–19, especially p. 16.

26 The anatomical reading of the pit is presented psychoanalytically in David Willbern, "Rape and Revenge in *Titus Andronicus*," *English Literary Renaissance* 8 (1978), 159–82. My own reading is political. The sexual punning with which Aaron introduces the hunting scene and his plot – e.g., "acquaint" Tamora with the plot (1.1.622/2.1.123), "coin a stratagem . . . [to be] cunningly effected [and] beget" villainy (2.2/3.5.5–7) – culminates in the serio-comic pit. As a site of sexual and textual displacements, the pit assumes dominant roles in the play's cultural criticism and in the audience's imaginations. The pit gains evocative power from its association with the pit of the Psalms. Sir Philip Sidney and the Countess of Pembroke (*The Psalms of Sir Philip Sidney and the Countess of Pembroke*, ed. J. C. A. Rathmell (New York: Doubleday, 1963), variously translate the pit as "ground-plotts" in which the architect himself will be "undunn" (11), "this gulph, this whirling hoale" in which the soul sinks (69), "pittfalls" which "entangle" (57), and a "pitt" dug to "ensnare" the speaker. Like the speaker in the Psalms, Titus is deeply afflicted by awareness that he is hedged about with treachery. The pit is a "ground-plott" crafted by Aaron, who gloats like a morality-play villain and, more powerfully, recreates the sense of engulfment vividly represented in Psalm 69: "Troublous seas my soule surround: / Save, O God, my sinking soule, / Sinking, where it feeles noe ground, / In this gulph, this whirling hoale" (1–4). Such epistemological unmooring brings Titus to exclaim, "I am the sea." The pit is a site where Roman imperial identity is undone.

27 In "Shakespearean Violence: a Preliminary Survey," *Violence in Drama*, ed. James Redmond (Cambridge University Press, 1991), Jonas Barish remarks that "with such conceits, reminiscent of Petrarchan blazonry, Marcus aims to transform" the physical violations, and that "Shakespeare is once again drawing on the resources of figurative language to turn to favor and to prettiness that which if directly gazed at, even verbally, is – in its extremity – not to be endured" (pp. 108–9). Questioning "whether this technique of combined horror and distancing works on the stage," Barish refers to Waith's claim, in "The Metamorphosis of Violence in *Titus Andronicus*," *Shakespeare Survey* 10 (Cambridge University Press, 1969), pp. 39–49, that Marcus' attempt to transform Lavinia fails because "in the presence of live actors the poetry cannot perform the necessary magic. The action frustrates, rather than re-enforces, the operation of poetry" (pp. 45–6). In "The Ceremonies of *Titus Andronicus*," *Patterns and Perspectives in English Renaissance Drama*

(Newark: University of Delaware Press, 1988), pp. 138–47, Waith reconsiders his earlier charge and blandly calls the discrepancy between rhetoric and spectacle a "kind of double vision" (p. 142) which he relates to the rhetorical *controversiae* popular in Shakespeare's day.

28 Richard A. Lanham, one of the first critics to discuss the importance of Ovid to renaissance rhetoric, describes the simultaneously ludic and political nature of the *Metamorphoses* in *The Motives of Eloquence: Literary Rhetoric in the Renaissance* (New Haven and London: Yale University Press, 1976).

29 Tereus cuts out Philomela's tongue, indignant and calling on her father's name, *indignantem et nomen patris usque vocantem* (6.555), words that may recall Turnus' death and criminalize Aeneas' disregard of Turnus' tacit plea for clemency by invoking his father's name. When Aeneas stabs Turnus in fury, Vergil chooses the same verb used for founding the walls of Rome in the fifth line of the poem. Although Aeneas views his act as sacrificial and judicial, Turnus' spirit flees to the Underworld *indignata*, resentful of an unworthy act. If Ovid's tale is taken as a commentary on the *Aeneid*'s ending, Aeneas loses the sacred character he claimed for the murder upon which he founds peace and the Roman empire. Although the murder retains its status as a founding political act, it is a precursor of familial violence that will ultimately destroy the community.

30 See Petrarch's sestina 30 for the image of the poet following the circle of the laurel's shadow, and John Freccero's argument about the petrarchan circle of obsession in "The Fig Tree and the Laurel: Petrarch's Poetics," *Literary Theory/Renaissance Texts*, ed. Patricia Parker and David Quint (Baltimore and London: The Johns Hopkins University Press, 1986), pp. 20–32. I here record a pleasureful debt to Robert Durling and John Freccero, teachers as inspiring as they are daunting in the scope of their knowledge. It will at once be recognized that what appears on my pages is a thin echo of their readings of Petrarch – exactly as thin, I hope, as the Elizabethan critique of petrarchism.

31 See Arthur F. Marotti, "'Love is not Love': Elizabethan Sonnet Sequences and the Social Order," *ELH* 49 (1982), 396–428; Louis Adrian Montrose, "*A Midsummer Night's Dream* and the Shaping Fantasies of Elizabethan Culture: Gender, Power, Form," *Rewriting the Renaissance: The Discourses of Sexual Difference in Early Modern Europe*, ed. Margaret W. Ferguson, Maureen Quilligan, and Nancy J. Vickers (University of Chicago Press, 1986), pp. 65–87; and Berry, *Of Chastity and Power*.

32 Freccero, "The Fig Tree and the Laurel," p. 29. Nancy Vickers, "Diana Described: Scattered Woman and Scattered Rhyme," *Writing and Sexual Difference*, ed. Elizabeth Abel (Chicago University Press, 1982), pp. 65–79, discusses Actaeon's relationship to the atomizing function of the blazon, which is intolerant of the image of a whole woman.

33 In the original *Arcadia*, Musidorus elopes with Pamela and, when they rest in the woods, he sings her to sleep, and "at leysure" beholds "her excellent Beutyes":

Hee thoughte her fayre Foreheade was a feelde, where her fancyes foughte, and every hayre of her heade seemed a stronge Chayne that tyed hym. Her fayre Liddes then hyding her fayrer eyes, seemed unto hym sweete Boxes of Mother of perle Riche in them selves but conteyning in them farr Richer Jewells: Her Cheekes with theyre Colour moste delicately myxed woulde have interteyned his eyes some while but that the Roses of her Lippes (whose seperating was wonte to be accompanyed with moste sweete speeches) now by force drewe his sighte, to marcke howe prittily they lay one over an other unyting theyr devided beutyes: And throwe them the Eye of his fancy delyvered to his memory, the lyinge as in Ambush under her Lippes those armed Ranckes, all armed in moste pure white, and keeping the moste precyse order of Military Disciplyn. And leste this Beuty mighte seeme the Picture of some excellent Artificer forthe there stale a softe Breathe carrying good Testimony of her Inwarde sweetenes, and so steallingly yt came oute, as yt seemed lothe to leave his contentfull Mansyon: But that yt hoped to bee drawne in agaene to that well closed Paradyse, that did so tyrannize over Musidorus affectes. . .

Musidorus is drawn by his *gradatio* ever closer to Pamela's body, "that well closed paradise" from the Song of Songs. Because Sidney changes his male protagonists from examples of idleness to heroism in the revisions that set the earlier *Arcadia* apart from the epic version of *The Countess of Pembroke's Arcadia*, the revised Musidorus does not follow his predecessor's example:

overmastered with the fury of delighte (having all his Senses parciall agaenst him selfe, and enclyned to his wellbeloved Adversary) hee was bent to take the vauntage of the weykenes of the watche, and see whether at that season hee could win the Bullwarck before tymely help mighte come . . .

See *The Prose Works of Sir Philip Sidney*, vol. 4, ed. Albert Feuillerat (Cambridge University Press, 1967), pp. 189–90.

34 Victor A. Doyno, ed., *Parthenophil and Parthenope* (Carbondale and Edwardsville: Southern Illinois University Press, 1971).

35 Marcus may use opulent rhetoric to begin the process of healing. In the 1988 Shakespeare Santa Cruz production, the actor playing Marcus spoke his lines soothingly while he tore his robe into strips and used them as tourniquets: the problems raised in the scene had nothing to do with failed characterization.

36 See Roland Greene, "Petrarchism among the Discourses of Imperialism," *America in European Consciousness, 1493–1750*, ed. Karen Ordahl Kupperman (Chapel Hill and London: University of North Carolina Press, 1995), pp. 130–65.

37 Jonathan Dollimore uses this formulation in *Radical Tragedy: Religion, Ideology, and Power in the Drama of Shakespeare and his Contemporaries* (Chicago University Press, 1984), p. 41, to introduce *Troilus and Cressida*'s fantasy of self-containment and support his argument about the powerfully disintegrative social forces which Troilus internalizes.

38 *The Living Monument*, pp. 38, 113.

39 Stanley Wells and Gary Taylor with John Jowett and William Montgomery, *William Shakespeare: a Textual Companion* (Oxford: Clarendon Press, 1987), p. 212.

40 "The Metamorphosis of Violence," p. 140. Waith defends the original text, supplies a useful note on its textual history, and characteristically treats the difficult scene as a challenge to a director.

41 Katherine Rowe, "Dismembering and Forgetting in *Titus Andronicus*," *Shakespeare Quarterly* (Fall, 1994), 279–303, esp. 280. Rowe reprints Paradin's "non sine causa" as a central emblem in a fascinating argument about the

problems of agency in the play: does the hand at the top of the sword confirm human agency or instrumentality? For her, too, Lavinia is the character who most economically represents agency as a conundrum. By accepting dismemberment as a template for revenge, Titus transforms his "effectless" (3.1.76) hand into a perversion of his once "victorious hand" (1.1.166). See also Mary Laughlin Fawcett, "Arms, / words / tears: language and the body in *Titus Andronicus,*" *ELH* 50 (1983), 61–77. Joan Pong Linton, in a paper delivered at MLA 1995, offered the wonderful suggestion that when Lavinia takes the stick in her mouth to write her attackers' names, she forms an emblem of a hand bearing a stylus. Coppèlia Kahn first noted the visual pun of Lavinia as a "handmaid of Revenge" in a paper delivered at Shakespeare Santa Cruz, 1988.

42 *Apius and Virginia* (1575), ed. Ronald B. McKerrow, The Malone Society Reprints (London, 1911). Another model for Shakespeare's audiences is Chaucer's Physician's tale.

43 If I am right to separate the "Philomelized" Lavinia from Lucrece, with whom Titus identifies in his quasi-suicide, it is worth noting further that Titus wrests control over political signification while Lavinia passively bears the "martyred signs" of his victimization. Shakespeare also uses her body to support his critique of the Virgin Queen. The reading generally supports Jonathan Crewe's aim in his provocative chapter on Shakespeare's Lucrece, "Shakespeare's Figure of Lucrece: Writing Rape," *Trials of Authorship: Anterior Forms and Poetic Reconstruction from Wyatt to Shakespeare* (Berkeley, Los Angeles, and Oxford: University of California Press, 1990), pp. 140–63, to question and test Shakespeare's capacity "to institute difference, not just systematically but systemically, in traditional representation" (p. 141). Also see Ian Donaldson, *The Rapes of Lucretia: A Myth and its Transformations* (Oxford: Clarendon Press, 1982).

44 Brower notes the allusion in *Hero and Saint,* p. 192.

45 *Astraea,* p. 75.

46 Waith's characterization of Titus appears in *The Herculean Hero in Marlowe, Chapman, Shakespeare and Dryden* (London: Chatto & Windus, 1962), p. 112, and the remark about Lucius in "Ceremonies," p. 146.

47 Larry S. Champion, *Shakespeare's Tragic Perspective* (University of Georgia Press, 1976); Sara Hanna, "Tamora's Rome: Raising Babel and Inferno in *Titus Andronicus,*" *Shakespeare Yearbook* 3 (1992), 11–29, and Henry Jacobs, "The Banquet of Blood and the Masque of Death: Social Ritual and Ideology in English Revenge Tragedy," *Renaissance Papers* (1985), 39–50.

48 *The Living Monument,* p. 115.

3 "TRICKS WE PLAY ON THE DEAD": MAKING HISTORY IN *TROILUS AND CRESSIDA*

1 *Orlando furioso,* ed. Eduardo Sanguineti (Aldo Garzanti Editore, 1974).

2 My summary of the Troy legend's ideological significance to Tudor and Reformation factions draws on the seminal account of Kendrick, *British Antiquity,* as well as the studies of Levy, *Tudor Historical Thought* and Ferguson, *Clio Unbound.*

3 Levy, *Tudor Historical Thought,* pp. 53–68.

4 Quoted in Kendrick, *British Antiquity*, p. 87.
5 Marie Tanner points out that Philip the Good of Burgundy commissioned Lefèvre's Trojan epic and that Lemaire's Trojan history culminated with Charles V. Her chapters on "The Revival of Epic Narrative" and "Mythic Genealogy," *The Last Descendant of Aeneas*, pp. 52–118, detail the efforts to substantiate Habsburg claims to imperial succession from Troy.
6 Samuel Rowlands, *The Letting of Humors Blood in the Head-Vaine, Complete Works* (Glasgow: Hunterian Club, 1880). Hyder E. Rollins, "The Troilus–Cressida Story from Chaucer to Shakespeare," *PMLA* 32 (1917), 383–429, established the reduction in Elizabethan verse of Troilus and Cressida to stereotypes.
7 J. S. P. Tatlock, "The Siege of Troy in Elizabethan Literature," *PMLA* 30 (1915), 673–770, extensively reviews the Troy legend's popularity in the renaissance. Douglas Bruster, *Drama and the Market in the Age of Shakespeare* (Cambridge University Press, 1992), stresses Elizabethan dramatic contexts. For studies of Shakespeare's use of Chaucer, see Muriel Bradbrook, "What Shakespeare Did to Chaucer's *Troilus and Criseyde*," *Shakespeare Quarterly* 9 (1958), 311–19; E. Talbot Donaldson, *The Swan at the Well: Shakespeare Reading Chaucer* (New Haven: Yale University Press, 1985); and Ann Thompson, *Shakespeare's Chaucer: a Study in Literary Origins* (Liverpool University Press, 1978).
8 Robert Kimbrough, *Shakespeare's Troilus and Cressida and Its Setting* (Cambridge, Mass.: Harvard University Press, 1964), p. 73.
9 In *Notorious Identity: Materializing the Subject in Shakespeare* (Cambridge, Mass.: Harvard University Press, 1993), Linda Charnes claims that *Troilus and Cressida* is "arguably the most 'neurotic' of the plays in terms of its skewed relations among and between characters, the play's generic inconsistencies, its resistance to a 'rehearsible' narrative, and its own self-proclaimed 'diseased' matter," p. 71.
10 See, for example, Oscar Campbell, *Comicall Satyre and Shakespeare's Troilus and Cressida* (San Marino, Calif.: The Huntington Library, 1959).
11 Nevill Coghill, *Shakespeare's Professional Skills* (Cambridge University Press, 1964). See also Gary Taylor, "*Troilus and Cressida:* Bibliography, Performance, and Interpretation," *Shakespeare Studies* 15 (1982), 99–136.
12 Joel Altman, "The Practice of Shakespeare's Text," *Style* 23 (1989), 466–500.
13 For the concept of a woman being "elsewhere," see Luce Irigaray, *This Sex Which Is Not One*, trans. Catherine Porter (Ithaca: Cornell University Press, 1985), p. 29.
14 Rosalie Colie, *Shakespeare's Living Art* (Princeton University Press, 1974), analyzes the play's abuse of petrarchan lyric; Bradbrook, "What Shakespeare Did," and Donaldson, *The Swan at the Well*, focus on the subversion of Chaucer; Graham Bradshaw, *Shakespeare's Skepticism* (Ithaca: Cornell University Press, 1987), incisively discusses the prologue.
15 Colie, *Shakespeare's Living Art,* p. 332.
16 Homer's seductive Helen discloses an intrigue to her relationship with Hector:

I wish I had been the wife of a better man than this is, / one who knew modesty and all things of shame that men say / . . . But come now, come in and rest on this chair, my brother, / since it is on your heart beyond all that the hard work has fallen / for the sake of dishonoured me and the blind act of Alexandros. (6.350–1, 354–6)

The Iliad of Homer, trans. Richmond Lattimore (University of Chicago Press, 1951, 1961).

17 See Roman Jakobson, "The Dominant," Language in Literature, ed. Krystyna Pomorska and Stephen Rudy (Cambridge, Mass.: Belknap Press, 1987). The satiric genre so dominates this scene that critics behave as if Pandarus' obscene ditty ends it. Mihoko Suzuki, a deft reader of literature's transformations of Helen, cuts off nine lines before the transition to verse and summarizes the scene by noting that "Helen as 'Nell' has been entirely stripped of her epic stature and appears callous and selfish, so unlike her former incarnation in the Iliad," Metamorphoses of Helen: Authority, Difference, and the Epic (Ithaca: Cornell University Press, 1989), p. 226. Although she does not consider the passage's oil-and-water relationship to the rest of the scene, Laura Levine aptly characterizes it as "the perfect emblem for beauty's dangerous disorganizing power" in Men In Women's Clothing, p. 38.

18 Jean-Joseph Goux, Symbolic Economies: After Marx and Freud, trans. Jennifer Curtiss Gage (Ithaca: Cornell University Press, 1990), p. 83.

19 See Cook's important essay, "Unbodied Figures of Desire," Theater Journal 38 (1986), 34–52, p. 50 and Knights' "The Theme of Appearance and Reality in Troilus and Cressida," Some Shakespearean Themes (Stanford University Press, 1960, 1959), p. 69. See also Elizabeth Freund's deconstructive reading, "'Ariachne's broken woof': the Rhetoric of Citation in Troilus and Cressida," Shakespeare and the Question of Theory, ed. Patricia Parker and Geoffrey Hartman (New York and London: Methuen, 1985), pp. 19–36.

20 Readers no longer assume that the play is tragic and that we are supposed to identify with Troilus as a hero, as do Coghill, Shakespeare's Professional Skills, and J. C. Maxwell, "Shakespeare: the Middle Plays," The Age of Shakespeare, ed. Boris Ford (Baltimore: Penguin Books, 1963, 1955). By refusing to preserve the Troilus who dies heartrendingly, Shakespeare reverses his stunning choice to alter another source and kill King Lear.

21 For the troping of the lovers, see Norman Rabkin, "Troilus and Cressida: the Uses of the Double Plot," Shakespeare Studies 1 (1969), 265–82, p. 265; and Colie, Shakespeare's Living Art, p. 323.

22 Margaret Ferguson discusses the tu quoque form of renaissance poetic defenses in Trials of Desire: Renaissance Defenses of Poetry (New Haven and London: Yale University Press, 1983).

23 Benjamin distinguishes between the stage actor, who retains his aura, and the film actor, who is estranged from his image: "aura is tied to . . . presence" and "there can be no replica of it," Illuminations, ed. with an introduction by Hannah Arendt, trans. Harry Zohn (New York: Harcourt, Brace, & World, 1968), p. 229. Benjamin concludes that when the camera replaces the public audience, "the aura that envelops the actor [playing Macbeth] vanishes, and with it the aura of the figure he portrays" (p. 229). The problem of transmitting aura and presence is no stranger to Shakespeare's stage. The chorus in Henry V craves real kings, countries, and wars to animate history.

Moreover, Shakespeare's legendary characters take no comfort in imagining their greatness boyed: Cleopatra and the Greek commanders view dramatic imitations as attacks on their authority. They are aware that their power to "be themselves" – a phrase recurrent in Shakespeare's public figures – depends on their unreplicated presence.

24 For the scene's importance to criticism, see Bradshaw, *Shakespeare's Scepticism* (Ithaca: Cornell University Press, 1987), pp. 132–44.

25 In his careless chivalry, Hector is reminiscent of Sidney and Essex, who issued a similar challenge to single combat at Lisbon in 1589 and whose heroics during his 1591 expedition in France earned the Queen's sharp reproof. See Richard McCoy, *The Rites of Knighthood: The Literature and Politics of Elizabethan Chivalry* (Berkeley: University of California Press, 1989), pp. 79–81, and G. B. Harrison, *The Elizabethan Journals, 1591–1603* (London: Routledge, 1938), pp. 50–3.

26 The phrase is from Geoffrey of Vinsauf, who also refers to Chaucer as "the fader and founder of ornate eloquence," and quoted in Doran, *Endeavors of Art*, p. 35.

27 John Bayley, *The Uses of Division: Unity and Disharmony in Literature* (London: Chatto and Windus, 1976), p. 191.

28 Discussing the erotics of spectatorship, Barbara E. Bowen notes Ulysses' pleasure in reproducing the theatrical camp of Patroclus: *Gender in the Theater of War: Shakespeare's Troilus and Cressida* (New York and London: Garland Publishing, 1993), pp. 129–33. While I do not find that Ulysses' "parody is liberating" (p. 132) for him, Bowen's remarks remind me of ways in which the characters perversely enjoy reducing companions to tropes even more than rivals.

29 Gayle Greene studies this problem in terms of comparison and tautology: "words suggest other words . . . [and] the subject slips away in a series of comparisons" (pp. 278, 282–3), "Language and Value in Shakespeare's *Troilus and Cressida,*" *Studies in English Literature* 21 (1981), 270–85. See Charnes' excellent account of the effects of comparison on the play's female characters, *Notorious Identity*, pp. 81–2.

30 I quote from Bullough, *Narrative and Dramatic Sources*, vol. 6, p. 158.

31 Cressida teasingly says that she knows a man if she has seen him before and known him; Thersites contends that Ajax should not be recognizable to others because he does not know himself; Thersites claims to be Patroclus' "knower"; and Aeneas maliciously pretends to Agamemnon himself that he does not know which of the Greeks is the general.

32 Achilles' Homeric struggle with Agamemnon recalls the Earl of Essex's resistance to his subjection under Elizabeth on the grounds of aristocratic ideology. As McCoy puts it, the Earl was deeply entangled in "the latent conflict between inherent distinction and that bestowed by the monarch– 'native' and 'dative' honor," *The Rites of Knighthood*, p. 89. For an influential discussion of the Essex revolt, see Mervyn James, *Society, Politics, and Culture: Studies in Early Modern England* (Cambridge University Press, 1986), ch. 9.

33 Achilles' classical and medieval incarnations are the subject of Katherine Callan King, *Achilles: Paradigms of the War Hero from Homer through the*

Middle Ages (Berkeley and Los Angeles: University of California Press, 1987). For Aeneas' evaluation, see Craig Kallendorf, *In Praise of Aeneas: Vergil and Epideictic Rhetoric in the Early Italian Renaissance* (Hanover, N.H.: University Press of New England, 1989).

34 Shakespeare adapts Marlowe's lines describing Helen of Troy in *Doctor Faustus* to emphasize her economic function. Thoroughly entrenched as the Trojan war's "general equivalent," she is faceless in an unmarlovian way: although the lines Troilus speaks are routinely attributed to Helen, they apply equally to Hesione, who is the referent closest to Troilus' "pearl." The context is as follows: "The Grecians keep our aunt. / Is she worth keeping? – Why, she is a pearl / Whose price hath launch'd above a thousand ships" (2.2.81–3). In *Troilus and Cressida*, the decrepit Hesione is as much a pearl as Helen, "whose youth and freshness / Wrinkles Apollo's, and makes stale the morning" (2.2.79–80).

35 In Horatian satire, Helen is the *taeterrima causa belli*, a reduction to a single anatomical part (the *cunus*) and to her function in a sexually and economically motivated war.

36 See Luce Irigaray, "Women on the Market"; Eve Kosofsky Sedgwick, *Between Men: English Literature and Male Homosocial Desire* (New York: Columbia University Press, 1985); and Gayle Rubin, "The Traffic in Women: Notes on the 'Political Economy' of Sex," *Toward an Anthropology of Women*, ed. Rayna R. Reiter (New York and London: Monthly Review Press, 1975), pp. 157–210. Carol Cook, Eric Mallin, and Linda Charnes treat the play's homoerotic concerns. Cook observes that the warriors "could all live and die in the eyes of one another. The exchange of recognition and admiration among men narcissistically reinforces their idealized images of themselves as heroes and soldiers 'worthy of all arms' " ("Unbodied Figures of Desire," pp. 43–4). Following Montrose's argument, in " 'Shaping Fantasies'," about the convergence of sexuality and politics in the Elizabethan court in order "to show the increasing ineffectiveness of the sexual and political mechanisms by which the Elizabethan court maintained its dangerous balance" (p. 175), Mallin applies some gains of feminist and psychoanalytic criticism to a new historicist reading in "Emulous Factions and the Collapse of Chivalry: *Troilus and Cressida*," *Representations* 29 (1990), 145–79.

37 With delightful acerbity, Raymond Southall, *"Troilus and Cressida* and the Spirit of Capitalism," *Shakespeare in a Changing World*, ed. Arnold Kettle (New York: International Publishers, 1964), pp. 217–32, insists that critics stop romanticizing the quality of Troilus' love: "It is extraordinarily difficult" to find "any intensity in the love of Troilus, or rather any love in the intensity of Troilus," p. 216. Southall's focus on the bankruptcy of petrarchan language relates to his Marxist reading of economics and capitalism in the play.

38 Leading defenders of Cressida are Gayle Greene, "Shakespeare's Cressida: A Kind of Self," *The Woman's Part*; Carolyn Asp, "In Defense of Cressida," *Studies in Philology* 74 (1977), 406–17; Grant L. Voth and Oliver H. Evans, "Cressida and the World of the Play," *Shakespeare Studies* 8 (1975), 231–9; and Janet Adelman, " 'This is and Is Not Cressid': The Characterization of Cressida," *The (M)other Tongue*, ed. S. N. Garner, C. Kahane, and M.

Sprengnether (Ithaca: Cornell University Press, 1985), pp. 119–41. By psychologizing her motivations, the critics attempt to combat Cressida's literary fate. Their sympathy with Cressida confirms the sense that Shakespeare is concerned with the costs to the subject of representational tactics meant to transmit authority to a privileged reader. Douglas Bruster, however, attractively argues that Cressida gains agency: "realizing that she is seen as a commodity, Cressida decides to take control of her commodity function," *Drama and the Market*, p. 98.

39 Janet Adelman analyzes Shakespeare's use of tragedy to meditate problems of uniting separate wills and minds in marriage: "Is thy Union Here?: Union and its Discontents in *Troilus and Cressida* and *Othello*," *Suffocating Mothers: Fantasies of Maternal Origin in Shakespeare's Plays, Hamlet to The Tempest* (London and New York: Routledge, 1992).

40 Noting the speech's relation to the petrarchan blazon, Cook relates it to pornography, "Unbodied Figure of Desire," pp. 49–50. Bruster, *Drama and the Market*, p. 103, develops the relationship of petrarchism to commerce, with particular reference to the image of the merchant-adventuring ship that Spenser, Donne, and Drayton adapt from Petrarch.

41 Quoted from Herford and Simpson, vol. 11 (1952), p. 271. Jonson further exhorts the poet not to let "the skin and coat" of language become "horrid, rough, wrinkled, gaping, or chapt" – the kind of language Shakespeare represents in Pandarus. Puttenham's comparison of poetic to courtly decorum, particularly in dress, appears in the *Arte of Poesie* III.xxv.

42 The *O.E.D.* defines "motive" as a moving limb or organ and specifies that this is an exclusively Shakespearean meaning. The other instance of this usage also meditates a complex state of agency and instrumentality: Bolingbroke swears that he will bite off his tongue as "the slavish motive of recanting fear" if he obeys King Richard's order to withdraw from combat with Mowbray (*Richard II* 1.1.193). Rather than allow his tongue to be the instrument of Richard's will, Bolingbroke would bite it off as a traitor to his own will.

43 "Shakespeare's *Will*: The Temporality of Rape," *Representations* 20 (Fall 1987), 25–76.

44 Troilus' ecstatic greeting of his ideal ego is, as Cook notes, reminiscent of Lacanian ideas of ego-formation, and particularly the role of "speculation." The great Myrmidon, however, can hardly be said to greet his identity "jubilantly": when he resumes his heroic identity by taking credit for Hector's death, Achilles goes about his business grimly.

45 To focus on the aubade scene calls for the audience or reader to tug against the play's and Troilus' pull toward closure and coherence. See Adelman, *Suffocating Mothers* and Rene Girard, "The Politics of Desire in *Troilus and Cressida*," *Shakespeare and the Question of Theory*, pp. 188–209, for detailed readings of this curiously misplaceable scene.

46 J. Hillis Miller, "Ariachne's Broken Woof," *Georgia Review* 31:1 (1977), 47–60, describes Troilus' shifts from illusory unity to doubling and finally fragmentation. Jonathan Dollimore reads the speech's linguistic and philosophical implications in terms of a disintegrating society in *Radical Tragedy*.

47 For a discussion of early modern London's neofeudal character and emerging capitalist market, see Lawrence Manley, *The Literature and Culture of Early*

Modern London. Also relevant to my concluding section are the studies of Lars Engle, Richard McCoy, and Raymond Southall, and Jean-Christophe Agnew, *Worlds Apart: the Market and the Theater in Anglo-American Thought, 1550–1750* (Cambridge University Press, 1986).

48 Jonson adapts the scene from Suetonius, where it is Augustus who presides over the bacchanalian dinner. In *The Boke Named The Governour* (London: J. M. Dent & Co., 1907), Sir Thomas Elyot describes the ignominy which spurred Augustus to self-reformation:

> The noble Emperor Augustus, who in all the residue of his life was for his moderation and temperance excellently commended, suffered no little reproach, forasmuch as he in a secret supper or banquet, having with him six noblemen, his friends, and six noble women, and naming himself at that time Apollo, and the other men and women the names of other gods and goddesses, fared sumptuously and delicately, the city of Rome at that time being vexed with scarcity of grain. He therefore was rent with curses and rebukes of the people, insomuch as he was openly called Apollo the tormenter, saying also that he with his gods had devoured their corn. With which liberty of speech, being more persuaded than discontented, from thenceforth he used . . . frugality or moderation of diet . . . (III.xxii)

49 Quoted from Braunmuller, ed., *A Seventeenth Century Letter-Book*, pp. 66–7.

50 William Cobbett, T. B. Howell, et al., *A Complete Collection of State Trials*, 42 vols. (London, 1816–98), vol. 1, pp. 1333–60. Essex was grateful to escape public execution: after his abrupt shift from honor-bound self-righteousness to pious self-condemnation, Elizabeth's government granted his request for a private execution in the Tower.

51 All references are to J. R. Tanner, *Tudor Constitutional Documents, 1485–1603* (Cambridge University Press, 1922), "The Law of Treason," pp. 375–451.

52 The body counts of these early Tudor rebellions were high: D. M. Loades, *Two Tudor Conspiracies* (Cambridge University Press, 1965), pp. 73, 113–14, notes that sixty to seventy men died in battle during Wyatt's rebellion and as many were executed for treason.

53 Alison Plowden discusses Walsingham's development of his secret service in response to Catholic plots, domestic and international, against the queen's life in *The Elizabethan Secret Service* (New York: St. Martin's Press, 1991). In *Treason in Tudor England: Politics and Paranoia* (London: Jonathan Cape, 1986) Lacey Baldwin Smith surveys educational, political, and behavior manuals as well as court politics to establish the culture of suspicion in England, and devotes several chapters to Essex. Drawing on seminal work in Keith Thomas, *Religion and the Decline of Magic* (New York: Scribners, 1971), Carole Levin, *"The Heart and Stomach of a King": Elizabeth I and the Politics of Sex and Power* (Philadelphia: University of Pennsylvania Press, 1994), pp. 91–120, describes less publicized or clearly motivated conspiracies of commoners against the queen.

54 Quoted from Tanner, *Tudor Constitutional Documents, 1485–1603*, p. 435.

55 Paul L. Hughes and James F. Larkin, *Tudor Royal Proclamations*, 3 vols. (New Haven and London: Yale University Press, 1969).

56 I quote Donne from H. J. C. Grierson, *Donne's Poetical Works*, 2 vols. (Oxford: Clarendon Press, 1912). In *The Augustan Idea in English Literature,*

a valuable guide to the literary, political, and religious contexts in which the renaissance understood the Augustan age, Howard Erskine-Hill notes the significance of the early manuscript reading (p. 81). His emphases on the law and politics in the chapter on Donne's satires furnish stimulating groundwork for understanding *Troilus and Cressida* as a translation of empire.

57 I quote from Erskine-Hill, *The Augustan Idea in English Literature*, p. 130, who takes the allusions to Augustus and Tiberius as reference to a providential pattern of rise and decline. Blair Worden elaborates Erskine-Hill's discussion of the late Tiberian–Elizabethan political scene in "Ben Jonson among the Historians," *Culture and Politics in Early Stuart England*, ed. Kevin Sharpe and Peter Lake (Stanford University Press, 1993), pp. 67–90. Malcolm Smuts, "Court-Centered Politics and Roman Historians," published in the same volume, pp. 21–43, stresses that Roman history reminded early seventeenth-century Englishmen of the vulnerability of "ancient constitutional forms," and notes that the collapse of the Republic and establishment of the empire, an intensively studied period of Roman history under Elizabeth and James, was "a story of constitutional instability and subversion" (p. 41).

58 Herford and Simpson, vol. 11, p. 574. On the institutional censorship of drama, see G. E. Bentley, "Regulation and Censorship," *The Professions of Dramatist and Player in Shakespeare's Time* (1971; rpt. Princeton University Press, 1984), pp. 145–96, and V. C. Gildersleeve, *Government Regulation of the Elizabethan Drama* (New York, 1908; rpt. New York: Columbia University Press, 1961).

59 Anticipating political misconstructions, Samuel Daniel burned his history of Cleopatra and Camden deferred his history of Queen Elizabeth's reign. John Hayward was imprisoned for publishing his *Life and Reign of King Henry IV* (1599), which "was interpreted as a parallel with recent events, and was alleged to be an apology for the Earl of Essex and an incitement to Elizabeth's subjects to overthrow her, as Henry IV had overthrown Richard II," Worden, "Ben Jonson among the Historians," p. 75. Suspicions were well-placed: Hayward dedicated the history to Essex and published it in 1599, just before Essex left for Ireland. Tacitean historiography, practiced by Hayward, Savile, and Bacon, found a home in the Essex circle. See James, *Society, Politics, and Culture*, ch. 9. The author and printer were brought to the Star Chamber, and the licenser, Samuel Harsnett, wriggled out of responsibility: see Greg, *London Publishing Between 1550 and 1650*, pp. 61–2.

60 Quoted from Manley, *London in the Age of Shakespeare*, pp. 277–8.

61 Frank Kermode notes the puns on Dido and Aeneas in Middleton's *The Roaring Girl* (1607/8) in the Arden edition of *The Tempest* (London and New York: Methuen, 1958), p. 47n. Rowlands dubs Cressida "Cresset-light" in *The Letting of Humors*, and Sir John Harington commemorates the scatological joke on a "jakes" in *A New Discourse of a Stale Subject, Called the Metamorphosis of Ajax* (1596).

4 TO EARN A PLACE IN THE STORY: RESISTING THE *AENEID* IN *ANTONY AND CLEOPATRA*

1 All references are from the Arden edition of *Antony and Cleopatra* by M. R. Ridley (London: Methuen, 1965).

2 Vivian Thomas, *Shakespeare's Roman Worlds* (London and New York: Routledge, 1989) and Barbara J. Bono, *Literary Transvaluation: From Vergilian Epic to Shakespearean Tragicomedy* (Berkeley: University of California Press, 1984), present detailed studies of Shakespeare's mostly harmonious relations to sources, even when he diverges from them to "transvalue" the characters of Antony and Cleopatra. The relation to source or, better, textual authority that I attempt to trace in this chapter is closer to the perspectival model described in Janet Adelman, *The Common Liar: An Essay on Antony and Cleopatra* (New Haven: Yale University Press, 1973). My model, more polemical and disruptive than Adelman's, is also more historically delimited than traditional source studies.

3 It seems fair to say that Antony and Cleopatra affiliate with Ovid against Vergil. My argument about Shakespeare's characteristic use of Ovid to destabilize Vergilian authority, originally tested in an article on *Titus Andronicus* published in *Violence in Drama, Themes in Drama*, 13 (Cambridge University Press, 1991), pp. 123–40, has found corroboration in Jonathan Bate's argument about Shakespeare's use of Ovid's *Heroides* to "destabilize a Vergilian, imperial idiom in *Antony and Cleopatra* and *The Tempest.*" See *Shakespeare and Ovid* (Oxford University Press, 1993), p. 103n.

4 Vergil by no means presents the misogynist words cited above as a divine oracle. He carefully separates the two appearances of Mercury: Mercury's first visit is authorized by Jupiter, who supplies exact wording to the messenger, while the second appearance of Mercury comes in Aeneas' dream, and the tone alters sharply from divine disgust at Aeneas to gynephobic fear of Dido. The second appearance is, I suggest, a Lucretian *simulacra* produced by Aeneas' anxious mind. In *De Rerum Natura*, Lucretius describes the experience of anxiety (*anxius angor*) and visions produced by the tormented mind. Dido becomes a dangerous and witchy figure after the line about feminine changefulness for some readers, who regard her alteration as proof of Mercury's words. I read the characterological inconsistency in terms of the imperial propaganda to which Dido must conform once Aeneas has made his pro-Roman choice. Noting that Vergil moves swiftly between emblematic and narrative modes, I attribute the problems in representation to Vergil's account of political myth-making rather than to dramatic and narrative causes.

5 Carol Thomas Neely, *Broken Nuptials in Shakespeare's Plays* (Urbana and Chicago: University of Illinois Press, 1993, rpt. from New Haven: Yale University Press, 1985), and Charnes, *Notorious Identity*.

6 In *Notorious Identity*, Linda Charnes mounts a strong argument about Caesar's control over the fictions generated to account for the civil war and victory. My argument about the political stakes in representing history at the end of the play stresses the concessive nature of Caesar's story of his opponents as romantic lovers and the ambivalence toward the terms of Augustus' victory that is powerfully recorded even in pro-Augustan literature and the divergences among Augustan authors. The play certainly "represents the ultimate triumph of Octavius, who will later sculpt himself into the Augustus of Vergil, Horace, and Ovid," but many tensions and questions are swept under the rug when one concludes that these writers, "who were to be

most influential in the Renaissance produced texts that would serve as Shakespeare's sources," produced a "monumental machinery of language" that was "at [Caesar's] disposal" (p. 108). It is misleading to assume that the three poets' works were fully complementary to each other and unswervingly committed to Augustus. As Janet Adelman notes, "the history of Antony, Cleopatra, and Augustus is inevitably history as told by propagandists; and propagandists with conflicting interests will disagree." Although Adelman writes that "Ovid, Vergil, and Horace were all good Augustans" for whom "Octavius's victory at Actium is the consolidation of all that toward which Roman history had been moving" (p. 54), her readings do not assume that the poets wholly endorse the official view. See *The Common Liar*, pp. 53–101.

7 Suetonius, *History of Twelve Caesars Translated into English by Philemon Holland anno 1606*, introduction by Charles Whibley, 2 volumes (London: David Nutt in the Strand, 1899), pp. 110–11.

8 Augustus himself seems to have promoted sexual and marital restrictions for pragmatic reasons – along the lines of Lear's "To't it, luxury, pell-mell, for I lack soldiers" (4.6.117) – if we judge by Suetonius' report of Antony's letter to Caesar, in which he wrote

> after a familiar sort, as yet being not fallen out flatly with him, nor a professed enemy: "What hath changed and altered you? Is it because I lie with a Queene, she is my wife? And is this the first time? Did I not so 9 yeares since? Alas good sir, you that wold have me company with Octavia my wife onely, tell me true: know you for your part none other women but Drucilla? Go to so may you fare well and have your health, as when you shall read this letter, you be not redy to deale carnally with Tertulla or Terentilla, or Rifilla, or Salvia Titiscenia, or with all of them. And thinke you it skilleth not, where and whom you lust after and meddle with? (p. 69)

9 I base my translation on that of Hans-Peter Stahl, in his compelling study, *Propertius: "Love" and "War": Individual and State Under Augustus* (Berkeley: University of California Press, 1985), pp. 140–1. On the history of the marriage law, see Ronald Syme, *Roman Revolution* (Oxford, 1960), pp. 443–4. Although the evidence of Augustus' early morality laws is uncertain, my argument relies only on the ideological shifts reflected in poetry of the period. The love poetry of Catullus, Propertius, and Ovid furnishes an appropriate context for the jarring effect of Aeneas' insistence on the authority of law over love.

10 Quint, *Epic and Empire*, p. 27. See chapter 1, for a succinct discussion of Vergil's play with cultural oppositions.

11 *Suffocating Mothers*, p. 179.

12 Discussions of the play's "gender trouble" include Adelman, "Making Defect Perfection," *Suffocating Mothers*; Jyontysna Singh, "Renaissance Anti-theatricality, Antifeminism, and Shakespeare's *Antony and Cleopatra*," *Renaissance Drama* 41 (1989), 77–90; Neely, "Gender and Genre in *Antony and Cleopatra*," *Broken Rituals*; Peter Erikson, *Patriarchal Structures in Shakespeare's Drama* (Berkeley: University of California Press, 1985); Madelon Gohlke (Sprengnether), " 'I wooed thee with my sword': Shakespeare's Tragic Paradigms," *The Woman's Part*, pp. 150–70; and Barbara Estrin, " 'Behind a Dream': Cleopatra and Sonnet 129," *Women's Studies* 9 (1982), 177–88.

13 My sense of Antony's rage against Cleopatra as an outburst of anxieties produced by the hostile cultural institutions setting in to define him is closer to Stephen Greenblatt's argument about the rousing and manipulation of anxieties in the renaissance than to psychoanalytic explanation. Greenblatt's argument about the rousing and manipulation of "salutary anxiety" – in this case, salutary for the emergent Augustan empire rather than for Antony – appears in "Martial Law in the Land of Cockaigne," *Shakespearean Negotiations*, pp. 129–163 and in "The Cultivation of Anxiety: *King Lear* and His Heirs," *Raritan* 2 (1982), 92–124, rpt. in *Learning To Curse*, pp. 80–98. Antony's tragic cooperation with Augustan ideology seems to me a more persuasive instance of a Shakespearean character rousing his own "salutary anxieties" than Prospero, whose intention to subject himself to the harrowing that purges Alonso seems to me far from clear.

14 Cleopatra does not, one of my students pointed out to me, wear the sword on her side. The sexual games between Cleopatra and Antony on that night are particularly vulnerable to the Roman charge of emasculation.

15 See Gordon Braden, *Renaissance Tragedy and the Senecan Tradition* (New Haven and London: Yale University Press, 1985).

16 Ronald R. MacDonald, "Playing Till Doomsday: Interpreting *Antony and Cleopatra*," *English Literary Renaissance* (1985), 78–99.

17 Dido's refusal of Aeneas is all Antony needs to claim victory over Vergil's hero. Yet Vergil himself undermines Aeneas' effort to offer and inspire emotional immediacy. For Aeneas' admission that he left Dido's shores unwillingly, Vergil adapts the line that Catullus assigns to the Egyptian queen Berenice's snipped lock in his mock epillion: "unwillingly, o queen, I left your head" (*invita o regina tuo de vertice cessi* (66.39) becomes "unwillingly, queen, I left your shore" (*invitus, regina, tuo de litore cessi*).

18 Shakespeare's Antony seems to conflate the stories of Ovid's Orpheus and Eurydice and Vergil's Dido and Aeneas. In *Metamorphoses* 11.61–6, Orpheus is overjoyed to rejoin Eurydice in death, and the two of them wander side by side through the "blessed fields" (*per arva piorum*) of the Underworld. Antony has reason to favor a mythological exemplar who was unable to restrain his desire at the crucial moment.

19 The phrase is G. K. Hunter's in *Dramatic Identities and Cultural Tradition: Studies in Shakespeare and his Contemporaries* (New York: Barnes & Noble Books, 1978), p. 266. Puttenham discusses the "Figure of transporte" as "a kinde of wresting of a single word from his owne right signification, to another not so natural, but yet of some affinitie or conueniencie with it," p. 178.

20 Malcolm Smuts, "Public Ceremony and Royal Charisma," *The First Modern State: Essays in English History in Honour of Lawrence Stone*, ed. A. L. Beier, David Cannadine, and James M. Rosenheim (Cambridge University Press, 1989), pp. 65–93. The marketplace scene reminds me of Elizabeth I's public ceremonies that drew on "the ancient custom of the acclamation, which in a remote period had expressed the idea that the assembled people must assent to the making of a King" (p. 78), a concept that Elizabeth I gratifyingly adapted and that both James I and Charles I repudiated for reasons of temperament and political theory. Since I believe that Shakespeare means to contrast the political styles and theories associated with Elizabeth and James

but not invoke their persons directly, I have confined Elizabeth I to the footnotes.

21 I quote from the translation of Philemon Holland (London, 1603).

22 The Ovidian character whose greying hairs are presented as examples of metamorphosis is, fortuitously, the warrior who cannot abide Caenus, the woman changed into a man. In *Metamorphoses* 12.464–5, he is described as a man whose years are between a youth and an old man, whose strength was youthful, and whose hair was changing at the temples (*aetas inter iuvenemque senemque, / vis iuvenalis erat, variabant tempora cani*).

23 Like Ovid, Vergil positively uses the idea of variety in conversation; he does not appear to condemn variety outside of the infamous assertion, *varium et mutabile semper / femina*. More often, the word comes up when a character feels torn by varied impulses, where it relates to epistemological and psychological complications.

24 Martin Spevack, *A New Variorum Edition of Antony and Cleopatra* (New York: Modern Language Association, 1990) records the responses of critics, starting with Swinburne, to "the woman of women, quintessential Eve" (p. 691).

25 St. Augustine rails against the love of eloquence which leads men to understand, all too well, the appeal of Jove's seductions in *Confessions* 1.16. He refers to the scene in Terence's *Eunuchus,* in which the youthful Chaerea rapes a woman and then rejoices in his exploit by recalling and describing a picture of Jove pouring himself in the lap of Danäe (*Eunuchus,* 3.5). Petrarch laments his inability either to gain his desires as Jove did or, following St. Augustine, to purge himself of the love of rhetoric and Ovidian myth.

26 As Susanne Wofford points out to me, the ecphrasis describing Cleopatra comes from Plutarch but may remind readers of Dido's links to rhetorical description in the *Aeneid* 1, where Dido appears at the end of the ecphrastic description of the Trojan war. Dido is first described in a pictorial simile to Diana leading her dancers and then presented, in tableau, passing laws and assigning tasks. Ecphrasis establishes the erotic appeal and political authority for both Cleopatra and Dido, who alone is disabled by the paradox.

27 Since Shakespeare delighted in "misusing" the blazon in order to call into question the sexual and gender norms it typically reinforces, it is in some ways not surprising to find ourselves dreaming of Cleopatra's little boys rather than her cheeks. When Petruchio and Kate pretend to mistake Vincentio for a "young budding virgin," they tease him with an inventory of his cheeks, in which white and red war, and his starry eyes (*Shrew* 4.5.27–49). In *As You Like It*, Phebe falls in love with Ganymede/Rosalind and immediately bursts into a lengthy blazon of his eye, leg, lip, and cheek, specifically admiring the feminine qualities of the supposed lad (3.5.109–35).

28 I quote from Bullough, *Narrative and Dramatic Sources of Shakespeare.*

29 I paraphrase John Freccero on the "radically fragmentary" effect of petrarchan comparison, in which Laura's "virtues and her beauties are scattered like the objects of fetish worship" (p. 29). He argues that Laura's body is reified, fragmented, and scattered in accordance to idolatrous poetics in "The Fig Tree and the Laurel: Petrarch's Poetics."

30 Stephen Orgel, *The Illusion of Power: Political Theater in the English Renaissance* (Berkeley: University of California Press, 1975), pp. 10–11.

31 Helen Morris notes the parallel of Elizabeth's water pageants on the Thames in "Queen Elizabeth I 'Shadowed' in Cleopatra," *Huntington Library Quarterly* 32 (1969), 271–8. An interesting reminiscence of her stately travel on the Thames appears in James Aske's *Elizabetha Triumphans*, when Elizabeth makes her way to Tilbury before the Armada. Through ranks of "brave and gallant men,"

> did passe our Queene most Dido-like
> (Whose stately heart doth so abound with love,
> As thousand thanks it yeelds unto them all)
> To water-side to take her Royall barge.

On this Vergilian occasion, the Thames is fortunate to find a "friendly king" in Aeolus, who "Recals his boysterous Boreas to his den," *Progresses of Queen Elizabeth* II, ed. John Nichols (New York: Burt Franklin, 1823), pp. 572–4.

32 In *Paradise Lost*, Milton analyzes romance in terms of the male imagination in its response to the ornamental female exterior when his Raphael chastises Adam for taking Eve's ornamental "outside" as a token of intellectual superiority. When Adam exclaims that sometimes she "Seems wisest, virtuousest, discreetest, best" (8.550), Raphael restores him to his sovereign place with the blistering rhetorical question, "what admir'st thou, what transports thee so, / An outside?" (lines 567–8).

33 Judith Butler, *Gender Trouble: Feminism and the Subversion of Identity* (New York and London: Routledge, 1990), pp. 140–1. See also D. N. Rodowick, *The Difficulty of Difference* (New York and London: Routledge, 1991) for critiques of Freud's binary conception of gender roles, particularly as analyzed in Laura Mulvey, "Visual Pleasure and Narrative Cinema," *Screen* 16.3 (1975), rpt. in Constance Penley, ed. *Feminism and Film Theory* (New York: Routledge, 1988), pp. 57–68.

34 Plutarch, *Moralia*, trans. Philemon Holland (London, 1603), pp. 1309 and 1294.

35 See Adelman's stimulating discussion of Cleopatra's role as Isis in *Suffocating Mothers*; see also Bono's lengthy consideration of the Isis myth in *Literary Transvaluation*. See also Eugene Waith's important discussion of Cleopatra's role as "the final custodian of [Antony's] image" as Herculean (p. 121) in *The Herculean Hero*, pp. 113–21.

36 My interest in these lines and the self-cancellation they attempt has been prompted by the reading of Laura Severt King, in "Blessed When She Was Riggish: Shakespeare's Cleopatra and Christianity's penitent prostitutes," *Journal of Medieval and Renaissance Studies* 22 (1992), 429–49. Although my conclusions about Cleopatra's agency and success differ, King's reading has enriched my sense of tragedy in Cleopatra's final performance.

37 For the play's evocations of Elizabeth I, see Morris, "Queen Elizabeth I 'Shadowed' in Cleopatra"; Keith Rinehart, "Shakespeare's Cleopatra and England's Elizabeth," *Shakespeare Quarterly* 22 (1972), 81–6; Clare Kinney, "The Queen's Two Bodies and the Divided Emperor: Some Problems of Identity in *Antony and Cleopatra*," *The Englishwoman in Print: Counterbalancing the Canon*, ed. Anne M. Haselkorn and Betty S. Travitskey,

(Amherst: University of Massachusetts Press, 1990); and Theodora Jankowski, *Women in Power in the Early Modern Drama* (Urbana: University of Illinois Press, 1992). Leonard Tennenhouse, *Power on Display: The Politics of Shakespeare's Genres* (London: Methuen, 1986), pp. 144–6, argues that Cleopatra represents a censorious Jacobean perspective on Elizabethan rule. H. Neville Davies offers a courtly reading of the play in "Jacobean *Antony and Cleopatra*," *Shakespeare Studies* 17 (1985), 123–58; and Jonathan Dollimore in *Radical Tragedy* reads of the play's discourse of honor and heroism in the context of the declining Jacobean military.

38 For the hostility of new historicist and cultural materialist criticism to psychoanalytic and Anglo-American feminism, see Stephen Greenblatt, "Psychoanalysis and Renaissance Culture," *Learning to Curse* and Jonathan Dollimore, "Shakespeare, Cultural Materialism, Feminism and Marxist Humanism," *New Literary History* 21 (1990), 471–94. Dollimore appropriates "sexual desire . . . [as] the vehicle of politics and power" (p. 486), neatly converting the language of sexual and psychic tensions into a metaphorical language bearing on political and social issues. While few would question the usefulness of attending to "the way diverse social anxieties are displaced onto or into sexuality" or to "the interconnections between women's subordination and other kinds of subordination," some have bridled at the dismissal of psychoanalytic and feminist concerns by the *fiat* of a dominant as opposed to a residual criticism, to borrow Raymond Williams' terms. Dollimore, it should be noted, is responding to an attack mounted by Carol Thomas Neely, "Constructing the Subject: Feminist Practice and the New Renaissance Discourses," *English Literary Renaissance* 18 (1988), 5–18.

39 Quoted in John Nichols, *Progresses of James I* (London, 1828), vol. 1, p. 500.

40 Quoted in Alvin Kernan, *The King's Playwright: Theater in the Stuart Court, 1603–1613* (New Haven and London: Yale University Press, 1995), p. 15.

41 For a broader consideration of the encounter of the boy actor, anti-theatrical censure, and homoerotic play with the vulnerable fictions of character and historical representation, see Kathleen McLuskie, "The Act, the Role, and the Actor: Boy Actresses on the Elizabethan Stage," *New Theatre Quarterly*, 3 (1987), 120–30. McLuskie considers different ways in which Elizabethan and Jacobean plays engage sexualities and the illusion by which a Rosalind protects "the true and essential character of her femininity, a fictional identity which transcends her clothes," p. 123.

5 *CYMBELINE*'S MINGLE-MANGLE: BRITAIN'S ROMAN HISTORIES

1 Shakespeare's project in *Cymbeline* is particularly compatible with Richard Helgerson's argument about the importance of literary form to the construction or "writing" of English nationhood. The chapter on law in *Forms of Nationhood* is apposite to *Cymbeline*'s interest in the constitution of political authority.

2 G. Wilson Knight, *The Crown of Life: Essays in Interpretation of Shakespeare's Final Plays* (Oxford University Press, 1947, rpt. in New York: Barnes & Noble, 1966), pp. 165–6.

3 Glenn Burgess, *The Politics of the Ancient Constitution: An Introduction to*

English Political Thought, 1603–1642 (University Park: Pennsylvania State University Press, 1992), discusses recent analyses of British insularity; the importance of "balance" between the king's prerogative and law – a balance *Cymbeline* achieves, unconvincingly, if royal prerogative is represented in Augustus' imperial claims and law in the customs established by Mulmutius; and the appeal to continuity or change in early modern theories of common law. Although Fortescue regarded custom as self-same from time immemorial, Selden's famous perception of continual change is anticipated in St. German. See also J. G. A. Pocock, *The Ancient Constitution and the Feudal Law: English Historical Thought in the Seventeenth Century* (Cambridge University Press, 1957).

4 See McCoy, *The Rites of Knighthood*, p. 89, for the distinction between "native" and "dative" honor.

5 It is useful to recall, from the Introduction, Heywood's frustration with Julius Caesar for seeking perpetual rather than elected power, an ambition that undermined the authority of the Roman officials whose posts equal London's Mayor and Sheriffs.

6 David Bergeron, *Shakespeare's Romances and the Royal Family* (Lawrence: University Press of Kansas, 1985) suggests a connection between the Queen and Tacitus' Livia, who administered poisons until her son Tiberius was advanced to power. If correct, his proposal affirms that the play melds ancient Roman and renaissance Italian sources in order to characterize the cultural degeneration of Italy. In general, the heritage of degeneration is best seen through Tacitean eyes as the corrupting effect of Empire. In the *Agricola*, Tacitus suggests that the Romans seduced the Britons and led, as Savile translates it, to "provocations of vices, to sumptuous galleries and baths, and exquisite banquetings; which things the ignorant termed civility, being indeed a point of their bondage," *The Ende of Nero and Beginning of Galba* (Oxford, 1591), p. 251. Quoted also in Smuts, "Court-Centered Politics and Roman Historians," p. 40.

7 I propose a more ambiguous and potentially distressing function for stage emblems in *Cymbeline* than is traditional in emblem study. Critics of *Titus Andronicus* and *Cymbeline* recognize the interest Shakespeare takes in emblems. See Peggy Muñoz Simonds, *Myth, Emblem, and Music in Shakespeare's Cymbeline: An Iconographic Reconstruction* (Newark: University of Delaware Press, 1992), Albert H. Tricomi, "The Mutilated Garden in *Titus Andronicus*," *Shakespeare Studies* 9 (1976), 89–105, and Ann Thompson, "Philomel in *Titus Andronicus* and *Cymbeline*," *Shakespeare Survey* 31 (1978), 23–32.

8 Knight, *The Crown of Life*, p. 140. Posthumus has by no means enjoyed universal approval. His ambiguous characterization receives fine commentary in Homer Swander, "*Cymbeline* and the 'Blameless Hero'," *English Literary History* 31 (1964), 259–70 and James Edward Seimon, "Noble Virtue in *Cymbeline*," *Shakespeare Survey* 29 (1976), 51–61.

9 Knight comments on the "mystery that shrouds [Posthumus'] descent," and notes that in so far as Posthumus symbolizes British strength, "Shakespeare is non-committal as to its origin." He suggests that Posthumus is "imaginatively at least a composite of the British and the Roman – his virtues are throughout

pre-eminently Roman" and his name sounds more Roman than British (*The Crown of Life*, pp. 141, 142).

10 My discussion of Cloten's unhappy relationship to behavior manuals draws on Norbert Elias, *The History of Table Manners* (New York: Pantheon Books, 1978). See also Daniel Javitch, *Poetry and Courtliness in Renaissance England* (Princeton University Press, 1978).

11 See Patricia Parker's illuminating reading of the play's engagement of the *Aeneid*, "Romance and Empire: Anachronistic *Cymbeline*," *Unfolded Tales: Essays on Renaissance Romance*, ed. George M. Logan and Gordon Teskey (Ithaca and London: Cornell University Press, 1989). Howard Felperin briefly notes the utility of the *Aeneid* in the dually romantic and political plot of *Cymbeline*, observing that the prophecies of Anchises and Merlin "converge in the accession of James I to the English throne" in *Shakespearean Romance* (Princeton University Press, 1972), p. 193.

12 My reading of the dream vision is particularly indebted to Parker's work in "Anachronistic *Cymbeline*."

13 See Homer Swander, "*Cymbeline* and the 'Blameless Hero'," who first criticized W. W. Lawrence's claim that modern audiences fail to understand the conventions of popular literature, in which a husband was entirely within his rights.

14 Knight notes that the speech gains a firmer grasp on the play's version of reality when one substitutes the Queen for Imogen (line 131). While Posthumus must correct his gynephobic impulses, the play does not.

15 In her informative essay on marriage contracts in Shakespeare, "'Wrying but a little': marriage, law, and sexuality in the plays of Shakespeare," *Essays, Mainly Shakespearean* (Cambridge University Press, 1994), pp. 3–30, Anne Barton makes the same point: "neither Posthumus nor we understand how deeply he does love Imogen until his remorse carries him not only to seek his own death, but completely to overturn the double standard" (p. 30). Barton's analyses of dramatists' engagement of problems in marriage laws are compelling throughout, although she offers more certainty than *Cymbeline* that Posthumus and Imogen are bound only by pre-contract. Arguments that assess the status of a Shakespearean marital contract by consummation run up against Shakespeare's delight in having his heroines both ways: Desdemona, Imogen, and Lavinia "are, and are not" virgins. When Lavinia is raped the day after her marriage, Shakespeare uses images of defloration.

16 See *The Two Books of Homilies Appointed to be Read in Churches*, ed. John Griffiths (Oxford University Press, 1859). The Homily of Marriage is reprinted in *Daughters, Wives, and Widows: Writings by Men about Women and Marriage in England, 1500–1640*, ed. Joan Larsen Klein (Urbana and Chicago: University of Illinois Press, 1992) and the Homily of Obedience in *Elizabethan Backgrounds*, ed. Arthur F. Kinney (Hamden, Connecticut: Archon Books, 1975).

17 Quoted from *The Miscellaneous Works in Prose and Verse of Sir Thomas Overbury, KNT*, ed. Edward F. Rimbault (London: Reeves & Turner, 1890).

18 Sir Thomas Smith preferred a model mutual subjection in marriage, in which husband and wife 'ech obeyeth and commaundeth other, and they two togeather rule the house.'" Debora Shuger, *Habits of Thought in the English*

Renaissance: Religion, Politics, and the Dominant Culture (Berkeley and Los Angeles: University of California Press, 1990), points out that the emphasis on mutual domestic rule would be inappropriately classed as "subversive" if orthodoxy were thought to be as unambiguous in the renaissance as it sometimes is in modern criticism. The orthodox remark is based on Pauline doctrine.

19 Marcus, *Puzzling Shakespeare*, p. 122. Hers is the strongest topical reading of *Cymbeline*'s relationship to the Union with Scotland and the problem of the Post Nati.

20 In a similar case near the end of Ariosto's *Orlando furioso*, Rinaldo encounters a man, maddened by the knowledge that he has been cuckolded, who offers Rinaldo a wine cup which spills its contents if the drinker is a cuckold. Rinaldo accepts the challenge and the cup, then hesitates, puts the cup down saying, "Let my faith remain undisturbed: it has stood me in good stead hitherto – what am I to gain by putting it to the test?" (43.6).

21 Michael Taylor focuses on the sexual implications of this image in "The Pastoral Reckoning in *Cymbeline*," *Shakespeare Survey* 36 (1983), 97–106.

22 Joan Carr dispels the scene's grotesque character through myths of resurrection. She reads the image of the headless body as Posthumus' redemption: "The reason for this bizarre identification [Orpheus and Cloten] is that, in an Orpheus-like regeneration, the chastened Posthumus will be returned to Imogen in Act V after he has purged himself of the violence and brutality of his now defunct *alter ego*, Cloten" (p. 319). See "*Cymbeline* and the Validity of Myth," *Studies in Philology* 75 (1978), 316–30.

23 Harry Berger Jr. analyzes the embedding of Orpheus' poetics in misogyny in "Orpheus, Pan, and the Poetics of Misogyny: Spenser's critique of Pastoral Love," *English Literary History* 50 (1983), 27–60. For a reading of Milton's critique of Orpheus in the post-lapsarian Adam of Book 10 of *Paradise Lost*, see my "Milton's Eve, Romance, and Ovid," *Comparative Literature* 45 (1993), 121–45.

24 Leonard Barkan observes that as Iachimo gazes about Imogen's room and then at her body, "he writes his own book, which the timing of the speech explicitly compares with the book on her bedside table. She went to bed reading of ancient rapes, and she becomes the book penetrated by the eyes of the modern rapist." *The Gods Made Flesh*, p. 250.

25 Patricia Parker suggests that the play's "imperial subject may also help to account for the complex overdetermination of Imogen herself, who, though, like Rosalind, in male disguise, also remains . . . more passive than her comic counterpart. She is, in the positions required of her in this imperial plot, not just the heroine in search of the husband who has turned against her but, in the kaleidoscopic subplot of the imagery, also an abandoned Dido, a passive Lavinia, and, in Iachimo's entry in the trunk, the potential British counterpart to ransacked Troy. Like Lavinia, she is the object of a rivalry between two suitors, one identified with a fierce local attachment, the other with the blending of both sides into the concord of a *Troia rediviva*," "Anachronistic *Cymbeline*," pp. 201–2.

26 Instead of following the pattern of Shakespeare's cross-dressing heroines, Imogen's fate and simplification parallel those of Desdemona and Cordelia,

whose masculine and assertive characters appear to demand their reduction to stereotypically feminine frailty and obedience. Perhaps the destruction brought down on the heads of the tragic heroines accounts in part for the blow Posthumus ignorantly unleashes on Imogen at their reunion.

27 *Court Culture*, pp. 28–9.

28 William Barry Thorne tries to put a positive spin on Knight's observation when he comments that "Cymbeline is the symbolic center of the tensions of the kingdom," and that it is in him that "the final reconciliations are effected," "*Cymbeline*: 'Lopp'd Branches' and the Concept of Regeneration," *Shakespeare Quarterly* 20 (1969), p. 143.

29 Leah Marcus, *Puzzling Shakespeare*, interprets Jupiter's clumsiness and Posthumus' opacity in terms of James' self-presentation. Felperin, *Shakespearean Romance*, relates Jupiter's imperiousness to the overbearing Cymbeline. He situates the god's limitations within the Christian design traditionally associated with Cymbeline's reign (p. 183–4). Meredith Skura archly points out that "while Jupiter does indeed descend, he neither does nor says anything of substance – no rescues, no revelations, and only the flimsiest, most circumstantially creaky, of oracles. Essentially all he does is say 'I am here'" in "Interpreting Posthumus' Dream from Above and Below: Families, Psychoanalysts, and Literary Critics," *Representing Shakespeare*, p. 211.

30 Philip J. Brockbank, "History and Histrionics in *Cymbeline*," *Shakespeare Survey* 11 (1958), 42–9, identifies and discusses Shakespeare's use of Holinshed in this passage.

31 All references are from *North's Plutarch*, 5 vols. (London: The Nonesuch Press, 1929).

32 All references are from *The Roman Historie of T. Livy*, tr. Philemon Holland, 1600.

33 The classic article on this subject is Emrys Jones, "Stuart *Cymbeline*," *Essays in Criticism* 11 (1961), 84–99.

34 For the characterization of the narrative principles of epic and romance as well as the epistemological and political implications of the creative opposition of the genres, see Patricia Parker, *Inescapable Romance: Studies in the Poetics of a Mode* (Princeton University Press, 1979).

35 The situation of *Cymbeline* within Jacobean politics has been thoroughly discussed. Emrys Jones, "Stuart *Cymbeline*," grounds Knight's suggestion that *Cymbeline* is a nationalistic play within the official propaganda of James' court. He cites abundant panegyrical writing and establishes the play's connection to Henry VII, James' royal ancestor, who landed at Milford Haven in 1485. In "From Tragedy to Tragi-Comedy: *King Lear* as Prologue," *Shakespeare Survey* 26 (1973), 33–48 and "Riddle and Emblem: A Study in the Dramatic Structure of *Cymbeline*," *English Renaissance Studies presented to Dame Helen Gardner*, ed. John Carey (Oxford University Press, 1980), Glynne Wickham amplifies Jones' findings.

36 James I, *The Political Works of James I*, rpt. from the edition of 1616, with an introduction by Charles Howard McIlwain (New York: Russell and Russell, 1965), p. 273.

37 The relationship between the revolution and images from political and artistic discourses is coincidental but felicitous.

6 "HOW CAME THAT WIDOW IN?": ALLUSION, POLITICS, AND THE THEATER IN *THE TEMPEST*

1 All references are to the Oxford edition of *The Tempest*, edited by Stephen Orgel (Oxford University Press, 1987).

2 Kernan, *Shakespeare, the King's Playwright*, pp. 150–68. For an opposed reading of Shakespeare's relationship to James I's absolutism, see Donna Hamilton, *Vergil and The Tempest: the Politics of Imitation* (Columbus: Ohio State University, 1990).

3 *Defence of Poesie, The Prose Works of Sir Philip Sidney*, vol. 3, ed. Albert Feuillerat (Cambridge University Press, 1963), p. 8. All references are to this edition.

4 *The Tempest*'s relationship to contemporary colonialist discourses has generated a large bibliography. See D. G. James, *The Dream of Prospero* (Oxford, 1967) and Charles Frey, "*The Tempest* and the New World," *Shakespeare Quarterly* 30 (1979), 29–41, who reviews the critical history of the subject and focuses on the play's deployment of new world vocabulary. Philip J. Brockbank, "*The Tempest*: Conventions of Art and Empire" and "The Island of *The Tempest*," *On Shakespeare: Jesus, Shakespeare, Karl Marx, and Other Essays* (Basil Blackwell, 1989), discusses the play's engagement of travel and colonialist literature in close detail; Trevor R. Griffiths, " 'This Island's Mine': Caliban and Colonialism," *Yearbook of English Studies* 13 (1983), 159–80, discusses production history. See also Paul Brown, " 'This thing of darkness I acknowledge mine': *The Tempest* and the discourse of colonialism," in *Political Shakespeare: New Essays in Cultural Materialism*, ed. Jonathan Dollimore and Alan Sinfield (Cornell University Press, 1985). pp. 48–71; Peter Hulme, *Colonial Encounters: Europe and the Native Caribbean, 1492–1794* (London: Methuen, 1986); Alden T. Vaughn, "Shakespeare's Indian: The Americanization of Caliban," *Shakespeare Quarterly* 39 (1988), 137–53; Stephen Greenblatt, *Shakespearean Negotiations, Marvelous Possessions: The Wonder of the New World* (Chicago University Press, 1991), and Stephen Greenblatt, ed., *New World Encounters* (Berkeley: University of California Press, 1993); Knapp, *An Empire Nowhere*; and Orgel, Introduction to *The Tempest*. For critiques of the tendency to conflate Prospero and Shakespeare and to assume that Shakespeare unhesitatingly endorses politically and socially normative positions, see Meredith Skura, "Discourse and the Individual: The Case of Colonialism in *The Tempest*," *Shakespeare Quarterly* 40 (1989), 42–69, and Deborah Willis, "Shakespeare's Tempest and the Discourse of Colonialism," *Studies in English Literature* 29 (1989), 277–89.

5 The choice of a providential storm and a Vergilian program indicates that Prospero may be a self-styled Jupiter, dispassionately surveying the scene of human history. Prospero appears to align himself with the Vergilian gods who understand the place of turbulent history within a larger design: he represents his power through a magic book by which he manipulates the "fates"; a staff like Jupiter's scepter; and Ariel, "Jove's thunderbolt," Mercury, and *avis Jovis* – "my bird," he calls the spirit. While Jupiter calms his anxious daughter Venus through his prophecy of the Roman future, Prospero assures Miranda

that the Italians have landed safely in harbor, without a hair suffering "perdition."

6 Bullough, *Narrative and Dramatic Sources of Shakespeare*, pp. 287, 292.
7 J. C. Davis, "Utopianism," in *The Cambridge History of Political Thought 1450–1700*, ed. J. H. Burns (Cambridge University Press, 1991), p. 332.
8 Ibid., pp. 240–1. See also Greenblatt, "Martial Law in the Land of Cockaigne," p. 154. The essay focuses on the prominence of authority and sedition as themes in the New World tracts and in *The Tempest*.
9 See J. H. Hexter, "Parliament, Liberty, and Freedom of Election," Johann P. Sommerville, "Parliament, Privilege, and the Liberties of the Subject," and David Harris Sacks, "Parliament, Liberty, and the Commonweal," *Parliament and Liberty from the Reign of Elizabeth to the English Civil War*, ed. J. H. Hexter (Stanford University Press, 1992), pp. 21–121.
10 McIlwain, *The Political Works of James I*, pp. 307–8. All references are to this edition.
11 Quoted in J Sommerville, *Politics and Ideology*, p. 101.
12 Sir Thomas Smith treats the household's mimetic relationship to the state, emphasizing its hierarchy and division of labor, in *De Republica Anglorum* 1.11, ed. Mary Dewar (Cambridge University Press, 1982), pp. 58–9. The idea of the ship as a figure for the state, law, and self-government is familiar from Horace's Ode 1.14, Aquinas – see *Cambridge History of Medieval Political Thought*, ed. J. H. Burns (Cambridge University Press, 1988), p. 327 – Fortescue, *De natura legis naturae* 1.46, and Petrarch *Rime* 189. For a discussion of Spenser's meditation of the ship as a figure for law, see Fowler, "The Failure of Moral Philosophy in the Work of Edmund Spenser," who cites Aquinas.
13 David Underdown, *Revel, Riot, and Rebellion: Popular Politics and Culture in England 1603–1660* (Oxford: Clarendon Press, 1985), p. 14.
14 Ibid. p. 21. Kett's rebellion inspired considerable political thought about the constitution of the commonwealth, such as Sir John Cheke's *Hurt of Sedition* (1549).
15 See Stephen Greenblatt's brilliant essay on linguistic colonialism, "Learning to Curse," rpt. in *Learning To Curse*, pp. 16–39.
16 J. M. Cowper, ed. *The Select Works of Robert Crowley*, E.E.T.S. (1872). p. 145.
17 Strachey praises Sir Thomas Gates for his readiness to set an example by his own labor, and Bullough notes that Prospero wants Ferdinand to learn this lesson. Prospero may approve of labor as a cure for idleness, but he takes the attitude towards his own labor that Crowley assigns the querulous gentry in "The Waie to Wealth." I argue that Prospero, who is extremely vulnerable on this score, personifies ideological tensions in the shifting attitudes towards work and laborers.
18 Underdown, *Revel, Riot, and Rebellion*, p. 35.
19 "Miraculous Harp: A Reading of Shakespeare's Tempest," *Shakespeare Studies I* (1969), 253–83, esp. p. 257. Prospero's aversion to labor forms one aspect of Berger's general concern with the disenchantment just beneath the surface of the idealizing mind.
20 Quoted from J. M. Cowper, ed. E.E.T.S. Extra Ser. XII (1871), p. 32. Starkey

went far beyond promoting the popular origins of kingship: his ideas about the free election of kings and possible right of citizens to "make him a prince and him that is a tyrant so to depose" (p. 167), so congenial to Caliban, but were not to be published for centuries, remaining a "dead letter," as Howell A. Lloyd puts it in his useful discussion of "Constitutionalism" in *The Cambridge History of Political Thought 1450–1700*, pp. 254–97.

21 John Gillies, "Shakespeare's Virginian Masque," *English Literary History* 53 (1986), 673–707. Although Gillies persuasively ties the fens of the plantation to Jamestown, the domestic fens, which caused tension between the gentry who wished to drain and enclose them and the laborers who regarded the land as common property, may also be of interest.

22 Frank Kermode, ed., *The Tempest* (London: Methuen, 1954).

23 "The *Aeneid* and *The Tempest*," p. 425. Kermode remarks that the allusion "has never been properly explained," and comments further that "nowhere in Shakespeare . . . is there anything resembling the apparent irrelevance of lines 73–97" (p. 47).

24 In his introduction to the play, pp. 41–2, Stephen Orgel proposes that "the notorious exchange . . . has proved baffling only because editors and critics have limited their attention to Vergil." Gonzalo refers to the historical tradition in which the exemplary Dido never met Aeneas, which Antonio and Sebastian "undercut [it] by invoking the alternative tradition in which Dido abandons her chastity to an equally unchaste 'widower Aeneas.'" This solution attractively suggests the way that *The Tempest* transposes the commentators' evaluative disputes over the two Didos. Since the fame of the historical Dido grew, however, with the number of times she was invoked to prove that Vergil lied, she relies on the canonicity of Vergil's Dido rather than the other way around. Vergil's phenomenally influential account of Dido emerges as the site of interpretive contest in a play which pervasively draws on Vergil's epic. In plays from *2 Henry VI* and *Titus Andronicus* to *Hamlet*, *Antony and Cleopatra*, *The Merchant of Venice*, *Othello*, and *Cymbeline*, Shakespeare's Dido is the compassionate Queen, with her "sad attending ear," who is about to plunge irreversibly into a fatal passion. See J. M. Hooker, "Widow Dido," *Notes and Queries* (March, 1985), 56–8, who finds in *The Tempest* a strong response to Vergil's sympathetic Dido; and Malcolm Pittock, who uses the same title in the same journal (September, 1986) to rebut Hooker on the grounds that Shakespeare refers to the historical Dido.

25 In the meantime, they may anticipate reasons to convey Dido into *The Tempest*. The queen was betrayed by her brother and, by heroism and ingenuity, converted her exile into a martial triumph. Prospero wants Miranda and Ferdinand to avoid Dido's fatal passion (*furor*), which turns to vengeful madness (*furor*) as Dido pores over entrails and fantasizes a Medea-like revenge. Sycorax may double as Dido's dark side, but she is not the play's closest analogue. A widower, duke, and magician, Prospero is also in exile because of a usurping brother. Dido neglected her city to pursue a private life with Aeneas, an affair which ultimately drove her to madness, the practice of black arts, and suicide. Prospero's story oddly reconfigures Dido's career: he neglected and lost his dukedom in the pursuit of arcane, magical knowledge; he has marital designs – for his daughter – on a shipwrecked prince; and he

discovers that he is driven by a vengeful "fury" that he must give up along with his magic. The allusion to Dido, locally irrelevant, generates significances during the course of the play as an "impertinent" allusion.

26 It is no wonder that the utopia fails to bring Alonso peace, since his councillor is dreaming of a commonwealth that needs no laws to curb the prince's wayward will and protect the subjects' rights. As Berger points out, Gonzalo was the chief minister of Prospero's ouster, so it is worth asking why Gonzalo is entitled to remain the "good old lord" (5.1.15) and be spared the grim fate of Antigonus, who exits "pursued by bear." In *The Tempest*, the councillor who remains loyal to a corrupt prince but never ceases to dream of an anodyne is rewarded with a good reputation.

27 Bullough, *Narrative and Dramatic Sources of Shakespeare*, p. 287.

28 Orgel notes the curious tension between Miranda's two claims about her curiosity, first that "more to know / Did never meddle with [her] thoughts" (1.2.22–3) and second that Prospero has often begun his tale only to cut it off, leaving her "to a bootless inquisition" (1.2.35). If Prospero has perpetually dangled and withdrawn his story, Miranda may be guarding her interest. She affirms that she does not need to know that Prospero is "more better / Than Prospero, master of a full poor cell, / And thy no greater father" (1.2.20–2). Miranda, who remembers that she once had three or four women attending her, may struggle somewhat with her memories of aristocratic living.

29 Amazement, or *miranda*, is Aeneas' response to marvels and wonders. Physical symptoms include shivers of horror, weakened joints, and "hair upstanding." Aeneas responds with amazement to portents such as the bleeding rushes that turn out to be Polidorus. Prospero uses Vergilian amazement successfully with Alonso, who reads the supernatural signs allegorically because he actively seeks punishment for the loss of his son. Prospero's devices have no effect on Antonio, the usurping brother who never moralizes when he can crack a cynical joke.

30 The choice of a harpy as an emblem of revenge has a comfortable valence when allegorized and applied to the Italian machiavels, for the harpy, with hooked claws and hungry pallor, represents greed. Yet Prospero's emblem is also Vergil's grasping, agile bird with a woman's face. Uncannily like Lear's model of women as half angel, half centaur, the harpy carries the taint of avid female sexuality:

> tristius haud illis monstrum, nec saevior ulla
> pestis et ira deum Stygiis sese extulit undis.
> virginei volucrum vultus, foedissima ventris
> proluvies uncaeque manus et pallida semper
> ora fame. (3.214–18)

From the waters of Styx there never arose a monster more grim and bitterly repulsive than these, nor a fiercer plague and wrath of the gods. These birds have the faces of virgins, but the most foul discharge drops from their wombs/bellies, and they have clawed hands and faces ever pale with hunger.

While Lear divides women at the girdle, finding all that the gods inherit above and hell, stench, and consumption below, Vergil seeks similarly nauseating effects in the line which sets the initial word "virgin" in opposition to the final word, "womb." The grotesqueness of the harpy's body seeps from the dense alliteration of "v's." Aeneas encounters the "foulest discharge from the wombs" they use offensively, charging upon Aeneas' food, soil it with their touch, shriek, and leave behind an evil stench (*taetrum odorem*, 228). Prospero's uses of the *Aeneid* tend to expose the motives, ambitions, and preoccupations that drive his project and harrow his imagination.

31 Gillies quotes the lines in an excellent discussion of the tropes of amorous courtship used to describe the English relationship to Virginia, "Shakespeare's Virginian Masque," p. 677.

32 *The Discoverie of the large and bewtiful Empire of Guiana*, ed. V. T. Harlow (London: The Argonaut Press, 1928), pp. 73 and 62–3. For a discussion of the courtly gallantry the English claimed in contrast with the Spanish treatment of natives, see Knapp, "The Triumph of Disgrace," *An Empire Nowhere*, pp. 175–219.

33 With his feet and neck manacled together, would the "traitor" Ferdinand resemble Sycorax, who "with age and envy / Was grown into a hoop" (1.2.257–8)? It is tempting to entertain a more political reason for her shape: apart from the rack and the manacles, Alison Plowden says of the instruments of torture described by the Jesuit Robert Southwell, "the most common forms of physical torture seem to have been 'Little Ease,' a dungeon so constructed that its inmate could neither stand nor lie, and 'The Scavenger's Daughter,' an iron ring which rolled victims into a ball and so crushed them 'that the blood sprouted out at divers parts of their bodies,'" *The Elizabethan Secret Service*, p. 135.

34 In addition to the Oxford edition, see Orgel's article, "Prospero's Wife," *Representations* 8 (1984), 1–13.

35 The cell transvalues the cave in which Dido and Aeneas made love, on the day of death and first cause of Rome's troubles (*ille dies primus leti primusque malorum / causa fuit*, 4.169–70). Kermode notes Bernard Smith's suggestion that the passage alludes to Dido and Aeneas' cave (*spelunx*), which Stanyhurst (1588) translates as "den." Ferdinand's thought is commonplace and needs no classical precedent, but his venue – the "murkiest den" – is off the beaten track.

36 Pitcher, "A Theatre of the Future: The Aeneid and The Tempest," *Essays in Criticism* (1984), pp. 193–215, pp. 204–5, discusses the masque's use of Vergilian passion. Gillies argues for the presence of Ovid's Ceres, goddess of fruitfulness, who reacts against the lust of "dusky Dis."

37 For Spenser's description of the Lucretian Venus, see *The Faerie Queene* 4.10.44–6.

38 Kermode notes that the reference to Juno's gait has a Vergilian root in the phrase, *divom procedo regina* from *Aeneid* 1.

39 The late William Nestrick drew my attention to the "ageyn bite of inwit" tradition inspiring Prospero's play on words and consciences.

40 Berger, "Miraculous Harp," describes the double pull, in which "the renunciation pattern is *there*, but only as a general tendency against which the main thrust of the play strains," and notes that the play should end with Gonzalo's speech, p. 254.

41 Greenblatt, "Martial Law and the Land of Cockaigne," pp. 144. See also the complementary chapter on distraction in *The Tempest* in Knapp, *An Empire Nowhere*, pp. 220–42. For a broader discussion of the problems with historicizing anxiety, see William Bouwsma, "Anxiety and the Formation of Early Modern Culture," *A Usable Past: Essays in European Cultural History* (Berkeley, Los Angeles, Oxford: University of California Press, 1990), pp. 157–189.

42 Gurr, *The Shakespearean Stage 1574–1642*, pp. 194–8.

43 *The Illusion of Power*, pp. 5–6, from which I quote Orgel's translation of Platter. Orgel pursues the question of the scope and limitation of social imitation, particularly as constituted by clothing, in *Impersonations: the Performance of Gender in Shakespeare's England* (Cambridge University Press, 1996), pp. 100–5, and specifically comments on the scene of the glistering apparel. For the Tudor emphasis on spectacle and finery to represent power, see Sydney Anglo, *Spectacle, Pageantry, and Early Tudor Politics* (Oxford: Clarendon Press, 1969), and Malcolm Smuts, *Court Culture*, esp. pp. 140–58.

Index

Cambridge Studies in Renaissance Literature and Culture

General editor
STEPHEN ORGEL
Jackson Eli Reynolds Professor of Humanities, Stanford University